HOW TO SUCCEED AS AN INDEPENDENT CONSULTANT

HERMAN HOLTZ and DAVID ZAHN

HOW TO SUCCEED AS AN INDEPENDENT CONSULTANT

FOURTH EDITION

WILEY

John Wiley & Sons, Inc.

Published by John Wiley & Sons, Inc., Hoboken, New Jersey.
Published simultaneously in Canada.

For general information on our other products and services please contact our Customer Care Department within the United States at (800) 762-2974, outside the United States at (317) 572-3993 or fax (317) 572-4002.

Wiley also publishes its books in a variety of electronic formats. Some content that appears in print may not be available in electronic books. For more information about Wiley products, visit our web site at www.wiley.com.

ISBN 0-471-46910-6

Printed in the United States of America.

10 9 8 7 6 5 4 3 2 1

Contents

scenarios. Who must you sell? Public- versus private-sector proposals. The evaluation system. The protest process. Sole-source procurement. Proposal formats and rationales. Format and general rationale. The necessary impact. Strategy and its evolution. Functional flowcharts. A few odds and ends.

Consulting means different things to different consultants. What are profit centers? Why other profit centers? The common denominator. Writing for profit. Publishing your own book. Marketing books. Other marketing means. Other publishing ventures.

Speaking for profit. The public speaking industry. The seminar business. Marketing the seminar.

The new meaning of independent. Desktop computers. The most popular functions. Desktop publishing. Database and spreadsheet functions. Communications software. Graphics developments. Printers. Modems. Facsimile machines. Tape drives, copying to CDs, and backing up. The computer as a general aide.

A standard of conduct. Conflicts of interest. Fees and related ethical considerations. Ethics and fees. A recommended code.

Books on retirement and second careers. Books on writing and publishing. Books on public speaking. Other books of interest. Periodicals of direct interest. Wholesalers and distributors. People and organizations in public speaking. Convention managers and planners. Speakers associations. Mailing list brokers. A few tips on writing direct mail copy. Associations of consultants. Miscellaneous resources. Internet resources. A few seminar tips. Proposal do's and don'ts. Outline for the preparation of a business plan.

Preface

WHY A NEW EDITION IS NEEDED NOW

Not every book has the good fortune to require a fourth edition. This book, however, has consistently been purchased by those interested in the collected wisdom of experiences acquired over many years of application and practice. Moreover, the book has been referred to and reread as opposed to purchased and never touched again. While it is inspiring to know that this book has become a vital resource for so many, it is also daunting when looking to update it. Knowing that there are likely to be so many eyes critically analyzing the recommendations made in this book and being aware of the high expectations readers have that the advice is of the highest caliber has ensured that this edition remain true to the original purpose of the first edition and every edition since then—to better elucidate the skills required to succeed as an independent consultant.

This fourth edition is necessary because in the 10 years since it was last updated much has changed within the worlds of business and technology, having tremendous impact on the consulting profession. As such, over time, this book has been developed according to the "give and take" of readers, practitioners, and professionals sharing the highlights and lowlights of their careers from their starts in the profession. In the preface to the third edition, one such exchange was shared when a man employed by his firm as an "internal consultant" reported that while he did not aspire to be self-employed or an independent businessperson, he still found the following insights to be "liberating eye-openers":

- Consulting is not of itself a profession, but how one practices a profession.
- Consultants need to market their services proactively as a planned part of the business, not as an afterthought.
- The client's perception defines the "truth" or reality of a consulting situation.
- Consultants need to make a profit in addition to making a living—pay themselves a salary.
- A consultant must be a specialist and a generalist at the same time.
- A proposal is a sales presentation. (Too often we write proposals as displays of erudite technical knowledge and clever phrasing.)

Over the last decade, there have been many "eye openers" for those of us who either are in the consulting industry, or have made it our business to study the industry. The very nature of the work has changed. For example, prior to 1990, it was rare to come across someone who identified themselves as an internal consultant. That job description is of recent vintage, and while it refers to an internal employee, the same requirements are made of that employee as would be made of an external consultant:

1.   Understand the client's needs. In the internal consultant's situation, the client may be another department or region or sister company.
2.   The necessity to sell oneself to the client as someone who can provide additional value. Asking an internal employee to assist in a formal consultative role is contrary to the way many executives would ordinarily have approached a resource. More uncommon is the internal consultant who can sell himself as a valuable entity to be included on a project, even if the fees or compensation are really little more than administrative transferring of funds within a corporate accounting system.
3.   Having to deal with a more savvy and experienced client. Given that many executives have worked with, or in some cases, for consulting firms during their careers, there is greater sophistication and knowledge on what to expect or demand from the relationship. This has led to more discerning consumerism on the part of clients who are now more experienced.

Additional changes that have occurred within the business world in general and consulting in particular are technology influenced and refer very specifically to the immediacy of performance and results. In speaking with consultants and clients who have either read the previous editions of this book, or in other instances, are living it in a sense, they share that:

1.   Video conferencing is now a relatively common reality for conducting meetings.
2.   E-mail has reduced the time required to communicate between clients and consultants, or between any two remotely located individuals, regardless of time zone or other logistical constraints.
3.   Cellular telephones and/or pagers keep people connected. Should someone be out of touch with their office due to travel or even if their work day has ended and they are at home or on vacation—the constant and instant access to one another through cellular telephones tethers people to each other instantaneously.
4.   Through the introduction of the Internet, remotely located people can share documents, exchange money, work in "virtual" groups without having to ever meet or speak to each other, and information (including pictures, video, narration, music, etc.) can be shared. Communication with clients, suppliers, vendors, peers, and others can occur simultaneously and can be customized to suit the needs of the information receiver (and be updated or customized without having to incur tremendous incremental expense). It is the rare business today that does not have a "presence" on the Web with at least a site or a

home page, if not the ability to transact business through selling or marketing through targeted communications to site visitors.

With all respect to Ben Franklin and his observation about the inevitability of death and taxes, he neglected to mention another thing (at least directly) that is inevitable in this world; it is change. Change is inevitable, it is constant, and, in the broad view, beneficial, although the immediate effects may not appear to be so. Many things about consulting have remained the same since the third edition of this book was published, but much has changed. This edition will reinforce that which is constant, but will also focus on the significant changes that must be taken into account if you are to continue succeeding as an independent consultant.

Some of the changes are minor, while others are of great importance, critical to success as a consultant. The fourth edition responds to these major changes and offers solutions for the problems arising from them.

THE GENERAL ECONOMIC ATMOSPHERE AND ITS INFLUENCE

We have survived the following economic changes since the last edition was released:

- The economic frenzy that accompanied the mid- to late-1990s, when many businesses exploited the rush of consumers to acquire and improve their lifestyles through purchases, and employees took advantage of the relative low unemployment to better themselves through frequent job changing and rapid career ascension.
- The dot-com explosion, when anything and everything related to electronic business portals, web sites, and Internet-facilitated businesses was deemed "golden." Investors and venture capitalists forgot that business models that are built on "eyeballs" and not on transactions, costs, revenue, profit, cash flow are doomed to fail. The ride, while exhilarating for awhile, came to its abrupt and unsightly end.
- The inevitable "dot bomb" was quick on the heels of the dot-com explosion. Eventually, businesses reliant on "future" earnings and mortgaging their horizon had to pay with something resembling currency and many of the "successes" of the prior few years were quickly dealt a death blow when creditors came for their money and there was none to be had.
- The loss of jobs that were integrally tied into Web companies that failed, companies servicing Web companies, and businesses reliant on employees or vendors/suppliers to Web companies that were no longer viable target consumers.
- September 11, 2001, as the airplanes crashed into the World Trade Towers, the ideology of being free from world pressures and terrorism evaporated, and we all came to realize how the United States was much more vulnerable than we ever understood and had thought. We are still sorting out all the repercussions

to business on that awakening (travel, security, trade, etc.). Political implications aside, the business impact of that event still ripples through our companies and the once insular approach and cloak of invincibility American businesses toiled under has been pricked (perhaps permanently).

- The greed and scandals of business management teams that did not perform their role and functions ethically. The names Arthur Andersen, Enron, Kmart, Ahold, and others have been sullied by the actions of the few who stood to gain at the expense of many innocent people who had entrusted them to execute their duties legally and ethically.

- In the spring of 2003, the United States entered into a military action against Iraq that while seemingly quick in achieving the military objective, has longer term ramifications for the world economically.

  - Does the United States have an obligation to rebuild other countries that are judged less advantaged than itself?

  - Should the cultural uniqueness of an area be modified in an effort to assist others to progress (using a definition of "progress" that may not be universally agreed on)?

  - How are contracts to accomplish these initiatives to be awarded?

The role of consultants within the dynamic and ever-changing business environment remains to be clarified, but it is clear that there will be business opportunities for the enterprising consultants savvy enough to recognize an opportunity to assist companies or individuals address professional and personal issues within the new business reality.

We know or ought to know that change is inevitable. We never succeed in going back. We must learn to live with the new situation. We must adjust and adapt, and market for today's conditions, not yesterday's or the hopes of tomorrow.

Many thousands of people have lost their jobs permanently; they were not laid off, to be recalled later; their jobs were terminated. They had to find new careers, those among them who could, but employers had retreated too, and jobs were less than abundant. Many of the newly unemployed therefore turned to independent consulting, and we suddenly saw a great many new shingles being hung out.

Is that good news or is it bad news for independent consultants? It is bad news in that it reflects both a shrinking market for at least some of us and increased competition for work in that market. But it is also good news for the aggressive and imaginative consultant, because in some respects the market has grown, and the opportunities are greater than ever. In this period, regardless of how accurately the government's economists perceive and interpret the economic signs that portend the future, employers have become bearish in hiring and turned to the independent consultant as the more desirable way to solve problems and meet needs.

All the foregoing problems are among many others, classic and new addressed in these pages. We assume in writing this, as in the earlier editions, that you bring to your independent consulting practice ample technical/professional expertise in your special field and need no guidance in helping your clients in that respect. But we assume also that you can benefit from general guidance in all the other elements necessary to establish and operate a successful independent consulting practice—in winning clients, especially. (The major focus here is not on how to *be* an independent consultant, but how to *succeed* as an independent consultant.) Here you will find guidance, suggestions, and ideas for all of these problems—for everything necessary to independent consulting success except that specialized technical/professional knowledge that you possess and wish to sell to (put at the disposal of) clients.

NEW AREAS TO BE CONSIDERED

One of the many compelling reasons for a new edition is the impact of changes and the need to bring them to you. The business of "objective advice giving" is not a black and white world at all; rather it has many shades and variations. Owing to the scandals at Enron and elsewhere, there has been a critical gaze cast upon the very nature of the business practices of the "advice providers" to ensure that there is nothing untoward in their methods and practices. There has also been an effort to separate the auditing and accounting efforts of clients from those of consulting organizations where possible.

The use (and avoiding the misuse) of the Internet, web sites, and e-mail requires attention as marketing tools, communication devices with their own protocols, and sales vehicles. With the ease of e-mailing and so-called "push" mailings that send out messages to a list of people, some of whom did not request solicitations, the creation of SPAM (unwanted e-mail messages) is a pervasive problem. Recently, the federal government created a national directory of telephone numbers that are not to be called for unwanted solicitations. Home owners register with this directory and are to then be excluded from sales pitches or other intrusive messages. It stands to reason that the next target will be e-mail messages that are unwanted. The number of solicitations for baldness cures, impotency cures, and weight loss or mortgage assistance far outnumber the actual mail messages for many e-mail users. As it happens, the mistake too often made by marketers, consultants included, is to emphasize the informality of the media and therefore cause an impression to be formed in the minds of customers that is rather difficult to change. A seemingly friendly e-mail message that is sent to someone who was not interested in the service offered is viewed as an intrusion and will damage that consultant's chance at ever getting business from that individual in the future.

One benefit of the Internet is that it provides the ability to "play bigger" than you can as an independent consultant competing with much larger (even multinational) firms. "Virtual organizations" or collections of cooperative vendors/suppliers of complementary services join together to provide services causing a dramatic shift in "go-to-market" strategies for many independents. Large firms are acquiring smaller firms or creating branding departments within larger consulting firms to give the appearance of flexible and dynamic consultation support most often associated with smaller firms, and in some instances the reality mirrors the perception with some firms actually creating and funding smaller organizations to address consulting issues that are best served this way (IBM and EDS have done this for ERP/CRM opportunities).

Through advances in targeting, attracting, and retaining small business clients, many credit providers are willing and encourage consultants to use credit cards for receipt of payment, offer credit to small businesses to improve their businesses, and are focused on the independent consultant as a fertile client base that requires servicing (as opposed to corporations that have "critical mass," the independents can form their "groups" by banding together to create large entities that allow credit providers to achieve the economies of scale they seek). Similarly, the health insurance industry previously did little to offer assistance to the small business or independent practitioner (in essence forcing the independent consultant to use a spouse's coverage option, or scramble for coverage that was likely to be insufficient and expensive to boot). While health insurance costs continue to rise, health insurance is available to independent consultants.

THE IRS VERSUS THE ON-SITE CONTRACTOR

One of the problems facing consultants is the attitude of the IRS: The IRS has been questioning the contractor status claimed by independent consultants who work on the client's premises and on long-term contracts. On the other hand, many consultants, those employed in large organizations and those functioning as independent consultants, work on their own premises or on both the client's and their own premises, usually under contract to do a specific job, rather than under an indefinite-term agreement to work for the client. Some independent consultants tend to short-term assignments by the nature of the work in which they consult, but this is not the case with all; many do consulting work that normally entails long-term contracts and assignments. Thus the IRS position can be a serious problem, and it will be discussed in these pages, with suggestions for overcoming it.

THE PLIGHT OF TODAY'S RETIREES

Early retirement and second careers have been an increasing trend for decades. Compounding the ebb and flow of people leaving their careers or jobs after many years and assuming a second career is the more recent phenomenon of people treating their careers as "serial positions" that often involve dramatic career shifts due to technological changes (printing is one industry that has dramatically changed as a result of technological changes, putting many people out of work well before they were of retirement age) or personal pursuits (after working in one career, a sizable segment of the working population chooses to give up their vocation to pursue an avocation or hobby as a career option). Finally, there are those that choose to leave work to improve their work conditions, have greater autonomy, or address disenchantment with the corporate lifestyle. As more and more companies undergo layoffs, downsizings, and other efforts to reduce the number of employees, the expectation of being "employed for life" and the paternalistic company looking out for the employees' interests is no longer the norm. This has left many employees disbelieving that the company truly values their input and is prepared to commit back to them. The end result is more people opting to "retire" from companies sooner than they would have in the past.

Additionally, as people maintain their health later in life, many retirees are still capable of, and desirous of living a vibrant lifestyle that includes working (either part-time or full-time) in a manner that accommodates their desires (time off, vacation, travel, working with clients of their choosing, etc.). Particularly for those workers that are not working solely for the income, but for the intellectual challenge or enjoyment of the endeavor, the freedom of working according to one's own preferences is very important.

THE EXPLOSION OF PERTINENT TECHNOLOGY

The technological revolution has greatly amplified a consultant's capabilities for expanding and addressing profit-making services and utilization of resources previously unavailable to business professionals. A few short years ago, having a desktop computer was considered progressive (that is, after the stigma of actually "typing" for oneself was overcome) and only the most technologically sophisticated consultants would have one. Now, business people have portable laptops and radio frequency devices that are easily carried along on trips or on cross country flights and that provide communication to home offices and clients in a nearly "real-time" mode. Laptop computers possess more computing power than whole offices of multiple users had access to only a decade ago. Along with the laptop on the business trip is the ever-present cellular phone that can also double as a fax machine and digital camera. The traveling consultant is quite likely to also have a personal data assistant (PDA) that replaces the rolodex holding all contacts' phone numbers and addresses. It doubles as a "to-do" list and provides some of the same capabilities as the laptop computer to run various applications or software.

The increase in memory capacity along with the miniaturization of microprocessors has created totally mobile offices that can be carried in a briefcase. You can now carry in a device about the size of a standard Swiss army knife the equivalent of an entire 1990s computer's memory capacity. You can carry whole presentations, graphics, sound, and even video examples of specific content you wish to present to your client without having to lug very expensive and unwieldy equipment around. The only requirement you currently need is to be able to plug your small device into the back of a computer that accepts a USB connection. Almost all computers that are less than five years old can accommodate that, so it is rare that you are unable to use your very miniature hard drive and present your reports or training materials through the use of the computers onsite at your client.

Should the cell phone and e-mail capabilities not be sufficiently comprehensive in performance, the consultant can always rely on higher end videophones or videoconferencing technology that includes the use of satellite transmissions. If the needs are less intensive, standard computers are now able to provide duplex (meaning two-way) transmissions of image and sound such that two people can conduct a meeting where they see each other via a monitor, share documents, and interact verbally.

There are a number of commercially available software communication programs to do this, and a visit to any office supply store can provide access to the latest programs and applications.

One of the drawbacks previously encountered by the traveling businessperson was the frustration of having to rely on telephone line transmissions to upload or download (communicate remotely with centralized computers that warehouse data) information that was graphically intensive or rather large files. Through improvements in services like DSL and cable modems, the rate of transmission has been increased exponentially over what it once was and that no longer is the issue it once was.

THE NEED FOR ENHANCED MARKETING

In these times of general business slowdown and increasing competition, marketing becomes a more critical need than ever, and it will get even more attention here than previously, with discussions of and suggestions for more efficient promotional schemes and materials. To offer additional and new insight into methods for marketing your services successfully, a large part of this fourth edition will focus sharply on specific marketing ideas and methods to consider and use, for those are the true ingredients of your success as an independent consultant.

NEW INFORMATION IN THIS EDITION

These are all matters to be addressed, along with many other new developments and current conditions. Thus, several completely re-worked chapters appear in this fourth edition; new and updated material appears in existing chapters; and the book overall has been reorganized to simplify your finding specific coverage and, more important, specific help for today's problems and the best opportunities to expand and increase your success.

HERMAN HOLTZ

Author's note: This edition is revised by David Zahn, a frequent speaker, author, and practicing consultant for leading companies such as Con Agra, Snapple, Hallmark, Clorox, and Johnson & Johnson. Herman Holtz, author of the first three editions of this book, passed away before the revision to this edition could be completed, but much of the content of this book is the result of his lucid thinking on the topic of consulting.

Introduction

Consulting has been a subject of great controversy from the time the first edition of this book was created because:

1. There is no unanimity on who among us is entitled to be called a consultant, and what work specifically is worthy of the definition of consulting. Many recently laid off employees explain their unemployed status to friends and family as "consulting."
2. The skills required to be a consultant are not universally understood and agreed upon.
3. There is still a sense among some executives that a consultant is a charlatan and little more than a well-packaged, sharp-tongued modern-day snake oil salesperson.

Consulting generally was then, and is now, a misunderstood profession by some of its own practitioners, occasionally misrepresented by its detractors, and misconstrued by the very clients who employ them. In part, this is due to the difficulty in defining the profession (and determining if it is a profession at all). While not a new problem, the lack of a definition continues to haunt those interested in consulting from any of the aforementioned perspectives as more "areas of expertise" are being carved out by those who wish to consult within those domains (web page design, electronic or communication security, international business, diversity, etc.). While the issue is not necessarily that the current definitions are too exclusionary (quite the contrary, the "walls" around consulting are rather porous and allow nearly anyone to consider him or herself to be a consultant). The issue of defining just what is "consulting" and who is a "consultant" will continue to gnaw at businesspeople and consultants alike as business practices become more global, requiring additional skills and insights to navigate the new challenges. Specialization in any one or more business disciplines becomes increasingly important to the survival and success of businesses looking to leverage the latest specialists' thinking and practices, and the desire to incorporate insights derived from competitors, customers, and even from within a company's own far-flung enterprise becomes more essential to remaining responsive to the needs of the business. To quell some of the uneasiness, I offer the following definition:

> Consulting is the science of providing objective business relevant guidance and counsel to decision makers without possessing an ownership stake in the decision.

Now, to dissect that definition a bit: Consulting is a science as opposed to an art form. As a science, it is subject to rigorous measurements and should be replicable by any practitioner equipped with the same skills. Obviously, not all consultants are equal in skills, but just as medical procedures can be completed by a whole host of different physicians with generally similar results, consulting can be done by a range of professionals. While there is still room for those who are better than others to be in higher demand, or for the business opportunities to differ by practitioner, the basis of the core skill of consulting is predicated on something other than the subjective interpretation or art form.

That leads us to the next important concept in the definition, the consultation must be objective. It must be based in reality and must not represent the impact of influences or be swayed by criteria that are not relevant to providing counsel that is in the best interests of the client. The consulting provided is to be business relevant and should further the objectives of the business or client.

The next part of our definition emphasizes the word, *guidance*. A consultant is *not* responsible for the actions of the client. A consultant provides advice and in some instances may produce a product, such as software programming. However, the consultant is no longer consulting when she is compensated for or manages the results of a project. If a consultant is responsible for results, she has become an employee in mind set and her counsel is no longer based on what is best for a client, but has evolved into acting on her best interests short term. This is controversial and is not without detractors. A consultant must be judged based on the appropriateness of the advice provided, and the client is responsible for the results. While they are very much linked, there must also remain a separation between them or the impact has repercussions that ripple through the entire business world as we saw with Enron and Arthur Andersen.

The last words in the definition remind us that you cannot consult with someone who cannot act on your consultation. Consulting is something done to build skills, provide insights, or develop positions or strategies. If you are engaged in sharing wisdom with anyone and everyone without discriminating between true users and others—then you are pontificating in the way that street corner evangelists do hoping to convert someone to their way of thinking. That is not consulting. Consulting must address a specific business need; be targeted to someone who can act upon it; and be based on objective, scientific, and replicable criteria.

Failing to adhere to these guidelines will result in our typifying one of the longest standing jokes about consultants: What's the definition of a consultant? Someone who takes your watch to tell you what time it is and then charges you for the answer.

INCREASING NEED FOR CONSULTANTS

The increasing complexity of society, in both the technological and sociopolitical senses (changes due at least in part to technological dynamism, political unrest and upheaval in certain countries that change the complexion of trade relations, and the ebb and flows of the cyclical nature of economies) increases the need for consultants, those with experience and insights, and people willing to guide or direct those with a need for their services. More broadly, we culturally are more comfortable as a society seeking the counsel of others to aid us in our own pursuits. Whether it is seeking the advice of a hairstylist, a wardrobe analyst, or even "consultants" on closets who "solve" the problem of storing the shoes and clothing that the wardrobe analyst suggested we had to have. Our businesses are more often than not becoming dependent on the interconnectivity of various computers, communication protocols, platforms, "software handshaking," and so on. In the not too distant past, purchasing hardware was searching for tools for home repair or building. Software was perhaps what we had hoped our jeans would become after repeated washings, and the only communication protocols we were concerned about were "minding our Ps and Qs." All of these revolutionary changes in how we conduct our business have opened up the portals to vast and complex needs for experts (consultants) to assist us in ensuring that we don't "hurt ourselves" by making mistakes (after all, we often can't program our own VCRs, how can we trust ourselves to build "firewalls" around web sites, ensure remotely located employees can communicate with headquarters, increase the speed of "paperless" order processing, and do the myriad other tasks that businesses are now pressured to do?).

The issue of who "is" and who "is not" a consultant may be moot in many instances. Is the attorney representing a victim acting as a consultant? Is the salesperson who identified a need for an improved telephone system and sold it to one of her accounts a consultant?

It is interesting to note that there are virtually no listings under the heading *Consultants* in my telephone company's directories, but only under such titles as *Management Consultants* and *Engineering Consultants*. The adjective, the profession in which one consults, is the prime identifier rather than consulting itself.

Thus, the qualifying adjective becomes important in identifying an individual consultant and defining his or her special technical or professional field and services. We have marketing consultants, editorial consultants, management consultants, and others. But those adjectival definers often prove to be too general also, so we have marketing consultants of many kinds—proposal consultants, direct mail consultants, advertising consultants. We therefore ought to bear in mind that consulting is probably a viable career alternative for anyone practicing any profession, subprofession, or paraprofession. And while we continue to refer to the consulting profession, as in the following paragraphs, that is for convenience of reference, and should not mask the understanding of what it really is—a means or special method of practicing a given professional specialty.

Many practitioners who regard themselves as consultants are reluctant to so identify themselves because of the sneers and epithets of critics and opponents of consulting. Lawyers, physicians, dentists, architects, and other professional or technical experts, for example, do not call themselves legal consultants or medical consultants even when they are extraordinarily specialized practitioners. Some, such as lawyers, do not generally use the term, as physicians do, even in the special circumstances of being asked by another lawyer to participate in a case as an adviser or associate. The words

associate or *co-counsel* are terms the legal profession prefers to *consultant*. In legal practices, even when an expert is brought in to depose or testify, the expert becomes an *expert witness,* not a consultant. (Consultants are often called upon to become expert
witnesses, and an entire class of independent consultants specialize in such support of
the legal profession, i.e., being expert witnesses and performing other support services. There is a great deal more to being an expert witness than appearing and testi-
fying on the stand.)

That is a major clue to defining one kind of consultant. It identifies a consultant
as a specialist within a profession, representing a mode of practicing the profession,
but not itself the profession. That definition seems consistent with all other evidence
of how consulting appears to others, as well as with how consultants themselves regard and define what they do. In one marketing consultant's business, he identified
himself as first a marketing specialist, second a specialist in marketing to government
agencies, and third a consultant to others requiring assistance in marketing, especially to government agencies and especially with regard to writing proposals. But he
might also regard himself as a writer who consults with others requiring assistance in
writing proposals, a must for certain types of ventures. Even those are only two of several possible ways in which he might identify and define what he is and what he does.
But the differences are more than semantics; they have a great deal to do with how
successful he is at marketing his services, specifically, what clients see him as *doing* for
them—what he can help clients perceive as what he *does* for them.

While on the subject, let us point out that the list in the telephone directory undoubtedly covers many services that one may not normally think of as technical or professional. The list includes movers, printers, tax return preparers, and travel agencies
and bureaus, while it fails to include dozens of technical, professional, and other highly
specialized categories in which many well-established consultants practice today.

For these reasons, we view consulting as a way of practicing a profession. That is,
it is not truly a profession in and of itself. A surgeon does not become something
other than a surgeon when he or she acts as consultant to others. Nor does a lawyer,
an engineer, a marketer, or any other professional, subprofessional, or paraprofessional
change his or her profession when acting as a consultant. The more we examine the
nature of consulting, the more we affirm the idea that consulting is a special way of
practicing a profession, subject to all the hazards, problems and opportunities of the
profession, but also subject to all the hazards, problems, and opportunities resulting
from the consultant mode of practicing the profession!

You will find, if you have not already perceived it, that independent consultants
are often defined or distinguished as much by the kinds of services they provide or by
the means by which they provide them as by the special fields in which they operate.
One of the most rapidly expanding fields of consulting is the area of Internet-based or
electronic commerce. Everything from setting up "stores on the web" to the logistics of
merging actual inventory in warehouses with the electronically generated demand,
through the marketing aspects of attracting consumers while shopping (those annoying pop-up ads through co-operative advertising campaigns with other complementary
web-based services, links off of related sites, etc.). Hot on the heels of this consulting

genre are the security issues related to processing payments in "real time" through the Internet and not risking exposing confidential information to competitors, hackers, or others without a "need to know" about the transaction being completed. In addition to these concerns, the same concerns that existed 10 years ago still exist now and are being addressed by consultants in the "information technology" fields:

1. How do we get the information that is centralized in headquarters and make it available to the field?
2. How do we convert to systems that can "talk" to each other instead of running parallel systems or doing twice the work?
3. What can we do to eliminate errors caused by having to rewrite or rekey the same information over and over again instead of having to enter it once and allow those departments or individuals within the company to all have exposure to the same information in one database?

In some instances, the same efforts addressed through the Internet can be used to solve these problems. In other instances, it may require separate projects or initiatives to fulfill the needs of a particular client.

DO CONSULTANTS HAVE AN IDENTITY CRISIS?

Previously, we mentioned that some professions (attorneys and physicians) shy away from using the term *consultant* to describe the role they assume or are performing at any given time. Other professions have sought to reflect in the shine of being referred to as *consultants* and view it as more desirable than their current job titles. Salespeople have come to recognize that the public's perception of a *salesperson* is quite a bit less trusting than that of a *customer service* or *customer care consultant.* The aura of a consultant is one that speaks of trust and wisdom in many people's minds. As such, many a self-respecting consultant takes umbrage at others co-opting the title of consultant and wish to exclude those who don't quite measure up to the requirements one has to possess before referring to oneself as consultant. The unspoken claim here is that the consultant making that charge knows what it takes to be a consultant and can determine who to exclude and who to include. The licensing issue has continued to be bandied back and forth with little success to date on whether there truly is an objective way to determine what skills are required and who is entitled to claim the title consultant.

Defining yourself as an independent consultant depends primarily on what you choose to be and do, on what kinds of assignments or contracts you choose to accept, and on how you deliver your services, but not on what you call yourself. You can accept only problem-solving jobs, if you wish, although you will probably limit your market if you do. You can refuse assignments that require you to write lengthy formal reports or make formal presentations to the client's assembled staff, if you rebel at writing or public speaking. You may confine yourself to assignments only in your local area and refuse to travel, if you dislike travel. You can, in fact, establish whatever rules, policies, and procedures you wish. In so doing, you may define just what that title *independent consultant* means for you and your own practice. In fact, *only* you can define the term for yourself and for what you do.

It Isn't Always a Conscious Decision

The evidence suggests that few people ever set out to become consultants; most consultants enter that mode of operation, apparently, as the result of chance. In fact, in some cases the transition into consulting is so gradual that the individual hardly realizes that he or she has become a consultant until the transition is complete. In many cases, there never is a specific decision to become a consultant; circumstances force the decision on the individual, perhaps even unconsciously, and propel him or her into the consulting profession almost before he or she realizes it.

My own case is one of those. I was a freelance writer for government agencies and other clients, after a career in high-tech companies contracting with the government, where I had served as engineer, technical writer, proposal specialist, director of marketing, and general manager, among other positions. Friends and acquaintances in quest of government and private-sector contracts, knowing of my success in winning government contracts over the years, often asked my advice and sometimes even asked for a bit of assistance in writing proposals and other aspects of pursuing government contracts. Like many people, I always found it difficult to refuse. But eventually I found this popularity interfering with my writing work, and I was forced to begin begging off, pleading lack of time and the necessity to earn my own living. To my surprise, most requesters immediately offered to pay me for my time to consult with them as an expert! They wanted help and wanted it badly enough to pay for it. I was thus launched into a new profession, almost involuntarily. Over time, the requests of clients dictated to me the kinds of services I offered, including seminars.

A great many other consultants are created by certain specific developments, some related to the many technological revolutions of recent decades, which created so many consultants in engineering and scientific fields, but others related to other developments. For example, Lyndon B. Johnson's administration, with its War on Poverty projects and related programs, inspired the creation of a great many new consultants in education, housing, and fields and activities related directly and indirectly to combating poverty in the United States. These new consultants sprang, of course, principally from the ranks of sociologists, psychologists, economists, educators, educational technologists (a rather new profession), and others in social sciences and humanities. Closely related programs to further the cause of civil rights and reduce the worst aspects of discrimination and persecution of minorities also served as the seedbed for many new consulting specialties. The advent of the new communication media—TV and orbiting satellites—created new situations (aside from the technological ones). The impact of these media on political campaigns alone inspired the rise of a great many political consultants and image consultants.

There are also government programs in reducing and controlling environmental pollution, in finding new sources of energy while conserving conventional sources, in developing affordable housing for everyone, in improving education, in providing better mass transportation, and dozens of kindred programs; each was responsible for seeding even more consulting specialties. So it is certainly not surprising that consulting is definitely a growth industry; circumstances compel it. It is an industry that is doing more than merely growing; it is virtually exploding.

HOW CONSULTANTS SPECIALIZE

Consulting is not a new profession. It probably started as a necessary support service to tribal chiefs and others of the earliest societies. We can easily imagine that the first primitive man who learned how to sharpen and point a stick to make a spear and was soon besieged by others eager to learn how to do the same! That was a simple situation. Today, few situations are that simple. Today, consultants may be defined or described in many ways.

Consulting is not itself a licensed or controlled profession, although consultants may be specialists in a licensed and controlled profession. Many job shops, those who supply technical/professional temporaries (technical writers, engineers, computer programmers, designers, trainers, physicists, illustrators, drafters, marketers, copywriters, and others), sometimes for short-term jobs, such as a week or two, but more often for long-term jobs of many months and even years, often identify themselves as consulting firms, and they often define the temporaries they supply as consultants. Many independent consultants hire themselves out on the same basis (as technical or professional temporaries), bypassing the job shop or broker. (The so-called job shops are really brokers dealing in human labor, very much like talent agencies or booking agents.) In recent years, there has grown up a business of brokering in which the broker takes on a contract with a client, requiring onsite work, and then subcontracts to independent consultants who will work on the client's premises, billing the broker rather than the client. The practical effect is the same; for the client, he or she has the onsite services of people who function as temporary employees. Legally, however, there is a wide distinction, the distinction between an employee and a subcontractor.

HOW DEFINITION RELATES TO CONSULTING (MARKETING) SUCCESS

Why trouble ourselves about defining what we do if we are completely free to call it whatever we wish, to define it however we wish, and to practice it however we wish?

The definition—and the knowledge that consulting is not itself a profession per se but is more often a specialty within a profession—is of critical importance. Later, when we probe the problems of marketing your services and methods for doing so most successfully, this will become more and more evident. You will see the absolute need to know what business you are in if you are to succeed in the all-important marketing aspect of your chosen field. And it is therefore marketing, more than anything else, that identifies and defines what this book is all about, for that is what business success is all about. In fact, while marketing—the vital ingredient to succeeding as an independent consultant—has always been the overall theme and underlying purpose of this book, the economic condition of today makes this more important to your success than ever before. More and more, you must *compete*successfully to survive, and this new edition addresses that need.

My perception of the independent consultant's need for help in marketing inspired much of what I wrote in the original book. To explain that undertaking and commitment to help others *succeed* as independent consultants, I stated as plainly as I could my major premise that most beginning independent consultants are perfectly capable in their chosen fields of technical or professional specialization and need no help from me there, even if I were capable of offering that kind of help. However, many—perhaps most—are badly in need of whatever help they can get in mastering the are of marketing their services—marketing themselves, that is.

Nothing since writing the first editions suggests that the original premise was wrong, in fact, it is as relevant now as it had been when this book was first introduced. This book has led to an ongoing dialogue of readers responding to, and reacting to, the importance of the premise that marketing of oneself is of core importance and have found the suggestions to be helpful and appreciated the direction offered.

THE MORE IMPORTANT VIEW: THAT OF THE CLIENT

However you view yourself and your practice, you do not control how a prospective client perceives you and your services. Does that matter? It certainly does matter, if you are to market successfully. You can sell successfully only to the client's perception and the client's *expectations,* not to your own. Perhaps you can shape the client's perception and expectations to some extend; marketers do that—or try to—constantly, sometimes with success, sometimes without it. But it can be risky to try to modify the client's perception. It requires great skill (and in many cases, it cannot be done at all), and the cost of failure is not to win the contract and sometimes to lose the contract you won earlier. It is usually more practical to determine what the client expects you to be, whether that is scholar, expert, trainer, troubleshooter, mentor, guide, hard worker, resident sage, father confessor, writer, and/or other functionary, and try to conform to that image. (Note, too, that the same client may have different expectations in different situations, depending on what the client perceives his or her immediate need to be in each situation.) Your success in marketing yourself as a consultant depends largely on these factors:

1. How accurately you have assessed the image you must project and how well you have succeeded in projecting that precise image.
2. How well you have estimated what your prospective clients want, including how *they* perceive their needs and problems.
3. How effectively you have convinced the prospective client that you—you and your image, that is—are exactly what he or she is looking for.
4. How effectively you have disseminated that image—made enough prospective clients aware of you, your image, and your availability to help them

overcome their problems and magnify their success. (In marketing, statistics and playing percentages are all important.)

Although presented in the context of achieving marketing success, these factors are equally important to achieving client satisfaction after you have won the contract (which is itself a factor in marketing). Everything you do after winning the assignment must confirm and reinforce the image and expectations you generated or confirmed earlier. As in all marketing, truth is whatever the client perceives as truth; it is the client who decides what he or she accepts, and you must understand the client's perception always. It is also no less important to create a favorable impression generally. You will always have difficulty satisfying a client who has an adverse impression of you. But you will find it rather easy to please the client who has a favorable image of you. Clients tend to see what they expect and want to see, just as we all do.

There are many hazards in consulting independently, many of them peculiar to being a one-person show. For one, as an independent practitioner, it is extremely difficult to cope with the feast-and-famine nature of consulting. It is difficult—frequently impossible—to backlog consulting assignments, and yet you have only so many hours a day available. How do you smooth out those peaks and valleys? Some jobs require several people; how do you cope with that successfully so that you do not lose the contract? Some clients simply cannot afford your regular, direct rates, although they have need of help. How can you help them—and yourself—without resorting to the dubious practice of cutting your standard rates?

Experience demonstrates clearly enough that there are still three especially noteworthy things about consulting:

1. Consulting has more than its share of detractors who question its merits and its necessity and the capabilities and integrity of its practitioners.
2. Consulting remains difficult to define; the debates and controversies over what it is (and what it is not!) continue to rage, although perhaps not as vigorously as in the past. (Are we gaining recognition?)
3. Despite these problems the markets for consulting—the *use* of consultants, that is—and the number of consultants in everyday practice continue to grow.

The need for specialists of all kinds keeps growing. Nor are the two trends—the growth in markets for consulting and in numbers of specialists hanging out their shingles as consultants—unrelated; they are the logical and inevitable consequence of several forces operating in the modern world, including at least the rapid increases in technological, political, economic, industrial, and other complexities of our society; and the rapidly rising average level of education, as young people go to college in ever greater numbers. It is inevitable that consulting will continue to grow and be a force in the business world and in society in general.

Yet, despite this, there is the strange phenomenon that consulting proves to be an elusive quantity, like quicksilver, when you attempt to capture it in a definition. Try, for example, to look up *Consultants* in the yellow pages telephone directory of any metropolitan area, and you will experience some frustration immediately; there is no such heading in most directories. But look it up in the index to the directory, and you will find a long string on consultant listings, at least in my own Washington, D.C. area.

The fact is that consulting is not a profession in itself, but a way of practicing a profession. The engineer who consults remains an engineer first, and a consultant only after that. The physician who consults does not give up being a physician first, nor do any of the others who turn to consulting change their professions. They change merely the arrangements under which they render their services, and often the kind of individuals and organizations to whom they render the services.

The latter aspect, who the clients are, gives us another clue to the nature of consulting and consultants, for we can divide the consultant's clients into two broad classes: peers and others. Most consultants serve one or the other, but some consultants serve both. the physician invariably serves his or her peers—other physicians—when called on to consult. But a public relations (PR) consultant would most often—almost invariably—serve a client who is a completely lay person at PR. An engineer would be most likely to serve other engineers as clients, but could easily be called upon by a client who is not an engineer.

This is an important point, one we shall discuss further. It has a great deal to do with how you conduct your practice and especially with how you do your marketing. But it also has a great deal to do with defining what you do as a consultant. And the necessity for doing that will also become more and more apparent as we proceed.

During the writing of the first edition of this book, the personal computer was just coming of age, though many people were still unaware of the impact it would have, indeed, the revolution it would cause. This book is being written on a laptop computer (not a desktop), during business trips away from a home office in untethered environments (using battery power during flights, plugging in and recharging once arriving at hotels or client sites, etc.). It is being transmitted to the publisher variously through cable connections, DSL and dial-up modems, and other times, it is being sent to the publisher on a CD-ROM that was copied remotely through software applications that reside within my laptop.

The impact on consulting may be obvious to you as the reader, but for one thing, it has created an entire new class and population of computer consultants, who specialize in electronic communication, microprocessing, miniaturization, and power management. These consultants help millions of businesspeople work independently and remotely without having to accomplish their tasks in a single location. But it has also placed a priceless tool in the hands of independent consultants, giving them resources that only large and powerful consulting firms enjoyed before.

The wise consultant will make it his or her business to be equipped with a suitable technology that permits "real-time" communications from remote locations. In this new edition, I will try to help you do this.

1 | What Does (Should) a Consultant Do?

Better to be proficient in one art than a smatterer in a hundred.

—Japanese Proverb

There is nothing especially unusual about the services provided by the typical consultant, nothing, at least, that distinguishes them from other contracted-for specialist services, such as those that might be rendered by an interior decorator, image counselor, financial advisor, or freelance package designer. The differences between these individuals and the consultants who provide similar services is the name by which the individual identifies him- or herself and what he or she does. In this chapter, we'll ignore the facade of titles and look at some of the most active fields for consulting and at several aspects of the consulting industry, especially as it pertains to independent consultants.

As a first step, we'll look at those consultants who are most often employed on the client's premises on a full-time basis, often long-term (many months, and even years, in more than a few cases), as a quasi-employee. That is a phenomenon of the modern technological age and especially in evidence, at least until now, in areas of high technology and large federal contracts. Among the most numerous of the warm bodies working as contractor personnel on clients' premises are the many varieties of computer-related specialists. Within those ranks are software application creators working on customized or proprietary applications, Internet gurus hammering out the client's needs for security and encryption technologies, and those that are focused on Customer Relationship Management (CRM) or Efficient Consumer response (ECR) which involves looking at all the points of contact between a client's customer and themselves and working to reduce "choke-spots," or areas of error in serving those customers.

COMPUTERS AND DATA PROCESSING

Given how ubiquitous computers are in today's culture where most people have personal computers and many are hobbyists owning multiple machines, it is hard to believe that there was a time not too long ago when computers were strictly the domain of large research institutions or extremely well-funded corporations.

Those early machines spawned a great many consulting jobs, especially jobs for consultants who specialized in writing custom programs. There were then relatively few ready-made programs, and even the available ones were rarely suitable for general applications. So hundreds of thousands of individuals became computer programmers, many of them independent consultants, others evolving into large consulting companies. But not all these computer specialists were programmers, literally; many were known by other titles, such as *systems analysts, systems designers, system engineers,* and *computer operators.* And there were often gradations within categories, to indicate levels of experience and capability, such as *senior systems analyst* and *junior systems analyst,* or they might be graded numerically. They might even be given other titles—*information analyst* or *data designer.* As the computer and, especially, the software industries grew, further modifiers and qualifiers were added to the descriptions of the individual's qualifications and capabilities, so that a programmer would also have to list the various computers and computer languages he or she was familiar with and, finally, the kinds of programs in which he or she was most experienced. There was a steady proliferation of areas of specialization and expertise, as the technologies of the hardware and software evolved.

In the hardware arena, for example, one of the most troublesome areas was data storage, and the improvements evolved through several stages beyond that of the familiar punched card, through banks of electronic (flip-flop) circuits, tape on large reels, magnetic drums, magnetic cores, and even a few other things before the more efficient hard- and floppy-disk systems evolved. Now disks are in common use. And at each stage manufacturers were eagerly seeking engineers experienced in whatever was the current latest method for storage of data. Not finding enough qualified applicants to accept jobs, many manufacturers turned to hiring consultants to work on-site as long-term contract labor—temporary employees, in effect.

The picture was the same in the software industry. Companies who could not hire enough qualified employees or could not wait for the relatively slow process of recruitment—seeking, finding, and selling—necessary to produce required staffs, often resorted to contracting for the services of technical/professional temporaries—consultants—to fill the gaps as contractors. (At the time, The National Association of Temporary Services reported six to eight weeks as the average time to fill a position with a new hire, a few days, often as little as one day, to fill the job with a temporary worker.)

A great deal of the cost was passed on directly to the federal government via cost-plus contracts, especially in military contracts, but also in others, such as the NASA space program. Hundreds of thousands of such consultants worked for the General Electric Company, RCA, General Dynamics, Boeing, North American Rockwell, McDonnell Douglas, Northrup, Hughes Aircraft, TRW, General Motors, Ford, and many other supercorporations as well as smaller, less well-known companies developing weapons and space systems under major government contracts. But it was not only contractors and private industry who made use of consultants working as contract labor or temporaries; many government agencies also found this an expedient way to get their own, in-house projects completed. The NASA bases, for example, employed many such consultants, as did many military bases where a great deal of R&D work was being conducted. Civilian agencies also used this method for hiring hard-to-find specialists. The U.S. Postal Service, for one, used many contract engineers, technicians, drafters, and designers, and many of the major computer installations in federal agencies were and are today operated by such contract personnel working on the government's premises. Many other kinds of government installations—the U.S. Army ordnance explosives plants, for example—are operated by contractors. In fact, there is a supply group classification for this in the federal procurement system. Relevant requirements are listed under category "M: Operation and Maintenance of Government-Owned Facility."

This is history, and much of it took place under the pressure of military needs and the drive to beat the Soviets in the race for both commercial and military use of space. The pace of it has abated now, with the end of the Soviet Union and the Cold War, but although less frantic, such hiring of consultants still goes on, and still on a large scale. For many consultants this type of work has become a way of life, a regular career. It can be a gypsy kind of life; to work regularly on contracts in these dynamic industries, one must be willing to go wherever the next job is. But that suits some individuals; there are those who like to keep moving and keep seeing new places. In fact, some of the most resourceful of these modern itinerant workers manage to find jobs in the climates of their choice, such as the Sun Belt in the winter and New England in the summer. It suits those, also, who want a much greater income than they are likely to make on a fixed job with an organization. Consultants generally can earn up to twice as much as regular employees would in the same jobs (and even more, in situations where specialists are in especially short supply or the assignment involves hazards and hardships), although with considerably fewer fringe benefits. (They also earn per-diem living allowances when more than 50 miles from their official home bases.)

This set of conditions, with its advantages and disadvantages, is not confined to the computer and data-processing industries; it is far more widespread and general than that. Today enough individuals earn their livings via such means that they have become a major part of the income-tax base. The most recent figures from the National Association of Personnel Services (the previously known National Association of Temporary Services, 2003 Annual Survey, posted on www.napsweb.org/aboutus /FAQAnswer.cfm?fid=1) provide an eye-opening view into just how pervasive this form of consulting is:

- There are in excess of 30,000 staffing, personnel services, and employment companies in the United States.
- Their revenues are nearly $65 Billion for 2002.
- The past seven years have seen average increases of 10 percent in temporary help services.
- It is estimated that 90 percent of the companies in the United States use temporary help services to fulfill their seasonal or heavier periods.

That has led the IRS to adopt regulations to define the legal and tax status of independent consultants and contractors, making it difficult for such independent workers to write off relevant expenses. It is no small problem to many independent consultants today. Later, we will discuss this problem at greater length.

The Job Shop or Supplier of Temporaries

Typically, the job shop must submit a bid for each contract to provide on-site consultants. In most cases, job shop employees are really potential employees, slated to be employed only as long as the job shop has a client to send them to and bill for their services. Therefore, employment by a job shop is a technicality and coincides exactly with assignment to a client, and not one hour longer.

Normally, the client does not simply order a number of anonymous warm bodies, but selects the bodies to be ordered; the client wants to see resumes of available consultants, and often wishes to interview before asking for quotation of rates, to satisfy himself or herself that the consultants are suitably qualified. Clients may not scrutinize these resumes quite as closely as they would those of prospective new hires, but they do study them with some care, and they do normally interview candidates.

Typically, the job shop quotes consultants by classes, asking the same rate for each person in a given class, although not necessarily paying each person in a given class the same rate! (Beginners in this kind of work almost always sign up too cheaply, but they soon learn what to demand.) The fringe benefits are scant, consisting of a few paid days off and perhaps a group hospitalization plan. And the employee often qualifies for paid days off only when he is employed for six months or a year, which is far from certain to happen in that work. (Most job shoppers change employers frequently, as opportunities are presented.)

This arrangement permits the job shops to operate at low overhead, an absolute necessity for survival in that field. Typical overhead rates are about 35 percent to 40 percent, which must cover insurance, taxes, miscellaneous costs, and profit; however, when the job shop is fortunate enough to hire well-qualified beginners, they may earn considerably more than 35 to 40 percent gross profit on those individuals.

Some hardy individuals far prefer the frequent changes of jobs and locales, the financial benefits of job shopping, and the many vacations they are able to take (between assignments), so they make a career of such work, earning at least half again as much as they would on salary, and in many cases considerably more than that. There are also some individuals who choose that mode of working because they are unable to win jobs on the regular payroll of a company, because either they are too old or can't pass a medical examination. Large companies often have rather rigid policies that bar older people, not necessarily because of their age alone, but because they cannot pass the insurance examinations. Job shopping is thus often a boon for people who are well beyond the typical retirement age, but are still active, alert, and capable of a full day's work everyday. (Many are, in fact, retired from lifelong careers, but unwilling to spend the rest of their lives sitting on the porch and rocking slowly.)

Although there are many hardy perennials in the field, there are a great many individuals who turn to that mode of working for a short while, attracted by the money or temporarily unable to find a job. Many soon tire of the uncertainty and the constant moving about necessary to work steadily in that field. Seasoned by the experience of a few assignments, they move on to work they find more satisfactory as employees or as independent consultants. In fact, it is not at all uncommon for job shoppers to make such a good impression on clients that the clients offer them permanent employment. All of this results in a steady turnover in the field, making it relatively easy to break into it as a port in a storm, a training ground, or a starting point in a career.

THE AEROSPACE INDUSTRIES

The use of consultant specialists as temporary employees predates the computer industry. As a direct result of World War II and its consequences, specifically the emergence of the Soviet Union as a major military power and potential threat to the western world, the U.S. government decided not to dismantle our huge military organization and lapse into typical peacetime somnolence, but rather to accept our new role as one of the only two remaining superpowers. We accepted what our government saw as our obligation to be the strongman of planet Earth and to develop powerful new weapons and systems. So, as cold war became the status quo, reorganized U.S. military organizations were given huge budgets and authority to begin developing supersystems of all kinds. Most of these weapons and systems involved the new high technologies of electronics applications—radar, sonar, missiles, computers, secure communications, jet aircraft, helicopters, and sundry other Buck Rogers-like technologies.

A new phenomenon appeared, reflecting a change in the thinking of the military developers; *equipments* (this new Pentagonese came into popular and accepted vogue quite quickly, as did another bit of Pentagonese contracting jargon, *deliverables*) were soon perceived not as singular, independent items, but as components of greater entities—of systems. They all became, in fact, military weapons, killing machines. A fighter aircraft was no longer an airplane, but a weapons-system, an entity involving radar, fire-control mechanisms (which means aiming and tracking systems), and other sophisticated defensive and offensive gear integrated as a system. This philosophy of collecting complete complements of equipment into single systems identified as weapons extended gradually to even larger, often city-size, entities, such as the Navy's destroyers and cruisers and the Air Force's largest bombers and reconnaissance airplanes. Airplanes became defensive and offensive systems. Self-contained in capabilities for detecting and neutralizing hostile attacks, they could also carry out their own attacks using a variety of individual weapons— machine guns, light cannon, and missiles—especially the latter, as the years wore on—while also using such other weapons as napalm, rockets, and bombs against ground targets. (Even helicopters became gunships, equipped as systems for specialized kinds of missions in the war we carried on in Southeast Asia.)

The concept of integrated systems spread rapidly and was reflected in what was now identified as systems engineering, which again called for the services of specialists who were in short supply. A great many systems engineers, individuals with broad enough interests and capabilities (both technical and managerial) to lead multidisciplinary teams, thus became consultants. And there were many stories of employees who resigned their jobs, but never left their desks. Instead, they merely changed status, now on the payroll of a job shop as consultants or professional temporaries, assigned to continue doing what they had done as employees of the client company, but now at a higher rate of pay. They had given themselves promotions and raises, in effect, by changing their status. Some even became independent consultants and contracted directly with former employers to stay on in a new capacity, doing the same work. (In fact, a great many independent consultants found their former employer to be their first and most enthusiastic client.)

A contributing factor was that a new era had dawned in the world of technology. The concept of interdisciplinary specialties had arrived, and new problems of hiring and staffing had to be solved; for example, what mix of specialists is needed, and what kind of specialist should lead a team requiring a mix of different kinds of specialists? Suppose you need to put together a team to develop a new missile system. You need to develop the rocket engine, airframe, launch system, guidance system, warheads, and perhaps telemetry. Because this is a highly complex system of many complex components, you must also design and manage complex tests to troubleshoot, debug, validate, and ultimately certify the resulting final system as an integrated entity. You must prepare operating and maintenance procedures, and full documentation for operation and maintenance. That spells out a need for mechanical engineers, stress analysts, chemical engineers, electronic engineers, test engineers, maintenance engineers, technical writers, illustrators, and more than a few other specialists to put the whole system together. Where and how will you get all these expert specialists, and who should lead that team? (To this day, that latter question has not been fully answered, and perhaps there is no satisfactory answer to it. Perhaps our knowledge and our ambitions have reached beyond the technical and managerial capabilities of even the most talented individual.)

The economics of doing business this way are relatively simple. The government might allow the contractor $30 an hour for some given type of specialist. The firm supplying the specialists might charge the government contractor $27 an hour for the specialist, and pay the specialist $19 or $20 an hour. This provides the specialist about 50 percent more than he or she might earn as the typical direct employee of the client company, while providing the supplier of the specialists some 10 percent net profit. (The actual numbers will almost surely vary quite widely from this hypothetical case, but the principles will be the same.)

That typical 50 percent differential between what the specialists could earn as the consultant/technical temporary and the direct employee explains why so few such specialists resisted the many offers they received to go direct with the client companies. It was easy to decline.

In fact, those specialists who choose to make a career of being job shoppers (the firms who hire them and assign them to client companies are known colloquially as job shops, although many refer to themselves as consulting firms and to their employees as consultants) are virtually a subculture of their own, jeering openly among themselves at the thought of going direct, referring to it almost as an act of heresy. By far the majority work for one of the many job shops, but many are independent even to the extent that they place themselves in their work assignments—contracting directly with the client companies, that is—thereby controlling their own situations entirely. (This generally comes about after the consultant has become thoroughly experienced in this way of doing business and knows many of the client companies and is well known to them as a competent and reliable individual.)

In many cases, the situation is quite complex, and the client for such services may be a sub-subcontractor, especially when the project and original contract are large ones. Even the largest corporations cannot and do not try to do everything. To perform on most of the huge government projects, even the largest of the supercorporations must award hundreds of subcontracts, many of those quite substantial and awarded to other great corporations. The basic contract for the Atlas missile system, for example, went to General Dynamics, who awarded a large contract for a supporting subsystem to RCA; IBM was a subcontractor to International Telephone & Telegraph (ITT) on a large Air Force logistics network (the 465L system); and GE developed heavy radar sets for the Ballistic Missile Early Warning System under contract to RCA, the prime contractor for the system.

In these circumstances, where the contracts are in the hundreds of millions and may even run to well over a billion dollars, there are usually several hundred subcontracts, many of them rather large, imposing a temporary labor burden on many of the subcontractors, as well as on the prime contractor. In many cases the contractor does not want to hire people as regular, permanent employees, knowing that the contract represents a temporary need for more people who would become surplus when the contract is finished. Although consultants are often hired as temporary employees because it is the only way to staff a project rapidly enough with qualified specialists, in many other cases consultants are hired as temporaries because it makes better economic and business sense to do so. It costs money to hire people, especially in the large organization; advertising, interviewing, paperwork, relocation, and numerous other costs are incurred in recruiting employees. Terminating no-long-needed personnel also costs money. And there are many legal obligations today in hiring people, as well as problems in terminating them. The technical temporaries represent a way around many of these problems. They can be hired quickly, with little paperwork and little legal obligation, since they work for a contractor, not for the client, and they can be terminated as easily when the need ends. Moreover, if and when a temporary proves to be unsatisfactory as an individual, there are no complications in having that individual's services ended, whereas it is not always a simple matter today to discharge a permanent employee for cause. (These are among the effective sales arguments employed in selling consultant services.)

The sizes of programs for temporaries—numbers employed and duration of assignments—vary widely. NASA has used rather large forces of such personnel, notably in engineering and computer-related work, and General Electric Company has almost traditionally employed large numbers of temporaries in the various engineering functions of their missile and space programs. In fact, where the project requires large number of temporaries, it is not unusual to have temporaries from a half-dozen or more firms working together on the premises.

As to duration, that also varies from a few days to several years. That is, a consultant may be employed on an indefinite basis, and be kept on for one project after another. At the Philadelphia-area plants of the GE missile and space systems many consultant temporaries were assigned there for as long as five years. Very much the same situation prevailed at the large training center Xerox Corporation established in Leesburg, Virginia, near Washington, where they hired several dozen training technologists, many of whom remained on assignment there for approximately five years. Those were all hired—placed under contract—as self-employed individuals or contractors working on the client's premises.

It is usually not by design that these assignments last so long. Frequently, the assignment starts as a relatively short-term one of several months, but new contracts come in, and the consultants are asked to remain. This can continue indefinitely, the client always acting on the reasonable assumption that the need is temporary. (The word *temporary* thus becomes rather flexible in definition.)

The practice of bringing in whole staffs of specialists, whether they are called consultants, contract labor, professional temporaries, on-site contractors, or contract labor—all of these terms are used—has become rather widespread in all sectors of the economy—in major government contracts, in commercial or non-government industry, and in government itself. Many federal institutions and facilities are staffed and operated by such personnel, especially by agencies doing technical work—NASA, EPA, and DOD, for example—but not exclusively so. The Air Force has contracted with private industry to manage and operate a warehouse in which it stores the many technical documents required to support its vast array of complex equipment systems. The Postal Service Training and Development Institute awarded a contract to have a private firm administer its correspondence courses in Norman, Oklahoma. The General Services Administration hired a private firm to run a chain of stores selling personal computers to government buyers. The NASA Scientific and Technical Information Facility in Maryland is staffed and run by a contractor. There are many more such situations, where it is more expedient or more efficient to contract out the management and operation of a government operation, even on government premises.

Most clients for consulting in this mode—hiring consulting specialists as temporary employees—have the common problem of needing a temporary force of specialists of one sort or another, usually to staff a special project that represents a nonrepetitive peak load. But this is not always the case. Some clients have more classical problems, problems that are solved not by the mere recruitment of a staff of specialists on a temporary basis, but by technical problems that the consultants are expected to solve for them.

One such case was that of Remington-Rand, once a computer division of Sperry Corporation (now Unisys). This organization had built a custom-designed, state-of-the-art computer for a California customer, and was approached by the U.S. Navy with an invitation to build another for them, albeit with a few changes, such as a much greater memory. The trouble began when the Navy rejected the user manuals the company offered. The Navy refused to pay until an acceptable set of manuals was produced for them, but the publications staff at Remington-Rand had been producing commercial manuals, and was not familiar with typical military requirements for technical manuals. The company thereupon felt forced to contract for consultant specialists to assist their publication staff in making the manuals acceptable to the customer, a project that consumed several months.

Today we have a great many computer consultants, and the number is growing steadily as a result of two influences. One, the number of computers is growing exponentially, since the advent of the low-cost, personal computer, which has made it possible for almost everyone in even the smallest business or professional practice to own at least one computer; two, the computer industry continues to become more and more sophisticated, and that means it has become and continues to become more and more complex in both the hardware and software aspects.

Still, there is more. There is a universe of possible configurations of these machines into systems, with various size of memories, drives, keyboards, monitors, software, accessories, add-on boards, operating system versions, and sundry other items, so that even an expert is soon confused.

Where the computer consultant of the prepersonal-computer days was probably called upon most often to help a client with the programming—software—problems, many of today's computer consultants find that clients want help in selecting the right system for their needs or are already in trouble. That is, they may be buying a first system, be ready to get a larger or more sophisticated system (e.g., multitasking, multiuser, or local area network), or have already bought a system that doesn't do what they need it to do. As the needs of the businesses serviced change, so too do the requests/requirements placed on the consultant serving that client. The need for expertise in; connectivity, cross-platform communication, portability, remote processing, and so on have supplanted the old requests of "tell me which system to buy." The client is savvy and has had experiences (positive and negative) with computers and is a more educated client about wants and requirements.

This is not to neglect the more classical consulting situation, in which the client not only has a problem to solve, but the problem is so highly specialized that part of it lies in finding the right consultant for the job. In one case, my own clients found themselves in need of a specialist in Tempest and EMP-hardening technology, areas concerned with data security and system survival under nuclear attack. There are many engineering people who know a great deal about these technologies, but in this case the work involved precise compliance with a highly detailed and sophisticated military technical specification. Esoteric although this subject is, there is enough demand to keep an expert busy advising electronic companies, even the largest ones, about it. They managed to find one such expert who turned in an excellent performance, but there are probably not a half-dozen others quite as knowledgeable as he about this specialized lore.

In the same vein, some years ago NASA commissioned a venerable Japanese scientist to write a definitive work on celestial mechanics because he was considered to be by far the most highly qualified person in the world for this assignment, and he was so well along in years that NASA feared the loss of his great knowledge if he did not soon record it.

Many consulting specialties are not in common supply, but also are not so rare that it is extraordinarily difficult to find qualified practitioners. My own specialty is one of these. I write, lecture, and consult on marketing generally, but especially on government marketing, and clients call on me often to help them write proposals, the key to government contracts. There are not a great many consultant, who can boast honestly of an impressive track record in writing winning proposals—good proposal writers must be sought out—but the skill is not so highly specialized that the talented proposal writer is a rare and much sought after expert.

During the Great Depression, there grew up a consulting class known popularly as *efficiency experts*. These were individuals who claimed an ability to raise operating efficiency in companies and so reduce costs, an unusually attractive prospect. Business people, even those operating large companies, found it difficult to resist the lure of relieving some of the economic pressure that threatened to force them. More than a few companies succumbed to their blandishments and brought teams of efficiency experts aboard to work their magic.

How good were they? It's hard to say for they ran into a buzz saw of opposition from employees and labor unions. Many of the latter were then struggling to establish and justify their very existence, and understandably, they saw efficiency experts as the enemy who was determined to eliminate jobs, and therefore did everything they could to discredit the whole idea. Efficiency experts vanished into history, at least in part as a result of having lost the battle of publicity and common acceptance. Well, perhaps vanished is not quite accurate. The term *efficiency expert* that vanished to be replaced by today's term for the discipline, *industrial engineer,* also called *methods engineer*—specialists in designing workplaces and work systems for greatest efficiency.

Industrial engineering and methods engineering are respectable professions today. Large industrial firms often have such experts on staff, sometimes serving the firm as internal consultants, but there are still many opportunities for independent industrial engineers to win consulting assignments with firms who have only occasional need for such capabilities.

THE CONSULTANT ORGANIZATION

There are at least two distinct types of consulting organizations, although there are the inevitable hybrids (it is never a black and white world!) that blur the distinctions. The first type is that which we have been discussing here: the supplier of technical/professional temporaries. The second type is the consulting organization that undertakes a project, generally under a contract, with a defined end-product or service to be delivered, and with work done most often on the consulting organization's own site, but if necessary on the client's site or on both sites.

THE CONSULTANT COMPANY

Many people do not consider the job shops to be true consulting organizations nor job shoppers to be true consultants. On the other hand, there is the well-known difficulty in defining consulting in today's business and industrial complex. For example, among the many procurement categories the government employs to classify and organize its purchasing, there is **H: Consultant and Expert Services.** You might expect that anything listed here would be consulting without question. Among the services requested here, however, are real estate appraisals, computer software programming, technical writing, surveys, and other pedestrian chores that we do not normally conceive of as consulting chores.

There are also a great many firms offering management consulting, among other services, because that term appears to encompass virtually any service a business or any other kind of organization might need.

It is not at all unusual for businesses that offer information systems to have consulting divisions, or to go out and purchase a major consulting firm to add to their portfolio of offerings to clients (not to mention create revenue streams for themselves that they otherwise would not have access to, and identify additional opportunities for them to pursue within their clients). Familiar names like IBM, EDS, Cambridge Technology Partners (bought by Novell), Ernst & Young bought by Cap Gemini, KPMG, LLC ultimately leading to the creation of BearingPoint, and others are all examples of firms that recognized the opportunities within consulting work and leveraging it for their businesses. Many accounting firms have attempted this and have been unsuccessful because of the perceived lack of objectivity that occurs when advice-giving activities were seen as being self-serving by clients, or one of the divisions was tainted by the scandals that rocked the other divisions.

Engineering firms have also migrated into management consulting, as have firms in training development, public relations, and a great many other successful firms in specialized businesses, service and otherwise. But it is not only already-established companies who make such transitions. Individuals launch their independent consulting practices from a base of experience in some given industry, for the potential for practicing as a counselor or consultant in any of today's many specialized fields is almost unlimited. In fact, although none of these firms or individual practitioners list themselves under a main heading of *consulting* as their basic category, they do make it clear that they offer consulting services, whether the listing is consultants or counselor, services, or others. Witness the lengthy, and yet only partial, list offered later in this chapter.

HYBRIDS

We have looked at two basic types, which may be considered to be at the extremes of consulting, one being rather classic consulting, recognized as such by even the purists, while the other barely qualified as consulting to some. But the world is not black and white, and a great many consultants and consulting firms fall between these extremes of definition. In fact, it is probably a fairly rare firm that does not fall between these extremes and have at least some of the characteristics of each case.

There is a distinct difference between supplying technical/professional temporaries and carrying out projects on-site (on the client's premises, that is). In providing technical/professional temporaries, the consultant firm is selling hours of professional effort, normally at a per-hour rate. The firm is obligated only to supply qualified personnel, as agreed to and contracted for, and does not incur responsibility for the project, whatever it is. It is up to the client to make best use of this labor—to manage the effort and the people. It is the client who is responsible for the result, and who must pay the hourly rate for every hour expended by the temporaries, regardless of result, just as with internal, direct employees. (Of course, the client may terminate summarily the services of the supplying firm or of any individual supplied.) In carrying out a project on-site (whether entirely or only partially on-site), the contractor must assume responsibility for the project overall—for the end result, which means also for the management of the staff, regardless of where they are physically employed. It is a critical difference. It should be noted here in passing that under federal laws, you must always manage your own employees when they are working on-site at some federal facility because the law prohibits civil-service employees from giving direct orders to or being given direct orders by contractor personnel. Ergo, the on-site contractor must always provide on-site supervision and management of the staff working on-site. (Civil-service employees provide only technical direction to the contract personnel working on federal premises.)

Aside from that, a great many firms who specialize in supplying professional temporaries also have in-house capabilities for staffing, managing, and carrying out projects on their own premises. But many of those firms whose main enterprise is handling projects in-house are quite willing to carry out projects on the client's premises or to supply professional temporaries, so that distinctions between the two tend to disappear.

THE CONSULTANT AS A SELF-EMPLOYED INDEPENDENT

Much of the foregoing discussion is outside the scope of this book because this book focuses on the individual, independent consultant. As an independent consultant, however, you should be familiar with all kinds of organizations and markets for their services, for you can take advantage of all these modes of selling your services too. But, the case is a little different with the individual, independent consultant working on the client's premises, even on government premises. Here you must manage yourself, and the distinction between technical direction and direct orders becomes somewhat blurred. Even in the case of the client in the commercial or private sector, when you are working on a client's premises as an independent consultant, you usually find it necessary to be project oriented—to be at least as much concerned with final results as with conscientious effort. In a career as a consultant, if you are aware of and alert for these opportunities, you will almost surely find yourself able to take advantage of them to sell your expert services in all these consulting modes.

Whether you find yourself working mostly on clients' premises or in your own office depends largely on the kind of consulting service you provide, and perhaps even more on the basic nature of your clients. If you counsel individuals in personal matters, it is likely that you will have to arrange to receive them in your own offices.

First, because fees are generally by the hour, usually running to only an hour or two per consultation and by appointment, you must see several clients a day, making it impractical to call on the clients. In addition, it is usually necessary to have a controlled environment—privacy and quiet, for example—something often difficult to achieve in a client's home. And in at least some cases, you need direct access to certain resources, such as a computer, a library, or files.

On the other hand, if you serve organizations and the nature of your work is such that most of your assignments run to at least several days and are billed by the day, it is likely that you will work largely and perhaps entirely on the clients' premises.

SUITABLE FIELDS AND SERVICES

Probably everyone who enters independent consulting (or perhaps any independent business venture, for that matter) has an education coming to him or her; the world we face is full of surprises, and the longer we live, the more we learn how little we really know of it. My own early experience in presenting seminars was an eye opener for me, but it reflects a common problem of underestimating the value of what we offer, as I did in the example I cite here.

The Graduate Course Seminar

Many of us tend to assume that what we ourselves know well is common knowledge. The first time I conducted a seminar on how to write proposals for government contracts, I assumed that it would be a waste of time to teach the rudiments. I therefore planned to focus my presentation on the grand strategies that distinguish the great proposals, and brush hurriedly by the basics I thought were common knowledge to everyone with an interest in proposals and marketing to the government. In fact, I stipulated in my advertising that it was a graduate course and not at all suitable for beginners in proposal writing.

To my surprise, a generous portion of the 54 attendees who registered for that first session proved to be beginners, lured by my promises to reveal a number of inside tips, techniques, and strategies I had learned or developed over the years. (In fact, the cautionary note that it was not for beginners proved to be more an attraction than anything else, and undoubtedly was at least partially responsible for the extraordinary results I got from my first venture into seminar promotion.) There were also a number of thoroughly experienced people, including two senior executives who were in the process of forming a new division of their large corporation. They had come to the seminar to see if they could pick up even a handful of useful ideas.

Until I conducted that session, I had doubts that I could reveal enough little-known information to justify the cost and the full day's time spent by each attendee. (I seriously underpriced that first seminar because of this fear.) I was amazed to discover that even senior, experienced people were unaware of many basic facts that I thought to be quite fundamental and even obvious about proposal writing, facts that I would have expected senior executives to know as well as I knew them. (Later, I had the satisfaction of having a senior executive of one large company bring groups from his staff to two successive sessions of my presentation, remarking that he found just one of the ideas I imparted to be worth the entire day's cost in dollars and time.)

Let the Client Choose the Services

I was quite surprised by the reaction to my coverage of the topic of costs—those cost analyses and detailed presentations required in most proposals. I had originally planned to do little more than mention these briefly in passing. To my amazement, that portion of my presentation proved to be one of the greatest areas of interest to the attendees. Even senior people tend to be somewhat confused and uncertain about direct and indirect costs, overhead, other direct, and many other basic cost elements and concepts, let alone the more esoteric jargon and concepts such as G&A and ex-pense pools. I had originally thought that even if the attendees did not know some-thing of the subject, they would be intensely bored by it.

This experience has been repeated in almost every seminar I have conducted, and I am always slightly surprised by it. Aside from my difficult-to-shed feeling that ac-counting is a boring subject to most people, I can never believe that experienced pro-posal writers in contracting companies have so little understanding of what costs are, how they are generated, how they proliferate, how they are classified, what they really mean, and how they must be analyzed and presented. That is because I found the matter of costs a fascinating and critically important one many years ago when I first became involved in proposal writing. Unlike many other proposal writers, I was not content to surrender this portion of the proposal effort to the accountants (maybe I was recalling what Clemenceau said about war being too serious a matter to be left to the generals and decided that costs were too serious a matter to be left to the ac-countants); I insisted that I would work out the costs and let the accountants review them. I would not submit (and be responsible for the success of) a proposal until and unless I personally approved of everything in the proposal. In time, I became so knowledgeable about the cost side of the business that I took such knowledge for granted and assumed that everyone writing proposals was equally knowledgeable. Therefore, I was too modest about what I had to offer in this respect.

It's a common enough error. Most of us assume that we have special knowledge or abilities to offer to those unfamiliar with our fields, but not to those who are our peers in whatever those fields are. Not so: You can probably sell your services to your technical/professional peers too, once you take the trouble to learn the areas in which they most need help, or what part of your special knowledge or skills will be helpful, yet is not widely known or available in your profession. (Examples: shortcuts, meth-ods, ideas, tricks of the trade you have learned from especially knowledgeable old timers, through extensive special reading and studies, or through your own experi-ence, introspection, and innovation.)

We often make the mistake of trying to decide for ourselves what our clients need and want, when we should be asking the clients. That is, we should be doing a great deal of experimenting by offering services and carefully listening and observing client reactions, to discover what works best.

This applies to virtually all professions and fields. Following, as the conclusion of this chapter, is a list of just a few of the many fields/areas in which consulting services are offered. Even these are, for the most part, generalized items, with various specializations possible within each. (Many were derived from the general index to the telephone company's Yellow Pages directory, which does not list consultants as a primary classification, but only as a subclassification within general headings.) Study this list to gain an appreciation of the diversity. You may find yourself qualified to consult in more than one field!

Even these are often too general. One security consultant, for example, may be a specialist in security devices—locks, alarms, barriers, safes, surveillance equipment, and other such items, while another is a specialist in guard forces, patrolling, background checking, and other security measures based on direct human surveillance. Most of the categories can be divided into several subcategories. Career and vocational counselors, for example, may easily specialize in at least a half-dozen areas. There are many kinds of engineers—civil, construction, mechanical, electrical, electronic, stress, and industrial—and these are all subdivided into many narrower specialties. Designers likewise fit into all kinds of categories—package designers, lighting designers, presentation designers—as do most of the specialists listed here. It is a rare field today that will not support a well-experienced specialist as a consultant.

Field Having Consulting Services

Accounting

Advertising

Agriculture/farming

Arbitration

Audiovisual presentations

Auditing

Automation

Aviation

Business and business planning

Business writing

Career and vocational counselors

Communications

Club management

Computer advisory services

Contract administration

Convention, conference, meeting
    planning/arrangement

Customer service

Data processing

Design

Drug and alcohol abuse

Editorial services

Educational counselors

Engineering, general

Executive compensation

Executive search

Financial management

Food preparation

Forecasting

Fund raising

Grantsmanship

Hotel management

Import/export

Industrial engineering

Industrial methods

Information management

Insurance

Labor relations

Lighting

Management

Marketing

Municipal services

Organizational development

Personal security

Public relations

Public speaking

Publishing

Quality control

Recreation program counselors

Restaurant management

Resume preparation

Safety

Sales management

Sales promotion

Security

Taxes

Technical writing services

Training

Transportation

Weddings and social affairs

Word processing services

Writing services

2 | Seizing Opportunity

A wise man will make more opportunity than he finds.
—Francis Bacon

The opportunities to become a consultant are far more numerous than is commonly supposed, especially in this technological and increasingly complex society. The examples surround us:

- Former academics George Dudley and Shannon Goodson were researching the reasons for salespeople's successes and failures and were able to isolate particular traits and behaviors that contributed to what they refer to as "Sales Call Reluctance" (the inability to perform certain sales-related behaviors). Recognizing the commercial potential in their findings, they formed Behavioral Sciences Research Press (BSRP) and publish assessments, tests, or inventories, as well as offer training and consultation on improving sales performance. They have expanded their testing capabilities to incorporate other business relevant needs and have licensed others to conduct the training sessions on their behalf.

- We are all familiar with "Dr. Phil" (Phillip McGraw, PhD) and how he was able to parlay helping media magnate Oprah Winfrey with his expertise in "reading juries" for a case she was involved in. Not content to allow an opportunity to pass him by, he was able to leverage that connection into a regular featured spot on her show and ultimately became a host of his own TV talk show and a best-selling author.

- Stephen Covey's name is synonymous with "Seven Habits of Highly Effective People." He has become one of the leading keynote speakers and is much in demand by corporations seeking guidance in "empowering their employees." Dr. Covey began his professional career as a professor in organizational behavior at Brigham Young University when he created his *principle-centered leadership* approach. Having the foresight to identify the opportunity, he grew that idea into a series of workshops, audiotapes, and eventually sold his firm to the Franklin Planner Company.

- Other examples are Michael Hammer who harnessed the power in his book, *Re-Engineering the Corporation* into a multimillion dollar opportunity, or Tom

Peters who has become nearly a legend from his co-authorship of *In Search of Excellence.*

On a much less lofty level, there are consultants who reside within the very communities that we live:

- Many individuals have started resume-writing services, but among them are also many who are counselors or consultants. They advise clients on how to best organize and present their (the clients') experience and other qualifications, along with other counsel on careers and job-finding. They are, in fact, job and career consultants.
- The locksmith can become a security consultant, and the accountant a tax consultant, and the list could go on almost indefinitely. The principles, however, would be the same: Almost any activity that is widely practiced and requires even modestly specialized knowledge and experience can become a consulting specialty. But how we practice our consulting specialties is a highly individual matter, varying widely according to circumstance. One basic problem in developing a consulting practice is deciding just how specialized you should be—how broad or narrow your specialty should be, that is, and just what services you ought to provide. That can have various consequences.

YOUR CONSULTING SPECIALTY VERSUS YOUR MARKETING NEEDS

There is at least a general relationship between the degree to which you specialize and your marketing success. You must be a specialist to be qualified in most clients' eyes as a true consultant, for one thing. The degree to which you specialize probably helps to determine how many competitors you have. It also determines the size of your market; it determines how many potential clients—people with problems and needs that call for such services as those you offer—are out there awaiting your services. Choosing the right degree and kind of specialization represents the classical trade-off, with success depending to at least some extent in finding the right compromise.

It isn't an entirely arbitrary decision. The market—the kinds of clients and types of projects available to you—may force the decision. One resume writer in the Washington, DC, area specializes in assisting law students and law school graduates in developing their resumes and cover letters. She is able to do this because there are many universities in the area, and at least one prestigious law school. Were she to locate her resume service in Detroit, the clientele most readily available to her would not include an outstandingly large number of law school students and graduates, so she would find it difficult to specialize in that aspect of resume services.

The decision is one of being *vertically* expert (that is, being fluent in the areas within an industry area). The adage "an inch wide, but a mile deep" is what to strive for. An example would be a consultant who was formerly a hospital administrator now specializing in working *only* with healthcare institutions. This consultant will not venture into manufacturing clients or accept assignments with not-for-profit charities, but is adroit at handling the multitude of tasks that cut across many departments or functional areas within that healthcare institution. On the other hand, a consultant may choose to specialize *horizontally* (has a functional specialty that can be applied in multiple environments). These consultants, for example, may have background in human resources and seek clients in *any* industry looking for guidance with selection, benefits, or succession planning, but *will not* accept assignments that require background in marketing or logistics. And there are hybrids of these two polarities. Some consultants may feel comfortable sticking to assignments that mirror their prior vast experience within a particular industry classification, but would be more narrow in their marketing of their expertise outside of that environment (but still feel comfortable handling some assignments).

Versatility Is the Answer for Some

Some individuals who have rather broad backgrounds of experience and are highly versatile have found an answer to the dilemma of finding the right specialty and services; they use their versatility to change their specialties, chameleon-like, according to the market opportunities of the moment.

This is a fairly common practice among those who devote themselves to accepting temporary assignments as job shoppers. Typical methods for finding such positions and qualifying for acceptance make this option quite viable. The individual needs to have more than one resume or the ability to create the right resume spontaneously for each opportunity. Some individuals have made up for themselves at least a dozen resumes, none of which give false testimony, but each of which presents a different kind of experience and capability as a consulting specialty. One individual I knew, for example, was an electrical/electronic engineer who could double rather easily as a technical writer or draftsman, and handle many mechanical engineering problems.

Actually, the clients are largely responsible for this need to have several resumes; many clients go overboard in the degree of specialization they call for as qualifications. A client seeking technical writers, for example, may demand the applicants be familiar with some given specification or specific kind of equipment. In fact, the competent technical writer usually has no serious problem working with and to any specification and any equipment within his or her field (e.g., electronic, chemical, mechanical).

On the other hand, this device of making oneself a chameleon as a consultant can present a potential ethical problem. Is it honest to be different kinds of a specialist on different occasions? Is that versatility? Or is it opportunism? That is something you must decide for yourself, but you need not decide yet; later we will discuss professional ethics, as it affects various aspects of your practice as a consultant.

WHAT DOES IT TAKE TO BE A CONSULTANT?

Over the years since the first edition of this book was published, would-be consultants have asked ingenious questions, such as what do I need to be a consultant? How do I get started? How do I get clients?

Faced with these questions, one is reminded almost automatically of the jest about the cost of a yacht, to wit: If you have to ask the price, you can't afford it. The truth is, however, that there are no simple answers to any of the questions that beginners and aspirants often ask. That's primarily because the answers that work for Smith are not the ones that work for Jones. Variables are involved to about the same extent and nature as they are in determining the kind of specialization and services you ought to offer. I can't tell you what these should be, nor can anyone but you yourself. You need to make some lists:

- What are your general and special skills?
- What kinds of relevant markets (people and organizations) can you somehow reach?
- What are their needs, general and specific?
- Where do these items coincide?

These are, for the most part, dependent variables, not independent ones, but when they are identified and matched up, they define your consulting service, at least the beginning one. In time and with experience, you will modify it to satisfy the facts on the ground, as you discover them.

THE SKILL OF A CONSULTANT

The foregoing addressed only the identification of the basic skills and services you will place at the disposal of your clients; however, as a consultant you need more than one set of skills. You need that set of skills that relates to your professional field—remember that consulting is not a profession itself, but is a way of practicing your profession. You also need the skills that any consultant normally needs—listening, analyzing, synthesizing, presenting, and a few others as necessary to the client-relations side of consulting as they are to the technical side.

The skills that will distinguish the successful consultant from the ineffective one are the ones related to maintaining a dual focus. On the one hand, the consultant needs to be technically proficient, but must also be able to think in "general management terms" (finance/cash flow, operations, legalities, staffing, etc.) with a comprehensive view of the project and its business rationale for the consultant (is this a good project to take on? Can I handle it? Will it lead to additional work? Is it something I would enjoy doing?). These can perhaps be bundled very broadly into two additional skill sets beyond the professional and the consultative soft skills of analyzing, listening, and others as (1) administration and (2) marketing.

I will not address professional skills. I assume here that you are entirely proficient in your own field and need no help from me, nor would I be qualified to help you in your own profession. It is in the other three sets of skills, and especially in marketing, that I offer help in becoming a successful consultant, for that is what this book set out to do in the first place. We will preview those three subjects briefly here and in much greater depth later.

Consulting Skills

As a consultant, you must have or develop certain skills and abilities that are necessary to consulting generally and to consulting independently especially, regardless of those professional skills you also require. You must, for example, be a good listener, a good analyst, and a good designer—able to analyze symptoms, identify the problem, and synthesize a solution or approach to solution. But consulting also requires abilities to make effective presentations, both in person (verbally, across a desk or from a dais), and in writing (via reports and articles). And consulting independently also requires an ability to interface effectively with a client—to build an image of competence and authority, to win the client's respect, and even to establish a relationship of mutual respect, if not amiability.

All of these are necessary capabilities for success as an independent consultant; however, although I have divided these sets of skills and functions into four classes or sets for purposes of discussion, in practice they are not so easily separated. They are, in fact, intertwined and even interdependent. Some of the skills so necessary to conducting a satisfactory consulting assignment are the same skills that help you market successfully and even administer successfully.

Management and Administration of the Independent Consultancy

Unlike internal assignments within a company as a full-time employee, consultants are rarely afforded the luxury to be just the technical expert without focusing on the other management skills that comprise a successful operation. As the full-time employee toiling away at a specialized task, you rarely consider the issues confronted by the person in the cubicle across the hall or in another department. However, when looking at running your own business, the proficient systems analyst who does not remain current with his or her billings will not last because the inability to manage cash flow will hamstring the consultant's ability to stay afloat. Many seemingly successful consultants believe that "sales covers all ailments" and that as long as there is business flowing in, the rest can take a backseat and get done when you have an opportunity. These consultants never know what hits them when the client falls behind in payments, when a supplier comes calling for monies owed, or when the bank sends out the third overdraft notice in a month.

To be fair, without sales (the fuel that runs the engines), the company cannot sustain itself. Yet, a company that has money owed to it and is tracking it and staying current can accommodate a lull in sales. A company that is selling and not collecting, on the other hand, will not be around for very long. That company will likely go out of business fastest because they will continue to incur variable costs in the creation of the sale, servicing of the sale, but will not receive payment, so they will reach their endpoint quickest.

Nothing is black and white in this world, and while it is useful in delivering explanations to segregate the functions and skills into separate classes, they overlap each other to such an extent that it is difficult to know where (and whether) they are distinct and separate from each other. And if marketing is the most important set of skills for success—even for mere survival—as I have maintained consistently, it is also the olio of all the skills, for all must be brought into play in building and maintaining a successful consulting practice. The following example is drawn from my personal experience.

One of my valued clients was a conglomerate, headquartered in New York City and comprising 20 or more companies. (The number changes, as the corporation acquired attractive companies and divests unprofitable ones.) They had done some business with the government, rather casually, but never actively pursued government business. One day they decided to look into government contracts, and that led them to send two people to a seminar I offered in marketing to the government.

As a result, I was invited to have lunch with the executive appointed by the corporation to head up their new government-marketing division to discuss what I might do for them. As an immediate result of that luncheon meeting and, I must confess, my own aggressive follow-up, several things happened:

1. I was retained to help prepare a capability brochure for the corporation. (In fact, they provided a draft, which I was to critique and offer my own contributions.)
2. I wrote a proposal for one of the companies.
3. I delivered a custom, in-house seminar for a group of marketing people from a number of the companies.
4. I continued to help several of the companies prepare proposals.
5. I was called on periodically for miscellaneous chores.

All of this was because I was a good listener and analyst (consciously and deliberately because listening does not come to me naturally). I listened carefully to the client's views, analyzed his real and felt needs, and responded with offers I thought not only relevant, but offers that the client would agree were relevant. (Remember that the client never grants you the right to make his or her decisions, but only to make recommendations.) It is critically important that you bear the client's orientation in mind—including any biases the client has—in making those recommendations. But compare that not atypical case with the following marketing rational I find many subscribe to.

Marketing Skills

On the face of it, at least until experience teaches you that this is an idealized view, the marketing challenge appears to be the simple one of finding and winning clients for typical consulting assignments. There is no doubt that the beginning independent consultant so views the marketing problem in general. That is at least partly because the beginning consultant has that traditional and classic view of consulting as the practice of advising distressed clients on how to solve their problems. Beginning consultants envision sitting with the client in his or her comfortable office, listening to a litany of woes and pleas for help, then dictating a substantial daily fee as the price of assistance, and having a grateful client agree immediately, after which a contract is signed and the consultant renders the wisdom that will solve the client's problems.

The marketing process, then, in this rational and based on this premise, consists of finding prospects with appropriate problems—clear need for the consultant's abilities—winning the prospect's consent to become a client, and negotiating a suitable daily or hourly rate of compensation.

Alas, it seldom works quite that way. Prospects often have a different view of what they need than the consultant does. They know they need help but they approach consulting with some skepticism and apprehension. They tend to resist agreeing to an hourly or daily rate in what they deem as open-ended arrangement, but want some bargain-counter means for getting the benefit of consulting services. Even when you succeed in winning a few of these ideal consulting contracts, they occur irregularly, so that you find yourself in the classic feast-or-famine cycle.

Take the case I cited of that major corporate client who started by retaining me to help write their capability brochure. They knew next to nothing of what a capability brochure should normally contain, and they had apparently been greatly influenced in writing that draft brochure by the copy in their corporate annual report. The brochure was all wrong for their purposes. Yet, to persuade them to change it meant criticizing what they had done, hardly an easy thing to do tactfully and diplomatically. The conflict is immediately between treating the client with great care and doing your work honestly and ethically. It calls for a great deal of tact to suggest and explain the need for drastic changes without condemning what has been already done.

Note, too, the variety of services I provided. Although perhaps the most valuable direct service I can render in many cases is actual proposal writing, I often find it necessary to spend a great deal of time selling the client on the need to do what I have done or propose to do in the proposal. My typical client is an intelligent, capable, and successful executive, scientist, or engineer, with ideas of his or her own, and requires me to be honest in my views and prepared to explain and justify my recommendations, especially when they clash with the client's ideas, as they often do.

All of this points up the need for some versatility in your capabilities and services. In the case I just cited, had I stubbornly insisted that my consulting service was restricted to advising clients on government marketing, I would probably have benefited with about 20 percent of the volume of work I actually was blessed with. Even if I had insisted that my services were restricted to advising on and/or writing and leading proposal efforts, I would have closed the door on much of the work, and perhaps on all of it, if the client had decided to seek a consultant more amenable to meeting all his needs. This brings up, once again, a marketing problem of a special kind that we have touched on briefly earlier: How specialized should you be?

Recognizing the business cycles of the clients' attractive to a consultant based on the alignment of the consultant's skills and likely client needs (new product launches, trade shows, quarterly or annual events, etc.) and what business needs they are looking to fulfill in that time can separate you as a consultant from competition in your client's eyes. No client thinks in terms of needing someone with background in "X" without also first thinking that, "I need to create 'Y' or address problem 'Z' and the best way for me to do that is to use someone with expertise 'X.'" The more the consultant can address the business issue and not lean too heavily on a supposed expertise within a particular discipline, the more broadly attractive that consultant becomes to clients and prospects. The consultant is viewed as a business resource and not merely a cog to fill a specific and unique need exclusively. This prevents the consultant from being pigeon-holed unnecessarily. (It will happen often enough without the consultant contributing to it.)

THE AVENUES OF SPECIALIZATION

The degree to which consultants specialize varies widely. In my own case, I tend to generalize within the field of proposal consultation and writing, but I am the exception; most proposal consultants specialize in given subject fields—engineering and technical (NASA and military/defense projects, especially), social science projects, training development, health programs, or other specialized areas, based primarily on the consultant's prior career experience. I work almost invariably on proposals submitted in pursuit of contracts, whereas there are consultants who serve clients pursuing grants, which also usually require proposals.

Regardless of whether the choice is ultimately to specialize narrowly, or provide broad-based consultation, it will be a requirement for many clients who hire you that you be prepared to speak about your personal experiences in conducting the project proposed. In selecting whether to specialize or not, remember that for many clients, the best indicator of your future success with them will be your previous success with others.

As in all things, there are trade-offs—advantages and disadvantages—in versatility as there are in a high degree of specialization. There are no really good guidelines here. You must be guided in making your choices by your personal judgment, your objectives, your standards, and—perhaps most of all—by the lessons of your experience, which is really the final arbiter.

CONSULTING ASSIGNMENTS EVOLVE

Early (original) decisions are or should always be regarded as premises, to be tried and tested by experience. What this means, in practice, for most independent consultants, is trial and error. You start at some position, one of the extremes or midstream, and you make adjustments as your experience reveals the need for adjustments, until you achieve the point at which you are satisfied with the results. This means keeping an open mind. Set out at the beginning with the knowledge that your first premises are almost certain to be considerably less than perfect for your purposes, and be prepared to learn from experience.

Again, I can cite one example from my own experience: After I had begun to offer seminars on an open registration basis—available to anyone who wished to attend—I began to build a reputation as something of a specialist in this field and found myself drawing inquiries from large corporations who were interested in having me deliver a custom, in-house training seminar in proposal writing. Each time I received such an inquiry, I cheerfully calculated the costs for customizing my seminar to the individual client's needs and quoted accordingly.

The results were disappointing. I failed to win a single contract for an in-house seminar. Obviously, I was doing something wrong, and my judgment was that these prospective clients were unwilling to pay the price for customizing a special seminar. I studied the problem and then switched tactics; I began to respond to such inquiries with a proposal to deliver my standard seminar, customized for them, but only insofar as I could do so spontaneously in my delivery, and principally through my choice of illustrative anecdotes and case histories, without extra cost.

I immediately began to win virtually all such contracts, and to this day I present a number of custom, in-house seminars every year. Moreover, whereas I began doing them at the equivalent of my daily consulting fee, I soon learned that this was a mistake and raised the cost. Interestingly enough, I also learned that the clients did not object to the cost per se and apparently never had; they objected only to the idea of paying a special fee for customizing the seminar. (This experience verified, once again, the idea that people buy emotionally, rather than rationally.)

Flexibility—A Basic Requirement

It is only from experience that you can learn these things. But there is another message here: No matter what your general specialty as a consultant is, either originally or as it ultimately evolves, be alert for opportunities to develop specialties within your consulting framework. It is not at all unusual for a consultant eventually to practice a specialty quite different from that which he or she embraced originally. (In fact, it is so common as to be almost a trend, rather than an occasional event.) For that matter, it is not unusual for any business venture to evolve into something quite different from what it started as. Some rather large companies do not today resemble their beginnings even remotely. Their ability to adapt rationally to the conditions they encounter is the factor that determines whether they survive or not.

A Special Case of Evolutionary Change

Changes in consulting specialties are not always the result of gradual evolution. Other factors compel change also, sometimes rather abruptly. The ability to switch fields rapidly and frequently—having a number of different resumes on hand—was pointed out earlier as one way some versatile consultants maximize their prospects for assignments. For instance, post 9/11, anyone with experience in airport security or antiterrorist recommendations was immediately a valuable asset to be consulted with by airports, airlines, federal and local governments, and others. So much so, that Rudy Giuliani was able to leverage his handling of the horrific event into his own consulting firm to meet with and prepare cities and countries on how to best avoid catastrophes of this nature, and how best to handle them, once they occur.

The effects of such changes in conditions are obvious. The consultant who has been highly specialized must move on or adapt in some other way, while those less highly specialized may well survive. For example, the reading specialist—an educator-trainer in reading skills for the functionally illiterate—may be totally without resources in the face of an abrupt shutdown of a major government project, whereas the consultant educational-technologist—a developer of training programs generally—can probably turn to other government training programs.

The Basis for Specialization

The focus on individual skill is quite important in resolving your own definition of what you offer to do for clients, for that inevitably becomes the chief focus of all your marketing. A technical writer, for example, must sometimes demonstrate to a prospective client that he or she is a radar writer or computer writer, because many clients are convinced that it is necessary to be that highly specialized, a fact noted earlier.

That points up another highly important factor: Truth is a subjective quantity, and in marketing the only truth that counts is the client's truth. No matter what you do, it is highly likely that the client will mentally tag and label you. I am truly a marketing strategist, in my own view, but some clients tend to perceive me as a proposal writer or as a lecturer on the subject, depending on their own needs and what they retain me to do for them. Moreover, most of my clients associate me with government marketing only. That is understandable, considering my extensive experience in that field, but the real reason for the perception is that most of my clients do not perceive a need for help in marketing commercially. Government marketing, however, is conceived as something of a mysterious and complicated project, in which they need help.

There is still another factor at work here: Many prospective clients, especially those in marketing and sales departments, would resist retaining me to help them in marketing commercially because they would regard that as an intrusion into their own domains and, more telling, a lack of faith in their own abilities. But government marketing is different, and they do not feel a blow to their egos in admitting to a need in this special field or to my special qualifications in it. So in the end, it serves my own best interests to encourage that view of my special abilities.

You are always the victim—and occasionally the beneficiary—of the client's own biases. Often you will be pigeonholed by clients according to their needs, regardless of how you represent your skills and specialties. Another problem I have often encountered when doing any kind of custom writing job is the bias most professionals have that they can write as well as anyone. Many refuse to acknowledge writing as a special skill or talent. They thus tend to treat the professional writer's work casually and almost with disdain. (Sometimes it seems as though everyone in the world wants to be an editor, even more than a writer, and is convinced that he or she is quite a good editor.) But that presents another kind of typical problem.

One prospect was outraged at the consulting fee I asked for. "That's too much money for a hired writer," she stormed.

"But you are not retaining me as a writer," I tried to explain. "I am a specialist in developing marketing strategies for proposals to win government contracts. The writing is incidental and not what people retain me for at all."

It was futile. I was unable to make my point because my prospect was simply unwilling to accept it under any circumstances. She insisted that I was a writer for hire and asking too much money for my services.

You must recognize that you do not always have an entirely free choice in deciding what you are and what you offer, as the *client* sees you. You must work at understanding the client's mind set and prejudices, and you may have to tailor yourself and your offerings accordingly.

In short, how you represent yourself and what you offer are not decisions to be made without analysis and deliberation, especially an examination of how the clients tend to perceive you and what you do and—even more important—how clients prefer to view you and what you offer.

That is not as cynical as it sounds, and it is not an exhortation to mislead or deceive your clients. It is simple realism to structure your presentations to complement your prospective clients' attitudes.

3 | Consulting as a Second Career

Retirement is not an ending, for many, but a beginning, as they opt for a second career. Consulting offers a wide variety of opportunities for those seeking a second career.

—*Herman Holtz*

WHAT IS A "SECOND CAREER"?

The concept of a second career is increasingly important in today's society, and entering into a second career is an ever-more common occurrence. This is even truer today than when this book was first published. The reasons for this include an inability to sustain lifestyle choices with income from a single job, the rate of technological change has rendered some career choices obsolete, the efficiencies of exporting tasks formerly done within our own shores to lower cost countries and then importing the products back to our shores in either a completed state or only requiring minimal further handling or work to complete the assembly.

According to the information collected for the well-researched and rather comprehensive book, "The State of Working America 2000–2001" by economists Lawrence Mishel, Jared Bernstein, and John Schmitt (Cornell University Press, 2001):

> The share of the workforce working more than one job—multiple job-holders—fell from 6.2% to 5.8%, reflecting fewer people working two part-time jobs or supplementing their full-time job with a part-time one. In terms of all types of nonstandard work—including regular part-time, temporary help agency, on-call, independent contracting, and contract firm work—the share of workers in these arrangements fell from 26.4% to 24.8% of total employment during 1995–1999.

Even though the numbers appear to be in a slight decline, the fact that approximately 6 percent of the workforce is actively engaged in more than one income-generating job is still noteworthy.

As one might expect or intuitively deduce, the ebb and flow of our national economy can lead to people feeling the need to pursue additional income opportunities through consulting projects to supplement their "full-time" job and/or determine to shift to a nonstandard work arrangement as referenced above. Clearly, when the sense is that families cannot accomplish their financial goals through the income derived from the "primary" job (or in the more common case of each spouse working, primary jobs), there will be efforts dedicated to enhancing the income potential through other opportunities.

However, that is not the complete picture on the composition of the "second careerists." There is a good portion of people (numbers are hard to come by since many of the projects are not "registered" by the people doing them in surveys, or other formal research means) who will offer their services outside the traditional reporting relationships to avoid paying taxes on the income. While illegal and certainly not condoned, to ignore it would be to derive a less complete view of the totality of the marketplace.

Additionally, there are those people who leave a job after acquiring enough time "in service" (military, civil servants, etc.) to secure a pension that suits them and yet are still energetic enough, vital, capable, and willing to work. These people will often look for opportunities to pursue passions, interests, or consulting engagements that fuel their curiosity and provide them with intellectual stimulation or other rewards that are less dependent on monetary rewards.

Still others had opted for the career path of working within corporate life and have (through no fault of their own) been outplaced, laid-off, downsized, or right-sized out of their jobs. Not having nearly the freedom that the young retirees referred to above have, these people often have to continue their personal revenue streams in order to make payments or continue their lifestyles as they currently are. These people will occasionally pick up "stray assignments" in the interim—while they pursue more secure full-time employment.

Last, there those that develop their expertise within the confines of the corporate environment and are given successive opportunities to expand their skills and experiences as they progress up the career ladder. Yet, these people find themselves with an itch that they are unable to scratch through their current employment. It might be happenstance that they "fall into" opportunities to speak on, or share their successes with others at conferences or other public events; it may be that they are being called on to assist others make transitions from one system to another or share their wisdom on best approaches to technological introductions. Regardless of how it comes about, there are those people that yearn to "do it for myself" and want to pounce on the opportunity to create something and at the same time have the ultimate freedom to determine the course of that business' fate. They are no longer sated with the rewards offered by their corporate employers. Even if it means a reduction in lifestyle, income, or prestige these people yearn to start their own businesses based on their (presumed) expertise and experience.

As a foundation beneath all of the above is the change in societal expectations and cultural acceptance of *serial careers*. It is not at all uncommon for people to have a series of successive careers (with one not being a natural extension or outgrowth of the previous). With the rate of technological change in contemporary society, many jobs will be modified or eliminated over the course of a standard career. Additionally, the covenant that many employees and employers believed they had entered into when the job was first accepted is less strong than it once had been. The notion of a company being paternalistic and caring for employees beyond the workplace and "being there" for the employees in exchange for their loyalty is anachronistic. While the debate rages as to whether that is a sign of progress or not, suffice it to say that it is reality and as such, employees do not have a fidelity to the company hiring them beyond the transactional exchange of performing work tasks admirably and receiving a commensurate reward. Should either party no longer view that transaction as appropriate or desired, then either party (within certain legal limits) may unilaterally decide to end it and pursue other opportunities and work relationships.

The American Association of Retired Persons (AARP) recently completed a research report, "Staying Ahead of the Curve" (September 2002) that analyzed the behaviors, motivations, and expectations of those approaching "traditional" retirement age, in retirement age, and even those still years away from retirement. Among their many findings were:

- The overwhelming majority of 45-year-old employees and older (69 percent) expect to work beyond reaching their retirement age.
- Of those that plan on working, a third (34 percent) wish to do so in part-time pursuits that appeal to them for interest and enjoyment.
- Perhaps surprising, less than a fifth (19 percent) are anticipating needing the income that their postretirement work will provide to live.
- 10 percent are anticipating going into their own businesses
- 6 percent will choose careers not related to their current work experience, but in keeping with an interest or avocation.

These numbers are perhaps startling in themselves, but when provided in the context that the over-the-age-of-45 employee represents the end of the Baby Boomer generation, the size of the working population that is considering these issues and that are pondering making these career choices becomes that much more impressive.

In a study done by Drake Beam & Morin (an outplacement firm), "Career Choices and Challenges of Younger and Older Workers" (2002) the previous insights were supplemented with the following facts:

- "Chemistry" (the relationships forged at work and the feeling of being valued and appreciated) was often cited as a reason for seeking a transition.
- Consulting as a profession was seen as gaining employees across all demographic groups (the "Gen X'ers", the Baby Boomers, and Mature Workers).

Clearly, there is high interest in changing one's level of being "tethered" to a single firm and accepting or yielding to the perceived "good with the bad" that is a necessity in larger companies. So you are certainly in good and abundant company if you choose to have a second career.

In the complex society of today, a second career can mean many things, including these:

1. A spare-time activity you pursue for added income or amusement.
2. A career change you voluntarily undertake for any of many possible reasons, such as a need to feel useful and valued.
3. A new and different kind of career you choose to embark on after retiring from an earlier career.

Consulting lends itself well to all of these applications. In the first case cited, not all career alternatives are suitable to be conducted effectively as part-time careers, but many can be, and so there are many spare-time workers and entrepreneurs of all kinds.

In the second case, modern conditions are an important factor: Many people today are forced to change careers. It may be the result of industrial changes; automation, for example, has put an end to many jobs and careers. The migration of many heavy industries to other countries—in the Orient and in the Third World—has contributed to the trend. Layoffs resulting from technological advances that minimized the number of employees required to do certain tasks (printing industry as an example), mergers and acquisitions that eliminated whole functions within the acquired company in an effort to streamline or reduce overhead, and the general economic cycles that at various times have led to a reduction in headcount have compelled many people to search for new careers suited to the changing business and industrial conditions.

That third case is probably the most significant one: The average age of retired people has declined sharply in recent decades. Where once 65 was considered retirement age, many people today retire as early as age 50 or 55. In a society where our life expectancy has increased considerably, and that alone is one reason more and more people retiring from long-term jobs choose to embark on new careers. Some do so because they relish the challenge of starting a new career, and they do so with great enthusiasm. Others choose to launch second careers because their retirement income is not great enough to satisfy their needs. There are also many published stories of people who contemplated retirement with great glee, envisioning a life of doing only what was enjoyable, but finding themselves bored beyond endurance after a few months and driven to find something to do as a career undertaking. Exacerbating that trend is that many companies are encouraging early retirement of employees and even offering them special inducements.

There is actually something of a crossover or hybrid situation among these cases. Some individuals embark on a spare-time second career while still working at a job, anticipating the time when they will retire and preparing for a smooth and easy changeover to a new career. Too, some who pursued a spare-time career for added income or as a hobby choose to continue that combination hobby-career on a full-time basis after retiring or being forced to change careers.

A perusal of the business books section in any library or bookstore will affirm that consulting as a career option for those seeking a change in jobs is an attractive option. The *boundaries of entry* (that is, how difficult it is to get into the business) are minimal. There is no inventory required, no special machinery, no demand for specific structures or office facilities. Business writers from Sylvia Porter in her books on planning for your retirement to Alan Weiss in his books on million-dollar consulting have addressed these issues.

In a great many cases, the new independent consultant's first and most important client is the very organization from which he or she has just retired. The logic of that is inescapable: Who is better qualified to understand and serve the interests of an organization than the individual who spent 25 or more years there and knows the organization thoroughly? Thus, a great many newly established independent consultants find their former employers highly receptive to retaining them as consultants.

In general, especially where the individual has completed a long career in specialized work or a senior position, he or she has excellent credentials for a consulting career, including the following:

- Many years of experience and highly developed specialized knowledge.
- Mature judgment, based on experience in the relevant fields.
- Wide knowledge of the common needs and problems in the industry or business.
- Knowledge of related industries, businesses, and professions.
- Acquaintance with many other senior professionals and executives in related industries, businesses, and professions—valuable contacts.
- Versatility in many relevant skills, highly developed and honed.
- Better listening skills, due partly to the greater patience that many of us develop with advancing maturity, but also due to greater understanding of the problems, needs, and various situations common in the industry.

ALMOST ANY SKILL/KNOWLEDGE/EXPERIENCE CAN BE THE BASIS

Consulting is essentially a service, even when products are involved. It is giving advice and assistance to clients in doing things at which you are skilled and knowledgeable and in which the client wants your help. Even if you sell a product or line of products, service is still a significant factor, for it is what your product or products *do* for the client that is important to him or her. It doesn't matter if it is a highly technical matter or a more mundane one; the principle is the same. It also does not matter if you call it consulting or by some other name, for example, freelancing or contracting. Thus, you can become a consultant specializing in any service or set of services, with or without products, for which there is demand—for which clients, individuals, and organizations, feel a need for help. That sense of need may be because the client lacks or feels a lack of adequate knowledge or skill, because the client simply lacks the time or manpower to do the job, because the client has a need to feel the security of having a professional expert/specialist handling the job, or because the client simply treasures the convenience of having a professional do it. (Never underestimate the power of these latter two considerations as motivators in selling.)

If you are retired from a long career in some field, you have a certain advantage in that you are a voice of authority. Your years of service *are* credentials. You don't have the problem of so many young people entering the consulting profession of lacking a track record—a lengthy record of accomplishment. Even if you cannot point to a great deal of specific experience doing whatever it is that you now propose to do, you will command respect for your years regardless of the service you offer.

One of the frailties from which many of us suffer is overestimating the knowledge of others. So often we have extensive knowledge of things that we believe everyone knows. You may assume, for example, that everyone knows how to organize a formal luncheon or dinner party. You may think that it is perfectly obvious that the words "black tie invited" are intended to indicate that the wearing of tuxedos would be entirely proper and is encouraged. You may believe that anyone with a high school education knows how to apply for a birth certificate or passport, or how to write a resume or post-graduate thesis or dissertation. You may be shocked to learn that many people *do not know* how to do many of the things you and I take for granted as common knowledge.

This principle applies to many small business owners, as well as to individuals. A surprisingly large number of business owners do not know many of the things you or I might assume a business owner ought to know. Nor is that confined to small business owners; I have encountered executives of large corporations who were sorely in need of help to read and understand official pronouncements, prepare a bid, and write help-wanted advertising. One executive was enormously impressed with my great wisdom in counseling his marketing people to be sure that they quantified whatever they were bidding, something I thought to be quite obvious and was mentioning only in passing. I have met senior executives in major corporations who could not understand clauses in contracts written in what I thought was simple English. I have known business executives who did not understand the common practice of discounting paper at a local bank or qualifying for a line of credit.

That is why consulting practices may be and often are based on what initiated executives consider rather mundane and simple services. It is necessary only that they be services you can perform capably. The following is a list of just a few examples of the many hundreds of opportunities for employing your skills, knowledge, and experience as an independent consultant, even if they are not based on unusually specialized knowledge and training. (On the other hand, do not underestimate the appeal or the value of your knowledge and skills.) Many individuals have built successful practices providing services such as the following:

- Menu planning—a service for individuals and organizations planning luncheons, award dinners, social dinner parties, or other events.
- Personal financial management—cost control, investments, long-term planning, solving financial problems.

- Automobile buyer's service—assistance in buying a new or used car, getting the right price, making a mechanical check of a used car, and related services.
- Job counseling—advice and assistance in planning the job search, writing the resume, handling the interview, and other elements necessary to success in job hunting.
- Recruiting—employees or members—advice and assistance in planning and organizing membership drives and other campaigns.
- Party planning—advice and assistance in ideas for parties, planning and organizing, arranging for pranks and/or other entertainment.
- Public speaking—counseling others in public speaking and/or writing speeches.
- Convention service for small clubs and/or associations—advice and assistance in arranging for meeting places, speakers, equipment, refreshments, and whatever else may be needed.
- Expert witness service—(litigation consulting). This includes much more than taking the witness stand, and in the bulk of the cases the expert witness is a consultant to the client (an attorney or firm of attorneys) but never does get to the courtroom.
- Bureaucratic guidance and services—advising and assisting clients in navigating the bureaucracy to get information, apply for various programs, and respond to official requirements.
- Letter writing—the day of the public scribe is not entirely ended; many people pay gladly to get assistance in writing letters of various kinds.
- Using a computer—how to set up the PC, install the software programs, and teach others how to use word processor, database manager, and other basic programs used in most offices.
- Information specialist/broker—research public databases for clients who lack time, patience, knowledge, or desire to do so for themselves.
- Dress for success—advising others, men and women, how to dress most effectively for various positions and functions in the business and professional worlds.
- Marketing specialty—advise clients on advertising, writing sales materials, setting up exhibits for conventions and trade fairs, other aspects or specialties of marketing.
- Office systems organization—organize office functions, filing systems, job duties, other necessities for an efficient office operation.
- Real estate advisor—help individuals find the right house at the right price and guide them through the mortgage and closing/settlement processes.
- Scholarship counselor—help students and their parents find scholarship opportunities, loan programs, and other assistance for getting into college.
- Quality control counseling—help companies set up quality control programs, especially today's total quality control.
- Security guidance—advice on security systems, including locks, fences, alarms, guard services, and other aspects of security.

The various relevant subjects of defining and marketing your services have been covered in earlier chapters, for the most part, and so will be treated here only briefly, as refreshers and reminders.

MARKETING—GETTING CLIENTS

To make any business or independently practiced profession succeed, it is necessary to carry out marketing, of course. Consulting is no exception to this, and what has been pointed out earlier about marketing applies here. If you are retired from a primary career, do take advantage of that track record you have of serving successfully and earning retirement. Study the items just listed and note those that best represent your own greatest strengths. Use them, then, as your primary sales arguments in developing brochures, sales letters, and in-person presentations. Stress not only experience, but *successful* experience. Assume the role of the prospect or customer/client and present your accomplishments with their needs in mind. Keep in mind that the person buying your time/service/expertise is often less interested in purchasing a single year of experience that you repeated 25 times over a career as opposed to being keenly interested in buying the expertise of a 25-year career of successively more varied experiences. Exceptions to this may be in a very highly specialized field, such as preferring a surgeon with many years of heart surgery as opposed to a general surgeon who has operated on different body parts. Generally speaking, it is best to include what you accomplished and what the results of your efforts were on the company for which you worked, or clients you have assisted. That is, develop a narrative of your most notable achievements that are relevant to the consulting services you offer. Make this a boilerplate reference, narrative and even tabular for some applications. (You may have to remind your former employer that it was you who developed and installed that much more efficient inventory control system, while you must also explain it to strangers.) Make sure to stress your achievements, as well as the years of experience. That is one of your most valuable assets as a consultant, they are credentials, and they are important whether you market to organizations or to individuals. Try to quantify, also. In my own case, the fact that I was once a manager and a director of marketing is not nearly so important nor so impressive as the fact that I wrote proposals that won over $360 million in contracts for my former employers and clients. Find the impressive numbers and cite them.

WHAT KINDS OF CLIENTS TO PURSUE

There are multiple approaches to determining what kind of clients would be appropriate targets for your consulting offerings. As we discussed earlier, you may choose to specialize within a particular industry or functional area, or you may feel capable of handling assignments across multiple industry "verticals" or comfortable addressing projects working with various departments. From a marketing perspective, however, the choice comes down to either assessing what the marketplace "needs" and then building a service or product to fulfill that need, or assessing what you can currently

offer and identifying places where that is needed. The trade-off is that in the first example, you may not have expertise in what is generally needed by the market at large
(for instance, your background is in marketing, but one of the commonly heard business needs just prior to the year 2000 was Y2K system analysis). In the other case,
you may tend to think in terms of having a "hammer" and therefore every prospect or
client has a "nail" that needs your attention. If you refer back to our definition of consulting, you will recall that consulting must be done in the best interests of the client
and is to be objectively provided. Matching clients to consulting skills must be done
in a way that provides the appropriate solution to them and not just the solution that
you happen to provide.

First identify if the prospect targets are more likely to be personal or individual
or corporate. For example, if your expertise is in nutrition, you may be able to strad-
dle the two (offering wellness programs for corporate clients and coaching on weight
reduction for individuals). If your background is in system encryption for Internet
transactions, there are few individuals who will require your services, but a good portion of corporate clients may be struggling with that issue and could benefit from
your counsel. If your area of expertise is child rearing, there are not many corporate
clients who would have an interest, but there may be many parents of school age children willing to pay you to share your insights or advice.

Services for Business Organizations

The following are just a few examples of services that are most appropriate to organizations—businesses, large or small, clubs and associations, government agencies, and
others: accounting, personnel, taxes, investments, mergers and divestitures, marketing,
seminar planning, publications guidance, expert witness/litigation services, enterprise
resource planning (ERP—the initiative to minimize costs and maximize efficiencies
through a sharing of information and flexible or dynamic use of data across an entire
organization as opposed to the maintenance of separate or discreet databases and methods for accessing information), customer relationship planning (CRP—a related effort
that focuses on the communication with and for customers and encompasses forecasting, accounts payable/accounts receivable functions, pricing, etc.), and Internet applications (home page design, "virtual stores" where customers can shop without having
to speak to anyone from within the company, electronic security, etc.). These skills are
typically honed and developed from working with any of the following functions or departments:

- Technology or information services integration projects.
- Advertising or marketing roles where contact with the customer was accomplished through the use of technology.
- Finance departments provide the skill to assess return on investment (ROI)
  calculations for these initiatives.

Many of these services have many possibilities for further specialization. Marketing, for example, may be retail, mail order, direct mail, discount, or even otherwise

specialized; few marketing consultants attempt to know or do it all. Of special interest now is databased marketing, a relatively new development, that is an improved method for marketing via any of those methods by increasing the sharpness of targeting prospects.

Services for Individuals

Many individuals go to specialists for help to satisfy personal needs or would be glad to get such help if they knew it was available. Examples of these kinds of services include letter writing, guidance through bureaucracies, buying new or used automobiles, buying new or used houses, making optimal arrangements for relocation, party planning, private dinner party catering, job-hunt counseling and assistance, cooking courses for brides and brides to be, guidance and counseling on house repairs or modernization, college admission application assistance, academic test preparation (ACT or SAT, GRE, etc.), and sundry others.

Services for Both Organizations and Individuals

A great many services have appeal and usefulness for both individuals and organizations. Both organizations and individuals have use for help in financial planning, social event planning for groups, writing and editing services, and computer services, to name only a few. You can specialize in any of these, however, and you may choose to pursue individuals as clients, organizations as clients, or both. There are pro and con considerations in all cases.

Consulting to Consultants

More and more individuals are becoming self-employed today, usually working from home, with the assistance of computers, modems, fax machines, laser printers, voice mail, and many other modern devices. They are in many enterprises, and many need help. In fact, many seek help in choosing a field and getting started, and will pay consulting fees for expert guidance. This is kind of a hybrid, a business service and yet a personal service. Among the kinds of help they seek are these: help in analyzing their assets and finding possible businesses they may turn their assets to, guidance in setting up businesses, selecting products, marketing products, creating brochures, finding suppliers, and other services relevant to launching a small business.

MARKETING YOUR SERVICES

If you are a recently retired worker, you may enjoy special advantages in getting a new consulting practice started. For one thing, your former employer may very well be your first client. This has been the case for a great many new independent consultants. You have immediate advantages: You know the people in the organization, and they know you. You know the organization's needs, wants, and problems. You know your way around in the organization. For these reasons, you have a great advantage in marketing, and you have the argument that you need no learning time; you are ready to start doing what has to be done without delay. You also can make a highly credible argument that it is less costly to retain you to help as a consultant than it would be to hire someone to learn the job.

You may also be familiar with other organizations and people in the field from which you have just retired. You have similar advantages vis-à-vis marketing to these other organizations, even if to a somewhat lesser degree. You know the people and can get in to see them far more easily than you can get in to see strangers.

In general, if you choose to consult in the field where you have worked, you have opportunities in networking because you know many people. You can and should maintain whatever memberships you maintained while active in that field, attend meetings and conventions, and remain in touch with old friends in the business.

For these reasons alone, you do well to stick to what you have been doing and to the industry, business, or profession in which you were employed. Success will almost surely come more easily there than in some new field. Still, you may be one of those who wants to try something entirely new and different. There are many retirees who reason thus.

PLOWING NEW FIELDS

Many people, on retiring, want to get into a new field. They are tired of doing what they have always done, and they want a change. They are ready, they believe, to tackle something new and different. Or they want to try to realize an ancient ambition they were never able to attempt before.

Many individuals have long cherished an ambition to be consultants. They have long believed that they can help others and that it would be pleasurable to do so as a main occupation. Consulting would be a new occupation, but they want to consult in a different area than the one in which they have worked. The expert accountant, for example, may have become expert with computers, and may wish to tackle computer consulting as a second career.

Breaking into a new field as a consultant is not all bad as an idea. There are advantages, as well as disadvantages. For one thing, you are likely to bring to it a fresh outlook and some new ideas, whereas there is always a tendency to keep doing things the same way when you continue on in the same field in which you have worked for many years. Too, there is a certain exhilaration in learning a new and interesting field of work. Obviously, it can't be a field in which you do not know the work at all; you can't decide to be a computer consultant if you know nothing about computers. However, you might be a consultant in editorial matters or training in the computer field, or you might apply your skills in other industries than the one in which you worked. For example, you might use your years of experience as a bank official to advise industrial companies in financial matters, counsel individuals in managing their finances, or advise clients on investments, to name just three ways in which you can put your broad experience to work. (Bear in mind that consulting is inherently usually highly specialized in the subjects it addresses and the services it provides.)

There are various other ways in which you can diversify. One is by adapting your specialized knowledge. The bulk of my proposal writing was in response to U.S. government requests for proposals (RFPs) and quite often for military organizations. With the decline of military procurement, I found it necessary to turn to the private sector for this work. However, I also found that my experience in writing proposals in response to RFPs works equally well in responding to private firms who solicit bids and proposals for subcontracts, and to foreign governments who issue tenders, rather than RFPs.

There is no requirement that you must base your consulting career on continuing to do what you did in your primary career. You may want to turn to some other things you know and are expert at. One man I know is an expert woodworker—he can turn out furniture of professional quality—and he has used that hobby as the basis for a second career in which he trains others in that craft and, more recently, has taken to writing books on the subject. Many people are as expert in some spare-time hobby as any professional. You need not be expert across the board, either; being expert in some aspect may be enough. Many of today's computer consultants are young people who had no formal training in computer technology, but became quite expert without the benefit of that preparation. (In fact, computer technology has long been dominated by youth.) Or you may be a collector antiques and become expert enough to offer a service to others who need help in finding genuine antiques. Or you may have become an expert collector of art, stamps, coins, or other hobby, and be able to turn that hobby to account as a consultant.

On the other hand, you may wish to plow a new field in terms of how you turn your knowledge and experience to account in helping others. For example, you might want to pass on your years of experience as valuable knowledge to younger people— more in a training mode or group presentation than in a one-on-one service. There are several ways to do this, as noted in other chapters—by writing and lecturing.

As long as you are aware of the caveat that consulting requires the client or prospect have a perception that you possess a level of expertise, there is nothing that prevents you from using your imagination to link your skills, aptitudes, experiences, and expertise with a client need. While not easy to do, consulting does afford someone the opportunity to create their own marketplace. Easier by far is to leverage your professional experiences and parlay them into a future consulting career. It is not outside the realm of possibility to use your own interests as the basis for a consulting career.

Lecturing and Seminars

Public speaking is itself a major field in which a great many consultants diversify their talents. You can develop a seminar (or even several seminars) to impart what you know about your specialty. You have the choice then of offering your seminar to the public at large, or offering it to interested groups under contract. That latter option has two aspects itself: There are seminar production companies who will produce your seminar and offer it to the public. They will hire you for a guaranteed minimum and percentage of the proceeds or for a flat sum to present your seminar. They will do the marketing, prepare all the materials you prescribe, and handle all the arrangements. You need only show up and deliver the presentation. But there is another way: Many organizations will retain you to present your seminar as an in-house event. I have presented my government marketing/proposal writing seminar many times to corporations, colleges, and associations, as well as to registrants drawn from the general public.

As an alternative, you can lecture at local colleges and universities. Most have extension courses of various kinds, and will entertain a proposal to add a lecture course. This not at all difficult to sell, if you wish to pursue it.

Publications

Publications—monographs and, especially, newsletters—are another way to pass on to others what you have learned. With today's resources, you can turn out a quite professional newsletter or monograph without being a publications expert. A recent wrinkle on the publishing angle that many successful consultants use is to create e-mailed newsletters that are sent to clients and prospects without the expense and effort of publishing and postage. Other consultants have used "webzines" that are essentially magazines posted at industry web sites for members or others to read, or have sent out when someone "opts-in" to receive (users or members choose to receive mailings or specific communication). This opens up the avenues of self-publishing e-mailed newsletters to an e-mail list, or relying on others to provide the bridge or link between your content and the eventual prospect or client.

For those that do consider using e-mail as the vehicle for communication, be very aware of the need for it to be *permission-based* and to allow receivers to *opt-out* or stop receiving the newsletter. Never share your client's e-mail address with anyone without prior authorization. It is a violation of good business practice and is a betrayal. SPAM or unsolicited e-mails plagues our business communications and is one of the easiest ways to annoy a client. Sending unwanted e-mails (especially if they are graphically intense and clog up the receivers ability to download needed information remotely) is a sure way to become a former consultant to that company.

In that connection—publications—there is another possibility that has not been covered earlier, and that is serving publishers as a consulting expert. Many writers offer publishers manuscripts—books and articles—on specialized subjects. The typical publisher has no internal means—in-house staff experts, that is—for checking these manuscripts for technical accuracy, but relies on outside consultants for help. You can make your name and specialties known to publishers and in time begin to win some of these assignments.

Classically, consulting contracts are project oriented. That means that you contract with a client to solve some specific problem, create a product, or otherwise pursue a defined goal or objective. You may be paid by the hour, by the day, or by some agreed-upon flat fee for the project. (Hourly or daily rates are probably the most common basis for billing clients.) Today a great many consultants work as temporaries, albeit in a technical, professional, or executive staff capacity. Modern business conditions are such that they encourage this as rewarding for both the consultant and the client.

CONSULTANTS AS TEMPORARIES

Many companies have come to the realization that they may not require full-time employees to address their needs, but rather, they only need expertise hired for a short duration. In these instances, companies will "rent an executive" to address situations as far ranging as, introducing a new product, installing a new inventory management system, managing a diversity program, or other projects that are self-contained and have a definable start and stop.

The temporary employment industry has traditionally been known for its ability to fill administrative positions or physical labor employment opportunities, but in addition to the clerks, typists, receptions, inventory takers, warehouse employees, and so on that we commonly think of, highly specialized and trained executives are also available to assist companies address their more senior level issues with the understanding that the project will cease at the conclusion of the system roll out, the product being launched, or some other agreed upon event.

That is, viewing this from your perspective, you can probably find temporary employment—as a W2 employee, that is—in whatever field you specialize, as many consultants do. It is the nature of our economy today that this is a desirable alternative but it is sometimes the only viable alternative. Many consultants have long accepted temporary assignments as a natural and appropriate mode of consulting, and there are those who prefer to work in this manner, for a number of reasons.

Working as a temporary rather than as a classic consultant is referred to as W2 employment (assignments that result in your being issued a W2 form certifying your earnings and taxes paid) versus being a 1099 consultant (referring to the 1099 form that is sent to you and the IRS in January when you work as a contractor).

Technical and Professional Temporaries

This special kind of consulting has long served the needs of government and industry and offered special opportunities to retired people who want to go on working but prefer temporary or part-time employment. In the post-World War II era, when the cold war inspired a huge program of weapons developments, the majority of such placements was in the offices and plants of major defense contractors who needed engineers, physicists, programmers, drafters, technical writers, designers, and hordes of other technical and professional workers. The industry has matured greatly since then, and today offers opportunities to workers in a much wider variety of fields. As you will see shortly, some of the companies in the industry even cater to retirees and older workers, recognizing their increasing presence in the markets.

The Temporaries Industry

By far, the majority of temporary workers are actually on the payrolls of companies who place them in clients' offices under contract. According to the American Staffing Association, there are about 7,000 firms focused on placing temporary employees with companies (ranging from entry level all the way to the most senior level positions) that have been in business longer than one year (and therefore, can be tracked by the association) and they operate from 21,400 offices nationwide. There has been a steady growth of this industry, although there are many old-timers, such as Volt Services Group, a division of Volt Information Sciences, Inc., a company that dates back to 1950, when it was one of many companies specializing in placing technical-professional workers in defense plants and government offices. (The U.S. Post Office Department of that time was one government agency using many temporaries, as was NASA, which is still a heavy user of such temporaries.)

Temporary Executives

As employers have come to recognize the advantages of hiring temporaries in many situations—it costs them less, in many ways—the scope of temping has expanded widely, not only in terms of numbers of temporary placements and companies offering this, but also in terms of the great variety of kinds of work for which temporaries are hired. Some occupations, such as nursing, have long been well suited to temping, as have been those highly technical occupations already identified. Today, however, even top-gun executives—chief executive officers (CEOs)—are being hired as temporaries. The most recent examples (though not always thought of in the most positive terms by employees) of temporary executives at the highest levels of an organization are the so-called *turnaround specialists* who often are brought in for the knowledge of how to make a company more attractive to stockholders or for a possible acquisition. There are boards of directors who will hire these executives for a period of time to create a large impact on the value of the business to raise capital, sell, or accomplish some other turnaround of the business. Hiring top executives, such as CEOs, comptrollers, marketing directors, and financial officers, as temporary executives is especially attractive to many companies today. The trade has taken to referring to these as interim executives.

Pros and Cons of "Temping"

The benefit of temporary employment to the hiring firm is that they need only expand their costs to accommodate the employee for the duration of the project and no longer than that. Upon completion, the costs of the temporary employee cease. Rather than incur the ongoing full-time costs commonly associated with employees (health insurance certainly being a major one, as well as the expected salary and associated benefits, office space, management time and effort, etc.), the company need only call on the expertise of the temporary employee on an "as-needed" basis.

From the perspective of the employee, the benefits include varied assignments, an opportunity to add to one's portfolio of experiences and accomplishments more quickly than most internal employee career progressions would allow, and the ability to interact with more companies, people, and their ideas in a shorter period of time. In essence, you are being paid to learn how to better complete your next assignment on an ongoing basis.

The downside to the company is that there is the need to explain "how we do things here" when it is germane to the completion of the project over and over again with each new temporary hire. The quality issue is always present as well. While the placement firms do their best to screen for true matches of assignment and personnel, it is not without hazards. The fit between an assignment and the person may not be ideal and the home-grown employee may be a known entity that could be molded to handle the assignment, whereas the external executive may not be as malleable. Of course, this is also why the person may have been hired in the first place—to provide a perspective not currently found within the hiring company.

The downside to the employee is that there may be no insurance (both in terms of actual health, disability, or life insurance, but also in terms of there being no guarantee) or certainty that there will be sufficient quantity of assignments to keep the executive in the lifestyle desired.

The flexibility it provides to both the employer and the employee may be seen as beneficial, but it does require concessions that some would find exciting and enticing and others may feel is inconsistent with their preferred approaches to conducting business.

FINDING ASSIGNMENTS

By far the majority of consultants and others working as temporaries are placed by the 7,000 companies who specialize in doing that. However, many consultants place themselves on clients' premises as temporaries. That is, they seek out clients who will hire them under contract at some hourly rate, rather than by the project, and they function more as employees than as contractors. Both methods for winning assignments are thus open to you.

Some consultants disdain temporary assignments or accept them only reluctantly when they find it necessary. They do so because they believe that they are compromising their principles and confessing failure as independent consultants when they accept temporary job assignments. They view that as being placed on someone's payroll as employees, even if they have placed themselves there. Many, however, embrace temping, via some broker or firm specializing in placing temporaries as a means for utilizing their full time in an earning capacity because they need not do any marketing. The firm that places them handles the marketing, or they may favor such employment because it represents a temporary commitment, one from which it is easy to disengage.

Finding temporary assignments is relatively easy, especially if you are willing to travel and to be placed by one of the firms specializing in this work. Some of these firms do this kind of work only, others, such as employment agencies and other corporations, have a separate division that does this kind of work.

There are a great many firms who advertise in the Yellow Pages and in the daily newspapers. You will also find a general starter list in Chapter 24, the Reference File, and a special list at the end of that chapter, of temporary-help agencies who specialize in and confine themselves to placing senior citizens in job positions as temporaries.

You will need a resume and basically it will be the same resume you would use if you were in pursuit of a permanent, full-time position. Because you are a consultant, as well as a temporary, you are likely to be hired for specialized work, and those who work regularly as temps tend to tailor their resumes for the specific assignment. In fact, it is likely that the firm seeking to place you will offer help in writing or revising your resume suitably. In fact, many who work always as temps by preference have several standard resumes, each for a slightly different specialty—an engineer might work also as a computer programmer, designer, technical writer, or marketing executive. With experience, you will probably develop several resumes of your own.

As a general modus operandi, you ought to follow a regimen along the following lines to maximize results:

- Develop a list of placement firms. (The starter list provided in Chapter 24 represents only a portion of the total.)
- Send each company a resume for their files. Be sure your address and telephone number, especially the latter, are listed prominently. (Fax number also, if you have one.)
- Monitor the help-wanted advertising in newspapers every day. Note placement firms you do not have on your list and add them. Note, also, the needs they list.
- Be flexible and consider assignments that may be corollary to your regular specialty, but well within your capabilities.
- Call the firms with advertisements of special interest. They may not perceive in your standard resume your qualifications for the assignment unless you point it out and are willing to revise your resume to stress the special abilities called for.

Networking

If you prefer to do your own marketing and place yourself directly with clients (whether on an hourly basis or by the project), you will have to establish some kind of marketing plan. Networking is a popular concept that many consultants use today, and about which much has been written elsewhere, describing and prescribing it as a highly organized and formal activity.

Networking is a rather modern development in marketing one's services. It consists of pursuing activities that will provoke and encourage word-of-mouth recommendations, although even that does not fully explain the concept. It is perhaps more precisely defined as marketing via the grapevine. That is, to put it into the most common terms, winning clients from those who have heard of you and heard good things about you. To turn the idea to your own application and purpose, then, you must identify and pursue the various means available to you to see to it that prospective clients will have heard of you. There are at least two approaches to this: (1) a rather informal, ad hoc set of activities and (2) a formal, organized activity.

There are many ways to accomplish this goal of being heard about via informal and even involuntary activities. The latter are the indirect result of something you did not control—a friend had the opportunity to recommend you to someone and did so—while others are most deliberate, results you have been at pains to provoke—you addressed a group and made your services clear to everyone. (Many of my consulting assignments result from individuals learning of me through my books, although I write them as a freelance writer and not to publicize my consulting service.)

Other informal methods are simply doing all the things that raise your general visibility—public speaking, joining associations and being active in them, attending conventions, and making sure to meet many people, letting them know what you do, and handing out many business cards and brochures. Join as many associations, and write and lecture as much as possible, because those activities produce clients and assignments. They raise your professional image and make people aware of you and what you offer, old, experienced professional that you are. In time, a great many consulting assignments will come to you spontaneously. Given the advent of the Internet, another opportunity to network is through electronic bulletin boards, discussion groups, or moderating topic areas. The Internet has many interest groups that have formed discussion groups, either conducted by people posting messages and others responding to the message in a serial fashion, as in posting things on a bulletin board, or through scheduled events that are more interactive (all go to a "room" or are provided with a password that allows entrance to a "private area" that only those with the password can enter and then they can interact in "real time" with each other and share ideas). By becoming associated with the group (often these groups are affiliated with industry or trade associations, or are self identified purchasers of a particular product—Ford SUV Owners, SAP Users, etc.), you can begin to interact with those that have needs in common and may be potential clients for your consultation.

COMPANIES FOR SENIORS

There are a number of national, multioffice labor contractors who have designated certain of their offices to specialize in the placement of retirees and other older workers—senior citizens. A list of such offices appears in Chapter 24, as a useful resource.

4 | Why Do So Many Consultants Fail? How to Succeed

> *Nothing in the world can take the place of persistence. Talent will not; nothing is more common than unsuccessful men with talent. Genius will not; unrewarded genius is almost a proverb. Education will not; the world is full of educated derelicts. Persistence and determination alone are omnipotent.*
>
> —*Calvin Coolidge*

It is a sad observation, but I must admit to as much surprise as delight when I find a newly established independent consultant still in everyday practice a year after launching the new consultancy. This is truer now than ever before. Unfortunately, quite a large number, possibly even a majority, of new practices perish within a year or less. But the real tragedy is that most of these failures are unnecessary; with just a little foresight and caution, most could be prevented. Most of those who fail could as easily survive that critical first year and all the succeeding years.

Every year, I receive many handsomely printed and dignified announcements of new consulting practices, with embossed business cards, brochures, letters, and other trappings. I receive many telephone calls from new independent consultants, advising me of their new ventures and offering to be available to me for future support and/or coventures in consulting.

Every year brings resumes and letters from these new consultants, almost pleading in their offers to support my own consulting projects. Most such offers are thinly disguised appeals for help (they have an undertone of desperation). I am saddened because each appeal represents trouble encountered and portends more trouble ahead for the individual. Such messages suggest that the individual has no active clients or current work assignments, and therefore no income and few prospects. It means that, in most cases, survival of the individual as an independent consultant is in question.

In many of these cases, I learn ultimately that the individual has joined the salaried staff of some organization, often that of a former client. That is not necessarily a tragic fate; often it is good news. Many consultants win excellent positions that way and are quite content with the result. In fact, some independent consultants never intend to remain in private practice permanently, and enter into consulting until they find a permanent post. But for the individual who has counted on building a solid practice to admit failure is almost tragic and is, at the least, traumatic. Yet, such events are not necessarily failures. For the individual with an aggressive, upbeat attitude—the indomitable entrepreneur—there are no failures, but only setbacks, temporary conditions.

THE ROOTS OF FAILURE

There are many reasons for the failures of independent consultants, some applicable generally to the failures of other kinds of businesses and professional practices. The U.S. Small Business Administration and almost anyone else with substantial entrepreneurial experience will agree that the first year of a new venture is almost always the most critical, the one with by far the majority of business failures. The failure rate for ventures that survive the first year is far lower than for the newly launched. If you survive the first year, your chances for overall success improve, and your chances for survival in the second year improve considerably. Many venture capitalists regard the third or fourth year as the watershed year; survive that, they believe, and you can count yourself a probable success for the long term. (In evaluating a prospective venture, they often calculate, as a major criterion of viability, its probability of starting to produce a profit by the end of the third or fourth year.) The IRS is similarly influenced, agreeing that it is not unusual for a venture to produce little or no profit for the first three years, but having serious doubts that a venture is truly a business venture and not a hobby if it fails to profit after three years. Paul and Sarah Edwards, two of the country's best-known experts, lecturers, and authors on small business (especially working-from-home ventures), appear more comfortable with the first five years as the trial by fire. After that, survival indicates the probability of long-range success.

Even for those who do not survive these critical years, the experiences are not always lost opportunities, as witness a thoughtful observation reported by the late Howard Shenson. Shenson was viewed as the "Consultant to the Consultant" for his time. He recounted the experience-based wisdom of a consultant who faltered three times, but was back on his feet and trying again a fourth time. This individual, Shenson related, observed that his first failed effort taught him the lesson of accounts receivable or too much easy credit extended. His second try foundered too, but, he said, taught him the lesson of accounts payable or failure to manage spending well. And his third unsuccessful run taught him the lesson of overhead—the disastrous effects of having too much of it. Now, trying for the fourth time, he was hopeful that the education he had paid so much for—the mistakes he had learned not to repeat—was complete and he would succeed.

He was not alone in that wisdom; a great many others have observed that what so many commonly refer to as failures are not that at all; they are simply lessons or experiments to discover what will and won't work. Edison conducted thousands of such experiments to find the right material for his incandescent-lamp filament; Charles Kettering tried many approaches before he solved the problem of building an automobile self-starter small enough to be practicable; Milton Hershey's hugely successful chocolate-candy corporation was not his first effort to launch a successful candy business; and U.S. success as putting a satellite into orbit required the education of several unsuccessful earlier efforts, as Werner von Braun and our other space scientists learned what not to do, as well as what to do. Succeeding without experiencing and overcoming setbacks is rare. Beware of the early success that comes without great effort or simply by chance; it sends up the wrong signals and can mislead you into making disastrous mistakes. It's Murphy's Law working in an insidious fashion.

There is a great deal of evidence that most successful entrepreneurs are individuals who failed a time or two—usually several times—before they found their major successes. It appears that failure is the school that teaches success. There are many successful people, some quite well known, who firmly believe that without the education of a few failures, true success is not possible. But this is not surprising; formal education cannot teach success in the business world. Here, the education that works most reliably is the education of experience. Despite the exceptions—those who are born successful or have success thrust upon them—the secret of success usually involves learning from various tries or mistakes. There are bad guesses, inaccurate estimates, and misfortunes, but there is no universal formula for success. That is, there are the normal mistakes, sometimes painful, usually costly, always educational, but there is no real failure if you use the experience wisely.

Whatever we call these—experience (as Oscar Wilde did in *Lady Windermere's Fan*), mistakes, or education—they are the latter. It helps to remember that education is never truly free; it has a cost. But then, all success has always had a price and required a willingness to pay that price. Early unexpected, unearned, and undeserved success—winning your first client or first project without effort through some stroke of luck—is itself a kind of failure. It misleads you and in so doing sets you back in your quest to learn what you need to know for your eventual, long-term success.

THE COMMON MISTAKES OF NEOPHYTE CONSULTANTS

I do not pretend to believe that you will not encounter disappointments and frustrations in abundance; you almost surely will. Still, while setbacks can be positive influences in building a practice, many can be avoided when you know what they are and how they are caused. Let's look at a few typical cases. These are all based on real people—they are factual accounts, suitably disguised—but they are absolutely typical of the mistakes a great many consultants make, usually the result of inexperience.

Jerry T. came to Washington, D.C., from the Midwest, fresh out of college and with a new wife. Making the rounds of government offices here, he soon ran into an official in the State Department who took an immediate liking to Jerry and offered him an assignment as a training consultant because he didn't have a slot open to offer him a job. The assignment was to set up and conduct a seminar for some State

Department staff. It went quite well and led to other consulting assignments, as Jerry's new friend recommended him to other government agencies. Before long, the volume of work expanded to a point where Jerry could not handle it alone. He then rented a suite of offices in downtown Washington and hung out his shingle as a training consultant. But he wanted to do things right, so he bought a stock of impressive stationery, had beautiful (and expensive) brochures printed, furnished his suite, and hired a secretary.

It was wonderful while it lasted, but government budgets have their ups and downs. The next year, Jerry's friend had no funds to continue his training program, and Jerry had no other clients of importance. He soon closed his downtown office suite and went in quest of a job again.

Consultant's Undoing: Increased overhead too rapidly without a suitable track record to support the increase in costs. Fixed costs are by their nature committed to regardless of business conditions, so when there is not sufficient revenue being generated to offset the costs, the reserves or savings of the firm must be used to pay expenses (a sure sign that the firm is in trouble).

Bobby S. is a fine illustrator. He worked for a major engineering firm, doing everything from detailed schematic drawings to artist's concepts for employers' engineering projects, documentation, and annual reports, and soon he was managing an entire department of illustrators and drafters.

His work brought him into direct contact with clients, and occasionally some of the clients tried to get Bobby to moonlight with them, and even to start his own independent service. Bobby was always reluctant to do so, fearful of leaving his steady job. But he was finally persuaded when his wife became pregnant and he was faced with a great many extra expenses. But the moonlighting still bothered him, and he did not like taking so much time from his home life, so he soon began to consider acting as a consultant. He set up a work area at home and quit his job.

Suddenly, all those clients who had encouraged Bobby to go out on his own evaporated. They had all kinds of apologetic excuses, but little work to offer. Bobby has survived and is managing well enough now, but he had a couple of very lean and difficult years. It will take more than a good year or two to make up what he lost.

Consultant's Undoing: Failure to secure commitment from prospects for their business prior to launching the firm. Promises made verbally or suggestions made (even if made with the best of intentions) are not sufficient to use for paying bills. Only contracts and firm assurances that demonstrate willingness to pay for services should be relied on (and even then, they are suspect as many projects are cancelled, delayed, or modified and may leave the consultant without the expected project revenue).

John R. is a somewhat different kind of case. A PhD—really Dr. John—he is a computer specialist and a bright fellow. Let go by his company in a general cutback when their principal contract ended, John let his business friends and acquaintances know that he was now available on a consulting basis.

John is a technical/professional specialist who happens to write well. He also thinks well and can devise strategies, which makes him an excellent proposal writer.

He found a number of clients eager to retain him to do just that, after a few telephone calls, and he was soon busy as many hours a week as he wished to work, at rates he stipulated. He even took in a partner to help him handle the workload, which had grown swiftly beyond his ability to handle it alone.

John's success lasted for several months. But proposal writing, while it is a year-around activity, also has its peak seasons, when organizations who normally write many proposals need extra help, and those who write only occasional proposals do not have the expert staff and must hire consultants. So the proposal consultant is as likely as anyone else to experience peaks and valleys of calls for services. The failure to recognize and plan for this was John's undoing. He neither diversified the services he offered nor did any serious marketing throughout those busy months. He was too busy writing proposals and invoicing clients to give even his thoughts, much less his time, to questing for new and additional clients. It was therefore almost inevitable and only a matter of time before he was forced to seek a salaried position again.

Consultant's Undoing: Inability or ignorance about building a business plan to recognize the ongoing needs of the consulting firm beyond the most immediate quarter. The need to sustain the business through constant marketing of existing or corollary services/products eluded Dr. John and he lost the business as a result of it.

Note the common mistakes, the most serious of which is the general failure to market until business slows or comes to a halt. But the failure to diversify a bit is also a severe handicap to a new consulting practice, because it affects your marketing in several ways: It limits your market prospects to only those who need that single, special service you offer; it limits the size of your projects to that single service; and it handicaps you against competitors who offer a wider diversity of services than you do.

THE BASIC TRADEOFFS

We make trade-offs throughout our lives, giving up one thing to gain another and otherwise compromising between alternatives—between what we wish for and what we can afford and must accept. One of my consultant friends, Al R., for example, makes a great deal of money every year—over six figures—but has traded off having a normal home life because he must travel more than 300 days a year to earn that much money. In my own case, I sampled that mode of professional life for a time, but eventually I refused to make that trade-off, despite the greater income possible.

Most trade-offs are deliberate decisions. You decide what alternatives you will choose and what compromises you will make. You decide what you will pay or sacrifice (sacrifice is payment, of course) for the gains you want. And this applies generally to your practice as a consultant; the more highly specialized the expertise and services you offer, the more sharply targeted your marketing must be, and the higher the fees you can charge (theoretically, at least!). But this usually means a more limited or restricted market, and thus may mean a more difficult quest for clients. Of course, the reverse is also true: Making your offering more generalized—a range of services, instead of a single, sharply defined and highly specialized service—broadens its appeal and increases the number of prospects. At the same time, it increases the number of direct competitors for contracts, and may tend to decrease the size of the fees you can command.

A somewhat more subtle effect is the psychological one: Broadening your field of claimed expertise tends to lessen your credibility as a consultant; clients usually equate consulting with specialization, and so they are likely to regard the most highly specialized consultants as the most highly qualified ones. In today's world, the generalist is not highly regarded. (There is a paradox here, which we shall discuss later.)

In practice, I find it necessary to trade off between the image of the scholarly expert counselor and that of the working marketer. Writing, lecturing, presenting seminars, training clients' staffs, doing market research, and performing other chores are all part of consulting, as I see it, and the refusal to offer a complete consulting service has hindered many independent consultants in their efforts to build a successful practice.

HOW SPECIALIZED SHOULD YOU BE?

There is more at stake here than where to draw the line as a specialist. The mistake is trying to decide from *your* viewpoint how specialized you ought to be. It is your clients who decide, in the end, whether you will or will not succeed in your undertaking. If they cannot get from you what they want, they will go elsewhere.

The question of what to trade off is one you must answer for yourself, because the right answer for someone else is probably not the right answer for you. When it comes to the breadth and diversity of the services you offer, however, you must be guided principally by what it takes to survive, especially in the early months. Ultimately, you will establish a pattern, as you discover what services are most salable, most profitable, and most suitable to your own talents, skills, and desires. You will probably wind up with a far different set of services than you visualized when you started a career as an independent consultant. (I had no intention nor even thought fleetingly of lecturing, offering seminars, or publishing a newsletter, when I started, much less of lecturing in local colleges and conducting regular courses.)

The argument that someone entering the consulting field must address is, "How unique do I wish to be?" Many consultants assume that their expertise is what sells them and their services to the client. There are dual tracks that the client/prospect is traveling down in making the decision: (1) does the person have the depth needed to handle the issue to be addressed and (2) does the person understand me/my company/my challenges. As often as not, it is number 2 that will either sell or undo a consultant's ability to secure projects. It is advisable for the novice consultant not to lose sight of the need to be "generalized" in consulting as a skill (aside from the expertise provided in the field of specialization).

It also is strongly recommended that a consultant research the prospect or client company to address how to best align one's specialty areas with the entire company's strategies, objectives, and stated plans. Talking to more than just one person in one department is critical. Getting a more comprehensive view of the company's needs is essential in linking your consultation expertise to the organization's requirements.

SPECIALIZE AND DIVERSIFY

There are two kinds of specialization for you to consider: specialization in the subjects of your expertise, and specialization in the modes in which you provide those expert services. I specialize in marketing to the government, especially in proposal writing, the key to custom contracts. But I diversify in the services I provide to those who want help in winning government contracts. I offer my personal services as a proposal writer, proposal manager, and proposal leader, but I also offer to provide proposal aid in other ways. One is study of requirements and advice on deciding to propose or not to propose on specific requirements. Another is the provision of counsel and strategy formulation to those who have adequate proposal-writing staffs. Another is proposal-writing training, usually in the form of seminars. Still another is an information service in the form of books and occasional monographs or manuals on the subject.

By operating in this manner, I am able to maintain the image of a specialist who focuses on areas of great concern to clients; yet I diversify so that I am not unduly constrained in revenue-producing activities.

This is an option open to every independent consultant. It is a way to have your cake and eat it, too; you can be a highly specialized professional, with all that such specialization bestows in the way of benefits, and yet be diversified in sources of income based on that specialization.

MARKETING

One basic mistake many newcomers to consulting make is offering too narrow a range of services—overspecialization; equally common is the mistake of marketing to too narrow a range of potential clients. Even worse is failing to understand the role of and need for marketing in the consulting enterprise. So often an individual launches a consulting enterprise on the basis of a single client or two, and assumes that the quest for clients need not be a concern until he or she needs more clients. Far too often, it is only a single client that inspires individuals to establish independent practices. Whether the access to an immediate paying client is the result of good fortune or is itself the catalyst for establishing the new practice, it often deceives the new consultant as to the ease or difficulty of winning clients and assignments. Too often, it is only after leaving a job, making an investment, incurring serious debt, and dedicating many months of effort, that the new practitioner begins to discover that most clients and contracts do not come as easily as that first one or two did.

Probably the deadliest of all marketing mistakes is the assumption that the right time to market is when business is slow and you have the time. This approach is based on the foolish assumption that you cannot afford to waste your time in marketing when you are busy serving paying clients, and the equally foolish assumption that there is no need to market when you are busy.

Such reasoning fails to recognize that in every enterprise there is a considerable time lag between the launching of marketing efforts and resulting sales. That is especially true in the field of professional services. Here the gap can be many months, for a variety of reasons. Even the most effective marketing of consulting services is likely to pay off substantially with contracts only months later, and only after months when income may be zero or near-zero. That is a period that most independent consultants have difficulty surviving. How long can *you* survive with zero income?

THE TEN LAWS OF SURVIVAL

This book is focused largely on survival. You will therefore be reading many highly specific items concerning survival, as well as success. And, unless you are extraordinarily fortunate, you are almost certain to come face to face with many disappointing and sometimes disheartening realities, such as Murphy's Law, which states (in its simplest form), "Anything that can go wrong will." (Additional Murphy's Laws make this perhaps the most optimistic one of all!) Here are some of the things that befall most of us, sooner or later (and usually sooner):

- The deceptively easy first assignment turns out to be a real bear, and almost induces you to give up being a consultant before you get the job under control and completed.
- That pleasant individual you accepted as a client without insisting on a written agreement (no need to sign paper for a small project that was in both your interests) fought you every inch of the way, misrepresenting what you thought was a clear understanding, and making you fight to get paid.
- That struggling little company who was so unconcerned about the cost of your services proved to be unconcerned because they didn't have any money anyway, and you never did get paid, or you settled for less than the full fee and had to pay an attorney or collection agency a third of that for helping you collect.
- One of those associates you brought in to help you handle a project that needed three people was a dud, and you wound up covering for him or her and working all kinds of extra hours to protect your own reputation. And the other one even tried to steal the client from you.

There were other problems. The accountant who set up your books billed you for a great deal more than the original estimate; he or she was full of long-faced and regretful explanations. The printer botched your stationery, and you had to have it all done over. The answering service lost several important messages—probably cost you a client or two. And almost everything you bought to furnish and equip your office cost more than you planned. (Your shopping was based on newspaper advertising and catalogs, and you trustingly believed the advertised prices when planning your budget.)

There are a few laws of survival that may help:

1. The First Law of Survival is to expect everything to go wrong and have alternatives ready to be implemented when needed.

2.   The Second Law of Survival is to make $50 mistakes, not $500 ones. You need that education, you usually get it only via the mistakes you make, and you should fully expect to make them, but you can learn just as much from $50 mistakes as you can for $500 or $5,000 mistakes.

3.   The Third Law of Survival is to avoid or at least delay every expenditure possible. If you don't get substantial prompt payment discounts, take 30, 45, or even more days to pay your bills, like the big companies do. Make the old printer do a little longer. Use your printer and computer to design your own letterhead. Do your own filing. Get that downtown office next year. Don't be in a big hurry to order the new brochure. Shop around for a better price; printers' prices vary all over the lot, and you can do better. If you have a good laser printer, print your own letterhead and labels; few customers will know the difference or care and you can cut costs for these items by about two-thirds.

4.   The Fourth Law of Survival is never to refuse a job on which you can earn a profit. Accept the small job that is offered, and never mind the big job you were promised; it may or may not—probably will not—ever material-ize, anyway, and you will have lost the small one that you can have now. Forget those vague promises; only the bird in the hand counts, especially when the landlord, the butcher, and the baker approach with their bills in one hand and the other hand outstretched expectantly.

5.   The Fifth Law of Survival is never to get so successful that you turn down jobs or fail to find and make time for marketing because you are too busy. (The failure to market when you are busy is the certain harbinger of ulti-mate disaster; tomorrow's contract is even more important than the one you are now working on because you don't have it yet.) The next time things are slow and you are desperate for a contract, you'll wish you had obeyed this Law. (And see the next Law.)

6.   The Sixth Law of Survival is forget the clock, and the calendar, too. Forty-hour weeks and two-week vacations are things of the past, at least until you are firmly established (if then, even). You'll rest and vacation when business is slow, if you put in those 50-, 60-, even 80-hour weeks when you have the work. Work now and rest later.

For those of you who are considering getting into consulting for "qual-ity-of-life" reasons, be aware that while you have the illusion of controlling your own schedule and which projects you wish to work on (only taking the interesting ones or the ones with people or companies you enjoy), it is a false hope for most consultants. Yes, you can turn down assignments or clear your calendar as you determine, but it comes with a peril that many are unwill-ing to accept (loss of revenue, contracts, or interest from clients willing to pay for your services). This is something that every consultant will need to confront on their own—if, and when, to say no to a project and prioritizing the "home life" with the "work life." There are no easy "how-to steps" on getting this right, but you will surely know if you don't!

7.   The Seventh Law of Survival is don't start believing your own press clippings. Don't overrate your own importance and become too much the discriminating specialist; don't, that is, start becoming a pompous ass. (Perhaps that is an occupational hazard, but some consultants booby-trap themselves this way.) You are never too big or important to earn a dollar doing honest consulting work, even if you think the task is not as prestigious or upscale as what you yearn to do.

8.   The Eight Law of Survival is to remember that you are worth what you cost, and discounting your rates—bargaining and agreeing to different rates on each occasion, even when you are badly in need of the work—is not only unprofessional, but demeans you in the eyes of the client and even in your own eyes. It eventually damages you, as word gets around that clients can bargain for your best rate. There are other ways to help the customer economize and win the job without compromising your professionalism, ways we'll discuss later. Especially, don't be led down the garden path by clients' promises of lots of business later, recommendations to friends, etc. Those are bargaining tactics, and you are almost certain to ultimately regret being influenced by them. (My own word-of-mouth recommendations are almost invariably from people who never promised them to me or expected to profit from them in any way.)

9.   The Ninth Law of Survival is to be totally businesslike in your dealings. Do stick to your guns on your rate (see Eighth Law) and unless there is good reason to make exceptions (for example, a formal purchase order or letter of commitment from a large and well-established company with A-1 credit), do ask for a retainer as earnest money upon signing an agreement, and do ask clients to sign a simple agreement with you, explaining the commitments of both parties clearly. (This is in no way at odds with the Tenth Law of Survival.)

10. The Tenth Law of Survival, and in many ways the most important Law, is to be totally ethical. That means being completely honest, respecting and keeping confidences, safeguarding clients' proprietary information from unauthorized disclosure, doing an honest day's work, honoring your contracts scrupulously, and rendering honest bills for your services.

These Laws summarize most of this book, but before getting on to the later chapters, let's have a closer look at some of these key points and injunctions.

Experience, Education, and $50 Mistakes

It is probably an apocryphal tale, credited variously to department store merchant John Wanamaker and many other executives, but he and the others are reported to have said, "I know that one-half of my advertising dollar is wasted, but my problem is that I don't know which half it is." The truth is that probably more than one-half many people's advertising dollar is wasted because there is rarely a reliable means for measuring the result of advertising dollars. Advertising is one of many areas where we spend money hopefully, usually without a reliable means for even estimating the outcome. It is hardly surprising that many expenditures do not pay off adequately, leading us to characterize those investments as mistakes, rather than as the price of education.

You are going to make many decisions that will not turn out as well as you hoped. Why not, therefore, knowing that you are buying an education, take a small advertisement in the Yellow Pages, rather than a large one, if you insist on trying that medium? If it works, you can always increase it next year. Why buy 1,000 expensive, two-color, embossed or engraved business cards and matching stationery when you don't even know whether you will soon change your address, telephone number, e-mail address, business name, copy, or services offered? You won't lose any clients by ordering 500 plain, white cards and stationery, tastefully printed on adequate—not costly—stock. Why buy a high-speed copier when you may find you do not need it at all and are able to get clients to produce manuals or binders by simply e-mailing them files or providing CD-ROMS with the master copy for them to reproduce in-house?

You will do well to establish your office in your own home, if it is at all possible. If it is not—and admittedly there are cases where it is not—you do not need to set up offices in the most expensive part of town or in the most recently built (and thus usually the most costly) office building. You can almost always find something a bit more modest, yet thoroughly adequate.

You never need be self-conscious, apologetic, or self-deprecating about running your enterprise on a sound financial footing and economizing wherever you can. On the contrary, many of your clients will be impressed that you are level-headed and practical. That is not a bad image to acquire.

There Are No Small Jobs

In the theater, they say that there are no small parts; only small actors and actresses. In that vein, there are no small consulting jobs. There are some months when there is no huge training session planned for a client, nor is there a consulting project on a pending proposal being worked on, yet they are still profitable months because there are the diversified services referenced earlier to sustain me during those times: ghost-writing, lectures, brochures, or other marketing collateral that requires polishing or editing.

Jeffrey Lant, a management consultant in Cambridge, Massachusetts, found a large market for the books he frequently writes and publishes to counsel and aid other consultants. He has made this a major activity of his practice, which includes seminars and general consulting services. Lant has continued to expand his activities and has built a large business which now includes how to use the Internet as a money-making venture for consultants and others.

Alan Weiss has had to re-invent his services over time as well to remain current with the needs of clients. In addition to his own thriving practice working with client issues of leadership, management, and personal productivity, Alan also has a thriving practice directed at assisting consultants with their practices. Not content with the occasional presentation to association groups, Alan has a successful newsletter that he sends to those interested and frequently speaks about and authors books on topics related to consulting skills.

The list could go on and on, and we will come back to meet these consultants and others again and to listen to some of what they have to say in advising beginning consultants. The message here, however, is that successful consultants are, in most cases, individuals who are enterprising, versatile, and unafraid to diversify and exploit opportunities. They all agree that the independent consultant is well-advised to be conservative in expenditures, as well as in inflating his or her self-image.

THE CONSULTANT'S IMAGE

By now, I hope, you understand that your own image of what you are is not the critical one; only the client's or prospective client's image of you really matters, in a business sense. And it is important that you recognize this, for you must understand the client's perspective: The client often does not perceive the transaction as one of buying something—product or service—from you, but rather as hiring you temporarily. Far too often, the client tends to regard you as an employee, albeit a temporary one, rather than as an independent entrepreneur selling a valuable service and entitled to function as an equal.

This misunderstanding of your role can lead to an unpleasant and unhappy consultant-client relationship. In most cases, however, the evolution of this client's perception of you as a temporary employee can be avoided, if you practice certain measures to establish and preserve the proper image.

First the Self-Image

First you must settle the relationship firmly in your own mind. You must think of yourself as an independent contractor, and you must value yourself and your services properly. You are delivering a service of value to your client, trading your services and special abilities for money. You are fully competent to do everything the client requires of you, and you have complete confidence in yourself and in your ability. Unless you firmly believe that, you are unlikely to persuade anyone else to believe it; no matter how brave a front you put up, your convictions about yourself manage to shine through the facade and are perceived by the client and the client's staff or associates. Most of all, however, bear this in mind: Your true value, what you are being paid for, is not your time. That's a very much mistaken notion. Time is only the measure by which you calculate your charges; it is not the commodity you sell. What you sell— or should sell—is results. You must help your clients understand that too.

Through the Client's Eyes

What has been said here in no way contradicts the truth that it is how the client perceives you that is most important in the relationship, much more important than how you see yourself. However, what you think of yourself colors the client's impressions.

The client does not have to like you, helpful although that would be; clients do business often with individuals they do not particularly like, when the business relationship is a brief one. Where you and the client must work closely together for a substantial period, however, amity between you helps a great deal, and if that is not possible, at the least you must be a person who is not abrasive in any way. The old adage that it is harder to fire friends applies here. While it is not advisable that you try to become "friends" with your clients just to curry favor at the expense of doing what is right for either your business or theirs, it is always better to be viewed positively by the client. You must see to it that your personality is compatible with the client's, at least to the degree that you do not strike sparks from each other.

The Roles You Must and Must Not Play

The don'ts of behavior are characteristics that may be acceptable in some places, but are definitely out of place in most places, in bad taste, and/or offensive to so many people that it is risky to exhibit such traits. In fact, we all play many roles in life, and most of us play more than one role—worker, father, mother, friend, confidante, supervisor. The consultant is a role, too, but consultants often play the wrong roles in the client's offices. Here are some roles to avoid:

- *Mr. or Ms. Personality.* They are full of good cheer and compliments for everyone in sight, memorizing everyone's name, bringing in doughnuts every morning, and otherwise buttering everyone up with unbearable cheerfulness and good will.
- *The Name Dropper.* Don't drop those names, not even if you really do know all those prominent and influential citizens.
- *The Militant, whether Male Chauvinist or Impassioned Libber.* These roles are akin to each other, all impassioned seekers after justice. Save these arguments, poses, and positions for another time and place.
- *The Supremely Confident Know It All.* Forget how stupid everyone who doesn't agree with you is; be patient with the less fortunate ignorami and forgive their ignorance if you want to get along.
- *The Hero.* Don't come on too strong—no braggadocio about your great feats of the past and your magnificent promises for the future.
- *The Night Club Comedian.* Don't tell racy, off-color stories, make ethnic jokes and slurs, be a backslapper, or try otherwise to be an amateur Jerry Seinfeld and a Las Vegas standup comedian combined. It's much harder than it seems, and even if you happen to be a good comedian, it doesn't help your image as a serious consultant.
- *The Great Polemicist and Orator.* Don't get into political, religious, or other discussions about which so many people get emotional—not even lengthy discussions of sports, which are often in that same category.
- *The Eager Beaver.* Don't rush about offering unsolicited help, especially in matters unrelated to the work you were retained to do. Be responsive if

you are asked—you may occasionally be asked for your opinion on some matter not related directly to the effort for which you were retained—but wait to be asked.

- *The Irrepressible Marketer.* Important although marketing is, don't make the mistake so many make of trying immediately to fatten your part, either by trying to expand the contract you have just won or by trying immediately to sell a next contract with the same client. (This can be related to the Eager Beaver problem, in which the consultant is busy poking into everything but the job for which he or she was hired, trying desperately to set up future business.) You can wear out your welcome very quickly this way.

On the other hand, there is a role you should play as a serious professional. Come as close as you can to this:

- *The Total and Complete Professional.* That means quit confidence, a courteous and friendly personality, a subdued manner, dedication to doing the job as quietly and efficiently as possible, and willingness to listen intently and actually hear what is being said. (So many listen—apparently listen, that is, but never actually hear.) Learn people's names, acknowledge others pleasantly with a nod, a hello, "Good morning," or whatever is most appropriate, but then go about the business you are there for and forsake the morning coffee club. (You are probably not accepted by the regular staff, and they may resent your efforts to be one of them temporarily.)

5 | A Few Keys to Success

There is no single secret of success in consulting. Success is a mix of many skills and functions.

THE ART OF LISTENING

Marketing is probably the most important function of any business because a business thrives or fails in proportion to its success in creating buyers for its goods and services. In consulting, what you sell is *you:* Your success depends primarily on how well you sell yourself—how much confidence and trust you inspire. One of the most important skills is listening. It comes naturally to some, but we can all learn how to listen.

A great deal has been made of the art of listening in recent years, because so often we tend to think about what we are going to say next, rather than truly listening and grasping what the other person is saying. "The art of listening" is a catchy phrase, but it doesn't really make the point; many people interpret listening to mean being silent while the other person is talking, rather than truly listening—hearing, that is. True listening is hearing what the other person is saying, hearing the words and having them penetrate your consciousness with meaning, rather than with sound only.

Former U.S. President Franklin D. Roosevelt delighted in telling a story that demonstrated how little most people listen. He said he tried sitting in his wheelchair (he was a polio victim, although few knew this in those pre-television days) at White House receptions and greeting each visitor or pair of visitors with his typically brilliant smile, a warm handshake, and a murmured, "How do you do. I've just murdered my grandmother." Not a single visitor or guest ever turned a hair, he said, because no one really listened. They simply did not hear what he had said. They heard only what they assumed he had said or should have said.

President Roosevelt's story refers to the pleasantries of formal and official functions, but it is almost as true for many other occasions. Listening—really listening and hearing—is relatively rare. One highly successful salesman reports that his major secret is listening. Once he gets his prospect going on a favorite topic, whether it is fishing, golf, or manufacturing ball bearings, his own prolonged listening and hearing invariably result in his prospect remarking on what a brilliant conversationalist the salesman is!

This sounds cynical, as though listening is purely a sales gambit. It is not. It is the means for determining what the prospect really needs or wants, which is the key to making the sale.

Let's analyze this a bit. We have already established that many prospects cannot tell you what their problem or need is; they can describe symptoms and nothing more. An important part of your function as a consultant is to be an analyst and determine what the problem is, even before you win the contract. That ability is the key to being able to furnish real help to your client. And you can accomplish the feat of analyzing your prospect's situation and offering a solution by listening to what the prospect has to say.

The successful salesperson is always a consultant in making the sales presentation, no matter what he or she is selling. Fuller Brush sellers are showing prospects how to solve housekeeping problems. Avon and Mary Kay salespeople are helping prospects find the answers to beauty and makeup problems. Clothing salespeople are helping prospects find the clothes that enhance appearance. Every successful salesperson is helping the prospect do something that is beneficial to the prospect. There is no other reason to buy from any salesperson, and thus there is no other reason for any salesperson to even exist. Many a salesperson makes the mistake of being in presentation or performance mode and tries to impress their prospect by demonstrating the depth of their own knowledge. This leaves most businesspeople feeling frustrated and thinking the consultant never took the time to understand their situation. The antidote to this is to ask questions and then listen to the responses. Through an informed series of questions, the salesperson can demonstrate the same level of understanding (leaving the prospect to wonder, "How did the saleperson know that there is a problem here?" Or, "that person clearly understands the issues I confront based on the questions I was asked.").

As an independent entrepreneur, regardless of the product or service you sell, you are a salesperson. You will succeed only to the extent that you can help your prospects get what they want. And only by listening can you learn (1) what the prospect thinks he or she needs and (2) what the prospect really needs.

DECIDING WHAT BUSINESS YOU ARE IN

In presenting seminars, I often startle and even outrage many of my listeners when I charge that they do not know what businesses they are in. This accusation may startle and outrage you, too. Still, it is probably true. Unless you happen to be that rare exception who has been exposed to the right kind of marketing indoctrination or has great instinct for sensing the truth necessary to effective marketing, you are almost surely defining your business from your own viewpoint—in terms of what you sell or wish to sell, what, that is, you wish the client to buy. If you are an office procedures expert, for example, and make a career of advising others on organizing their office procedures or doing it for them, you may define your business as management consulting or perhaps more narrowly as office management.

That seems a logical enough way to define your business, does it not? It describes what you do, does it not? And what is the difference, anyway? Isn't definition an entirely academic question?

Definition of your business is not a mere academic question; it is a critical question, and the answer is likely to have a great deal to do with your success or lack of it.

In fact, your success depends largely on how wise you are in deciding or perceiving what business you are in from the client's viewpoint. (In marketing, that's the viewpoint that counts.) You may or may not be able to change your decision as to where, how, and in what you will specialize, after you have launched your practice, but you must be able to perceive your offer through the client's eyes if you are to sell your services effectively. It is that, the perception of the client, that defines your business. The client may be buying something he or she defines quite differently than you define it. More times than not, the client is buying a *solution* to a problem. The problem may be one of efficiency, accuracy, morale, or any other business issue. What the consultant is selling is the opportunity to have that problem resolved, or at least minimized. Thus, the answer to the question posed here is not always a simple one or one arrived at easily. But, before trying to find an easy answer or an easy way to find the answer, consider some related ideas that may be helpful.

Business Definition as Advertisement

The definition of your business is, or should be, a commercial for it. To be effective, a sales appeal (whether we call it a commercial, an advertisement, or a sales presentation) is most effective when it explains to the prospect what the product or service does for the customer. Keep that in mind as we discuss sales and advertising, for that explains the why, how, and what of defining your business.

A Common Denominator of All Businesses

Sophisticated marketers have sometimes made the point that every business is a service business, meaning that every customer buys what the business sells for the benefit he or she derives or expects to derive—for what the item will do for him or her. The buyer of a wristwatch has a primary motivation of being able to determine what time it is immediately, at his or her convenience. Everyone today has an electric refrigerator to store food. We have TVs primarily for entertainment, automobiles to give us mobility.

Yes, there are other motivations, and it will be necessary to discuss them later, in a more detailed examination of marketing. But, simply stated, everyone buys something, even a manufactured product, to gain some primary benefit from it, something it will do for them. Thus, whatever the actual item, ultimately it is the service that item does for the buyer that we really sell. (In fact, even this is not close enough to the buyer's motivation to fully explain it.)

What Customers Really Buy

Consultants are in the problem-solving business generally because clients tend to call on consultants when they need help. Perhaps everyone is in that business, in the final analysis, but a great many people associate consulting specifically with problem solving, so it is a good place to begin the analysis of your venture. Everyone has problems, and the reason for retaining a consultant is to solve the problem by the most efficient—and usually most rapid—means possible. But even that does not always tell the story. Sometimes the client is an executive in trouble—under great pressure to straighten out some situation. When he retains a consultant, the consultant is in the rescue-service business! On the other hand, when the client is an executive who is trying desperately to establish himself or herself in the organization—to get recognition and become a hero or heroine—the consultant is in the hero-making business!

Clients are organizations, but they are represented by individuals with whom you must do business. Perhaps your contract or purchase order says PDQ Corporation, but your client may very well be Harry P. Executive personally. To get PDQ Corporation to pay you and to do business with you again, you must satisfy client Harry P. Executive. Thus, you must know what Harry P. Executive wants and demonstrate an ability to satisfy that want. Moral: Be sure you know who your client is.

Many consultants (new and established) forget that the consulting business is a person-to-person business, and without the subjective approval of someone willing to spend money for services offered, there is no objective determination of value provided or worth. Contrast that with the mistake that some new consultants, and even some experienced ones make of assessing their value or worth based on their own income needs or desires. The erroneous thinking would maintain that if I need or want to earn $100,000 a year, and only work on 10 projects a year, then each project must generate at least $10,000 in fees. The project may not be worth that much, or may be worth significantly more—but this consultant is blinded to the project and the client's needs and is only viewing it from a self-centered perception and is blinded to the value being provided.

THE KEY TO THE DEFINITION

If your business is satisfying clients' wants, finding out what your clients really want is the key to discovering what business you are in. There is certain to be variation among the wants of your clients, but there must be some common ground from which to start. All clients for my proposal-writing service wanted to win government contracts, and I could arouse the interest of every one of them with my promise of assistance. That interest established, we could move on to a more detailed discussion of what the client wanted and whether we could reach agreement.

Thus, you begin with a general, and yet specific, understanding of the client's want, and then work at defining that more precisely. You cannot base your appeal on a specific promise to get the client off the hot spot or to make the client a hero or heroine; your appeal must be far more subtle than that. But, you must understand the client's true motive if you are to make the most effective appeal, and it is quite often necessary for you to help the client understand and recognize his or her want.

In many cases, where the client does not consciously perceive his or her want in these terms (although it may be an unconscious desire), you can help the client see one of these possibilities as the chief benefit of your services. It is safe to say that all organizations have problems, and individuals have the responsibilities for solving the problems, so the basic appeal to solving problems is always a sound one. But, it is likely that every executive, especially young ones still working at establishing their images, yearns at least subconsciously to gain special recognition by doing something heroic for the organization. Many successful marketing campaigns are based on arousing the Walter Mitty that is buried in most of us.

All customers buy love, prestige, ego gratification, security, success, recognition, and many other emotional satisfactions. Like all other people, they need to be in on things, to belong, to be recognized as having worth, to be appreciated, to feel important, to be loved, to be admired, and to be successful.

A wise consultant will view the definition problem in terms of corporate needs (improve competitive position in the marketplace, reduce costs, develop new products, etc.), departmental or functional needs (marketing department needs to create sales collateral material, advertisements, and maintain the web site), and personal needs (this project can get me promoted, earn me a bonus, or reduce the heat I am feeling from management on the loss of our top three salespeople), and then articulate how the proposed solution meets all three needs.

Clients Are People!

As far as marketing is concerned, all truth lies in the client's perception. You may be sure that you are delivering a major benefit, the ideal answer to the client's problem, or the means for making him or her a hero or heroine in the organization, but none of this matters if you cannot persuade the client to believe it.

On the other hand, clients are sensitive, and you must take care to avoid giving offense. You need to have regard for the client's own pride. The fact that a client has called on you for help does not mean that he or she necessarily feels less competent than you to do the job. A large number of clients believe that they are perfectly capable of doing the job themselves but are just too busy to do it or that it is not a wise allocation of their time. This may even be true in many cases, but what difference does it make if it is true or not? Ordinary diplomacy dictates that you must not flaunt your knowledge and ability. Even when the client is perfectly willing to admit to a capability or knowledge he or she does not have, it is risky to appear patronizing or condescending. Remember, in any case, that you will often be called in by a client who can, indeed, do the job as well as you but truly does not have the time or believes that it makes better sense to hire you and not tie himself or herself up with the project. To assume otherwise can be hazardous.

Even when the client is wrong—perhaps especially when the client is wrong— you must exercise great tact. Many executives and professionals freely admit that they do not write well and are happy to turn the job over to a professional writer. Unfortunately, many others insist that they write as well as anyone, when they have the time, but are usually too busy to do their own writing. (It may even be true.) There are countless cases where the client has called on a free-lance writer, offering a hopelessly inept draft of a proposal or other manuscript, asking for a quotation to edit and clean it up a bit. The client does not wish to admit, even to him- or herself, that the writing is inadequate, or that the manuscript should be trashed in favor of an entirely fresh effort. The foolish consultant remonstrates that the manuscript needs complete rewriting, a tactic that will probably cost him or her the job. The smart consultant agrees that a heavy edit is needed, furnishes a quotation for the total rewrite he or she actually plans to do, and winds up with the job and a satisfied client. (There is nothing unethical or dishonest in calling the job editing, when you know it will be writing, if you are charging a fair price to do what you know must be done and then doing it.)

Most of us want to believe that we are the best at whatever we do, and we think that the client ought to be able to recognize that obvious fact. The client, however, unless he or she has had some experience that has made him or her wiser, has no way of knowing that one computer consultant is better than the next. All the consultants the client talks to claim total competence in all matters relating to computers, so how is a mere client to know the difference? In those circumstances why not simply call for bids and award the project to the lowest bidder?

Helping the client perceive the difference—educating the client—is a major requirement in the successful marketing of consulting services. Even if you were willing to try to be the low bidder—generally a self-defeating practice in itself—it would not be the winning strategy in a great many cases. In fact, to win in the marketing of technical and professional services generally you must be able to prove yourself and/or your plans superior to those of competitors.

There is also a *buyer's psychology* at work here. The perceived value is often related to the actual costs (the client will convince him or herself that, if I pay $5,000 for services, I will have purchased a "better" service than the one available for $3,000). Clients will occasionally shy away from the low-cost provider, thinking that the "worth" of the service cannot be as good as the consultant charging a higher fee. While it is difficult to suggest a fee guideline to you because of the many specialties represented by the readers of this book, a very broad suggestion might be to aim for the middle 50 percent of what the market typically sees. In this way, you are not discounting your services to the bottom 25 percent and leaving potential project money on the table and you are not likely to lose business by overpricing yourself by being more costly than 75 percent or more of the consultants likely to be seen by the client.

THE TWO BASIC SALES SITUATIONS

There are two basic sales situations. In the first, there is a felt need: The client is aware of and accepts the need for consulting services to solve a problem of some sort, whether it is a technical problem that requires an expert or a staff shortage that requires a professional temporary or two. In the second case, you must create a need for consulting services: The client may or may not be aware of a problem or need, but even if he or she agrees that there is a problem to be solved, he or she has not yet decided that outside services are the best answer.

These are two entirely different selling problems. In the first case, you are selling against competition. You know the contract will be awarded to someone, and it's your task to convince the client that it be awarded to you. In the second case, you are sell-ing against bias, perhaps, if the client has not yet decided that retaining a consultant is the thing to do. Instead of persuading the client that you and your plan are better than your competitors and their plans, you must convince the client that your ser-vices are needed and provide valuable benefits. There is the hazard here that after you persuade the client to retain a consultant, the client may wish to conduct a competi-tion, rather than making the award directly to you, so that you will have created an opportunity for your competition.

In either case, you are likely to be required to do some analysis and propose a spe-cific plan to satisfy the client's need, as well as furnish an estimate of costs—submit a proposal, that is. It is probably in your own interest to encourage the client to require this. The client will very likely rate you on how well you understand and appraise the problem your services must solve, as well as on how effective your plan appears to be.

The failure to listen carefully to what the client has to say can be fatal to your mar-keting effort and even to your entire company, as it was to Sam and his small, but growing engineering-services company. Sam was a former employee of a major com-pany in the Washington, DC, area in their engineering department. His small com-pany did the majority of its work for his former employer. Having worked for and with them over a good number of years, Sam began to believe that he "knew" their needs and did not need to seek to understand the needs from the client's perspective. Sam thought that his experience was such that he already knew more than the client about what they needed or should pursue. He reached a point where he was sure that he knew more about what they needed and wanted than they did, and he began to ignore their stated requirements in favor of his own mandates of what they would get from him. He didn't hesitate to tell his former employers management that they need not tell him what they wanted him to do; he knew all he needed to know already.

This arrogance began to cost Sam the contracts he had once been able to gather in, and it was not very long before his prosperous little service organization was no more. The client had no difficulty in finding other competent engineering consul-tants who were more compliant and responsive in listening to their statements and satisfying their needs.

THE INDEPENDENT CONSULTANT: SPECIALIST OR GENERALIST?

It is ironic that the independent consultant must be both specialist and general-ist—very much the specialist, technically and in the perception of the client—while also very much the generalist in practice as a one-man band, doing all or nearly all the things (technical, managerial, and administrative) necessary to the successful operation and survival of a small business. In a very real sense, even the functions necessary to the technical side of consulting are highly diverse. While you may be able to call on outside help or associates to carry out some of your functions, the main burden for all of them falls on you.

The Independent Consultant as a Technical/Professional Specialist

The special technical skills that you must have as a consultant depend on the field in which you consult. In general, however, the practice of consulting requires the application of certain technical/professional skills, and as an independent consultant you must usually be capable of personally doing all of them. Every consulting assignment requires at least some of the following six direct-support functions, and many require all:

1. Listening.
2. Analysis and problem definition.
3. Problem solving.
4. Doing.
5. Public speaking.
6. Writing.

Listening and doing are functions required for virtually all consulting assignments or projects. You must master and practice the art of listening to—hearing—what the client says, as well as to what those whom you interview and/or must work with have to say. And you must actually do the engineering, computer programming, office-procedures design, training development, or whatever constitutes the basis of your consulting specialty. It would be rare indeed that a client would not require you to at least lead and guide the effort. (Even in major proposal-writing jobs, where the client's staff must do much of the writing, the proposal consultant must lead, edit, supervise, write, and be totally responsible for the final result.)

Analysis, problem definition, and problem solving are functions you must carry out in a majority of instances Even when clients identify their problems quite clearly and dictate the desired solution, you should be able to analyze the symptoms and verify the clients' statements or discuss them with the client if you find them not entirely accurate.

It is not enough for the client to have a vision of the recommended solution, or for you to feel that you know the right approach to take to resolve a client's problem. Before a consultant can receive a project, the client must perceive that the consultant truly understands what is needed. Being able to demonstrate that you are worthy of trust and confidence is achieved only through listening, analysis and problem definition, and problem solving (before you ever get to demonstrate the "doing, public speaking, and writing" skills in most instances).

There is frequent need and always good use for public speaking and writing. At the minimum you may be called on to make presentations and/or train or brief the client's staff, but you will also find speaking before groups valuable as a marketing tool and as the basis for another consulting income center. Writing falls into the same category, and perhaps ought to be included as a necessary function of consulting because for many types of consultancies you must write reports and proposals as part of all or nearly all assignments. Like speaking, writing may also be the basis for an important income center in your practice.

The Independent Consultant as a Businessperson

Consulting is a profession, but it is also a business, and you must be a businessperson to succeed. That means being a manager and administrator. The functions and skills required for management and administration of any business include at least these:

- Accounting and related record keeping.
- Cost estimating and pricing.
- Scheduling and time management.
- Financial management.
- Marketing and sales.

Other skills are elements of general business management and administration for many kinds of enterprises, but those listed above are usually the main functions in managing and administering a consulting practice. In general, the first four elements are the same in principle for all business enterprises. Not so marketing, however. Marketing for you as an independent consultant is a special problem, and something of a gray area of management and administration. It is not readily separable from the technical/professional side of consulting. It will therefore be discussed briefly here, in a separate discussion, and in much greater depth and detail later, since help in marketing your consulting services is the single most important objective of this book overall.

Accounting and Record Keeping

Many individuals entering a small business immediately enroll a certified public accountant to set up a complete accounting system and handle all bookkeeping and accounting work. A major motivation underlying this is the belief that accounting is something of a black art—a mysterious ritual that most mere mortals cannot hope even to fathom, much less practice. (Perhaps this mythology is encouraged by the jargon with which most professional accountants disguise, whether by intent or not, perfectly ordinary and commonsense functions.) This motivation is reinforced heavily by a dreadful fear of the Internal Revenue Service and the mistaken belief that the chief purpose of keeping books is to comply with the legal statutes and preferences of the IRS.

There is nothing wrong with retaining a professional accountant to handle all your accounting needs. There are good arguments for doing it yourself, however, and it is far less difficult than you might imagine. In fact, there are several ways to handle the problem as a compromise between the extremes of turning it all over to a professional accountant and doing it all yourself. (I have tried both extremes and have for years used a compromise solution quite successfully.) Here are the basic alternatives in adopting a hybrid system or compromise between the alternatives:

1. The accountant sets up your books and a system for you to follow, so you do the day-to-day journalizing, check-stub maintenance, invoicing, and other such chores. The accountant comes in periodically—once a week or once a month—and does your formal postings, balancing, reconciling the bank statement, making up estimated tax returns and other tax papers when necessary, and so on.

2. The accountant sets up the system and instructs you in how to do posting and keep the books. Periodically, perhaps every quarter- or half-year, the accountant goes over your books to do all your taxes and prepare the standard reports (profit and loss statement, balance sheet, and others).

3. You use one of the standard computerized or traditional accounting systems designed especially for very small businesses—you can buy the traditional journal/ledger and instructions that constitute such a simplified system in almost any good office-supplies store—and get an accountant's help to do your taxes and prepare your standard reports.

4. Purchase one of the commercially available software applications that provide "intuitive" interfaces (or at least they are fairly "user friendly") and enter information into fields as prompted (often these software applications will also provide guidance in report generation with standard or templated reports, tax preparation, and even go so far as to aid in establishing savings plans, monitoring investments, and other financial requirements small businesses may encounter).

There are some variants on even these basic hybrids. You may find an individual accountant who will come to your office to work, but you are more likely to deal with an accounting firm who will want you to bundle up your books and papers periodically and carry them to their offices, where they will do the work. Of course, you do not have to follow any of the arrangements exactly as described here; you may make various adjustments between what you will do and what your accountant will do. The arrangements cited here are mere examples, and you can adjust these to your own needs and wants.

In my own case, I use the last-named hybrid, and my accountant does little more than end-of-year state and federal corporate and personal income taxes for me. I had previously tried having an accountant handle it all for me, and I was dissatisfied with the arrangement for several reasons, especially that I had to hold my breath for three months to find out how I was doing. I needed to know immediately when things were going wrong, and I found that those little do-it-yourself systems actually let you know every day how you are doing if you pay attention. Moreover, it's a great deal less expensive and a great deal simpler. (Most consultants have a rather limited number of transactions to record.)

The purpose of accounting is not to make life easier for the IRS, although the law requires you to keep some kind of record. The primary purpose of any accounting system is furnishing you information on which to make sound decisions—on which to manage your practice to your own best advantage. And of course you want that information while there is time to make beneficial adjustments—discontinue something that is costing you money, for example, or renew a marketing effort that is producing good results—not when it is too late to correct a mistake or take advantage of an opportunity. (It is quite easy to be entirely unaware of such things if you do not have a system that automatically alerts you.)

In short, to be useful and do what it ought to do for you, the system must furnish information that satisfies three requirements:

1.   It must be accurate information.
2.   It must be timely information.
3.   It must be the right (i.e., useful) information.

The need for accurate information needs no discussion. Inaccurate information is not only of no help, but it is a burden and a hazard.

Timeliness is of the essence, as already noted. You need to know how things are going in real time, while you can take corrective action.

Only you know what information is useful or right for your purposes, and even you may not know that until you have had some experience and determined what information helps you make good decisions and what information is of no help. Keeping your own books and making your own postings teaches you this and may be the only way to learn it.

It is just not possible for a public accountant to do for you what you can do for yourself. Moreover, the accountant has an understandable tendency to burden you with a system that is not only far more complex and sophisticated than you need, but actually tends to conceal the facts from you, rather than high-lighting and dramatizing them, as it should.

The large corporation has a comptroller or chief accountant who is expert at reading the figures and devotes full time to analyzing them, but you have to do it for yourself. That is why you need a simple system, one that you can understand and interpret easily.

In addition, remember that the accountant is simply not familiar with your profession, let alone the circumstances of your individual practice, and cannot possibly anticipate what you need. Those simple systems, however, give you absolutely up-to-date information, if you keep the system up. You can usually identify every cost center you have, what it has cost you in the past week (or month, if you prefer to keep records on a monthly period), and what it has cost you in total for the year to date. You have the same figures for all costs, and for all income, so that you can make comparisons as often as you like and spot changes in a trend immediately.

Financial Management and Cost Analyses

Some organizations also use their accountants or comptrollers as financial managers. I believe this can be a mistake. Accountants and comptrollers are ordinarily more focused on day-to-day operations, including establishing and maintaining records, making up reports, verifying expenses, and getting the data to various managers who need the information. Financial managers, on the other hand, are or should be concerned with future projects and overall management affecting the organization's finances, such as the following:

1. Cost analyses, to ensure that work is estimated and priced accurately. This is not a simple matter, and some organizations operate at a loss for a long time without realizing it because they have failed to make a realistic and accurate analysis of all their costs.
2. Optimizing the organization's cash flow and financial position by ensuring prompt invoicing, taking advantage of all discounts, managing assets to minimize interest payments and maximize return on investment, and other such measures.
3. Cost control, including the use of available cost reduction and cost avoidance practices.
4. Funding operations, including equity funding, debt financing, and other available measures.

Scheduling and Time Management

Scheduling and time management are executive functions that as an independent consultant you will normally do for yourself. They can be complex in the large company but are usually quite simple in the small organization. If you get into work situations in which you must keep accurate time records, however, you will have to organize some sort of formal system.

As was mentioned in the discussion about cost analysis, knowing the actual time devoted to projects and billing or proposing fees accurately ensures a well-run consulting practice, whereas never confirming the facts against the time you believe you have dedicated can lead to conflicts that could potentially damage the expectations of your practice.

Marketing

Marketing is rarely a simple function; in the case of selling consulting services it usually gets quite complex because such services can rarely be sold through conventional or traditional methods. Many consultants who have tried such methods—media advertising, brochures, and personal calls on prospects—have been puzzled and dismayed to find that results are often zero and rarely more than absolutely minimal.

To some degree, this reflects a failure to formulate a specific and detailed marketing plan in advance, especially the detail of identifying the specific benefits you offer via your services and the specific kinds of prospects to whom you wish to appeal. Many new consultants believe that if enough people are made aware that they (the consultants) are now ready to solve clients' problems, the telephone will start ringing.

The opposite is true. Rarely does a client choose a consultant casually as a result of a conventional advertisement or sales call. Quite the contrary; clients find consultants through indirect means, such as recommendations by friends, meeting consultants at business meetings and conventions, hearing consultants speak at such events, reading about consultants in articles, and reading articles and books written by the consultant.

Many of these activities of consultants are marketing functions, and they call for the application of certain skills listed earlier as technical/professional skills. It is partly for this reason that the subject of marketing is handled separately here as a kind of gray area between the two sets of skills. However, the importance of marketing to consulting success is itself enough to merit and justify treating the subject separately. The message in this chapter is how to survive the first year and set the survival and success patterns for succeeding years. The secret of that survival and success has been for me, and for a great many other independent consultants, having more than one consulting service and/or related product to sell (other profit centers, that is) and effectively marketing all the services.

DO'S AND DON'TS, ESPECIALLY FOR THE FIRST YEAR

The first year of a new venture is the most critical one. The sensible main objective of the first year is not success; it is survival. The second and only slightly less important objective of the first year is education—learning what works and what doesn't work for you, what to do and what to avoid doing, and whatever else only experience can really teach you.

General Suggestions for Minimizing Costs

Don't get carried away with the enthusiasm of a new venture. Enthusiasm is a great asset and will help you considerably, but it should not blind you to the reality of that first year, when it is quite possible that you will pay more money out than you take in, especially if you are not careful. Remember that what you spend this first year—and possibly even in succeeding years—is the cost of your education, but the education need not be disastrously expensive. Businessman and 1992 presidential candidate Ross Perot, who is reported to have assets of about $3 billion, started his Electronic Data Systems company as a one-man enterprise in an office he rented for $100 a month, with only $1,000 in borrowed capital. He still has simple tastes, claims that no painting or lithograph in his office cost more than $25, and says he drives a late model Oldsmobile. The late Sam Walton, of Wal-Mart stores, reported to have built personal assets of between $7 and $8 billion, was also a man of simple tastes; he drove a pickup truck.

Here are some suggestions for conserving your cash and minimizing your first-year expenses:

- Make no long-term advertising commitments, such as Yellow Pages advertising or an advertising term contract with a newspaper.
- Set up your first office in your home, if at all possible. If you must have an office outside your home, choose a modestly priced one in the nearest business district, where you do not have to pay monthly parking fees.

- If you cannot set up an office at home, rent a single office, not a suite, or sublease an office from someone with a suite. This can be quite inexpensive and comfortable. (It may even offer certain business advantages.)
- Consider desk space in a communal office. These are offices in which you pay a modest sum for your own desk in a large room, with answering service and access to a conference room, copier, stenographic services, and a mail room. This is a good arrangement if you will not spend much time in your office. It gives you a telephone number, business address, mail address, and place for the occasional conference with clients on your premises. It also saves you the cost of furnishing an office, minimizing initial investment.
- Be conservative in furnishing your office. You can buy a decent desk new for about $150 to $200, for example. But you can do even better by seeking out one of the companies who rent office furniture and sell left-overs. They often have great bargains in nearly-new office furniture. Also, watch the classified sections of your newspapers for salvage sales—furniture slightly damaged in accidents of one sort or another—bankruptcies, and other such events.
- Be modest in ordering your business cards and stationery. Plain white thermographed (raised printing) stationery (cards, letterhead, and envelopes) in black ink on good quality stock is entirely adequate. Expensive cards and stationery will not produce one extra dollar's worth of income for you.
- Shop around. The market for most things is competitive. You can easily spend $5,000 for a personal computer and printer, for example, but you can also get a quite adequate system for well under $1,000 today.

A Few Special Tips for Cost Avoidance

We seem to have forgotten that ours is a competitive economic system. *We* refers to both buyers and sellers in America but, fortunately, not all buyers and sellers. A few sellers still deal competitively, and a few buyers still seek out the best offers. It is easy to pay too much for things if you fail to take advantage of the competitive system. Here is an example:

When I made the move to my own home from a costly downtown suite of offices with monthly parking costs for my car, I had to seek out some new suppliers. Of special importance to me was a good supplier of printing, since I was publishing a newsletter and using a great deal of printing regularly.

I turned to the Yellow Pages to get quotations and was dismayed by the exorbitant figures I was quoted. They were even higher than those in downtown Washington. I soon realized that I had been calling only printers who had large advertisements in the directory, and so I next tried printers who had a one-line listing and no display advertisement. Immediately, I began to find prices I deemed competitive. I soon chose one printer for my work, and not only did this printer offer modest prices, but he gave excellent service and entirely satisfactory quality.

I learned a lesson from that and have since used the same philosophy in seeking out other suppliers. It is not foolproof; you must still exercise good judgment in your choices. But it is a sound basis for beginning a search.

The same philosophy applies to other areas. Buying nearly-new office items from renters of office furniture is a good practice generally, but that does not guarantee a fair price. I have discovered some renters of office furniture who wanted to recover the original price plus a profit, despite the fact that the item was no longer new and had probably earned back all its original cost for the merchant. And you need not be an expert to know what a fair price is: A little comparative shopping will soon educate you as to the proper market for any item.

I shopped very carefully when the time came to buy my first personal computer. I studied all the personal-computer advertising I could find, first of all. I reviewed articles in a number of computer magazines, as well, to compare what the writers—presumably experts all—had to say on the subject. I had no illusions about what I wanted: I wanted a personal computer for word processing, nothing else. That any personal computer can do other work was irrelevant; I intended to buy a good word processor and not be attracted by other features, which would not be of any use to me and which would cost many dollars nevertheless.

I wound up with a $1,900 system, which included a printer (it cost a few hundred more than that because I upgraded a few items—got a bigger and faster model printer, for example) at a time when most systems cost about twice that. Given the rapid technological breakthroughs occurring in technology (microprocessor speeds, miniaturization, display clarity, etc.), systems purchased will be "previous generation" technology within six months. The challenge for consultants is to truly determine what technology is suitable for the applications needed. Keeping up with the pace of technological change for the sake of having "the newest toy" is a one-way ticket to unsupportable costs. Because I was careful in that and subsequent investments in computers and related equipment. I did not hesitate long to trade up when it seemed the time to do so. Perhaps if I had invested more money in earlier systems, I would have been reluctant to upgrade and so would have denied myself the advantages of the newer systems. That's another advantage of being cautious and conservative in what you buy; it's far easier to endure the pain of writing it off and replacing it with something better a bit later when you have managed to keep your original investment as small as possible.

Occasions arise when you win assignments you can't handle alone. Sometimes you need others with skills similar to your own, and sometimes you need others with complementary or supporting skills. At times, I have had to find other proposal consultants to help me handle a proposal task too big for one person; at other times, I have needed specialists in logistics or some other discipline I have no skills in; and sometimes I have had to have drafting or illustrating help to support me. (And unless you are trying to build up an organization, these are temporary arrangements, usually with other self-employed individuals.)

The results have often been disappointing and costly. More than once, I have paid off the associates or hired help and worked late into the night to do their work over because I considered it not up to my own standard. Perhaps the client would have accepted it, but I would not, for reputation is fragile and once damaged almost impossible to repair. I am unwilling to submit work I believe to represent less than my best effort.

I learned to follow certain principles:

- Do require references and check them out carefully. (An amazingly large number of people take others at face value and fail to verify references.)
- Don't hire people by the hour. Doing so compels you to pay them for each hour worked, no matter how productive or unproductive they are, no matter how satisfactory or unsatisfactory the result is. (Even when the result is satisfactory, why should you be penalized if the other person is a slow worker? And perhaps the hourly rate inspires slower work!)
- Do retain the other party as a subcontractor, not as an employee or even as an associate. Reach agreement on what is to be done, when it is to be done, what the quality standard is to be, and the price. Then write that agreement up in some simple letter form.
- Do make it clear that payment will be made when you accept the product as meeting the quality standard agreed on.

A great many people can talk a good game—speak knowledgeably and be quite convincing about how good they are at what they do, and yet turn out to be rather poor performers. I tend to subscribe to Pareto's Law, also referred to as the 80-20 Rule.

Vilfredo Pareto (1848–1923) was a French-born economist who did his significant work in Italy and is therefore mistakenly referred to as an Italian economist (and even as a Swiss economist sometimes). He discovered that in the Italian economy and in a great many other things—perhaps in most things—a small proportion of the applied cause is responsible for a large—a most disproportionately large—part of the result.

For example, 20 percent of any production team normally produces 80 percent of the output, and vice versa; unfortunately, the other 80 percent of the team produces only 20 percent of the output. Eighty percent of the money in a bank is deposited by 20 percent of the depositors. Twenty percent of the workers in a project produce 80 percent of the result. And, as value engineers have discovered, 20 percent of the parts in a machine do 80 percent of the work.

Even that probably apocryphal executive who thought that half his advertising dollars were wasted but wondered which half, was probably mistaken: Probably 80 cents of his advertising dollar was wasted, and almost all the result produced by the remaining 20 cents.

This demonstrates a law of inverse ratios, revealing a horrible inefficiency and waste: 80 percent of the cost is incurred to produce 20 percent of the result, and 20 percent of the cost produces the other 80 percent of the result; in sales organizations, for example, it is not at all unusual to find that 20 percent of the salespeople produce 80 percent of the sales, and the remaining 80 percent of the sales force produces only 20 percent of the sales. This has been found to be largely true in all sorts of applications and activities. Applied to people, probably not more than 20 percent of the performers in my field are truly good, and the other 80 percent range along a spectrum from pretty good to pretty poor.

The real hazard is semi-competence. It's easy to recognize the truly competent and truly incompetent, but it is usually difficult to be sure about the semi-competent individual, who often gets away with substandard work for a long, long time before you are sure that the work is really not good enough. I found semi-competence in accountants who had good references and could say all the right things, but whose books never balanced, whose invoices were always being sent back to correct errors, and who could never come up with the right answers to ordinary questions asked by management. I found it in technical writers who diligently put in long hours, but who, in the end, resigned when the time came to surrender a manuscript, leaving nothing but a large notebook filled with indecipherable notes and in some cases not even that. And I found it in engineers who discussed the work convincingly enough but whose designs and prototypes never met the specifications or matched the reports they wrote. I was grateful when I found someone whose work I heartily approved of because it assured me that I did have reasonable standards, when sometimes my disillusioning experiences were causing me to wonder whether I was excessively and unjustly critical.

Beware of being deceived by appearances. Many of these semi-competents are experts at creating the appearance of competence and success in what they are doing. Judge by results and by results only. It's the only way to be sure.

Even taking the relatively safe route of acting on friends' recommendations and doing business with large, successful vendors has its hazards, I agreed to develop a sales brochure for a rather large firm, who asked me to have a quantity of them printed after I had finished preparing the manuscript and final copy. A friend and subcontractor, who was handling art work and preparation of camera-ready copy, recommended a local printer who had a large shop and did fine work. My friend didn't tell me what kind of business ethics the firm practiced, however. I furnished a maximum estimate of the size of the final document, number of photographs, and so on, and got a price. I delivered copy that was more than 10 percent less than my estimate, and the printer, who should have thereupon reduced his price, attempted to charge me over 20 percent more than he had originally estimated! Only the fact that I had his estimate in writing and challenged him to sue me in court persuaded him to settle for his original estimate, which was, nevertheless, more than I should have paid, under the circumstances.

Finally, beware of moonlighters. I hesitate to condemn them as a class, but I have had many bad experiences. Many are excellent performers, but you would be wise to check their references most carefully. Unfortunately, many are unreliable because they have regular, steady jobs and are not dependent on their moonlighting. They often tend to get tired and begin fading long before the job is done. They take off time for a movie or a party at critical junctures. They balk at redoing their work when it is unacceptable. And sometimes they simply disappear and are not heard from again. I have had all these discouraging experiences with moonlighters, and I prefer to trust subcontracts to full-time self-employed individuals who depend on the work for their survival. They are almost invariably far more reliable.

The odds are, therefore, not exactly in your favor, and you will be wise to practice defensive tactics when entrusting some portion of your success to others.

6 | Founding the Consulting Practice

Well begun is half done.

—*Horace*

IF YOU HAD IT TO DO OVER

What were your mistakes or major problems when you started? How did you handle them?

What would you do differently today?

What advice would you offer beginners?

These are some of the questions asked of a number of successful independent consultants in preparation for the second edition of this book. They were followed up with the same questions asked of the original group of consultants responding prior to the third edition. Now, the same questions are being addressed again (the knowledge gleaned from the prior responses has already been included in earlier editions of this book).

The initial reaction of many experienced consultants was that the earlier editions of this book would have been more helpful to them when they were first starting out as opposed to after they were more firmly rooted and entrenched in their practices. Yet, as the dialogue continued with them about their suggestions and what they were able to apply from the book to their current practices, an unexpected phenomenon began to emerge. Many consultants admitted that they could still learn to apply lessons they had never learned or had learned previously and then neglected later in their careers. One of the more salient examples was, overlooking the importance of constantly marketing and being vigilant in marketing for tomorrow before today's project ends.

Let me note here, before proceeding further, that at least some of the advice and opinions I gathered from others were in variance with my own opinions and the counsel I offer you in these pages. That is as it should be; each of us mirrors his or her own experiences and draws conclusions therefrom. But none of us has experienced exactly what you will experience, so none of us can give you advice totally specific to your own need. Take from what follows, therefore, only whatever is relevant and helpful to you.

David Moskowitz was one helpful respondent. He is an independent computer consultant based in the suburbs of Philadelphia. He states that if at all possible, you should have enough capital to support him- or herself for a year before launching an independent practice. That is a piece of advice offered frequently, I found. Unfortunately, it isn't always possible. Many independent consultants confess that they were forced to launch their ventures on short notice and without much preparation, as was Moskowitz, and were forced to manage somehow without adequate reserves.

He stresses also the need to have a clear concept of what you want to do as a consultant, rather than embark on the venture with some vague idea of what you will offer, and he agrees heartily on the need for marketing knowledge and sales training. He also pointed out the need to develop negotiation skills. (These are really part of, or at least an extension of, sales skills.)

A great many readers agreed that my book gave them an entirely new view and appreciation of the function and purpose of accounting as critically important to management needs. Esther Schindler admitted that she has always thought of accounting as an incredibly boring subject, but found it suddenly became incredibly fascinating when it concerned her money and her business! Later, Esther admitted that she and her partner, husband Bill Schindler, had made the common errors of the typical too-eager new entrepreneurs, such as accepting contracts with nothing in writing and suffering predictable consequences of being victimized by clients who demanded (and got) too much and sometimes failed to pay their bills even then.

Most recently, Rick King, currently vice president for sales training and distributor development at Snapple Beverages Group shared the story of a thriving consulting practice he had at one point that was torpedoed by a client who said all the right things, but did not follow through. He ultimately received Rick's best efforts without ever paying for them. Rick was unable to sustain his consulting practice due to the cash flow crunch that inevitably occurred.

There were also a few rueful comments from others who had suffered from their failure to establish a suitable accounting system at the beginning.

I found consensus about the need for continuous marketing, even when you have a full schedule. Many had learned the hard lessons of failing to market for tomorrow's contracts and projects, assuming that the time to market was when they were not busy doing work for clients. They reported a variety of experiences that stressed the need for more attention to marketing. One consultant, for example, was relaxing with what appeared to be a comfortable backlog of contracts, when suddenly he was faced with three contract cancellations and subsequent large gaps in his working schedules.

The need to do careful credit checks of clients and to get retainers or deposits up front was also a common lesson learned. The failure to verify credit and the reluctance to risk losing a contract by requiring a retainer have cost many consultants heavily. One reported a loss of over $5,000 in printing costs alone when a client simply refused to pay.

Several consultants agreed with the opinion of Gerre Jones, reported in an earlier edition, that incorporating as a Sub-Chapter S Corporation is a good plan, although some pointed out that this is a mixed blessing because not all states treat such a corporation benevolently—with tax breaks. This is a matter to discuss with an expert accountant or attorney familiar with the relevant laws in your own state. Too, the tax laws undergo frequent change, and that is an influence on the form of your business organization.

There is more, a great deal more, but most of it repeats the lessons summarized here.

GENERAL CONSIDERATIONS SUCH AS LICENSING

Unless your basic profession is one that requires licensing or your local statutes compel you to have a mercantile license, you probably do not need a license, for consulting is not itself a licensed or regulated enterprise. If you are uncertain about it, you can seek information or guidance from any of a number of sources to determine whether you need licensing or permits of any sort and, if so, how to proceed:

- A local lawyer.
- The local Chamber of Commerce.
- Clerk of your county/city/town hall.
- The business editor of the local newspaper.
- Local business owners.
- The local U.S. Small Business Administration (district) office.
- State or local government small-business office.

Even when licensing of some sort is required, there may be special provisions, as in Miami, where one is required to have a mercantile license, but a war veteran is entitled to a very much reduced fee. Moreover, the licensing authority was kind enough to suggest (and allow) that I conduct my business without a license until the beginning of the new license year.

Small Business Administration (SBA)

The SBA operates about 90 district offices throughout the United States. Your local telephone directory will furnish the address of one near you. The SBA usually has several services available to small business owners, including at least two consultant services available free of charge. One of these is furnished by volunteers, usually retired business executives, who have joined SBA's Service Corps Of Retired Executives (SCORE). The other is furnished under contract to SBA by private firms located where they can serve the country's large population of small businesses. It is probably worth your time to visit the nearest SBA office to see what they may be able to offer you.

State/Local Government Programs

Many state and local governments have instituted socioeconomic programs to aid small businesses and minority-owned businesses. In many cases, general counseling is among the services offered. It is a good idea to check with these programs to see what they can offer to help you in getting started. A description of these will be found in Chapter 24 along with names and addresses.

THE MATTER OF A BUSINESS NAME

A government executive whose work required him to review many consultants' proposals was fond of remarking. "The bigger the name, the smaller the company."

He always made this observation with a sigh and a tolerant smile because he applauded all enterprise and truly wanted to award contracts to new, small firms. Still, there was an ambivalence in his reaction because he was also an admirer of complete honesty. Because of that, he always felt a grandiose business name such as International Computer Systems & Information Consultants, Ltd. was an effort to impress and deceive him into believing that he was dealing with a major organization. That led him to wonder what else in the proposal, brochure, or sales presentation was false or super-hyperbole of some sort.

There is great dignity in simplicity and understatement. Witness the names of many major corporations, even their original, full names, further simplified to acronyms or abbreviations, in many cases:

RCA (Radio Corporation of America)

IBM (International Business Machines)

Xerox Corporation

GE (General Electric)

GMC (General Motors Corporation)

USI (U.S. Industries, Inc.)

Most of these supercorporations became so well known by their initial letters that many people do not even know the full names. It is not necessary to adopt a long and elaborate name to reflect competence and success, and it may be to your disadvantage to do so.

The two most popular practices of consultants in identifying their practices is to identify themselves and what they specialize in by their personal name or by adding the word associates, as in these examples:

Gordon W. Honeycutt
Marketing Consultant

Gordon W. Honeycutt & Associates
Marketing Consultants

Usually the consultant will have another line or two, in addition to an address and telephone number, elaborating a bit of the exact nature of the services offered such as marketing plans, direct-mail services, and/or market surveys.

One immediate advantage of using your personal name in this manner, if you operate as a sole proprietorship, is that you have no legal complications. On the other hand, if you use a dba (doing business as) or trade name of some sort such as International Market Consultants, you ordinarily have to register that name. If you incorporate, that business name is registered in filing your documents of incorporation, but if you are a sole proprietorship or partnership, you usually have to comply with state and local statutes requiring that you file fictitious names or dba names. That is so that the authorities (and anyone else) can always determine the true and proper owner/s of any business operating under a business name.

This is not an especially costly procedure, normally, and you can do it all yourself, if you wish, although probably most people retain a lawyer to handle it. (A clerk in the Philadelphia City Hall was able to advise me completely on proper procedures for doing this, even to exact working of the required advertisements, when I registered a business name in that city some years ago.) It normally amounts to filing statements with state and local governments and placing an advertisement in the local daily newspaper or in a special legal periodical (*The Legal Intelligencer*) for three insertions advising readers (the public at large) about your enterprise and its actual proprietor/s.

Even if you use part of your own name (rather than your complete name) as part of the fictitious business name—for example, Honeycutt Marketing Associates—you are probably required to file that name since it does not really identify you as the proprietor. (It is best to consult a lawyer in such a case, since these are general observations based on my personal experience and are not intended to be taken as specific legal advice.)

Consultants who are embarking on naming their firms often wonder whether it is better to use their names in the firm's name or choose another more industry relevant name. When co-author David Zahn was choosing to name his own firm (Clow Zahn Associates, LLC), he at first wanted to name it "Transition Consulting" under the belief that it would be more impressive sounding. What he came to understand is that it was ambiguous as to what it was he was offering by using that name. (Was he a family psychotherapist aiding empty nesters adapt to loss of children underfoot? An aesthetician offering to help people remove wrinkles? A travel agent?) If there are opportunities to create a name that is specific to the function or type of consultation provided, then it may make good sense to use that in the company name. A firm that calls itself Younger Skin, Inc. is not likely to get confused for a travel agency just as a consulting firm that is named Better Leads and Prospects Company is clearly identifiable as a company focused on sales and marketing contacts. The use of his name in the title of the firm allowed clients and prospects to reach out for him quickly when they thought of a project he could handle and not have to make that translation (what was it that Zahn called his firm . . . is it Training Consultation, Transitions Associates, Training Transitions, etc.?). The other thing to consider is the name be reflective of the company in years to come. Had 3M remained as Minnesota Mining and Manufacturing, would we associate Post-It Notes with that firm? What about videotapes? By virtue of shortening the name to 3M, it no longer has the local or provincial narrowness that a firm associated with solely Minnesota and uniquely Manufacturing and Mining would conjure. Be aware that your firm may evolve into related or even different businesses from the one that you currently envision and that your name may stifle client's ability to connect you to that capability by virtue of the chosen name.

WHAT TYPE OF BUSINESS ORGANIZATION SHOULD YOU USE?

An amazingly large number of fledgling, one-person consulting enterprises spring to life as corporations, often on an accountant's or lawyer's advice but equally often on some mistaken notion of the new entrepreneur that incorporation is a must for success (very much as some believe in a lofty name) and/or a mandatory safeguard against liability.

There is nothing wrong with incorporating, and it may well turn out to be the best route for you, but first consider the other ways to organize your venture. There are other ways—several, in fact—and you ought to consider all before making a decision. Please note that the observations made here are not qualified legal advice nor represented to be such.

Sole Proprietorship

If you won the business and all its assets in your own name, whether you work alone or have help (or even associates), you have a sole proprietorship. That means exactly what it says: you are the sole proprietor. The assets are entirely yours and you are also solely and entirely responsible for the liabilities. This is by far the simplest way to operate, but some consultants are increasing apprehensive about the potential liabilities of being totally and personally responsible in these times of excessive litigation, and many find this a persuasive argument for incorporating.

Partnerships

A formal partnership is suggested when you have one or more partners, of course. Proprietorship, in a simple partnership, is vested in all partners, equally or according to whatever agreement exists between or among you. You share responsibility for all liabilities, as well as ownership of all assets. You should have a detailed agreement drawn up, properly notarized and witnessed. It is a good idea to have an attorney handle this for you; in fact, it is usually wise for each partner to have an attorney to represent his or her interests. Even if you operate as a sole proprietor, however, you may find advantages in having your spouse named as a partner. Consult an attorney to learn the pros and cons of doing this.

Limited Partnerships

A limited partnership is somewhat like a corporation in that although it has the legal and tax characteristics of a simple partnership, the liability of the partners can be limited to the capital invested. Consult an attorney and/or accountant to learn the pros and cons of this approach to business ownership.

Limited Liability Corporation

A relative recent innovation in business ownership is the Limited Liability Corporation (LLC). As many states have differing laws governing the establishment of an LLC and what are the implications, it is strongly suggested that you consult with an attorney or accountant to sift through the appropriateness of this approach to business ownership. Generally speaking, this form of business ownership caps the liability of the owner/partners, while at the same time, not obligating the business to paying corporate taxes as if it were an "entity" as defined next.

Corporations

Corporations are entities, in the legal sense, just as every human is an entity. The United States Supreme Court defined a corporation as "an artificial being, invisible, intangible, and existing only in contemplation of law," a definition that has been echoed frequently in other courts and in legal texts.

The corporation is treated as though it were a person in many ways, although not in all. That is why the corporation, not you personally, is ordinarily responsible and liable for the obligations of the corporation. (Ltd, standing for Limited, which some people use in preference to Inc. or Incorporated, refers to limited liability.)

There are a number of types of corporation. Some are public, accepting investors by selling stock in the corporation. Most independent consultants who incorporate, however, form close corporations. (You can sell stock privately, to the limits prescribed, in a close corporation, but you cannot offer stock to the general public. That is a far more complex proposition.)

You can incorporate also as a nonprofit corporation, but again that has many drawbacks, although it also has a few advantages. You can draw a salary and expenses, plus normal fringe benefits, and you can treat yourself well as an employee, but the corporation cannot accumulate a reserve of profits and you never have an equity position—a business you own personally, in part or in whole, and can sell.

Some individuals opt for a Sub-Chapter S Corporation, an entity that does not have to pay corporate taxes. To qualify for this, you must have stockholders and draw income from operations, not investment, again an arrangement that may or may not be suitable for you. (You have noted that one of the consultants quoted earlier, Gerre Jones, believes firmly that this is a must for the independent consultant, but conditions for an S Corporation vary from one state to another and from one tax year to another.)

Most individuals who incorporate tend to form a close corporation, one help closely with limited participation. It is possible, in fact, to hold all the offices yourself. Most who form corporations, however, bring in family members and sometimes close friends to act as other officers and directors of the corporation.

One strong caveat to offer is that if you in any way can foresee or anticipate that you and the other parties may have a disagreement over management somewhere in the future, or anticipate a changing family circumstance (through marriage, divorce, births, etc.), be *very specific* as to how ownership changes hands, how disputes are to be resolved, and what the roles and powers of each officer or board member are in the entity. An ounce of prevention early (even when you are giddy with the possibilities upon start-up) can avert a disaster sometime later on when people's motivations change, circumstances shift, or needs are altered from those that were known initially. A reputable accountant and attorney familiar with incorporation issues in the start-up phase may turn out to be worth more than you could ever imagine some years after the launching of the firm.

Pros and Cons of Incorporation

While attorneys and accountants are prepared to advise you, it behooves you to do all that you can up front to learn the benefits and detractions of incorporation for yourself before trusting the advice of the paid professionals. While you need not be as "expert" as they are, you should know enough to ask intelligent questions and challenge what you are being told when appropriate. With the advent of the Internet search engines being so readily available (www.google.com among the more popular), it is not a difficult task to prepare yourself with some preliminary understanding *before* approaching an expert to seek advice.

Cynically speaking, accountants and lawyers tend to encourage you to incorporate. Probably they are sincere in their belief that everyone in business ought to be incorporated; the nature of their work almost mandates that conviction. However, each stands to benefit directly if you incorporate—lawyers charge fees to do the paper work and accountants get much more work to do when you are incorporated—so there is always the question of whether they are being as objective as they think in recommending that step.

There are pros and cons in incorporating, as there are in most things. Aside from the possible (and dubious) benefits of adding prestige to your professional image, there is the real consideration of limiting your liability; if someone sues your corporation, and gets a judgment against it, your personal property is normally immune to that judgment. On the other hand, being incorporated may add a great deal of bookkeeping and accounting and a few extra taxes as well. Balancing this added paperwork burden is the use of a corporation as a tax shelter. Unless the tax code changes considerably— as it may very well in these times—the corporation offers some opportunities to manage your affairs so as to lower your overall taxes. Many individuals have the notion that if they incorporate their businesses, they will immediately and automatically be allowed many more deductions for business expenses and thereby enjoy lower tax rates, as well as sundry other benefits.

That is both true and untrue. First of all, you will still pay whatever your individual tax rate is on the money you draw from the corporation for personal use, whether you pay yourself a regular salary or simply draw money from time to time. The lower corporate tax rate—assuming that it is lower, which may or may not be the case for you, depending on certain circumstances—applies only to the money left in the corporation, money that the corporation banks as profit or earned income.

The deductions you take for business expenses are essentially the same, whether you are incorporated or not. Your insurance, other taxes, interest paid, rent, and other expenses are deductible under all kinds of business organization. As a corporation, however, you may be able to give yourself certain benefits that are not taxable as income and are deductible business expenses for the corporation. (Your tax expert should advise you on that.) In general, the tax benefits begin to accrue more significantly when you earn substantially from your work than they do when you are earning only a modest income.

Another reason many incorporate is in the mistaken notion that being incorporated adds to prestige and heightens the professional image. That simply is not true, especially since you can incorporate in most states today for under $100 and can even use web sites on the Internet to complete the process fairly easily. The forms are quite simple—an attorney may draw up a thick document to apply to the state, but there are usually simple forms you can fill in (a single page, in Maryland) for a simple, close corporation.

Even the matter of bylaws and other necessary trappings of corporate life does not represent a problem. There are suppliers of all these things in all metropolitan areas. My own local telephone directory lists under the heading "Corporation Supplies" three in this suburb alone, offering such supplies as corporate seals, stock certificates, printed bylaws, resolution forms, record books, and other such items. In fact, these suppliers are quite expert in the whole matte of incorporation and can usually advise you as to where to go to get the necessary forms and how to go about filling them out and filing your application for incorporation. Nor is this especially expensive. I paid only about $40 or $50 for my complete corporate kit when I incorporated.

Don't be misled. I have met individuals who believed that they could not incorporate because they worked from their homes. They thought that incorporating would require them to set up offices in commercial locations. But the state really does not care where you conduct your business, as far as a legal address in concerned. That's a matter possibly for the local zoning commission, but it has nothing to do with the state government.

Even if you wish to incorporate, you do not have to do so immediately. You can incorporate when you wish to. There is the disadvantage that you will have some additional taxes to pay and a good bit more accounting work to do when you incorporate, but you will also gain some useful options.

Where Should You Incorporate?

The State of Delaware has long been the favorite state for companies because Delaware has made incorporation simple. Consequently, it enjoys by far the largest number of corporations, even though few of those corporations maintain headquarters in or even operate in that state! Wherever they do operate, however, they are a foreign corporation and must register as such, which involves a few penalties, such as taxes. At the same time, they must keep a registered agent in the state of their incorporation.

Most states have liberalized their requirements for incorporation so that it is usually inexpensive and easy to incorporate in your own state. That eliminates the problems of being forced to register as a foreign corporation and paying someone to act as your registered agent in the state of your incorporation. (You are your own registered agent when you operate in the state of incorporation.)

Consider, then, your own needs, your own problems, your local laws, federal tax laws that exist at the moment (they do change, sometimes significantly with respect to corporations), and whatever else applies to your individual situation, and be governed accordingly.

DO YOU NEED A LAWYER?

There are many reasons to retain a lawyer. Many are good reasons; some are not. A good lawyer can ease your path in a number of ways:

1. Doing things for you that require legal expertise and/or familiarity with the system.
2. Advising you as a legal expert.
3. Advising you as an objective observer.
4. Representing you and your interests.

You can also do a great many things for yourself and save a great deal of money in the process. Ordinarily you can handle your own incorporation, registration of business name, applications for licenses, drafting simple letter agreements, and similar chores that are feasible as do-it-yourself projects. If you choose to do it yourself, there are books available in abundant supply to help you learn how to carry out these tasks. This information is abundantly available online as well by simply entering a request into a search engine and placing appropriate parameters around the request (state, specific need or form being requested, etc.). (Many of these are listed in Chapter 24.) These books and sites include sample forms you may use and guidance in how to handle corporate tasks (such as writing resolutions, holding directors meetings, and opening corporate bank accounts) and how to derive maximum benefits from incorporation. You can also get from these sources a complete set of bylaws you may use, perhaps with some minor adaptations, as your own corporate bylaws. (Or you can buy a standard set from one of the suppliers of corporation supplies, mentioned earlier.)

One word of caution: Do not ask your lawyer to make your business decisions. Some lawyers may make it clear that what they offer is simply advice and to help you reach decisions; others may urge their recommended courses of action on you, even prophesying dark and ominous events if you fail to heed their good advice. (My inclination would be to change lawyers, at this point.) Even the best lawyer is only an advisor, no matter how sound the advice offered; you must make the decision, as a result of all advice and your own good judgment. But that good judgment depends on your own complete understanding. Require that your lawyer couch the advice and the rational for it—and do insist on knowing the rational—in lay English, language that you can understand. Otherwise, you are being snowed, rather than advised, because you do not understand the basis for the advice, and so you cannot possibly make a sound decision, except by pure chance.

DO YOU NEED AN ACCOUNTANT?

Virtually everything said with regard to your need for and use of a lawyer applies with equal validity to accountants. Strictly speaking, you do not need an accountant; it is possible to manage without one (especially if you use the simple proprietorship method of doing business), using one of the several alternatives suggested earlier. There is this difference to consider, however: You would probably make good and perhaps even extensive use of a lawyer's services in setting up and organizing your practice, but after that you would need legal services only intermittently, if and as legal problems arose. Accounting, however you must do regularly, keeping records of every day's events and generating appropriate reports and tax returns. Here is a list of the functions that must be performed in all accounting systems, including your own:

1. *Journalizing.* Entering bills, receivables, and other items into the daily journals spontaneously, as they appear. (A small system may have only a single day journal for everything, whereas a large system may have a number of day journals, each devoted to a different kind of accounting event.)
2. *Posting.* Transferring the journal entries to their proper pages and columns in the ledgers. (As in the case of day journals, the size and number of ledgers used depends on the size and complexity of the business and the accounting system.)
3. *Balancing and auditing.* Validating the correctness of the entries posted through verifying various mathematical balances and checking specific items to track down the problems when accounts do not balance.
4. *Calculating overhead.* Determining the cost of doing business as a mathematical rate—percentage of direct labor and/or other direct costs.
5. *Generating various reports and statements.* Preparing such items as the profit & loss statement, the balance sheet, net worth statements, and various monthly quarterly, semi-annual, and annual reports necessary for legal and/or management purposes.
6. *Tax work.* Making out tax returns for the various government agencies (federal, state, and local) to which taxes must be remitted, along with whatever forms, reports, and statements are required.
7. *Scheduling payables.* Listing invoices to be paid, with schedules for the payment dates, calculated for maximum cash flow and other financial advantages.
8. *Invoicing receivables.* Sending out invoices for money due you.

9. *Miscellaneous.* Follow-up statements and notices urging payment of invoices, preparing special reports, making estimates, calculating and preparing payroll checks, and whatever other tasks arise.

These are the general tasks of accounting, and while all accounting systems must do these kinds of things, the actual functions and elements may vary widely from one organization to another, depending on several factors, chief of which are the size of the organization, the nature of the organization's activities, and the nature of the accounting system itself.

For the consultant just starting out, there are many high-quality software applications that are relatively intuitive to use and require only the most fundamental understanding of what constitutes a "cost" or "expense" and what is "cash" or "asset" in order to use. Among the more popular computer applications is the QuickBooks series by Intuit. With prompted guides and questions, and requiring only enough accounting dexterity to use a keyboard sufficiently well enough to enter checks/deposits and "buckets" or categories of expenses commonly incurred and/or clients frequently serviced, the consultant can perform all of the tasks listed above with ease.

The application allows totals to be tallied on a rolling basis, charts and graphs to be created to use for analysis of spending versus cash flow, or any other of the hundred different ways we each will have of managing the financial side of our businesses (estimate accuracy, accounts receivables, etc.). The application has become so easy to use that it can steer the layperson through accounting without fear or discomfort (and, let's face it, for most consultants, this chore will be given short shrift if there is any possibility of doing "other tasks" that are more rewarding or more fun). This tool allows you to do what you must to track your business' performance and to do so in a way that supports your efforts and does not detract from them.

DO YOU NEED A BUSINESS PLAN?

The business plan comes up often as a problem, especially for the newly launched independent consultant or the aspirant contemplating such a venture, usually in terms of such questions as these:

- Do I need a business plan?
- If so, what is it supposed to do for me?
- What should it look like?
- Where can I find out more about it?

The term *business plan* means different things to different people. For some, it is a euphemism for loan proposal. That is because thee are two kinds of business plans—or perhaps it is more accurate to say that there are two uses for a business plan, and thus two ways in which it might be slanted. A business plan can be designed to help the entrepreneur raise capital for a new enterprise or designed to help the entrepreneur think out what must be done and make plans to do it, that is, to think out precisely where the entrepreneur wishes to go and how he or she proposes to get there, with all the necessary anticipation of difficulties to overcome, as well as of objectives to establish and reach. Actually, that is the thrust of a business plan regardless of whether it is actually a planning guide for a start-up or a prospectus to persuade bankers or investors to provide capital.

Neophytes are likely to think of a business plan entirely in terms of preparation for a startup, whereas one's business plan should be reviewed periodically and revised as circumstances dictate. Often, in fact, the original business plan should be scrapped and a new one drawn up, accommodating the inevitable changes that take place in the course of conducting a business and making corrections of earlier estimates.

Every business venture ought to be based on a business plan, but the enormous variability in business ventures mandates an almost equally enormous variability in the plans. Many features are common to all, of course, but many others must be peculiar to the industry or business and to individual circumstances. These must be reflected in either of the two business plans.

An outline is offered at the end of this chapter for your guidance. Study each element of the outline carefully and be sure that it is appropriate and fits the practice you plan. Make whatever changes ensure that fit.

Consider business conditions of the moment and make any changes necessary to make your plan a sensible one vis-à-vis market and financial conditions. Too, be prepared to review periodically to revise, update, and/or otherwise modify the plan to meet sudden or unexpected changes in conditions.

The model represented here would be adequate for launching a relatively large venture. To adapt it to a small venture, merely reduce the scope of the coverage, eliminate irrelevant/unneeded items, and so on.

SOME GENERAL OBSERVATIONS ABOUT BUSINESS PLANS

The executive summary is important. This is a brief summary—two to three pages, in most cases. It is an overview and a reminder of your major goal and major approach.

The plan must be highly *specific*. It must specify products and/or services to be developed and marketed, and where and how these things will be done. To whom will you sell? (Identify markets.) How will you reach your markets? Avoid vague generalizations here.

Shun *hyperbole*. Facts are much more impressive and much more convincing. Use nouns and verbs, not adjectives. Avoid superlatives and sweeping generalizations. Be rigidly factual and practical.

The chapters or sections normally found in even the simplest business plans include most or all of the following:

1. The service(s)/products
2. The organization
3. The market(s)

4.   Marketing/sales strategy/plans
5.   Administrative plans and projections.

They are presented in this order here, but this is not necessarily the best order. The best order varies from one case to another, according to what is most *important* in terms of the *purpose* of the business plan.

GENERALIZED OUTLINE

Here are some major items that should be covered:

- Start-up capital requirement.
- Start-up decisions:
  Office location.
  Starting fixtures, furniture, equipment, supplies.
  Specific services to be offered.
  Products to be offered.
  Short- and long-term goals and objectives.
- Marketing plan strategies:
  Profile(s) of client(s).
  Competition.
  Advertising.
  Promotion.
- Staffing (what are the unique strengths, backgrounds, roles of the business owners—especially if more than one owner).
- Size of market (what is the size of the market being pursued).
- Financial projections over 3 to 5 years.
- Rate structure.
- Potential for diversification.
- Contingency plans.

See Chapter 24 for a more thorough sample plan.

7 | Finances, Taxes, and Related Problems

Business is about money and problems related to money as much as it is about what you sell and how you sell it.

USING WHAT YOUR ACCOUNTANT TELLS YOU

Accountants have their own jargon, just as lawyers, doctors, engineers, and insurance experts do. It can be confusing because words that you and I believe we understand have different meanings when accountants use them. You might take cost of sales to mean marketing or selling cost—what it cost you to get the order. That's not what it means in the accountant's office. There it refers to all the costs incurred in fulfillment of the sale—filling the order. A sale is not an order there; it's money received. Having your system on a cash basis doesn't mean what you think it means; it means you post a payment, that is, payable when you pay it and a receipt, that is, receivable when you get the money, whereas in some systems you post a payable when you get the bill and a receivable when you send out the invoice.

I do not understand most of the jargon. I manage to live with it by ignoring it. I am not the least bit afraid to ask dumb questions. The fear of asking such questions often leads to serious trouble. As with your lawyer, be sure that you understand what your accountant tells you. Make him explain it in everyday English, ask all the questions you like, without inhibition, and make sure that you understand and agree with the rationale before you bow to your accountant's recommendation.

In short, use your accountant as a doer of things you can't or don't want to do yourself and as an advisor whose opinions are worth serious consideration but not necessarily indicative of the course you will finally pursue. You, then, and no one else, must make the decisions.

The main purpose of accounting is to support management, to furnish information for management. Management is a topic of never-ending fascination in the business world, probably second only to marketing. Hundreds of books are published on the subject every year, and it is discussed in thousands of other books. It is taught to thousands of college students. It is offered in thousands of seminars and special training courses. And every few years there comes a new Messiah of Management with a new wrinkle that will, it is alleged, take the pain and mystery out of what seems almost a black art.

Management is not that mystical or complex, nor is the mastery of it that simple. Management is the art of getting maximum desired results from available resources. Anyone can manage the most difficult situations with unlimited resources of time, money, labor, and whatever other functions are needed, but one rarely has all the resources desired. In fact, the best managers are those who manage to get the job done despite limits on the available resources. Moreover, management may or may not have to do with directing or guiding other people. Even the smallest enterprise, where one person does everything, must be managed!

Management is thus mostly a matter of objective thinking and sound judgment, qualities that cannot be reduced to mechanical functions or built into simple tools. Most of all, even given our capacity to reason objectively and then arrive at sound judgments, management is a matter of information; no one can think objectively and make sound judgments without having the essential information. A decision, any decision, is not and cannot be any better than the information upon which it is based. Ergo, the information produced by accounting is essential to good management, and the production of sound management information is therefore the major objective of and reason for accounting.

THE INFORMATION YOU NEED

Here are some of the kinds of information—the most critically important items—that your accounting system ought to deliver to put you in full and total control of your enterprise:

- *Overhead costs.* Rend, heat, light, telephone, advertising, postage, bad debt, and equipment used in production of product/service, etc.; what and how much they are and whether they are approximately constant or are trending up or down.
- *Sales figures.* Dollar figures, frequency of sales, types of sales/clients, trends up or down, if any, Days of Sales Outstanding (DSOs) to the Cost of Sales (how long does it take to get a "receivable" or payment after delivery of service).
- *Cost of sales.* Total cost of winning and completing every project or assignment.
- *Margin/markup.* How much you are adding to your total estimated cost of each project so that you can meet all expenses and realize a profit.
- *Profit.* Surplus over all costs for each job, in total, and as an average, calculate the profitability of each client and/or project type.

Studying this kind of information regularly will enable you to discover almost immediately any increase in costs, decline in sales, slippage in profitability, and relative profitability of one type of sale or project over another. These are all key factors in the success of your enterprise. It is a fact of business life that even in a small enterprise you can be so busily engaged that you can go on for a long time—months—losing money without being aware of it. Unfortunately, if enough time elapses before you discover that costs have gotten out of hand or you are marking up your costs insufficiently and therefore losing money, it may be too late to recover. More than one business has succumbed to such unpleasant surprises; hence the urgency of current information on the health of your enterprise.

When I required a great deal of printing on a regular basis, I kept a close watch over printing costs. If they appeared to be climbing more steeply than they should, I conferred with my printer or even changed printers. Sometimes one printer had the best price on one type of work, while another had the best price on another kind of work. And in some cases, where the schedules permitted it, I had the work done out of town, via mail order, which often reduced the cost.

Accounting information also told me clearly what types of activities were most and least profitable. This is certainly indispensable information for planning future action—what types of sales and contracts to pursue and which to steer clear of. Many of us succumb to the lure of accepting work we enjoy but that does not pay us enough.

On the other hand, I was well aware of what were reportedly the typical seasons—peaks and valleys of activity and sales volume—and I monitored my own sales accordingly. Surprisingly often, I found that my own sales did not follow the reported pattern, but were even the exact opposite, peaking when the conventional wisdom said sales should be in a lull. (That is the signal to increase sales efforts at that time.) The conventional wisdom is only opinion; the ledger figures are facts.

SOME COMMON MISTAKES

Business savants of such institutions as the U.S. Small Business Administration and Dun & Bradstreet often report and remark on the high rate of small-business failures, often as high as 70 percent of new starts. This indicates a success rate of 30 or more percent. This may seem minuscule, but given (1) the fact that a large majority of these new starts are by beginners with no prior business experience, and (2) the enormous opportunity (possibilities) to make fatal mistakes, it is perhaps little short of marvelous that as many as 30 percent do survive and succeed. Here are some of those typical mistakes that often prove fatal to the newly launched small business:

- Failing to understand the meaning of profit. A great many beginners in business think that everything left after recovering costs is profit, but they fail to assign themselves a salary and fail to count that as one of the costs. (Your own salary is cost, not profit.) Be aware that depending on the type of business organization created, the owner(s) may receive a distribution as opposed to a salary. In either case, the monies taken out of the firm to handle personal living expenses must be accounted for as an expense prior to the determination of a firm's profitability.
- Assuming that successful marketing means being the low bidder, thereby underpricing everything they bid on and believing, naively, that they will somehow manage to muddle through, since their principal cost is their own labor (failing, that is, to have and use a realistic—objective—estimating system and failing to place a suitable value on their own labor as a major cost item).

- Going to the opposite extreme and overpricing everything they bid on, so that they rarely win a job (again, failing to have and use a sound estimating system).
- Failing to charge their enterprises for—count as business costs—facilities they provide from personal possessions, such as use of their personal automobile, telephone, office space at home, and other such necessary resources, under the naive premise that they are going to have and pay for these anyway!

The goals of the business must be factored into how success or profitability is measured. Clearly, if the business is designed to provide a pleasant diversion for the owner and is not required to create substantial sums for the owner, the threshold for determining success is much lower than if the business must support a large family with a large debt load.

Independent consultants who operate this way do not necessarily fail to remain in practice—many go on for years eking out a living of sorts—but their practices are, nevertheless, failures as business enterprises. Success means, or should mean, being able to realize personal income that is at least as much as you could earn on someone else's payroll and yet showing a reasonable profit—at least 5 percent to 10 percent after taxes—each year. It is commonly accepted that a business that is not growing is a failure, and no business can grow without a profit.

SOME BASIC RULES

Here, in a recapitulation, are the basic rules:

- You must know and charge on your books each and every cost incurred for and in your practice.
- Your personal draw or salary is a cost, chargeable to the practice. It is not part of profit.
- Anything you supply in kind, such as office space in your home or a personal computer you already own, must be evaluated and charged at fair value. (Prorate the cost or sell the property to your practice, as appropriate. The IRS allows charges only for space that is totally dedicated to the business.)
- All costs must be recovered by the practice, and you must price work so as to recover all costs and show some profit.
- Despite all this, you must still be competitive in price. That means you must keep close control over your costs.

BASIC COST CENTERS AND COST DEFINITIONS

It is not the purpose of this book to teach you accounting, nor am I at all qualified to do so. But finding success in any business venture is difficult enough, and a failure to have a good grasp on costs—fully understand what they are and recognize them for what they are—can easily prove fatal, as it has for many enterprises. My years of experience in delivering seminars and consulting services to the owners of small businesses—especially those in consulting enterprises—have demonstrated to me quite clearly the need for this kind of information.

Were you to take a formal course in accounting, you would soon find yourself learning a large number of technical terms to communicate a number of complicated ideas about the many accounts recorded in ledgers and the various financial reports. But here we will consider only the most basic concepts concerning costs so that you will have a general understanding of this most important subject and know enough about it to ask the right questions when you do not understand something.

You should become familiar with these terms for at least two reasons. One has already been stated—so that you understand costs and the language accountants use. The other is because these special terms designating and defining costs are in themselves management information. You need to know exactly where in your cost structure—*what* costs, that is—are out of control when costs get out of control, as they sometimes do. You need to know when you are paying too high a price for something or buying too much of it. And you need to know, also, what costs are bringing adequate returns—represent good investments—and which are a waste of your money.

Before we get into this subject, let us consider a basic truism that often becomes lost in the jargon and complexity of accounting systems and accounting language: There are only two kinds of dollars, those you take in and those you pay out. Don't allow any jargon to cloud your view on this. Every dollar discussed or posted in any accounting system is in one of those two classes—income or outgo—no matter what the accountant calls it. (Dollars invested in plant, inventory, or other centers are not an exception to this; they are neither income nor outgo, but are simply dollars converted to some other form.)

Later in this book, we will talk extensively about profit centers, also a most important subject. But here we want to discuss first the concept of cost centers. That's a simple idea. It means, simply, that there are a number of main categories of cost, each a center of cost. For example, there are *fixed plant costs,* the cost of your practice of your physical facility, with its several subcategories—heat, light maintenance, and so forth. *Payroll* or *labor costs* is another cost center, as are *marketing* and *printing,* if you have appreciable quantities of these costs.

Does it appear that *cost center* is a somewhat arbitrary term, which you may assign as you wish? It certainly is. Each enterprise has its own cost centers, and they vary from one to another. Advertising is a cost center only if you spend a significant portion of your operating budget on advertising and you want to establish it as a cost center. (Then again you may want it to be a subcategory of marketing costs.) You may or may not want to make it a major consideration in your accounting system by setting up a special account or even a separate ledger for it. That is not as important as recognizing that it represents some significant portion of your total costs and distinguishing it, at least in your mind, as one that merits keeping under control.

There are other ways to define or identify costs, again as arbitrary identifiers, often with functional names. Certain costs, for example, may be identified as *variable costs* for obvious reasons. Telephone toll charges, travel expense, and printing costs may fall into this class, if they do vary a good bit. On the other hand, rent and yellow-page advertising are obviously *fixed costs,* at least for some extended period, usually a year at a time.

Other common categories are *overhead costs, material costs,* and *G&A,* a type of cost similar to that of overhead. There is also the indirect cost known as G&A—general and administrative costs. That is a special category of relatively recent origin—since World War II and vast increases in government procurement—and it requires explanation.

The G&A expense pool includes certain special classes of expenses, typically those costs incurred to support the central corporate core of large organizations. A multi-division corporation would assign all costs of operating the central headquarters or corporate offices to the G&A pool, for example. However, not everyone keeps a G&A account, although it is an especially good idea to have one when doing business with government agencies. In fact, in many cases it is essential to doing business with governments.

This can get confusing if you do not bear in mind that these are principally functional names, assigned to remind you of the nature of the costs and help you understand where the money is going. For example, advertising may be a fixed cost or a variable cost, and it may also be an overhead cost, depending on where and how you choose to assign it. But it is nevertheless a cost. Regardless of these terms and concepts, these are all *costs,* money going *out,* and no amount of jargon or idiom changes that.

One major distinction in type of costs that is essential, however, is that of direct and indirect costs.

Direct and Indirect Costs

It costs money to operate any kind of business venture, large or small; however, the ratio of direct to indirect costs varies widely for different types of enterprises, as inherent in the nature of the enterprise. What is direct cost in one kind of venture may be indirect cost in another enterprise. This may be the case to some extent even in different ventures in the same industry, such as two independent consulting practices. The difference may be inherent in the nature of the enterprise; it may be the result of an individual accounting system; or it may simply reflect the owner's personal preferences. This will become clearer as we proceed.

For many enterprises, it is critically important to understand fully the nature of these two broad categories of cost. In some circumstances, such as most marketing to governments and their agencies, success in winning the contract depends on this understanding, as reflected in your proposals.

These discussions will focus on the small, independent consulting practice, naturally, but will necessarily refer occasionally to other kinds of ventures in order to make certain concepts clear. First, here are some basic definitions to distinguish direct from indirect costs:

- Any cost incurred specifically and exclusively for and assignable totally to a given project, task, assignment, or client is a *direct* cost.

- Any cost incurred in general and not assignable to or identifiable as having been incurred specifically and exclusively for some project, task, assignment, or client is an *indirect* cost.

Consulting Is Labor Intensive

The term *labor intensive* is often used to describe enterprises or activities that consist primarily of services and do not normally require a significant investment in or operating cost of equipment and/or inventory. That is, it applies to most industries and ventures wherein the client is billed primarily for the services rendered, with other items of cost only incidental in magnitude.

Consulting fits that description, despite occasional exceptions. As an independent consultant, you usually bill your client mainly for your services, based on the time you have devoted to the client. Consulting is unusual when compared with other industries in that "the inventory goes home each night and returns the next morning."

Direct Costs

In most cases, the chief item of direct cost on your bill is that for *direct labor,* which is probably your own labor, but might be that of associates or employees. You often have some other direct costs, even if they are not significant portions of the entire bill. In my own case, I often have travel costs and per diem living costs—lodging and meals—to bill clients for, but you might have some other costs that you have incurred for your client. Here is a list of costs typically incurred in consulting and often representing enough dollars to justify listing on your invoice for reimbursement:

Travel (air, taxis, car rentals).	ISP services.
Per diem (food and lodging).	Online database charges.
Telephone toll charges.	Messenger services.
Printing/copying (reports, etc.).	Secretarial/stenographic support.
Express-delivery charges.	

There are occasional exceptions, of course. Some consultants must normally add significant charges to their bills for computer time, printing, travel, and other costs, and any consultant might occasionally encounter such a situation. Normal practices for accounting and billing cope with this without difficulty, as you will soon see.

Another exception is the result of individual systems or preferences. For example, if your own system gives you no way of distinguishing those printing costs or those telephone toll charges incurred for a given client from other charges incurred for other clients or other purposes, you obviously cannot bill your client directly for such charges. Still, you must recover those costs if you are merely to break even and stay in business, let alone turn a profit. That leaves you no alternative; you are compelled to recover these costs in your overhead rate, as indirect costs.

It is not to your advantage, in the end, to lump extraneous costs into your overhead. That offers only the slight advantage of simplifying your record keeping to a small extent. On the other hand, treating these costs as direct costs wherever possible offers certain distinct advantages, not the least of which is that it minimizes your overhead rate and is thus beneficial to your marketing and sales efforts. It places the costs where they belong. For example, if you make a number of long-distance calls in connection with a specific project, those calls ought to be charged to that project—to that client. And to do so you must keep records of the costs of those calls.

The same thing applies to printing, messenger service, travel, and other expenses. They are, properly, *other direct costs* (other than direct labor, that is), and are normally recorded as such in cost estimates. If you do not take the trouble to keep track of such other direct costs and charge them to the proper contract and client, you are inflating your overhead unnecessarily and inflicting those costs on other clients, not to mention adding to your own burdens in marketing your services at the same time.

There is one exception to this: Costs incurred for what are essentially overhead activities—marketing—should be recorded and logged so that you can determine the cost of the activity, but the cost is entirely an indirect cost.

Indirect Costs

Most ventures have many indirect costs, and these fall into several broad categories, according to the choices made in setting up the system. Before discussing the several categories, here is a more complete list of typical indirect costs:

- Rent (which may or may not include heat, light, and other utility expenses).
- Parking.
- Insurance (usually several kinds, some required by law, others by prudence).
- Taxes, various (depending on location and local laws).
- Licenses (as appropriate, if and as required by local laws).
- Depreciation (recovering the cost of major equipment, furniture, and other capital items).
- Stationery (business cards, letterhead, and envelopes, at the least).
- Computer/printer related supplies (ink or toner, paper, diskettes or CD-ROMs, etc.).
- Advertising (any/all).
- Telephone (at least that portion covering the general service, not assignable to specific projects).
- Travel (general, including auto expense, unless assignable to specific projects).
- Printing and copying (general, that portion not assignable).
- Contributions to charitable causes, political campaigns, and so on (you can be sure that you will be solicited).
- Subscriptions (you will subscribe to several journals, at least).
- Memberships (you'll want to belong to an association or two).
- Entertainment (business lunches and the like).

Some of these costs or portions of them may appear as other direct costs in some projects. It is possible that a project will call for you to travel, have printing done, or advertise as part of a contracted project. (I have done so on occasion.) *Those* (printing, travel, or advertising) are then direct costs.

Kinds of Indirect Costs

Many people equate indirect cost with overhead, using the two terms interchangeably. In fact, in some systems, especially very small enterprises where the accounting system is simplicity itself, the two terms may be used interchangeably. Generically, however, *indirect costs* is the broader term, and *overhead* is one of several possible categories of indirect cost. (Moreover, in some types of enterprise it is possible to have more than one type of overhead.)

In some accounting systems, the cost of fringe benefits—paid time off (holidays and leave), free group insurance, stock options, bonuses, and other such items—are accounted for and posted separately from the rest of the normal overhead, so *fringe benefits* becomes another category of indirect costs.

Overhead Is a *Rate*

Overhead and G&A are dollars, of course, as all costs are; however, for estimating purposes, it is generally necessary to establish an overhead *rate,* the ratio of the overhead dollars to some other factor. In labor-intensive operations such as consulting, the something else is generally the direct-labor figure. If, for example, you find at the end of a year that you have incurred direct-labor costs of $100,000 and your various overhead charges for the year total $65,000, the rate is 65,000/100,000 = 0.65 or 65 percent.

To put this into another perspective for clarity, for every dollar paid out for direct labor you had to pay out 65 cents for overhead expenses, so that your total labor cost—direct plus indirect—was actually $165,000 for the year. To that must be added whatever other direct and indirect costs you may have incurred—perhaps you experienced another $14,000 worth of such costs—so that your total cost for the year was $179,000. You can see that if you had not separated out those other direct costs your overhead rate would have been somewhat higher—1,000,000/79,000 = 79 percent.

The first year presents something of a problem because you have no last-year's figures so you have no basis for an historical overhead rate. You must therefore make the best estimate you can and use that. You should be able to accommodate an overhead rate of 65 to 85 percent in a typical independent consultancy if you keep track of all charges that should be recorded as direct costs and thus do not burden your overhead rate unfairly. That would be a reasonable expectation for an established consultancy, one in which you were kept busy with billable time a reasonable proportion of your time—say two-thirds—in billable projects. Unfortunately, that is not often the case in newly established practices. Time and money spent in marketing is likely to be your chief overhead activity the first year, and may well occupy more than one-half your time.

That does not mean that you should shoot for a 100- or 150-percent overhead rate the first year. To do so is likely to make your marketing even more difficult, unless you compensate for the high rate with a modest direct rate for your time. Either way, you will have to be competitive, and you may have to subsidize your first-year operations extensively.

In today's consulting market, there are probably few fully capable consultants accepting a daily rate of less than $750, although that may vary somewhat with local conditions and individual policies. For example, $750 works out to be $93.75 per hour on the basis of an 8-hour working day, but one $750/day consultant does not charge for overtime—10- or 12-hour days—while another does. Or one may charge a $85 hourly rate, but charge premiums for overtime, weekends, and holidays.

Let's take a hypothetical case in which you decide that you ought to pay yourself $50 an hour (a $104,000 salary), but you estimate that your first-year's overhead rate will be about 125 percent. That means that you must charge the client $50 + $62.50 = $112.50 (cost) + $100 (pretax profit) = $1,000 a day. That is generally a competitive rate in today's market. (In fact, it is a modest rate in many localities today.) If you are doing billable work about one-third of the time, you are billing at the rate of about $85,800 a year, not recovering your own salary, much less all the costs, which your estimate will have established as $234,000 ($104,000 + 1.25 × $104,000.)

Even if you raise your rate a little to equal $1,200 a day, you will have increased total income by only about $5,200. However, if you have succeeded in keeping overhead down to, say, 65 percent, while charging $1,000/day and paying yourself a more modest $40 an hour, the figures are quite different:

Total estimated costs for year: Salary	$ 83,200
Overhead	$ 20,280
Total	$103,480
Total billing (income):	$ 85,800 (approximately)
Gross profit (loss)	($ 17,680)

While still a loss figure, the latter is considerably more tolerable and a great deal closer to the break-even point. Only a few percentage points of billable days—an increase of about seven percent—would sop up the loss and put your practice into a profitable position. On the other hand, increasing the number of billable days is not the only answer. While this illustrates the need to be especially conservative in generating and controlling costs, as well as in minimizing what you draw personally that first year, it illustrates two other cogent points:

1. You need to market aggressively and continuously. There is probably never a time when it is safe to relax in the quest for new clients.
2. You need to maximize the number and type of profit-potential activities in your practice, for there are many ways of practicing your consultancy—of providing your consulting services to clients.

Both of these are matters of prime concern in this book. Somewhat later we will approach and explore the matter of other profit potentials. But now let us turn our attention to insurance—another basic cost of business.

INSURANCE

To most of us, the subject of insurance is mysterious, straddling the special jargon of the legal and accounting professions, with heavy overtones of probability statistics. It is complex enough to intimidate most of us, and cause us to surrender decision making to the experts—the sellers of insurance—often to our great cost.

Buy Only What You Need

You do need to be insured, of course, though not over-insured, as so many of us are. Many of us are victims of persuasive presentations by insurance professionals trading on our fears. (Insurance is most commonly sold via fear motivation.) So we play it safe, or so we think, paying heavily—buying $100,000 coverage of $50,000 worth of assets, for example.

Paying extra for insurance when renting an automobile is usually a waste of money. Most of us are covered by the insurance on our own automobiles. Insuring rental property, such as rented offices or equipment, may be duplication of insurance already held by the property owner. Check on all such possibilities before buying insurance. Ask plenty of questions before you sign up. One of the basic problems is that the harried business executive either thinks that insurance policies are too complicated to be understood by ordinary humans or he or she is too busy to spend the time. The result is placing the decision in the hands of the seller of insurance. "Just sign me up for what I need," are words uttered too often, an invitation for some to put their hands in your pocket and help themselves. If the seller cannot answer all your questions so that you understand what you are buying, become alarmed immediately and refuse to buy until you do understand what you are getting. There are some general truths to be considered:

- You buy insurance for protection of your business against disasters, such as fire, flood, and burglary.
- You need some kind of medical or health insurance.
- You may need some kind of liability insurance guarding against the risk of someone being injured on your property or as a result of what you do.

These facts you can ascertain for yourself, but other insurance matters are more specialized and require guidance from insurance experts. No matter how many questions you ask, there will always be questions you should have asked but did not because you didn't know them. You need professional guidance. Where will you get it? From an insurance direct writer? The direct writer works for his company, the underwriter, not for you. It is in his or her interest to sell you as much insurance as you are willing to pay for, and he or she is locked into that single underwriter, although there is a possible advantage in having all or most of your insurance with one underwriter and possibly getting a slightly lower rate. A broker or agent? He or she usually represents more than one underwriter, and can offer greater flexibility. A good broker is an honest broker and will give you honest advice, but you must be the final judge. Insurance people, like lawyers, appear to have a prejudice against the use of everyday English when discussing their professional speciality; they use all sorts of legalistic terms that often do not mean what you think they mean or simply leave you completely baffled. Ask questions.

Getting medical and health insurance is a major concern and problem for many self-employed individuals. Individual rates are, of course, much higher than are group rates. The best solution for many independent consultants is to get group insurance via some association. In fact, when considering what association or associations to join, it is a good idea to make an assessment of group insurance plans one of the major criteria in your choice. The association may be a professional one of some sort, but not necessarily. The NASE (National Association of Self Employed) or any of many other associations offer group insurance plans. A number of associations are listed in Chapter 24.

Some consultants may wish to consider a type of insurance known as errors and omissions (E&O). This insurance protects "advice givers" in the case of oversights on the part of the consultant or a client claiming that a poor outcome was a result of actions either taken or not taken by the consultant. Seek the counsel of a trusted insurance agent and/or attorney to learn more about this kind of insurance protection.

TAXES: AVOIDANCE IS LEGAL

Tax evasion is illegal, and you can go to jail for it. Tax avoidance is perfectly legal and honorable, and you are foolish if you fail to take advantage of it. It is perfectly proper to arrange your affairs, personal and business, in such a way as to incur the minimum possible tax obligations.

As a business owner, your tax situation is different from that of a typical wage earner, although you may be one of many consultants who derives part of your earnings from wages. That is, if you work part of the time via a labor broker or job shop as a W2 temporary, part of your income will be in the form of wages, from which taxes will have been deducted. For that part of your income that is 1099 income—named for the form the client must fill out and send to you and to the IRS identifying the payment—you will have to calculate what you owe and pay it directly to the IRS.

Unless you are yourself an accountant, you probably will retain an accountant or other professional tax preparer, although it is not excessively difficult or complex to file a tax return for a simple, one-person business. If you are incorporated, however, that adds complications, since you must file both corporate and personal tax returns. You will probably find it useful then to turn to an accountant to handle your tax calculation and reporting. Software programs such as QuickBooks by Intuit and TaxCut by H&R Block have made the filing of taxes easier for the small businessperson and provide prompts to trigger possible areas of concern in the filing and/or suggest possible deductions allowable, but not taken. While these programs are useful, you still may wish to consult with a tax preparer or accountant before solely relying on them. Nevertheless, you need to know the basics of what you can and cannot do under current tax laws. Since I am neither a lawyer nor an accountant, I cannot represent these suggestions as technically irreproachable. They are based on my own experience and what lawyers, accountants, and IRS officials have told me in the past. Still, I have found that even advice given me by IRS staff is not always dependable; I have acted on such advice and found it reversed by the IRS when they reviewed my tax returns. So qualified, the following points are ones I have found to be generally true, but it may pay you to check with the IRS or other authority—your accountant—when considering a specific application. Too, the tax codes change, as new legislation in enacted, so what is true now may not be true when you read this. You must thus ascertain what is the law at the time.

Taking Deductions

Probably the most common question asked about taxes concerns deductions for office expenses at home. Probably that is also the most misunderstood aspect of tax obligations and deductions. The position of the IRS is, at least in principle, clear enough: Anything deducted as a business expense must be dedicated to—used solely for—that business. That means that you can make a deduction for a spare room or den you have converted to office space and used exclusively for your business, but you cannot take a deduction for the use of your kitchen table to address envelopes or do your books. You cannot charge off to your business more than the business takes in, however. If you are running a business, whether sideline or full-time, and it is not yet profitable, the nominal charge for space and other deductions may be greater than the total income of the business, but you are limited to your total business income for deductions. That means, too, that if you have other income, losses from the business cannot be used to reduce your tax obligations arising out of the other income you receive.

To calculate the deduction for business space, prorate the cost of the space. If you have 1,600 square feet in your home and it costs you $800 a month in rent, you may use a factor of 50 cents per square foot to calculate the monthly cost of the space you have dedicated to business use. Use the same principle to allocate deductibles for your personal telephone, automobile, and other costs, if your business shares any of these. You will have to either keep a log or make a reasonable estimate to calculate the allocations. Don't forget, when you do this, that your telephone costs mount up for other business uses than voice communication, if you have a fax of your own and use a computer for communications (via a modem, that is).

If you buy equipment for your business, it is totally deductible, and may be depreciated over five years or charged off the year it is bought, if the cost is not more than $10,000; you may charge off the first $10,000 of the cost the year it is bought, if the total exceeds $10,000. As this number changes from year to year, confirm amounts with an accountant.

Travel, lodging, and meal costs for business purposes are 50 percent deductible if they are not reimbursed by your client. You can handle this by deducting the costs as expense and then crediting reimbursement as income. That amounts to the same thing.

Some expenses incurred in starting a business may be written off. These do not include expenses incurred in the general search for and investigation of business opportunities, other than market research for an established business. Expenses incurred in actually acquiring, taking over, and/or starting a business are deductible, however, if it is to be an active business, as defined by the IRS, and if the expenses are amortized over 60 months or longer. Typical deductible expenses are legal fees, costs of incorporation, market research, consulting fees, organization of distribution, research into supply sources, and travel expenses, among others. The amortization period begins when you begin efforts to acquire or start up the new venture. If, having incurred expenses to acquire and take over a business, the deal falls through, you may deduct the expenses incurred as a capital loss.

You Must Keep Records

It is too late to create records after deductions are disallowed. The IRS does not welcome belated explanations of expenditures without documentation. A credit card receipt for lunch or rooms is not enough by itself, but an abundance of relevant records lubricated the process effectively. Record names and make notations about purpose, organizations, and other items that indicate the business purpose of the expense. Keep a diary or log of dinner, hotel room, airline ticket, car rental, or other such expenses. Have canceled checks, receipted invoices, bank statements, and other records readily available.

Timing Events

Arranging your affairs to minimize your tax obligations includes the freedom to decide when to make purchases of capital items. Often it is in your interest, with respect to tax obligations, to time a purchase to take place in the current tax year or to postpone it until the next tax year.

The same philosophy applies to income. It can sometimes be in your interest to collect receivables after the start of a new tax year, and you may therefore be a bit tardy in sending out your invoices near the end of a year. (In some account systems, the money due you is received—becomes a cash asset—as soon as it is billed.)

Job Shops and Taxes

This topic is covered in more detail in Chapter 10, but some pertinent tax issues are worth mentioning here.

Job shopping is that simple proposition of becoming a professional temporary on a job assignment that may last a few weeks, or many months, and even years. You become an employee of the job shop, paid an hourly rate, and assigned to work on a client's site for whatever period is necessary. Your fringe benefits are scanty, but your hourly rate is considerably higher than what you would get as a permanent employee of the client organization.

You can negotiate terms with the job shop, although on a somewhat limited scale. You are an employee, getting a W2 form, and the job shop must pay the employer's share of FICA and other taxes, plus some minimal fringe benefits. The job shop must therefore be able to earn about one-third of your direct rate as overhead and profit.

There is a variant of this arrangement that is practiced in many places: you become a subcontractor, rather than an intermediate employee. You and others undertake to subcontract your services to a broker who has agreed with a client to provide as many on-site computer specialists as the client requires at rates agreed upon. In this arrangement, you work on the site of the prime contractor's client, under a contract you have signed with the prime contractor or broker, and you are given a 1099 form, rather than a W2 at the end of the year. You must take care of your own FICA—self-employment tax—income tax, and other obligations of an independent contractor.

The distinctions are not sharp at all. To many, the job shop is always the firm that hires specialists as temporaries and assigns them to client premises; however, some organizations referred to as job shops enter into contracts, as brokers do. The net effect is the same: The prime contractor undertakes to provide qualified bodies to work for the client on the client's premises for as long as the client requires them.

Unfortunately, the IRS is not at all fond of this arrangement. They believe that consultants who work this way are really employees disguised as independent contractors to reduce tax burdens. The IRS therefore presses hard on brokers to make these 1099 subcontractors their W2 employees, and this had produced a sharp reduction in 1099 subcontracting and an increase in W2 temporary employment. Brokers are increasingly reluctant to use a subcontracting arrangement and prefer hiring the consultants as W2 temporary employees.

Factors that tend to support and prove the IRS argument that a consultant is a disguised employee, rather than a 1099 subcontractor include:

- Working for only one or two clients or prime contractors during the year.
- Working entirely on a client's site, rather than on one's own site.
- Being directed by the client and taking orders directly from the client.
- Having no specific responsibility for results, but only for carrying out assigned tasks.
- Working for a contractor who is responsible only for producing the bodies and has no project responsibility.

Accordingly, some consultants believe that it helps support their claims of being independent contractors to incorporate themselves and become W2 employees of their own corporations.

If you subcontract with a prime contractor who does have prime responsibility—referred to by some as a technical services firm—for project results and, if your subcontract permits you to work at least part of the time in your own facility, you have a much stronger case and can probably resist the IRS effort to classify you as an employee of the client or of the prime contractor.

8 | Marketing and Sales: Finding Leads and Closing Them

*There are several ways to judge the health of an enterprise, and a
close study of the sales log is a good place to start the evaluation.*

SUCCESS IN MARKETING IS ALWAYS A TONIC

Among the causes of small-business failure, according to experts such as the executives of the U.S. Small Business Administration, is what they characterize as undercapitalization. That's a somewhat euphemistic term that means, in simple English, not enough money. But not enough money for what? Not enough to make a proper original investment? Not enough to advertise adequately? Not enough to market properly? Not enough to survive many months of negative cash flow? (That latter term is itself another euphemism, meaning more money going out than coming in, or operating at a loss.) These expert observers, unfortunately, rarely focus their diagnoses more closely than these generalizations, which are broad enough to be safe from contradiction.

Other causes cited frequently for the many failures of small businesses are inadequacies of or inexperience in matters such as management, accounting, inventory control, purchasing, and other equally inexact catchalls.

The one cause of failure that seems to be cited most rarely is the failure of marketing. Yet that is almost surely the most common cause of business failures, small and large. It is why even well-established businesses who do not have the dread disease of undercapitalization ultimately vanish from view into bankruptcy, dissolution, or acquisition of their assets by more successful companies.

We can find many causes for these failures: That the companies didn't keep up with the times is one popular explanation. And of course the organizations can be accused of poor management, failing to meet competition, and similar obvious shortcomings. Still, these are more in the nature of rationalizations than of explanations; they evade the ultimate translation of what failing to keep up with the times, poor management, and those other alleged derelictions really mean. Almost all business failures ultimately translate into failures in the marketing functions of the organization. Their *sales* begin to slip, and continue to slip until, yes, the organization begins to experience negative cash flow—losing money. Ultimately they are out of capital and over their heads in debt. Yes, they fail to keep up with competition and the times—inevitable changes in the marketplace, changes in popular merchandise, changes in methods of marketing, and many other changes. Perhaps they become complacent and fail to detect or choose to ignore the changes and the slippage taking place. Perhaps they smugly assure themselves that they have become household words, have built such secure niches that they cannot perish. But even mighty Chrysler would have perished as a result of declining sales, without federal government rescue operations and a chief executive officer who did something about their lagging sales, and almost single-handedly persuaded the federal government that the economy of the United States could not afford the failure of Chrysler. Once Chrysler chief Lee Iacocca had persuaded the government to furnish relief for the immediate problem of financial distress, he turned immediately to the marketing problem and personally led a massive and successful sales campaign.

Success resolves ultimately into marketing—sales success. It resolves into being hungry and fighting vigorously for sales. Those failures just referred to were the failures of organizations who no longer felt hungry enough to fight for sales, who thought that they could take their customers—*former customers,* as it turned out—for granted.

After the business press and analysts had done all of the post mortems on the rise and demise of the dot-com businesses, this point was reinforced to an extent by the realization that "clicks and counting eyeballs" on a site did not always cleanly translate to sales and revenue production. Many businesspeople and investors temporarily lost sight of that important concept in the frenzied excitement of the "new economy," only to have it come crashing down on them when the realities of producing sales and managing costs caught up with them.

All the most brilliant management, superb accounting systems, totally efficient inventory control, tough-minded and shrewd purchasing, and other good management will not save the organization that does not make enough sales. Nor will the normal deficiencies in all these important functions of management and administration bring about the collapse of an organization with great marketing success. A great many shortcomings of management can be found in every company and probably in every division of every company, but the company that is highly successful in the marketplace can and does survive these problems. It is actually difficult to fail when your marketing is producing enough sales. Conversely, it is impossible to succeed when your marketing success is marginal.

It is therefore no exaggeration to say that marketing has heightened importance in the established organization, but far more so of the new venture. Neither survival nor overall success is possible without successful marketing. Every other problem can be solved or overcome when sales are producing the energy and income that are the muscles and blood of the organization.

WHAT IS MARKETING?

There is a great deal of confusion about marketing, beginning with understanding—or, more exactly, *trying* to understand—just what marketing is.

Many people, including those who ought to know better, believe that *marketing* and *sales* are synonymous terms and functions. That is not so, and the difference is more than semantic.

For one thing, marketing is not confined to businesses or other organizations dedicated to earning profits; every organization, from the smallest to the largest, markets, *must* market to survive. Churches and temples seek additions to their congregations and donations. Military organizations seek recruits. Associations seek members. Politicians seek voters and campaign contributors. Political parties seek volunteer workers. The Red Cross seeks blood donors. Even the U.S. Postal Service and the Federal Supply Service have marketing organizations, and all government agencies lobby—market to—their legislatures, seeking supporters for larger budgets every year.

It's all marketing. Marketing is the pursuit of whatever or whomever provides the sustenance for the organization—customers, clients, contracts, members, donors, contributors, volunteers, enlistees, or other results that represent successful accomplishment of the organization's mission.

That begins to sound very much like sales, and in many ways it is difficult to distinguish the two from each other, especially when we study marketing in terms of independent consulting. It is far to consider that the sales function is part of marketing, the final act of marketing, whereas the earlier actions include preparatory and necessary activities and functions. Here are the major steps illustrating this progression:

- Decide (define/identify) exactly what you want to market—what is to be your service (and/or product, if there is one).
- Decide (define/identify) your market—*who* you are going to sell to—those who are the right prospects for your service.
- Determine how you will reach those prospects with your presentation.
- Define your *specific offer.*
- Distinguish yourself from competition.
- Design your sales campaign.
- Carry out your sales campaign.

Decide What You Want to Market

There is a built-in dilemma in deciding exactly what your service is to be. Making the service too narrow limits your market—the number of prospects. But making your service too broad dilutes and weakens your image as a consultant, who is by definition a specialist and not a generalist. This is the classic trade-off problem in consulting, one we have discussed earlier, and the answer has already been offered: Start with whatever appears to you to be the right answer—a compromise between the two extremes—and use your experience, as you go, to shape modifications in your services (and/or product) until you are satisfied you have found what you need and want.

Decide What Your Market Is

As an independent consultant, you can't market effectively to the entire world. (Even supercorporations have difficulty trying this.) Having decided, at least on a provisional basis, what services you will provide, you must next identify the right prospects for those services—those most likely to need or want those services, hence most likely to become your clients. *Note:* This is a critically important step that is all too often neglected.

Determine How You Will Reach Those Prospects

You must be able to reach your prospects with a presentation of what you have to offer if the prospect list is to be of any value to you. In my own case, I tried to rent mailing lists of the kinds of prospects I wanted to reach—those who were most likely to need help in writing proposals—and found that I couldn't do so. Despite the enormous variety of mailing lists handled by the list brokers, and despite the many ways in which they could have their computers manipulate, sort, merge, organize, and reorganize all those lists that made up the databases, they could not produce a specialized list of government contractors of the types that I wanted. It was not their fault; none of the lists were coded in such a manner because few of their customers have need for such lists.

I had to build my own mailing lists, which meant that I had to find or invent the means for doing so. Being able to reach the prospects you have targeted is a critical test of your prospect definition. To succeed, you must reach those prospects with your sales appeal.

Distinguish from Competition

As much as we may want to believe that by virtue of our deciding to pursue business, it will automatically be available to us, the truth is far from that. It is not enough to merely decide what to market, where to market it, and how best to communicate the message to your intended market. Clients and customers are inundated with marketing messages constantly. With the advent of e-mail, the number of marketing messages all of us have been exposed to has increased exponentially (from product promises to remove wrinkles to solicitations to enter contests where we may win trips and vacations, through to some messages that assure us of some increase in business productivity, etc.). The challenge for the independent consultant is to identify a niche or competitive advantage over other suppliers/vendors offering same or similar services. That unique advantage (proprietary approaches, previous experiences, service levels, etc.) can separate you and your offer (more on that later) from your competitors.

Define Your Specific Offer

In defining your specific offer, you draw much closer to the sales function, to devising a sales *strategy*. Here, too, we get to some rather fine points of definition about what the word *offer* really means. Probably to most people, even to a great many market specialists, the offer is simply what they wish to sell. In my case, were I to use that concept, my offer would be services in writing or helping to write proposals, plus whatever other services I provide in that connection. But that is not what I mean by the term *offer*, as used here and in the list of marketing functions. (It took a great deal of patient experimentation—trying and testing, really—to develop this truth about what the word *offer* ought to mean.) For while I do help my clients develop proposals and train their staffs in proposal writing, my *offer* is that of help in *winning* contracts. *That* is what my clients really want, and it is the hope that I can help them achieve that which inspires them to retain me and pay me the fees I charge.

The offer is therefore what you promise to *do* for the client as a *benefit* resulting from your services, and *it must be based on whatever you believe is the client's most ardent wish of end-result*. It is the reason for retaining you and paying you. It is a recognition of the fact that the client wants the result, not the means to it. Not all of those who attend aerobic exercise classes enjoy the exercises (some even hate them), but they submit to them in the hope of losing weight. Therefore, don't offer them aerobic exercises; offer them weight loss. To define your offer properly is to understand the client's mind—to know what benefit he or she hopes to achieve in retaining you.

The offer should assume the perspective of the client/customer and *not* the consultant. Rather than thinking in terms of, "Graphics Package Training" as the offer (which is somewhat limiting and very much a commodity that will not have high value to a client), the offer is, "more efficient communication, organization, and presentation management" (which has more inherent value than the prior topic).

Design Your Sales Campaign

Once you know what you wish to sell; to whom you wish to sell it; how you will reach those prospects to present your offer; and what your offer is to be, you are finally ready to design your sales campaign.

You reach prospective clients in any or all of several possible ways—networking, organized or spontaneous; making direct calls; mailing literature; becoming active in associations; lecturing; writing; getting your name on bidders lists; and registering with agents or brokers who can help you win assignments or subcontract to you.

In this phase of marketing, you prepare the sales materials you need, and plan the methods and schedules. The more carefully you design this campaign, the more successful it is likely to be. But design includes all those earlier marketing steps enumerated, so that the effectiveness of your sales campaign depends in great measure on how well you have done the marketing work earlier. Thus the difficulty in separating the two terms. Both refer to winning business—clients, in this case—but while sales is the business of wooing and winning clients, marketing is all the things you need to do preparatory to making sales, including deciding on strategies, determining what clients to woo and win, and how to do so.

Networking

Some readers of the first and second editions of this book complained that there was little or no coverage of networking as a marketing measure, while there appeared to be agreement that it was useful to be active in associations, write articles, publish newsletters, and otherwise work at raising your image and becoming as visible as possible. Perhaps no one recognized that these *are* networking activities, informal ones, rather than formal ones. They are the means for inspiring the word-of-mouth advertising and referrals that so many consultants point out as their chief sources of business. Strangely enough, I have found that many people who have no real experience with you and your work will recommend you to others because they have gained a favorable impression of you in some manner, perhaps hearing you speak or reading something you have written. This is an informal way of networking, but it is nevertheless a networking activity.

There is also a formal, organized networking that some professionals pursue successfully. It consists of joining or organizing your own business meets, meetings of individuals in various trades and professions who get together for the express purposes of getting acquainted—establishing contacts—and exchanging business cards, brochures, and conversation, during which some referrals and leads are passed out immediately, and the bases for future ones are established.

Networking versus Word-of-Mouth Marketing

Whether formal and organized or informal and spontaneous, all these activities are aspects of networking. Work well done often leads to word-of-mouth recommendations and referrals from satisfied clients, and many consultants claim to get all their work from word-of-mouth referrals and recommendations. That is a pleasant way to market; it costs you virtually nothing in time or money—at least for as long as it lasts. It cannot happen until you have had the opportunities—the projects—in which to satisfy enough clients to inspire such referrals. (It should be apparent, from both logical analysis and from the accounts of many consultants, that getting enough work via word-of-mouth usually happens only after a few years of practice and patient buildup of your reputation.)

Not every satisfied client has the occasion to recommend you or bothers to do so. Further, there are some consulting activities—marketing support, for example—of such a nature that clients are not likely to want to recommend you to others, most of whom are the clients' competitors. Finally, this kind of marketing is shortsighted: it is marketing by chance, hopeful marketing over which you have almost zero control.

The source of such referrals from existing and former clients often runs dry, and leaves you with no marketing structure and no marketing resources in place. Word-of-mouth marketing is therefore a passive and rather high-risk kind of marketing, if you depend on it and abandon or never undertake more aggressive marketing initiatives.

One way to exploit this approach while still relying on networking and word-of-mouth that is less passive is to ask for referrals. Most insurance salespeople or other personal services salespeople have been taught to ask for referrals at the conclusion of a sales pitch (regardless of whether the prospect purchased or not, the standard question: "Do you know anyone that could use these services/products?" is frequently asked). Consultants could benefit from a similar approach in asking their current clients or even nonclient business associates for leads, recommendations, or networking referrals. While the consultant does not want to appear to be a "huckster" selling his or her wares, asking for referrals is just good salesmanship.

DISCOVERING WHAT CLIENTS WISH TO BUY

Deciding what services to sell cannot be a unilateral decision—cannot be based, that is, on what *you* want, but must be based on what clients want. But, you say, how can I know what clients want?

In some cases, you can anticipate or estimate clients' wants accurately, but that is not always the case. When it is not, the question can be answered in two words— *ask them.* That may seem to be an unsatisfying answer, but it is not to be taken literally. I do not mean literally to begin approaching strangers who appear to be good prospects and saying, "Hello, what kind of consulting services do you want to buy?" And yet, in effect that's what I do propose. For there are several ways to ask the prospective clients what they want or what it will take to persuade them to become your clients.

First, let's start with a few generalities we know to be true:

- Everyone has problems.
- Everyone wants to solve those problems.
- Everyone has at least one problem that is more worrisome than the others, more urgently in need of solution.
- Everyone has desires, things they want to gain.
- Everyone has fears, things they want to avoid.

These simple statements are the basis for all advertising and sales success. It is through taking advantage of these truths that all successful sales and marketing are achieved, for these are the motivators, the reasons people buy, why they say yes to various sales appeals. Sales and advertising success is dependent on choosing and using the most effective motivators.

Consider how insurance is sold, for example. Probably a few people buy insurance as a means for saving money, but by far the majority of people buy insurance out of fear, the fear of being defenseless in an emergency. They are motivated by the sense of insecurity most of us have, and insurance salespeople fully understand and use this in reminding us of the need to have a hedge against disaster.

Basic Motivations

All marketing and sales efforts are based on some preconceived motivational factor. If fear or the desire to avoid some result is one basic motivation, the desire to gain is the other one. Most efforts to sell material items are based on that gain motivation. (More dramatically put, people are induced to buy out of either fear or greed.) Every effective sales appeal conforms with this concept. Consider just a few possible consulting specialties, listed next, and mentally check off the motivational factor—fear or gain—most likely to inspire prospects to become clients:

Plant/office/home security measures	_____ Fear	_____ Gain
Engineering	_____ Fear	_____ Gain
Financial advisor	_____ Fear	_____ Gain
Executive search	_____ Fear	_____ Gain
Convention planning	_____ Fear	_____ Gain
Hearing aid	_____ Fear	_____ Gain
Public relations	_____ Fear	_____ Gain
Safety	_____ Fear	_____ Gain
Training	_____ Fear	_____ Gain
Mergers and acquisitions	_____ Fear	_____ Gain
Receptions and party planning	_____ Fear	_____ Gain
Taxes	_____ Fear	_____ Gain
Industrial methods	_____ Fear	_____ Gain
Transportation	_____ Fear	_____ Gain
Office organization	_____ Fear	_____ Gain

In some of these cases, the optimal choice is obvious. The first one, services in behalf of physical security, is obviously a service to be sold via the fear motivation dictated by the nature of the service. On the other hand, anyone wishing to get executive-search help wishes to gain something.

But there is another factor to consider. In most cases, the motivation could be either fear or gain. Even in the case of plant security, the motive could be gain, under certain circumstances. Suppose, for example, that a given company has a person on staff charged with seeing to plant security, and that person, for whatever reason, wants help. While the reason for having the security function is fear, the motive in retaining a consultant is gain—gaining help in doing the job.

The same consideration applies to some other items and can be applied to marketing them, given certain circumstances or kinds of needs. That is, the owner of the plant needs to make it secure, but the individual responsible for making it secure needs help in doing so. Each might retain a security consultant, but each has a different problem than the other, and that is at the heart of the marketing strategy. You must know—or estimate accurately—what the problem is to make the most effective appeal—to make the right *offer,* that is.

Identifying the problem to be solved is the key to developing the strategies of the marketing and sales campaign. It is a cliche of marketing that every salesperson must be a consultant to be effective, in the sense that every salesperson should be offering a solution to the prospect's problem in making the sales appeal. That is the basis of our definition of an offer, which can be defined as an offer to solve the prospect's problem. But it is necessary to determine what the problem is, and that is what we are really discussing here.

It would be a most useful exercise for you to pause now, before reading on, and go back to scan the list again, deciding which items could be sold via either or both basic motivations and the circumstances or needs under which one or the other appeal would be used. This analysis leads directly to the formulation of the offer because it is based on determining what the prospect's need is—what want must be satisfied. And that is the key to the entire appeal. It is the final objective of the marketing effort—making the right appeal to the right prospect.

*   *   *

I hope you found in the exercise of once again scanning the consulting-services list that most—probably all—the services listed could be sold by either or both fear and gain motivation. That is a general truth, although it does not mean that all sales appeals ought to be based on both motivations. In most cases, one is far more useful than the other and applicable to far more situations; the natural solution is the one that is more likely to appeal to the majority of prospects. Even in selling life insurance, gain motivation—gaining peace-of-mind—might be used with some effect, but the fear motivation is almost invariably far more effective.

Occasionally, someone finds a means to utilize both fear and greed as sales motivators in the same presentation. Recent best sellers, *Rich Dad/Poor Dad* and *The Millionaire Next Door* both raised the notion that there are others that are doing better financially with the same or fewer resources to begin with than the reader. For those who are unfamiliar with these books, a comparison is made on life choices and lifestyles and what impact that has on ultimate success. The books point out that contrary to conventional wisdom, the people who have achieved financial success do not necessarily look or act all that differently from those that have not, but rather, have made conscious decisions to be frugal and conserve resources without negatively impacting their lifestyles. The greed factor is exploited by the implied promise of wealth, and the fear factor is invoked by the thought that the reader is less successful than peers or neighbors and is falling behind. The titles of these books alone are a great help in persuading people to buy them. The implied threat that friends or others are "onto something" that you are not and are exploiting it while you are ignorantly unaware motivates many would-be readers to purchase the book.

Motivation versus Prospect

The matter of *who* the prospect is may be the determining factor in what the motivation must be. In the plant-security example, the difference was in what the plant owner and the security manager wanted; each had a different problem as a result of his or her different responsibilities. Simply knowing the prospect's identity (in terms of job responsibility, in this case) furnishes the major clue to proper motivation. Suppose you were a security specialist and had decided that the prospects you would target (and could reach effectively) were all individuals responsible for plant security. But you knew that these prospects were not themselves expert in the field of security, and they didn't have much time to research the subject because they were all general administrators in industrial plants with many duties to perform. That would dictate your general strategy of offering your help and special expertise, perhaps in a "Don't go it alone; special, expert help is readily available" kind of appeal. But even so, you might find a fear motivation workable in the argument "Your plant is not as secure as you think it is; let an expert show you the most modern methods."

In short, it is essential to know who and what your prospect is (and/or to have selected a target audience of prospects most carefully and thoughtfully) when devising your strategies.

It might be helpful to go back and scan that list of consulting specialists and motivations once again, considering the different types of prospects you might target and how each choice would affect the motivator you would use and the general strategies upon which you would base your offer. At the least, it would dramatize the extreme importance of identifying the prospects for your services.

Motivational Research Methods

There is an entire field of activity in marketing, especially in the subordinate field of advertising, given over to motivational research—to what inspires people generally to buy. But that is for the general consumer market. In marketing your consulting services, the research you do is far different, and depends on how, as well as to whom, you propose to sell your services.

Most Basic Method

We have been discussing a first method of research, a method based on your own advance knowledge of your field and of the prospect to whom your appeal is addressed, combined with a simple analysis of probabilities. Many marketing campaigns are based on nothing more than that, and that is sufficient in many cases. But there are other research methods available, some of them far more specific and more precisely focused.

Personal Interviews

If your chosen method of marketing includes making personal calls, you have an excellent opportunity to conduct the kind of research that leads to effective sales presentations. Until now we have been discussing common problems, problems stated on a broad and general basis, as they apply to a large number of prospects. In personal discussions with prospects, however, you have the opportunity to discover and address the specific problem(s) of the individual prospect, as well as learning (over the course of many calls and interviews) the general problems of your chosen population of prospects.

Identifying problems ought to be the first order of business in such calls. When I was devoting much of my time to developing training programs for government agencies, I once called on an executive in the training office of the Occupational Safety and Health Administration (OSHA)—an agency of the U.S. Labor Department. I introduced myself briefly and inquired as to the nature of the work in that office. I learned very quickly that the major focus of the moment was the installation of courses to train occupational safety and health technicians, and the immediate problem was developing a junior-college curriculum based on a new training program that a contractor had developed for the office.

The contractor had delivered two manuals, a student manual and an instructor's manual, but not a word prescribing the implementation of these into a formal course of instruction. The manuals themselves were complete in their coverage, but the instructor's manual failed to lay out any guidelines for its use.

A simple proposal offering to solve the problem and explaining the general rationale for doing so won an immediate purchase order and, subsequently, a great deal more work from that office and others to which my services were later recommended by this satisfied client.

The key is to do more listening than talking, especially in the early stages of the visit. Encourage the prospective client to talk, have (and show) a healthy and sincere interest in learning more. There is a pattern for this:

- Learn in advance—before the actual visit—as much as you can about the general and immediate organization and the individual upon whom you are calling. The more advance information you have, the more inspired and more productive your questioning (it's actually research into the client's wants) will be.
- Ask a few general questions, phrasing them so as to make it clear that you have done your homework and know something of the organization, but want to learn a little more. The typical client is pleased to know that you are familiar with the organization and equally unhappy to learn that you know absolutely nothing about it.
- Guide the conversation so as to learn about the problems generally—the routine, everyday problems of the organization, but particularly any special problem that urgently needs solution. Learning that can be the most important objective of your visit.

- Continue to zero in on the most troublesome problem(s) of the moment (the chief worry item or problem the prospect appears most eager to solve).
- Ask what the company has tried to do previously to address the issue. Why was it successful (or not)? What prevents the company from resolving the problem? What would a successful solution include? What does the company hope to accomplish?
- Discuss possible solution approaches to determine where the prospect's interests lie or what approach appears most acceptable. (The client may very well have some ideas of his or her own.)
- Offer your specific services to test general reaction, discover organization's normal methods for purchasing services, and getting clues to best follow-up.
- Propose specific follow-up, such as telephone call, submittal of a proposal, arranging a presentation, or other measure, as discussion has suggested. Never leave the matter hanging or with some vague understanding as to future action. It is essential to have specific follow-up agreed on, and that almost invariably means an action by *you,* not the client. You must retain the initiative if you are to have control, and control is essential if you are to close, finally, and win a contract.

Usually this kind of call and interview is itself a follow-up of a lead gained earlier via some method; it is difficult (although not impossible) to arrange a meeting spontaneously in the course of making cold calls. It is an important step, however, for most consulting assignments of any reasonably large size. The purpose of such calls is to make sales, of course, with research a fallout of the calls, rather than the objective. The research benefit should not be neglected, however; it is important input to your marketing program.

This entire approach may not be suitable for you. One individual who counts himself an independent consultant is a hypnotist who focuses his services on helping people overcome phobias. Because of the widespread interest in giving up cigarettes, he has made special efforts to help individuals quit smoking, and he conducts both individual sessions and group sessions. For him, obviously, the personal call on prospective clients (or are they patients?) is not a viable marketing plan. The same consideration would apply to others who deal in services to individuals or groups and charge by the hour, by the visit, or by the series constituting a program, such as financial advisors, investment counselors, and resume consultants. You can only call on clients via telephone, mail, and broadcast media. (There is an exception to this, however, in that you may be able to sell your services to organizations, many of which will sponsor seminars or classes to employees or members of the client organization.)

More recently, the Internet and corresponding improvement in computing and communication software applications have allowed communication that is not "face-to-face" in the more traditional sense, but can allow for video conferencing or personal interviews to occur either "live" or captured for future review. Currently, it is possible to use chatrooms or other electronic means of having remotely located people all communicating in "real-time" simultaneously and interactively. As the technology improves, this may broaden the scope, reach, and depth of personal interview usage.

Surveys and Questionnaires

Surveys and questionnaires are traditional methods of gaining information from a large number of people. This may or may not be suitable for your purposes, depending on whether you have or can acquire a suitable mailing list and can devote the time and money to what is usually a rather tedious and expensive program. If your practice already includes a direct-mail element, such as a newsletter, you are well equipped to conduct such a research program.

Using Inquiry Advertising for Motivational Research

There is a special way to use the survey/questionnaire method to focus your offers. It has the enormous advantage of being a cost-free spinoff or fallout from normal marketing methods, from a lead-generation program. But that subject itself merits a few words.

Except for special situations such as those sought by the hypnotist and the investment counselor, consulting assignments are normally fairly sizable, running to at least several hundred dollars and more often to several thousand dollars or more. This consideration alone (although there are also others) dictates that the marketing of consulting services is not a one-call business: You rarely win a significantly large or long-term contract in a single call or sales appeal to a prospective client. These contracts almost always require a series of contacts, appeals, and/or presentations to a prospect to acquire a new client, or even to win a new project from an old client.

This means, in practical terms, that making sales of your consulting service normally involves and requires at least two distinct steps: one, getting sales leads—people and situations that appear to be good prospects for contacts; and two, following up the leads to sell and close, as describer earlier.

To a large degree, the first step, generating the leads, is the real heart of marketing, the step that determines ultimate success. It is no exaggeration to say that sales success is largely dependent on the quality of the marketing, on the quality of the prospecting and the resulting sales leads—even on the legitimacy of the sales leads. No one closes all leads, but if the prospecting is not done well, too many leads prove to be not really leads at all. It is thus the quality of the leads generally that is the chief factor determining what proportion of leads you can close.

There are many ways to prospect for sales leads, some of which we will explore later. For now we will consider one basic method—inquiry advertising—which can be carried out through advertisements in periodicals, through direct mail, and through some miscellaneous methods related to these.

Inquiry advertising is advertising designed specifically to generate leads. Those in direct mail sometimes run advertisements offering something free or for a nominal cost—a newsletter, a special report, or a device of some sort—designed to elicit responses from only those who would be good prospects for—truly interested in—whatever the mailer wishes to sell. The direct-mail dealer does this to build a mailing list. But automobile dealers, real estate brokers, home-improvement firms, and many others who are in enterprises that are not one-call businesses use the same idea. The automobile dealer or real estate broker may offer to buy the respondent's lunch or provide a free floor mat to anyone who calls to see the new models and listen to the sales presentation, while the home-improvement dealer probably sends a salesperson to call or follows up with a telephone call and an effort to set up an appointment with the respondent.

Judicious mailings or advertisements of your own will soon provide you with the clues you need, while they also develop leads for you to follow up. By experimenting with what you offer as an inducement to respond, you can soon determine what the respondents' chief interests and concerns are. As an example, let us return to our general administrator who has been charged with being the plant security expert and who may or may not have knowledge of the subject and time to devote to it. You want to evoke responses from such individuals to develop leads. You have a mailing list developed from association directories, advertising, the Yellow Pages, and other sources, so you decide to make a mailing.

You construct a simple sales letter in which you introduce yourself briefly and advise the reader that, if his plant is using security devices and systems that are more than 10 years old, they are woefully out of date and not at all effective. But if he or she will send you a request on a formal letterhead or accompanied by a business card, you will send, free of charge, a special report explaining what it takes to be up to date in plant security today.

You construct a slight variation of that letter, too. The second version explains that plant security is not a part-time job; it requires frequent inspections. You'll be happy to send a free report explaining how to make such inspections, if the respondent makes the request on a letterhead and/or with a business card.

A third variation says that there are at least a half-dozen common mistakes made in designing plant security systems, as a free report you have points out and explains. Again, you make the offer of the helpful report free of charge to anyone who requests it on a business letterhead or with a proper business card enclosed.

You code each of these letters so you can tell which one each request responds to. (The report you are going to send is the same in each case, and covers all the points made in all the letters.) You can do this coding by making variations in your name—J. F. Smith, John F. Smith, J. Frederick Smith—or by adding Dept. 23, Drawer 46, or Security Specialties to your address—or by other such devices.

You print and mail an equal number of each letter to portions of your mailing list—perhaps 500 or 1,000 names each—and wait for results. The responses tell you which was the most productive appeal—which produced the largest number of sales leads to follow up.

You could offer to make a free plant inspection to anyone who requests it, but that is likely to produce fewer responses because it will be taken by many as saying, "Yes, I am interested. Please send a salesperson to see me." Probably a better time to offer that free security inspection, if you wish to offer it (it is probably an excellent gambit), is in following up the first response, when you are trying to set up a personal call and interview.

Alternatives to Mailing

There are other ways to reach prospects, if you do not have a mailing list, don't want to run advertisements, or want to supplement these. One is to make up that letter (or those several letters) into a simple brochure to distribute on literature tables at conventions, conferences, seminars, workshops, association meetings, and other events and occasions.

You can often manage to run your simple print advertisement, offering your brochure or special report, as an editorial or news item in local newspapers, trade magazines, association journals, and newsletters. You can also make your offer by mailing news releases, about which we will have a great deal more to say presently.

As mentioned previously, the use of the Internet has expanded the possibilities to reach clients and prospects, but comes with a strong caveat—do not send e-mail or post messages to electronic bulletin boards that are not wanted or appropriate. Sending e-mail to people who have not opted-in or at the very least do not have the option to refuse future e-mails is not only poor business and deplorably rude, it is also subject to criminal prosecution in some instances. Posting SPAM or uncalled for messages to web sites/bulletin boards is equally unappreciated and discouraged.

A smart consultant may choose to post responses to questions asked on a web site/bulletin board and demonstrate competence that can potentially lead to business opportunities offline (that is, through contacts made through the Internet, but then further elaborated on and discussed privately and not through the web site for all other readers, subscribers, and posters to the web site to see).

"I KNOW IT WHEN I SEE IT"

All the foregoing discussion was based on the assumption that the client knows what he or she wants—recognizes not only the existence of a problem, but knows what the problem is and what is necessary to solve or eliminate it. That is, the client has what is sometimes referred to as a felt need. However, there are at least two other cases of needs or wants. One is the client who feels a need but has not identified precisely what that need is. A few authors have written about this in books bearing titles and/or philosophies expressed as "I know it when I see it." In fact, the client probably observes certain symptoms but has not been able to decide what the problem or the remedy is. Often the situation is like the nail in your shoe; it's an annoying condition, but not intolerable, and you are too busy to take care of it right now. You'll get around to it one day, when you have the time.

To carry the analogy a bit further, if you happen to be standing in front of a shoe-repair shop while waiting for a bus, you might pop in and have the nail removed or pounded down, simply because it is suddenly and by chance convenient to do so. Many sales are made spontaneously because it has suddenly become convenient for the client to settle that troublesome problem without further delay.

That is the exceptional case. In most cases, this condition requires that you help the client perceive what you offer as what he or she needs. Your presentation ought to include a description of symptoms to help the client recognize the applicability of your services. A gentleman named Sheridan Cody, marketed a correspondence course in English successfully for years by asking, "Do you make these embarrassing mistakes in English?" But you need not be quite that blunt or that direct to help the prospect recognize the applicability of the benefits to his or her own situation. Simply listing ore describing the benefits in clear terms will accomplish the same purpose. For example, less than a decade ago, computer owners had to essentially choose whether they were going to use Apple MacIntosh computers and the operating system that those systems used or a Microsoft Windows based system. While each had their strengths and were appropriate for many of the same tasks, they were not able to easily use the same files or communicate with each other. It was not easy to transfer work between the two systems.

Identifying the problem in having what was for many businesses viewed as "incompatible" systems, software engineers and application specialists created programs and then products that could allow the open system communication between and among computers that we now enjoy.

You must bear this in mind and help the client make the connection between what you offer and the symptoms that trouble him or her. The mistake lies in assuming that the client will perceive exactly what you hope. Vain hope; it rarely happens: You must operate on the assumption that the client knows what you tell him or her, but no more.

CREATING NEEDS—FUDs

There is at least one other kind of prospective client to consider; this is a prospective client who is untroubled at the moment, and does not have any problems that might relate to your services. At least, they do not know that they have a problem! Not yet. Not until you help them discover their problem and their need or want. In other words, *you* create the worry item. Consultants often refer to this as the *FUD factor.* Create fear, uncertainty, or doubt in the prospective client's mind that they are in trouble and don't recognize it, are about to be in trouble and need to either be prepared for it or avoid it, or are less certain than they believed about whether they are in trouble or not (perhaps some competitor is gaining a lead on them, maybe the marketplace is changing, federal legislation is about to be enacted that will impact the business, etc.).

Some marketers or advertising specialists speak of creating a need. Actually, that is a convenient idiom, for you cannot literally create a need, and you cannot persuade anyone to want something they truly do not want, although it may appear sometimes that you have done so. However, for convenience of reference, we sometimes speak of creating needs as though we actually can do so, and we will use the term here in that idiomatic usage.

There are two ways to create a need. One is by creating a new service or product. The mere fact of offering your consulting services as something new creates a need, especially if the services you offer are unique. Anyone who becomes your client thus confesses to a need or a want that did not exist before. (It could not have existed before because the service did not exist before—one did not want a television 100 years ago because it did not yet exist.) Ergo, the mere availability or offer of something new may be said to create a need. But even that is not entirely valid, as we will soon see when we press a bit harder on defining what a need is.

The other way to create a need is by educating the client—by *giving* him or her the problem and then the solution. We all have seen the Goodyear Tire television commercial of the young infant sitting inside of a tire cooing and happily playing as the narrator reminds us of the importance of having high-quality tires in good repair. Most drivers give very little thought to the condition of their tires, but seeing the commercial and being reminded that the tires on our cars are what transports our children around led to many drivers suddenly giving a lot more thought to replacing and maintaining the upkeep of their tires. No driver (and especially a parent of a child being driven) wants to be responsible for an accident or a blowout that injures a child passenger because of their inaction in tire care.

Are You Curious?

When selling to businesses, there is another technique that often provides good results for consultants. If a consultant assumes that a client has a problem and the consultant has the recommendation or solution, many would-be clients will be offended or will refuse to acknowledge the existence of the problem (the client or prospect thinks, "Who is the consultant to assume that I have a problem," and "How dare this person tell me that I am somehow not doing my job well, or could do better?"). It is difficult to sell anything to a prospective client who does not see or recognize the need for the service and is not in a buying mode at all.

What many businesspeople will respond to, though, is an approach that essentially asks them, "Are you curious?" If a consultant offers to share how a competitor to the prospect achieved results, or how a well-known company in the industry known to the prospect accomplished an impressive business result, many businesspeople will not be able to curb their curiosity to find out. Especially if the referenced company is one that the prospect fears, respects, or competes against. The natural inclination is to stay at least as current as that company on new initiatives or approaches. The prospect may choose to have the consultant share the story or approach with an eye toward having the consultant provide the same (or better) result for them. This works best when the consultant was actually involved in the referenced company's initiative and can speak from the experience of having been a part of the effort.

FACE-TO-FACE CLOSING

In most sales situations, you must come face to face with the client to close. To many, that word means getting the order, as in closing the sale. To the professional sales expert, the word has a second and more subtle meaning. It means *asking* for the order. That is, it refers to closing the sales presentation by asking for the order. In the classic sales situation, especially when a big-tag item such as an automobile or large contract is involved, it is an accepted premise that the salesperson must close—ask for the order—many times before getting the desired signature on the order form. So at some point you must consummate your presentation and try to complete the sale.

Even on modestly priced items this is often true. How many times did you get a solicitation for *Time* magazine or some other item sold via mail before you finally ordered it—if you did? The seller would be surprised if you responded to the first solicitation with an order, although a few prospects do. Far more sales are closed on second, third, fourth, or even subsequent closes than on first ones. Perseverance and patience are keys to success here, as they are in so many things.

Selling consulting services may not appear to work quite that way. But it does, albeit on a more indirect and less obvious—and usually more protracted—basis. You send out many brochures and letters, speak at numerous gatherings, chat with dozens of people at conventions, follow up with innumerable telephone calls and perhaps lunches, submit more than a few written bids and proposals, make frequent presentations, and ultimately you wind up with a few signed contracts or purchase orders. You probably came in second many times before you won the prize. Even after you have won good leads, you had to make several closes to most of those leads before you won a contract.

Are there exceptions? There are exceptions to everything. Once in a while you get lucky and get the lead, make the sale, and close the order all on one occasion. If you get lucky on your first try—and that has happened, unfortunately, to some beginners—don't let it destroy your good judgment and cloud your vision. Such a stroke of fortune is a fluke that will probably happen only rarely, if ever again, and you can destroy yourself with disappointment and frustration at your inability to make it happen again. You must recognize it for what it is.

Marketing is playing percentages. You do everything possible to stack the odds in your favor by trying to generate the best possible leads and by every other means available. But in the end, your success is controlled by numbers, by probability statistics. You cannot close every lead, only a percentage of the leads. The more leads you generate, the higher the percentage of sales you will make, normally. That means that you must do something to reduce the time wasted on prospects you are most unlikely to sell—determine who the poor prospects are before you spend too much time on them, that is.

Some of the more enthusiastic zealots among sales experts will assure you that you should be able to close each and every lead. But there are some leads—prospects— you cannot close for any of many possible reasons. You will sometimes run into a prospect, especially in a large organization, who has nothing better to do than to chat with you, but who has no authority or perhaps no sincere desire to do business with you. (Don't be misled by sumptuous offices and what appears to be serious interest.) You may run into a prospect who is simply picking your brain so he or she can become a big hero/heroine in the organization, using the information and ideas stolen from you. Or perhaps there is no budget available and the prospect is probing possibilities for a future project that is not likely to materialize. (Sometimes an idle executive is desperately seeking to develop a project to protect his or her own job, but wasting your time in the process.)

There have been times where executives sitting around a table at lunch will read an article in the daily newspaper or trade publication mentioning some initiative or approach that another company is taking and will desire to have you provide free education on the details for how to go about doing it and applying it to their company. Unfortunately for the consultant, there is no commitment from management to do it and the project exists only in the mind of the hopeful executive seeking to better his own understanding of a business dynamic or new initiative.

Because these kinds of things do happen, it is wise—nay, essential—to practice a defensive measure known as qualifying the prospect.

QUALIFYING PROSPECTS

Qualifying a prospect means simply taking some measures to assure yourself that the individual you are spending your time with is indeed a true prospect, one who *can* retain you and is serious about retaining a consultant.

Here are the kinds of qualifications the prospect must have to be truly a prospect for you:

- A need appropriate to your specialty—one that you can satisfy.
- The money necessary to retain you.
- The authority to retain you.
- The sincere intention of doing business with someone.

There is first that matter of making sure that you are not wasting your time discussing some vague need that may be outside your field. The only practical way you can address this is to probe until you are satisfied that you know what the client will require. Be aware, however, that frequently the client really does not know what the need or problem is, but can describe and list only symptoms or complaints and may be vague about those, too. You will have to probe until you gather enough information to reach at least a preliminary conclusion. A word of caution here: Keep that conclusion to yourself, for now. You have not yet been retained or paid for your time; disclosure here would be premature and might result in your analysis being passed on to other consultants as a definition of need.

The question of money to retain you has different practical interpretations. In some cases, the question might be literally whether the individual has the cash in hand. In others, as when dealing with organizations rather than individuals, it is a question of whether the individual has both budget and authority or has access to and influence with someone else who has the spending authority.

That is an important consideration. In many cases, someone in an organization can recommend and help sell you to the right individual in the organization, although lacking personally in the authority to retain you.

Finally, try somehow to determine whether you are discussing a project that will come to pass or wasting time on an imaginary project.

A suitable euphemism for asking about money tactfully is, "Are funds currently available for this project?" Another way to put it is, "Is this project budgeted yet?" Or, "Has this been funded yet?" Any question along these lines, delivered quietly and matter-of-factly, will usually be accepted as an objective, businesslike query, asked strictly for information and not as a challenge or intimation of mistrust.

All questions you ask in qualifying a prospect must be tactfully phrased, and asked in that same quiet, matter-of-fact tone. That's especially the case in asking a question or two to establish the authority—or lack of it—of the individual you are talking to. Among the questions you might ask are these:

- Who will have to sign off on this?
- What's the decision-making (or approval) process on this?
- Will somebody besides you have to okay this?

If you find that you need to probe the matter of the client's intent, you may have to ask some rather direct questions. Here are a few leading questions that ought to steer the discussion in the right direction:

- Has an official decision been made yet to go ahead with this project?
- Is this exploratory, or is there definite commitment already to the project we are discussing here?
- How soon do you expect this project to begin?
- When would you need me to start on this?
- Has this project been budgeted yet?

From the answers you get to these questions, you can generally judge whether you are discussing a definitely planned project or wasting your time on a prospect's wish that is likely to never materialize, or even on being used cynically, for that happens occasionally, too.

9 | Releases, Brochures, and Other Materials

Miscellaneous tools for and routes to marketing successfully.

MARKETING AND MESSAGES

Marketing requires getting messages to prospective clients. Doing that takes many forms. The messages are diverse, although your purpose is to build an image—one of competence, dependability, and integrity—and explain what it is that you do for your clients—how they benefit from your services.

Writing is important in this because we depend heavily on written presentations to broadcast our marketing messages and sales arguments. The role of writing in marketing is a dual one. The presentation must be persuasive enough to carry out the mission of image building and benefits definition, but readers must be persuaded to read the message. That is itself a difficult marketing job. Persuading readers to read and digest messages is not easy, when so much competes for our attention—radio, TV, newspapers, and magazines. The task of seizing and holding the reader's attention is no minor chore.

Is this familiar? It should be. It's the same set of principles we discussed as the prerequisites of the sales presentation: Get and hold the subject's interest. Consider first the task of developing a publicity release (also known as a news release or press release).

RELEASES AND NEWSWORTHINESS

Publishers and broadcasters are aware that you and other millions—yes, millions—who send out releases every day are asking for free media space or time to advertise your product and/or your service. They are aware that you are using the release for marketing, free advertising. But the editor does not use your release and give you free space or time without getting something in return. The editor will *trade* space/time for something *newsworthy*. You can buy that space with something the editor can use, something the editor's readers/listeners/viewers would find interesting.

That is the key: newsworthiness. I use the term rather loosely, for the typical publicity release is not newsworthy in the sense of hard news, but in the sense of reader/listener/viewer interest. The editor is not concerned with what interests him or her personally, but what will interest the audience.

The broad lines of those interests are easy to draw. The subscriber to *Jones' Daily Investor's Report* does not expect to read a piece on inventory management, *even if that is of personal interest,* so don't send that inventory-management release to Jones; he won't use it. Send it to *Management Daily, Manager's Monthly,* and *Inventory Weekly.* It is *their* readers who will want to read that release, who will be able to identify with it.

The physical format of a release may vary, as Figures 9.1, 9.2, and 9.3 reveal. The minimum requirements are that the piece must identify itself as a release and identify its origin or source—who issued it. There are other considerations—perhaps not musts because many violate these principles—but considerations that can make a considerable difference in whether you do or do not get the publicity you are after. Here are some do's and don'ts:

- Do double-space the copy. The editor will want to edit your copy in most cases.
- Do put a date on the piece.
- Do provide release information—"For immediate release," if it is not embargoed, but a specific release date if it is embargoed. (Copies of speeches are sent out in advance, but embargoed until the speech has been delivered, for example.)
- Do provide a contact—someone to call for more details if the editor wants more information.
- Do indicate where the copy ends with a standard notations, such as "End" or "30" (an old telegrapher's sign off).
- Do type on one side of the paper only.
- Do try to use the journalist's style of summarizing all the key points of who, what, when, where, and why in the first sentence, if your release purports to be news—a new product or service or a discovery in your field. If the piece is a feature type, try for an attention getter in the headline and follow it up immediately in the first sentence.
- Don't be cryptic and don't get cute or clever if you use a headline (I recommend that you include a headline, although others sometimes counsel not to, for what I think to be irrelevant reasons). The purpose of the headline is to get attention and summarize the main point of the release so the editor can judge swiftly how it fits into the scheme of things. The easier you make it for the editor, the more likely you are to sell the piece.
- Don't get literary. Use the simplest language and the most straightforward explanations possible. That is the best kind of writing.

It is always possible to find attention-getting and interesting items for releases, even if it is not easy. But it is worth the effort; by far the vast majority of releases are

For immediate release

Contact: Mike Onorato
(201) 748-6361/monorato@wiley.com

Lateral Marketing:
New Techniques for Finding Breakthrough Ideas

By

Philip Kotler and Fernando Trias de Bes

Today's marketers face a difficult challenge: how to innovate in a hyper competitive, super-segmented marketplace. In a consumer economy saturated with homogeneous products and inhabited by customers who are more and more immune to advertising messages, traditional vertical marketing—with its fundamentals of market segmentation and brand proliferation—is beginning to fail us.

LATERAL MARKETING: New Techniques for Finding Breakthrough Ideas (Wiley; September 2003; $24.95; Cloth) by Philip Kotler and Fernando Trias de Bes introduces a new paradigm for the creation of big marketing ideas: lateral marketing. Not intended to replace existing structures of segmentation, targeting and positioning, lateral marketing will instead expand the vision of marketing beyond the sequential and logic process in which it is based, with an infusion of creative thought.

These innovations include new products like Honey Nut Cheerios Milk N' Cereal bars, a quick alternative to actual cereal with milk, or new business concepts, such as CyberCafes, where computers with Internet access are placed inside cafeterias, or supermarkets inside gas stations. LATERAL MARKETING explains the concept of using old products in a new way, such as promoting Bayer aspirin as a heart attack preventative, or using apples in hotels reception desks as a way of welcoming guests. This means expanding the utility, needs, or targets of old products, which will allow incremental sales.

The new marketing concepts that led to these products are the direct result of a different creative process than the endless vertical segmentation of yesterday. LATERAL MARKETING offers a framework for thinking up new marketing concepts as these ones, by putting together the marketing thinking with the lateral thinking.

Kotler is widely considered one of the architects of modern marketing and is sometimes referred to as the "Father of Marketing". He was the first recipient of the American Marketing Association's Distinguished Marketing Educator Award in 1985; and it is largely due to his presence that *Business Week* calls Kellogg the "Best Business School" for teaching and marketing. The awards and honors he has accrued in his forty-year career are staggering.

<u>About the Authors:</u>

PHILIP KOTLER is the S. C. Johnson Distinguished Professor of International Marketing at Northwestern University's Kellogg School of Management. Considered the father of modern marketing, he is the author of twenty-five books, including *Marketing Insights from A to Z*, also available from Wiley. He has worked as a consultant to corporations such as IBM, Bank of America, General Electric, and AT&T.

FERNANDO TRIAS de BES is founder and Partner of Salvetti & Llombart, a firm specializing in consulting and market research with an international scope and clients such as PepsiCo, Sony, Hewlett-Packard, McKinsey & Co., Nestlé, and Dannon. He is also a consultant on innovation in marketing. He is an Associate Professor of the Marketing Department at ESADE Business School in Barcelona.

LATERAL MARKETING:
New Techniques for Finding Breakthrough Ideas
By Philip Kotler and Fernando Trias de Bes
John Wiley & Sons, Inc.
Publication Date: September 2003
$24.95; Cloth; ISBN: 0-471-45516-4

<u>ATTENTION REVIEWERS</u>

For the convenience of your readers, please include the following in your review: **Wiley books are available at your local bookstore or by calling 1-800-225-5945.** In Canada, call 1-800-567-4797.

Figure 9.1   Typical publicity release.

PRESS RELEASE

NATIONAL ASSOCIATION OF TEMPORARY SERVICES
119 SOUTH SAINT ASAPH ST. ALEXANDRIA VA 22314

TELEPHONE:	703/549-6287	**FOR RELEASE:**
CONTACT:	Bruce Steinberg	Friday, December 11, 1992

TEMPORARY HELP INDUSTRY RELEASES PAST PERFORMANCE
Industry Study Necessitated by Change in Govenment Statistics

(Alexandria, VA) –– The temporary help industry grew modestly from 1990–1991 and at a significantly slower rate than throughout the 1980s according to an independent study released by the National Association of Temporary Services (NATS).

Annual payroll grew 2.0% to more than $14 billion ($14,002,000,000) in 1991. Industry receipts, which had never been previously collected or reported by NATS, reached more than $20 billion ($20,456,000,000) in 1991, which was a 2.2% gain over 1990.

In response to a change by the government to include non-temporary help arrangements of employment in its measurements, the trade association, which represents an estimated 85% of the industry, contracted with DRI/McGraw Hill, an internationally recognized economic/market research firm to conduct the study of NATS and non NATS members.

One widely followed measurement of the industry –– average daily employment (ADE) –– could not be definitively determined due to the lack of valid data from both the DRI study or government sources. However, industry sources estimate the ADE dropped slightly in 1991 to barely more than 1 million in 1991, or approximately 1% of the workforce.

According to Samuel R. Sacco, executive vice president of NATS, "These results show that temporary help companies have been able to continue to provide workers with much needed flexible employment opportunities throughout a rather lackluster economic period."

– more –

Figure 9.2   First page of news release.

dull, self-serving, and poorly written, and find their way into the circular file swiftly. When I was trying to use interesting items for my own releases, I found opportunities among the government's procurements, and came up with headlines like these:

- The government paid me $6,000 to answer their mail.
- Government contract issued for go-go dancing.
- Federal agency rents mules and handlers.

You won't always find material that is attention-getting, novel, amusing, or intriguing, nor should you use such headlines unless they are truly appropriate and

News Release

GSA #9064 IRMS

September 22, 1992

GSA Awards $1.7 Million Contract to Washington D.C. Firm

A contract worth an estimated $1,700,000 has been awarded by the U.S. General Services Administration (GSA) to a small business firm, VMX, Inc., Washington, D.C., to provide voice messaging and call processing systems to federal agencies.

The contract is for one year, Oct. 1, 1992 through Sept. 30, 1993. It was awarded through the multiple award schedules procurement program under which GSA negotiates with vendors for goods and services required by federal agencies. The agencies then order directly from vendors at the GSA-negotiated price.

The estimated contract value is GSA's expectation of the purchases federal agencies will make from the firm during the contract year.

# # #

U. S. General Services Administration, Washington, DC 20405 (202) 501-1231

Figure 9.3   A federal agency news release.

accurate. The most clever headline won't help if it has nothing to do with the content of the release. It is not always necessary to have a blockbuster of a headline because you are usually addressing readers with special interests. Any appeal to those interests—to what is new and potentially profitable or useful—will do the job you want it to do, *provided that the editor understands that appeal.*

The headline may or may not be one the editor will like and use—editors have their own ideas about what readers want and how to command their attention—but that is not important at the moment. The important point here is to create a headline that tells the editor why he or she ought to use your story. (No matter what the item is, many journalists refer to it as the story.) The headline is an *announcement,* in fact, crying, "Hey! Look!" You must remember, however, that unless the release is going to a specialized trade periodical, the editor will probably not understand special jargon or references peculiar to the special field. That is, editors of *Personal Computing* would probably have no difficulty understanding the significance of TECHNOCOMP COR-PORATION ANNOUNCES 4.0 GIGAHERTZ COMPUTER, but the lay person or the editor of the *Millersville Times* would have difficulty judging the newsworthiness (much less the attention-getting power) of that headline. You would do far better to use something such as NEW, SUPERFAST (4.0 GHZ) COMPUTER ANNOUNCED BY TECHNOCOMP. That enables any editor to grasp the idea that this is a new and newsworthy development, whether he or she knows anything about computers. (Of course, the body of the release will go on to provide the details and clarify further the significance of the headline announcement.)

Typical Items for Releases

Straight news in a release is practically never of the front-page-headline type. There are exceptions, such as news released by government offices and agencies, but news in a release tends to interest only those within some kind of special-interest group, such as a given industry or profession. When releases are of interest to readers of a popular publication, such as a magazine or newspaper, they are most suitable for specialized sections of the periodical, such as the financial pages or food section. Following are a few examples of the kinds of news items found in releases:

- Information about people within the industry or sphere of interest, includ-ing notices of newcomers, retirees, promotions, and deaths, particularly of prominent figures.
- Announcements or advance notices of mergers, new starts, contract awards, divestitures, stock offerings, new constructions, expansions, and other such stories.
- Stories behind the story—inside or little-known information about such de-velopments as mergers, divestitures, sell-offs, new products, and cutbacks.
- Technical details of new product, stock offering, merger, financial manipula-tion, or other development of interest.
- Government activities affecting the readers, such as new legislation, regula-tions, reports.
- Announcements of relevant new books.
- Notices and/or reviews of new products and services.
- Announcements of special events, such as conventions, association meetings, and trade show.
- Copies of speeches by individuals at special events, such as those just listed.
- Statements by individuals prominent in the field.

What Is Interesting?

I happen to be interested in computers and electronics, subjects that bore some to tears. But most sports are of little interest to me. On the other hand, like almost ev-eryone, I am interested in remaining healthy, being successful, and enjoying life.

Health, success, and happiness involve *self-interest,* and you can almost always capture and retain someone's attention when you get into the subject of his or her self-interest. Even this varies to some extent. Everyone needs to feel secure, for example, but security has different meanings for different individuals. To some, a job that appears to be steady and pays a decent wage represents security, but others require far more, such as substantial savings, a retirement account, and perhaps a great deal of insurance.

Such motivations will inspire people to do things they might never do otherwise. Who would arise every morning before dawn, put on a special outfit for which they have paid a great deal of money, and run themselves to exhaustion before breakfast had they not been led to believe that this would assure better health?

The most basic drives are to avoid the undesirable and to gain the desirable—fear and greed. These drives get attention and arouse interest. Fear drove thousands of people to build and stock elaborate bomb shelters in the fifties, for example. Insurance, locks, and many other goods and services are sold principally through fear motivation, appealing to the insecurity that is inherent in most of us.

Desire for gain also commands attention and interest. There is no apparent end to the appeal and the supply of books and newsletters purporting to guide people in the stock market and in other kinds of investments. The late Joe Karbo reportedly sold more than 600,000 copies (at $10 each) of his little paperback titled *The Lazy Man's Way to Riches.*

There are other appeals that many find interesting, all of which are time-tested and apparently never wear out their welcome:

- Inside information or tips. Most of us have that all-too-human desire to gain access to information denied to most—information that is even, perhaps, a little illicit.
- FREE! How that word endures as a lure! It truly never wears out.
- SALE or BARGAIN. Like FREE, these words endure forever. There are successful businesses who have everything on special sale every day of the year, and most shoppers appear to have no trouble with this idea. (How easy it is for us to persuade ourselves to believe what we want to believe.)
- How it works. Few people can resist the mystery of how things work, whether you are talking about satellites or legislative horsetrading. Make such subjects easy to understand, and you have an audience.

Humor helps, but it is double-edged. The ability to be humorous, especially in writing, is rare. Despite the fact that almost everyone likes a laugh, humor that doesn't succeed is a deadly bore. Best course: Report the facts without editorializing (as I did when I reported that the government had contracted for go-go dancing) or trying to *make* the item a humorous one. No one will criticize you for straight reporting, if you report accurately. Humor is inherent in many items, and requires no embellishment.

A show-business cliché says there are no small parts but only small actors. There are also no dull subjects but only dull presentations. Every subject has interesting facets, amenable to being discovered and presented. Lancelot Hogben, an engineer in Great Britain, passed the time during a lengthy illness by writing *Mathematics for the Million,* a book on the history of mathematics, published by W.W. Norton in 1937. Millions who find mathematics otherwise uninteresting still love Lancelot Hogben's accounts of mathematical developments and disciplines.

You can find something interesting to report about any and every subject imaginable. Use the public library and do some research.

Linkages: Keeping Your Eye on the Ball

Copywriters often get carried away with the challenge of writing effectively and forget what they set out to do—generate leads for future contracts, for example. An excellent release that is widely published is not a success if it fails to generate sales leads for you. To succeed, your release must do two things beyond getting published: It must somehow provoke readers into responding directly to you, and it must be selective so that those who respond are *qualified* leads, good prospects as clients for consulting services—clients for *your* consulting services.

The release must make it clear that you are a consultant, and define the general area of your consulting expertise and services. That definition must provide a clue of what your services do for your clients—kinds of problems solved and/or benefits delivered.

Probably the easiest and most direct way to establish the correct linkage is to have your specialty incorporated into your business name or subtitle, as in the following examples:

- Accurate Real Estate Appraisers
- Government Marketing Consultants
- Convention Planners, Inc.
- Editorial Experts, Inc.
- Office Systems Designers, Ltd.

If you link that with the content of the release—if the connection is obvious—most readers will perceive where, how, and why your services can be of interest. Given that much, if your release is widely circulated, it will probably produce at least a few leads, in time. But you can improve the odds by doing something to stimulate the response.

The how-to success story is often effective, especially when it is the inside story. Promise to tell readers how so-and-so (e.g., the president of a prominent metalworking company) increased productivity 18 percent through a simple method available to everybody. That kind of thing almost always commands attention. Even better, promise to show readers how *you* helped that individual get results. You can offer a set of several such reports and get even greater impact, especially if those reports show how your services can deliver the same benefits to different kinds of industries or clients.

That means offering to provide some kind of brochure or report to any reader who requests it. That is exactly what you want: requests from those interested in learning how to increase productivity. You send them your report—and it need not be elaborate: A report typed on regular paper and reproduced inexpensively in perfectly suitable—and your sales literature, and you follow up with telephone calls.

Powerful although this kind of response device—inducement to respond—is, it is not the only kind by any means. Study the junk mail you receive, and you will discover a great many ideas for response devices—free appraisals, free estimates, samples, free newsletters, and others that you may wish to adopt. (As we proceed, we will discuss newsletters, seminars, and other things as both profit-makers and marketing tools.)

News releases are not the only way to make these offers and to prospect for sales leads, and not the only way to put your pen to work (or your fingers to a keyboard) in developing good sales leads. Let's talk about some of the other ways.

BROCHURES AS MARKETING TOOLS

Of all the many written instruments used for marketing, brochures are the most abundant. Brochures are the basic marketing tool for many, if not most, consultants and can be found in every possible size, color, format, quality, and application. The very word, *brochure,* has almost infinite interpretations. It is possible to produce brochures that cost a fraction of a cent each, but you can also produce brochures that cost several dollars each. Many brochures are a single typewriter-sized sheet folded to fit into an ordinary business envelope; others are dozens of pages, formally bound, requiring a large envelope for mailing.

There are situations justifying those elaborate brochures. In most cases, however, it is unnecessary to go to such extremes. Even a brochure made up of a single sheet folded to fit a business envelope is adequate if properly typeset and printed on reasonably good paper. Bear in mind that the brochure is not intended to land a contract; even elaborate and costly ones can't do that. Brochures help you generate marketing leads for follow-up. That is all they *can* do.

A 3- × 9-inch brochure offers many advantages. It fits into a standard business size envelope, and it is convenient to carry in an inside pocket, a purse, or a briefcase. That enables you to have a supply with you at all times.

That convenience extends to anyone to whom you hand such a brochure: Not faced with something awkwardly large, the recipient may slip your brochure easily into pocket or purse. In fact, a 3 × 9 brochure is often more useful than a business card; it is not only a convenient size, but it carries a message far beyond that possible for a little card.

You can use your brochure as you might use a release, offering the same inducements to respond and similar copy. But the resemblance is superficial. One major difference is that you have total control over distribution of your brochures. It's a trade-off, of course. You have complete control over the distribution of your brochures, but that distribution is up to you primarily. The alternatives are to do the actual physical distribution yourself via direct mail, at business and professional convocations (conventions, conferences, trade shows, and other such gatherings), or have mailers and other marketing support specialists do it for you. It is wasteful to mail brochures alone; if you are going to the expense and labor of a direct-mail program, make up a complete direct-mail package, which includes a salesletter, a brochure, and a return envelope, as a minimum.

This does not rule out having one of those more elaborate brochures—an 8½- × 11-inch format, with stiff covers, and other refinements. But that kind of brochure should be reserved for follow-up contacts and should be in addition to, not in place of, the smaller brochure.

OTHER SALES MATERIALS

There are many marketing applications for your writing. Properly developed, they are likely to be your most productive and fruitful marketing activities. Put your pen to use to develop salesletters, bids and proposals, advertising copy, newsletters, e-mail campaigns, books, and articles for periodicals.

Salesletters

The typical salesletter tends to be high-pressure, with bold type, capital letters, two- and three-color inks, circles, exclamation marks, handwritten notations, and other high-excitement symbols. This is as appropriate for selling consulting services as huckstering on the streets. If a salesletter is to be of any use at all to you, it has to be quiet and dignified, while still observing all the valid principles of selling effectively (Figure 9.4).

There are several other relevant items—bids, proposals, capability brochures, and newsletters—that will be discussed in much greater detail later, and so will be passed over here.

Articles published under your byline in suitable periodicals can be an important marketing tool, and you should make every effort to write such articles and have them published. They do a great deal for your professional image—potential clients tend to be impressed by them; they certify your authority in your special field; and reprints are useful as inserts in mailing packages and appendices or exhibits of your proposals. Q&A (question and answer) columns are excellent, if you can persuade some editor to allow you to write these on a more or less regular basis. The idea is to prove your capability and the worth of your services by offering a few samples, but the mere fact of being published is itself an impressive credential to many people and a great help to you in marketing.

In that same philosophy, when you do manage to speak publicly to groups, invite questions and even comments from or open discussion by the audience. That not only gives you a chance to display your wares, but it helps you understand prospective clients' views, attitudes, problems, needs, biases, and other characteristics that aid your marketing. Learn as much as you can about how your prospects think, for in marketing the only view that counts is the client's view. Your main goal in every

Consulting Opportunities Journal

P.O. Box 17674, Washington, DC 20041

$500 and more per day consulting, or grossing up to $10,000 and more in a single day working a favorite profit center, today's consultants are cashing in on growing demands for their knowledge. The age of the consultant-entrepreneur is here!

Dear Colleague,

You are sitting in a great position to turn your knowledge into "gold" in the months and years just ahead. And it doesn't matter if you're just starting out or an "old" pro in consulting, or whether you are part or full time in your practice.

The months and years ahead will bring unprecedented consulting opportunities to those men and women, in all fields, who are prepared for them.

Consulting Opportunities Journal (COJ) was founded to bring you information on those opportunities. We also report on trends, tips and techniques on how to most efficiently market yourself in today's potential-laden environment.

The response to COJ has been great. Being founded and written by consultants for consultants, the COJ has earned the reputation of a no-nonsense, straight-from-the-shoulder 'How-To' publication. No "ivory tower" stuff here.

Its writers earn their living from consulting in their various fields. So you can be assured that COJ's writers cannot afford (and neither can you) the luxury of writing about theory versus how it actually is "on the street." Each one of our consultant-writers, now and in the future, has faced and overcome the marketing problems, difficult client relationships, proposal-writing struggles and outright loneliness and more that we've all faced at one time or another.

Consulting is as much a leadership business as it is a people business. The COJ covers the people giving advice to the leaders of our society. The COJ is the only publication of its kind in the world. We are dedicated to your success in consulting, now, more than ever before.

It is to this end, to maintain our place of leadership in the consulting profession, that we are making you, what I believe, the most generous offer you have seen—from any national publisher in any field. First, let me tell you what subscribers are seeing in the COJ:

- How and Where to Get Consulting Leads (Self-Marketing Strategies that Can Be Used in Any Field)
- How to Set Fees (Also, What Others are Charging)
- How to Write Winning Proposals & Reports
- What Goes Into Launching a Successful Seminar or Newsletter (Information that can save you plenty!)
- IRS Proposals and Tax Considerations Affecting the Independent Consultant
- How and Where to Find Writing and Speaking Opportunities
- Consultant Networks, Consultant Brokerages: What They Are, How They Work, and How to Work with Them (Are They the Ultimate Income Source?)
- How to Discover, Develop and Market Information Products and Other Profit Centers of Your Own
- Data Banks, Research Centers, Make Them Work For You or Your Client, Telephone Marketing and much, much more!

Figure 9.4 Sample of typical sales letter.

Along with covering scores of publications to bring you the happenings in the booming consulting industry, we have just acquired Consultant's Digest and merged it into COJ—at no extra cost to subscribers. There's even a Q & A column where you can get specific answers from specific questions from COJ's own consultant to consultant editor, Herman Holtz.

When you come right down to it, the COJ could be broken up into several newsletters—each with the same or higher subscription rates. There could be one on Self-Marketing Strategies, Consulting Contracts/Fee Negotiation, Direct Mail Marketing/Advertising Strategies for Consultants, Developing and Marketing Seminar and Newsletter Properties and others. But these are all included in your COJ subscription.

A year's subscription to COJ is only $24 for six full issues. And it's totally tax-deductible along with a money-back guarantee. Plus, there's no extra charge if we increase our publishing schedule during your subscription term. (Saves $6.00 over single copy)

Those watching the mushrooming consulting industry tell us that, within two short years, a weekly publishing schedule will be needed to touch all the bases. We don't know about weekly, but from the looks of things now, a monthly publishing schedule is not far off!

A 2-year subscription is just $39 (a savings of $21.00 off the single-copy price), and a 3-year term is only $57, a big $33.00 savings over single-copy!

Now, let's get back to my "most generous" offer I mentioned earlier. We've just made a special purchase of 7 top-selling titles of consulting guidebooks from The Consultant's Library, the nation's leading consulting book publisher (See the attached list).

As if all the foregoing benefits of a COJ subscription weren't enough, now you can get up to 3 (THREE) books FREE—up to an $80 value with your paid subscription! You simply select one book FREE for each year of your chosen subscription term.

This is a limited-time offer and may be withdrawn soon. To ensure your selections, order today on the special order form enclosed. Use the handy postage-paid envelope for additional speed and savings.

Isn't it time you discovered all the benefits to you and your family from your own consulting practice?

Yours for a successful consultancy,

J. Stephen Lanning
Publisher

Figure 9.4   Continued.

contact, especially face-to-face contacts, should be to learn about the prospective client. Do more listening than talking—much more.

Books

Even more than articles in periodicals, books published under your byline help establish and confirm your technical/professional authority, and lend you a great deal of prestige. Many successful consultants are the authors of books about their own special fields. Among the best known of these is management consultant Peter Drucker. The late consultant's consultant, Howard Shenson, authored several books, as has Hubert Bermont, publisher of *The Consultant's Library* and Director of the American Consultant's League, and many other independent consultants. Consultant Jeffrey Lant chooses to be his own publisher, and has written a number of books about consulting, marketing, and other business subjects. He markets them aggressively, partly through a column he self-syndicates in a number of periodicals, and he has gained prominence through these activities.

Ironically, in some ways it is easier to get a book published than to get an article accepted for publication. Many consultants have managed to do both, however, and both are worthwhile. (Admittedly, you may not earn a great deal of money from your books, unless you publish and market them yourself, as Lant does, but you will reap benefits in publicity and image building to help you market your services as a consultant.)

A WORD ON E-MAILS

Electronic means of communicating—through e-mails and other Internet forms of messaging—have reduced the costs of many marketing campaigns, while at the same time allowing for broader coverage and more immediate responsiveness. These benefits, however, have come at a price that needs to be considered before being used by the eager consultant.

Executives are being asked to "do more with less" in contemporary business, but that translates to accomplish more with less reliance on being able to delegate tasks to subordinates. It is more common for an executive to be responsible for his or her own correspondence and communication (making the thought of someone taking dictation seem quaint and outdated, and even having people solely tasked with being part of a typing pool may seem antiquated) and often are accountable for their own presentations made to customers or others within the same organization. Given that executives are flooded with messages via their e-mail systems, and often have to work remotely from hotels or other locations with slower download times, a consultant can risk annoying a frustrated executive looking to send urgent correspondence or time sensitive information.

Therefore, some hints on using e-mail as a marketing device:

- Try to keep files to a very manageable size (less than 1 megabyte).
- Allow the recipient to "opt out" of mailings that may not be of interest to them (newsletters, releases, or advertisements).
- Keep messages to one screen length (as opposed to requiring scrolling down to see the entire message).
- Let the reader know what the e-mail is about in the first sentence (some e-mail systems allow "previews" of the message by showing the first two lines, you want to be sure that your message is not deleted because you failed to generate interest until much later in the correspondence).
- Refrain from using all capital letters (it reads as if you are shouting).
- Be aware that humor may not be "read" as it is intended (your vocal tone, body posture, or smiles/winks/nods cannot be seen in a written message). I once received an e-mail response to a proposal I had submitted that in part

read, "What do you think I am, made of money?" I did not read this as a sarcastic comment that was actually telling me that I had come in well below the expected budget. Had I not called to inquire what the problem was with what I had believed to be a fair price quote, I would have run the risk of either dismissing the client as a kook not deserving of my time, or maybe further lowering my price to my own disadvantage.

- Don't fall into the trap of thinking because it is an "informal" medium that you can forget rules of grammar or get away with lackadaisical writing skills. If anything, it is *more* important than in other mediums, because the classic devices of formality—letterhead, signature, and so on—are missing.
- Be aware that many companies have spam filters or virus protection software to protect their "intranet" or internal networks from receiving unsolicited mail. If you choose to use a commercially available software for e-mailing advertisements or newsletters, they may not be received by the intended target due to it being "trapped in a security net" by the client's company.

Advertising Copy and Writing Sales Materials

We tend to think of advertising as the printed notices in periodicals, written by professional copywriters in the advertising industry. All those items we have been discussing are advertising, however, and the principles enunciated here apply to all of them.

The mark of the amateur writer and the kiss of death in advertising copy is overwriting, especially extravagant use of laudatory adjectives and adverbs, superlatives, and other hyperbole. The novice copywriter apparently reasons that readers will accept any claim that is outrageous enough and repeated often enough. We find brochures peppered with such words and terms as these:

expert/expertise	adept	renowned	worldwide
highest standards	leading	tremendous	unique
remarkable	superb	sensational	outstanding
national authority	peerless	unmatched	incredible

Not one of these terms is objective. Without exception, they mirror opinions, claims, bias. Perhaps such words were effective once, in a less sophisticated time, but today they are an assault on one's senses and intelligence. Today's reader hardly pauses over such words or pays them any heed. In fact, if today's reader thinks about it at all, it is merely to snort in disbelief at such Madison-Avenuese (or Hollywoodese?). Such words are virtually invisible to readers, because of overuse; we read past them at speeds exceeding that of light, which Einsteinian physics assures us, makes them vanish from view!

10 | The New Marketing

Extraordinary times call for extraordinary measures in marketing, as they do in other areas of business. Thus, your marketing, as an independent consultant, must be enhanced—buttressed in some way—to cope with the times. Increased marketing aggressiveness is one approach. New and better marketing ideas are another.

We are, at this writing, still in the throes of the terrorist attacks of September 11, 2001, and the resultant impact of that horrific event on the world economy. The airline industry has been significantly impacted, tourism is down, and companies are behaving in far less optimistic ways than they were in the mid-1990s. Senior management at high profile firms (WorldCom, Enron, Ahold, etc.) have come under attack for actions that, if not strictly criminal, have been widely criticized as being motivated by self-interest and not by the common good of shareholders or employees. The post "dot-bomb" era has seen a general slowdown of the economy. Despite the efforts of the U.S. government to facilitate consumer confidence through reduced interest rates and tax reductions, recovery has been slow, uneven, and almost invariably behind the predictions.

Typically, the economy is in constant cyclical movements, and the alert entrepreneur must always be aware of these movements and react accordingly. Still, it is a strange kind of economic situation today: Unemployment is distressingly high, with layoffs in even the largest corporations continuing—the euphemism *downsizing* is currently in vogue to describe this spreading trend—retail sales are disappointing, bankruptcies are frequent, foreclosures are at a high rate, and there is a growing excess of space in new office buildings. (*Overbuilding* is a word used today to describe this condition.) Nevertheless, there are paradoxes: Prices are still rising for many commodities and services, and inflation has been slowed but not halted. At the same time, many new jobs are being created, but not in enough numbers to absorb all the entrants into the labor force or reduce the overall rate of unemployment.

RECESSION OR "ADJUSTMENT"

Perhaps we are misreading the signals and do not understand what is happening. Perhaps this is not a recession at all, but an adjustment from the abnormal prosperity of the past few decades, especially the past decade. If this is the case, we may never return to these conditions; perhaps this more modest growth and increased need for competitiveness are normal economic conditions for the nineties. In any case, it is a good idea to operate on this premise, for the signs seem to be clear enough: We are in a more straitened economic condition than at any time in the recent past. We must thus, each of us, pay more attention than ever to marketing and surviving.

THE GOOD NEWS

The news is not all bad. One silver lining for consultants is the current reluctance of many employers to recruit new employees, even when workloads appear to be increasing. That is a natural consequence of recession and reservations about—bearishness in—estimates of long-term workloads. It is also an advantage for consultants willing to work on the client's premises; many employers now see advantages in turning to temporaries and independent consultants to see them through short-term peaks or special projects. The availability of independent consultants/contractors represents labor pools that can be turned on and off at short notice with a minimum of the start-up and phase-down costs that are always a problem in recruiting or terminating permanent employees. This job shopping or temporary work (and temporary is relative, for some of the assignments last for months and even years) has been mentioned earlier and will be discussed again. However, there are other considerations, including data-based marketing, the essence of what has been called by some the new marketing.

WHAT'S WRONG WITH THE "OLD" MARKETING

Just as mass production was the key to producing a superabundance of goods that most of us could afford, mass marketing was the way to sell those goods, and it also became the way to sell many services. Several media are used for mass marketing. The principal ones are broadcast: radio and TV; print advertising: newspapers and magazines; and direct mail. Mass marketing was effective, and it was cheap. A tiny return, often as little as a fraction of one percent of the prospects reached, produced enough sales to make the campaign profitable.

But now, the cost has changed. Postage, printing, airtime, and all the other costs have skyrocketed. It is increasingly difficult to make a marketing campaign successful with only miniscule response rates. With today's costs, it is increasingly difficult to absorb the waste that has been an accepted condition of mass marketing.

As mentioned previously, e-mail has filled the marketing void fairly cost efficiently in many instances, but there are other efforts underway that point to a change in how marketing is done. Concepts of "one-to-one marketing" or targeting consumers or businesses based on their specific or unique purchase habits or previous performance (think of www.amazon.com and their approach to suggesting possible books or other products to you each time you click on their site). Another example of this is the proliferation of Loyalty Cards or Frequent Shopper Cards at retailers. By collecting minimal amounts of data about each of us and then tracking our purchase habits, stores can tailor their coupons or other offers to us to match the lifestyle or life stage we may be in, or base it on the product categories we purchase.

IS MASS MARKETING DEAD?

Some enthusiasts of databased marketing pronounce mass marketing moribund, if not expired. That probably overstates the case. In fact, it probably misstates the case: Mass marketing is not moribund, and it is not going to die, but it is going to change. It must change, and databased marketing points the way. Where the targeting for classic mass marketing was broad—the appearance of your name on a list of those who had bought a set of golf clubs or a package of golf balls was enough to ensure that you would get golf-oriented literature, even if you had bought the clubs as a present and never ventured onto a golf course yourself. Mailers were flying blindly, with limited knowledge of how likely it was that the average individual on the list or in the audience would become a buyer. The new mass marketing will put your name on the list only if you are known to be a golfer. In short, the mass in mass marketing will be a smaller mass because the individuals on the list will be much more highly qualified—the targeting will be far more precise. Databased marketing produces greater information about each individual and so raises the response rate by reducing the waste.

WHY CONSULTING IS NOT SOLD VIA MASS MARKETING

Consulting services cannot normally be sold by conventional mass marketing. At the same time, databased marketing is appropriate enough, possibly even especially appropriate, for most independent consultants. It is based on the idea of having enough *individual* information about each of our clients and prospective clients to target our sales appeals more closely than ever before. The possibilities are even more diverse and sophisticated than that; there are several aspects or possible outcomes:

- You can tailor your presentations to the client—find common elements that will permit you to create a presentation for everyone listed in your database.
- You can select those in your database who represent the best prospects and address them especially.
- You can tailor your services/products to the interests of those in your database, or tailor services/products to various subgroups in the database.
- You can use the information to develop a profile of your ideal client, and, thus your best prospective client. This becomes an excellent marketing tool.
- You can define one or more market segments or niche markets that are well suited to your needs and what you offer. That is one of the most important uses of databased marketing.

THE MARKETING DATABASE

You cannot rent a marketing database, as you might rent a mailing list; you must build your own. It will contain the usual fields for name, address, and other data, but it must provide for many other fields—data you can use for marketing. It should be a relational database, rather than a flat file type, for reasons that will become apparent shortly, as we discuss the kinds of information. You may decide that you ought to build and maintain more than one marketing database, but, for purposes of discussion, we will assume that one marketing database will serve your needs. The marketing database is the heart of the strategy.

Clients versus Prospects

The original idea underlying databased marketing was to build a database with detailed information relevant to each individual's needs and preferences vis-à-vis buying whatever you sell. When you read what others say on the subject, you are likely to find all discussions focused on databases of existing customers.

That focus is of great use to those who sell a diverse set of products or services, and those whose success depends on repeat business with established customers. It has rather limited application to those who sell only a few narrowly defined services, and especially to those whose services are typically one-time purchases by clients—clients who will need your services infrequently and perhaps only once or twice in their lives. For that reason alone, but also for other reasons, the marketing database should not be confined to clients only, but should include prospects who appear to be likely clients.

Kinds of Information

The information in the database should be data released to marketing what you sell, but restricted to that—if you sell computer services, you are not interested in the individual's preferences in literature and education. That is why you must build your own marketing database; it must be tailored precisely to your own needs. You want to know what each prospect feels a need for, prefers to buy, likes and dislikes, is motivated by, and whatever else furnishes clues for your marketing.

Here are just a few kinds of information typical for any marketing database, insofar as they pertain to what you market:

- Demographic data and lifestyle—age, occupation, income level, and so on.
- Purchasing history—purchases from you or others, relevant to your own services.
- Hobbies, outside interests.
- Memberships.

Sources of Information

There are many sources of information. You already have some information on established clients because you have done business with them. You probably have invoice files, for example, and perhaps logs, copies of reports, and personal recall from casual or formal conversations. You may very well have information about your clients in several different files (hopefully, all computer files). That is why a relational database is best: You then have no need to duplicate information in the marketing database, but can simply summon it up from other files.

The best source for information is the individual. Organizations most actively engaged in building extensive marketing databases take the initiative in encouraging input from customers and prospects. They do so by asking for relevant information when customers and others send for rebates, enter contests, join clubs, request free goods offered (e.g., recipes), and whenever there is an opportunity for any kind of dialogue with customers and prospective customers.

If you have a newsletter, use it to gather information for your marketing database. If you run a booth or exhibit at a trade show, think up some device to gather starting data from each visitor. Think of other ways to elicit information for your marketing database. You can gather information by passive means through secondary sources, but the most valuable information comes to you only through proactive measures you take to provoke the information directly from the individual. In effect, you are asking, "What must I do to do business with you?"

Market Segments and Niche Markets

As your marketing database grows, use it to discover market segments or niche markets, two names for the same thing. (Advertising people tend to talk about market segments, whereas marketers tend to talk about niche markets.) This alone justifies the work of building a marketing database; it identifies the smaller and more efficient mass for modern marketing. Often, it also identifies the market that has lain undiscovered. You may find, for example, that your best clients are always businesses of a certain size or nature. Focusing your marketing efforts on businesses matching that description may quadruple your effectiveness, as it did for me when I discovered that small software-development firms were my best clients for proposal-writing and proposal-seminar services. The effectiveness of all business activity, especially marketing, depends on the quantity and quality of the information upon which decisions are based—the *available* information, that is. Most of us never realize how much we base our judgments and actions on hunches, rather than on real data. Databased marketing allows us to base decisions on data instead of intuition, and the payoff is new and profitable markets.

NETWORKING FOR CLIENTS

The term *networking* is fairly new, although the concept is old, and is used to refer to a method for marketing oneself—for salaried jobs, as well as for independent ventures, although we are concerned here with the latter. Networking is complex enough to justify some discussion.

A large number of consultants report that their principal method of advertising and their principal source of new business is word of mouth—recommendations from one individual to another. The stimulus for such person-to-person recommendation is usually unknown to them. They like to think that they are being recommended because of the superior quality of what they do and sell, and perhaps because they are regarded as honest, fair, and honorable. Probably there is no single cause, but many causes; your superior performance and professional behavior are undoubtedly key factors. In others, it is the result of your having been warm and friendly; many people are impressed by that, whereas they really have no basis for judging how good you are at what you do. But in a surprising number of cases, it is pure chance; someone who needs help does not know where to turn and welcomes any recommendation from any source. I have been amazed at how often someone who does not know me, but has only heard of me, will recommend me to someone else.

That is not to demean the beneficiaries of such serendipitous recommendations, but only to place the situation into a reference frame of reality. That is, such marketing is marketing by chance, and its success is in direct proportion to the state of the economy, the tenure of your consulting practice, and the degree to which you and your reputation have become known—the level of your visibility. It works, to a degree, but it is probably hazardous to rely on this chance method if your practice is still rather new and not yet well established. These times call for more organized, more regimented, more controlled conditions.

Networking can be pursued via casual or directed means. Both work, although probably with different degrees of effectiveness. At the same time, whether you pursue formal, organized networking or informal, casual networking depends on your own needs. Let's have a look at each.

Informal, Casual Networking

Informal or casual networking is carried out by:

- Belonging to and being active in associations and local organizations—business clubs—where you meet and associate with prospective clients or with those who may recommend you to prospective clients.
- Appearing at conventions, symposiums, and other gatherings and meeting with prospective clients and with those who can recommend you to prospective clients.
- Being a guest speaker at seminars and other occasions where you can make yourself known as a professional and consultant in your field.
- Being active in community affairs and becoming well known locally as the expert and consultant in whatever you do.

Networking in this manner requires no special effort, beyond what you would probably do anyway—belonging to associations and being generally gregarious and friendly. It requires no special allotment of time, money, or attention. The downside is that it is largely a chance method.

Formal, Organized Networking

It is possible to organize your networking and make a formal practice of it. The formal method is usually based on gathering special groups of individuals for the sole purpose of joining or creating a network. For example, entrepreneur Jerry Rubin (once a prominent "Yippie," along with the late Abbie Hoffman) organized network meetings at the famous Club 52 in New York. Each individual paid a fee to attend, and the club on New York's 52nd Street offered a bar and many places to sit and chat. The idea was to hand out your business cards and brochures freely, jot notes as you met others who might be in a position to recommend you to someone immediately, or would keep you in mind for future recommendation. The goal was to meet and chat with as many people as possible during the course of the evening, exchanging information of mutual interest for business and professional reasons (not social ones).

If you cannot find a group that is suitable for you, organize your own or get together with some acquaintances to organize a starter group. (The gatherings are called mixers, for obvious reasons, since mixing is their prime purpose.) If you are doing this with the help of personal acquaintances, each of you should be handing out invitations to attract people to the group, or you may be able to advertise the group and the event, as Rubin did. (He used direct mail.) If you have a computer and modem, you can get coverage by placing notices on electronic bulletin boards and urging readers to proliferate the notices to other bulletin boards. You may have a notice printed and post it in supermarkets, public libraries, and other public places.

The pros of this method are principally the controllability and the intensity of the networking; it will probably produce more results and produce them more rapidly than the informal methods. However, it does require time and effort, and perhaps money (although you may choose to ask for admittance fees to cover costs).

MISCELLANEOUS MARKETING CONSIDERATIONS

Newsletter Publishing

The idea of publishing a newsletter has been raised before (even in this chapter) and will be raised and discussed again in these pages. There are several ways in which newsletters and the publishing of newsletters become a subject of interest in connection with consulting. You might, for example, publish a newsletter of your own as a marketing tool.

Newsletter publishing may not be for everyone, but it can be used effectively for marketing in any serious business venture or professional practice. To an independent consultant, it is a means for establishing and maintaining contact with clients and prospective clients. (As we have mentioned in connection with databased marketing activities, a newsletter is also an excellent method for obtaining feedback from clients and prospects to help build your marketing databases.) In general, a newsletter is better than a brochure or salesletter because people rarely discard a newsletter without glancing through it for items of interest. The details of publishing a newsletter are covered elsewhere. Too, you do not necessarily have to create your own newsletter: You can buy newsletters published by others, have your own name imprinted, and even include material of your own so that you do not have to create the newsletter every month (or at whatever frequency you choose). Whichever method you use, do consider a newsletter for marketing purposes.

Seminars

There are many ways to promote your practice; one is giving seminars. Like newsletters, the subject of seminars is covered in other chapters; this mention is merely to point out that seminar presentations are an excellent marketing tool for consulting services. Bear that in mind as you read the various discussions of seminars elsewhere in these chapters.

Booths and Exhibits

Engaging a booth and presenting an exhibit at conventions and other such occasions is a workable marketing tool for many consultants. If you choose the right occasion, you will be able to do a great deal of prospecting for new clients. You can hand out business cards, brochures, newsletters, and sundry other marketing and sales materials. You may also, in some cases, be able to gather a small crowd for a miniseminar several times a day, while you gather names and addresses of prospects.

BROKERS, JOB SHOPS, SUBCONTRACTS, AND THE IRS

One way to win clients and contracts is via middlemen—brokers, that is—and many independent consultants turn to that expedient, because they dislike marketing or for other reasons. There are, however, problems in this, problems that affect one's very status as an independent consultant, and even that ancient problem of how one defines consulting and consultants.

The very word *consultant,* especially *independent consultant,* is not easy to define because it has more than one definition. Independent consultants work under a wide variety of conditions. Some hire themselves out as technical and professional temporaries, working on the client's premises. Some undertake contracts and subcontracts, and work on either their own or the clients' premises, according to the individual project. Some find projects independently or for themselves, while others use brokers to find the projects or assignments, make all the arrangements, and take a brokerage fee for themselves. Some specialize in working under just one of these methods, while others employ all the methods, as opportunities and/or needs arise. Thus, an independent consultant may be just that: a consultant. But he or she may also be a technical or professional temporary, an independent contractor or subcontractor, or some hybrid of these.

Even this does not fully explain the complexities. Certain legal questions, centering on taxes and tax liabilities, arise and have their own effects. They do not have an impact on consulting and contracting generally, but they do have a pronounced impact on independent consulting and independent contracting.

Four terms in common use are *independent consultant, independent contractor, job shop,* and *broker.* These terms have been used here before and will be again, but unless we clarify them now, confusion will result. Despite my experience with the functions referred to by these terms, I was confused for a time because these terms do not mean the same things to all people, in all situations, or in all places. Hence, the need to clarify them. We will also introduce a new term, *Technical Services Firm* or TSF.

The subject of job shops and brokers is very much a part of the world of independent consultants and contractors. It is difficult, however, to discriminate between the two terms. The need to be absolutely clear about these matters is important enough for us to tolerate some repetition here.

Job Shops and Brokers

The term *job shop* originally referred to small machine-tool shops who undertook small jobs—subcontracts—to manufacture or process small parts, such as to grind down or polish a rough casting. (One of my clients was a small job shop in the South Bronx, New York, who retained me to help write a proposal for a contract to manufacture tail fin assemblies for a missile used by the Navy.) The term was later borrowed and is now used to identify suppliers of technical/professional temporaries—engineers, programmers, designers, writers, and others. (Some suppliers, who don't like the term *job shop,* prefer to call themselves *labor contractors.*) The job shop recruits skilled individuals, puts them on the job shop's payroll, and assigns them to work on the client's premises, just as in the case of office temporaries. That is the mode of operation for job shops: The consultant assigned to a project by a job shop is an employee of the job shop and receives limited hospitalization, leave, and other benefits.

In some cases, suppliers of temporary specialists operate as brokers or prime contractors. Instead of hiring the specialists, the broker writes a prime contract with the client and subcontracts with each individual consultant specialist to work on the client's premises, ordinarily at an hourly rate, and usually with little defined beyond this. This nominally makes the consultant an independent contractor, solely responsible for taxes, hospitalization, and other overhead costs. At least, that is the intention and presumption under that arrangement.

Generally speaking, the firms who provide consultants as independent subcontractors are called *brokers,* but they may be known also as job shops. In neither case is the shop responsible for producing a product; they are responsible only for producing bodies—specialists to work on-site for the client. That is a significant factor, for it creates what many refer to as *body shops.*

For the consultant, the consideration in turning to a broker or job shop is marketing. Using job shops and brokers means freedom from marketing for oneself, although it also means a much reduced degree of independence. (Working for a job shop means even less independence than subcontracting to a broker.) For that reason, many independent consultants shun brokers and job shops, unless they cannot avoid it. (Some consultants I interviewed took pride in saying that they never used brokers or job shops, but always did their own marketing and found their own clients and projects.) Marketing is often the most difficult task facing the independent consultants, driving them into the arms of middlemen. That, however, is not the issue here: A more important question arises as a result of IRS enforcement of Section 1706 of the Tax Reform Act of 1986, a subject we will take up in a moment. It threatens the consultant's status as an independent operator.

In the meanwhile, the term itself, broker or job shop, is not significant; the contractual arrangement is. One makes the independent consultant an employee; the other makes him or her an independent contractor. As an independent contractor—IC—the consultant is legally entitled to have an overhead and deduct expenses for travel, tools, marketing, office expenses, equipment, and other legitimate overhead items. As somebody's employee, however, whether temporary or permanent, the consultant can deduct none of these.

IRS and Section 1706

The IRS resists recognizing consultants working full time on the client's premises as contractors or subcontractors entitled to take deductions for overhead. The IRS has disallowed IC status regularly for consultants in this kind of work situation, especially when the assignment, while technically temporary, is actually long term—months and even years. The IRS regards such consultants as employees, temporary perhaps, but W2 employees nevertheless, who must have taxes deducted and who are not entitled to file tax returns in which they deduct the normal overhead items of any business owner.

A major disadvantage is that the consultant is denied the right to deduct a variety of business expenses, but that is not the argument the IRS raised in lobbying for the passage of Section 1706 of the Tax Reform Act of 1986. Instead, the IRS argued that compliance would be greater if consultants were recognized only as employees from whose salaries taxes had to be withheld. They assumed that independent contractors could not be relied upon to pay their taxes, and, thus, the chief justification for 1706 was to ensure compliance.

The law permits the IRS to apply 20 tests to determine the status of the consultant as an independent contractor or employee under the provisions of the Act. Some of the indications that the individual is an employee, rather than an IC, are that the individual is, has, or does the following:

- Has only one client.
- Works entirely on the client's premises.
- Is obligated only on the basis of hours to be available on the job (has no mission statement and deliverable item specified).
- May be terminated immediately and arbitrarily by the client.
- Takes orders during the day from the client or client's staff.

These and the remaining items are taken as indicators of employee status, and that conclusion does appear reasonable enough, at least superficially.

Indicators that the individual is truly an independent contractor are that the individual is, has, or does the following:

- Is incorporated as a business.
- Has several sources of income from business operations.
- Keeps formal time, expense, and income records.
- Maintains a formal business office.

- Is contracted to deliver a specified end product.
- Works at least part of the time in own facilities.

Some consultants report that incorporating their practices has made it easier to satisfy the IRS that they are, in fact, independent consultants and independent contractors. Others report that the IRS does not accept incorporation alone as prima facie evidence of independent status, but looks for other supporting evidence. Some consultants have reported being required to fill out a 16-page document to prove their independent status. One consultant reported that the IRS was not satisfied even by the fact that he maintained offices in commercial space and employed several people!

As a result, brokers have become more and more bearish about using technical/professional specialists on a contracting or subcontracting basis. Many brokers have turned to hiring the consultants as W2 employees, rather than as 1099 subcontractors. Thus, to work as an independent contractor via a broker today is increasingly difficult. All of this applies to clients also, with respect to contracting directly with consultants; they are equally apprehensive where there seems to be a clear possibility that they may have to wrangle with the IRS.

Under the provisions of 1706, it does not matter whether you subcontract with a broker or contract directly with a client for your services. The Act treats both cases equally and requires the same bona fides in either case.

There appears to be some regional influence. In some areas of the country, many independent consultants are subcontracting via brokers and maintaining a 1099 status with no apparent difficulty, whereas in other areas—Phoenix, Arizona, for example—consultants report virtually all such work done as W2 employees only.

TECHNICAL SERVICES FIRMS

In addition to job shops and brokers, there is another category that is of interest. It is the Technical Services Firm, which many consultants refer to as a TSF. That kind of firm does accept project responsibility and contracts to produce a specific result, a defined deliverable item. If you are yourself a TSF or subcontract with one of these, you have a much stronger argument to prove IC status, even if you are assigned to work on the client's premises, for you have contracted to help produce some specific item, and you take your orders from the prime contractor and not from the client.

11 | Marketing to the Public Sector: Federal, State, and Local Government

American governments are not only the biggest buyers in the world; they are also the biggest buyers of consulting services and certainly a major market.

A BRIEF GLIMPSE OF GOVERNMENT MARKETS

Despite cutbacks, federal agencies make over 15 million purchases and spend nearly $200 billion annually. That does not cover everything; there are government corporations whose procurement is off budget and not included in official reports of the Office of Federal Procurement Policy. The U.S. Postal Service, which employs over 700,000 people (although the current postmaster general has announced an impending cutback), spends (approximately) an unreported $20+ billion for salaries, goods, and services every year. Federal procurement is thus in excess of even the $210+ billion reported.

Even that great number is dwarfed by the aggregate of state and local government spending for goods and services. The federal government consists of 14 departments, some 60 independent agencies, and several dozen assorted bureaus, commissions, and other organizations. Each of these is divided further into subordinate agencies, so that the total begins to approach 2,000. Moreover, most of these have offices throughout the United States, offices that do most of their buying independently. State and local governments present this staggering array of what the U.S. Census Bureau (1998) refers to as governmental units:

State governments:	50
Counties:	3,043
Municipalities:	19,372
Townships:	16,629
Local school districts:	13,726
Special districts:	34,683

Each of these lower-level government entities has its own complement of bureaus, agencies, and institutions, often rivaling the federal establishment in number and size. That makes it easier to understand why this array of government agencies together spends twice as much as the federal government, even today in a much straitened general economy, with public budgets much tighter. Still, we are talking about more than $640 billion annually in government purchasing, a significant portion of that for various consulting services.

WHAT GOVERNMENTS BUY

The nature of public purchasing has changed a great deal in this century. Once, governments represented markets for public works primarily: construction of streets, highways, bridges, dams, and public buildings, except in wartime, when needs would change. Today, there are few goods or services the governments do not buy, even in peacetime, and in many cases the governments are the only customers for certain items. Who else will rent mules and handlers today or issue contracts for baggers in military supermarkets?

Even after significant cuts in military spending due to shifts over the last few years in the public's perception of its importance over social welfare programs that were believed to have higher relevance and priority to most taxpayers, it still represents the highest percentage of governmental purchasing and is a fertile ground for many consulting projects for the consultant that meets the criteria established by the government for contracting with consulting organizations. Aside from that, the procurement practices of state and local governments do not differ much from those of the federal government. Here are a few typical public procurements:

R&D (research and development) projects	ADP services
Insect and disease control	Program evaluation
Crime prevention and control	Studies and surveys
Communications	Technology transfer
Education	Operations research
Housing	Public relations
Health services	Training
Social services	

HOW GOVERNMENTS BUY

Some agencies have permanent or semipermanent requirements and authorization for consultants, usually some specific number of slots. For example, one office in OSHA (Occupational Safety and Health Administration, Department of Labor), for whom I did considerable work, had three consultant slots authorized and had three consultants devoting three days a week each to the office. I had won several small projects there, but my major project for OSHA was to occupy my full time for eight months, working on government premises. They furnished me office space, a typewriter, and secretarial services—a not-unusual arrangement.

Government agencies may need consultants for almost any kind of work, including work that most organizations carry out with their regular employees. Governments, however, are generally motivated by political considerations more than efficiency. Here, to illustrate this, are a few examples of consulting work I have been involved in or observed, despite the fact that the work is similar to that ordinarily handled by regular employees:

- Public information/PR services (including, in some cases, running the entire public information office).
- Developing work statements and other elements of requests for proposals (especially when the work is highly specialized in some respect).
- Reviewing, evaluating, and scoring proposals received (again, especially when the work is highly technical or greatly specialized).
- Answering government's mail and telephones.
- Managing the administering government correspondence courses.
- Operating government facilities, such as computer systems, laboratories, training establishments, and warehouses.

THE PROCUREMENT SYSTEM

All bureaucracies are given to excesses. In the case of our own, at least one excess is an overabundance of supply categories. The general supply groups in the federal system, a system closely emulated by most state and local governments, number over 200, with many subcategories. As one consequence, the total of consulting services is obscured; by far the majority of such services and not called consulting, although the government is a major purchaser of all and sundry technical and professional services. (It is difficult to judge which category is most suitable for listing a given requirement, so the decision is often arbitrary and may surprise you.) Study the *Commerce Business Daily*, the federal government's daily announcement of the agencies' needs and lists of solicitation packages available. You soon discover that consulting services are solicited under a number of categories, these especially:

- Experimental, developmental, test, and research work.
- Expert and consultant services.
- Technical representative services.
- Architect-engineer services.
- Photographic, mapping, printing, and publication services.
- Training services.
- Miscellaneous.

That is not all; many of the needs listed under other categories actually call for consulting services. So you are likely to find opportunities for government consulting contracts listed under even these categories:

- Maintenance and repair of equipment.
- Modification, alteration, and rebuilding of equipment.
- Operation and maintenance of government-owned facility.

- Installation of equipment.
- Funeral and chaplain services.
- Salvage services.
- Medical services.
- Training aids and devices.
- General purpose automated data processing (ADP) equipment, software, supplies, and support equipment.

Basic Procurement Philosophy

The aim of all public purchasing is selection by competition, which is the basic philosophy of our free enterprise system. This is theoretically the fairest way to afford everyone an equal opportunity to win a share of government business, while it supposedly keeps suppliers honest and assures the government the best possible prices and quality. As with all systems, it is less than perfect but it is, on the whole, a clean system that achieves its main objectives reasonably well, despite the occasional procurement horrors reported in the press. Whatever scandals we do have concerning government procurement are much more scandals of bureaucratic inefficiency and stupidity, rather than venality and corruption.

Procurement officials would prefer to make all purchasing price competitive, with sealed bids and awards to the lowest bidders. Unfortunately, this is not possible, and is impracticable in a growing number of procurements, for reasons that become apparent on reflection.

The humorist observes wryly that no one wants to fly in a plane built by the lowest bidder. But wry or not, the statement sums up the situation; price is only one consideration in these times of ever-more complex and sophisticated systems, and it is a secondary consideration where there are other important factors to consider such as safety, quality, performance, durability, reliability, maintainability, practicality or viability of plan, ability to perform, and all the other items that must be appraised as figures of merit, rather than as absolutes. Nor is it only the military, with their tanks, missile systems, and sophisticated equipment, who must be concerned with these other factors in making their purchases. Concern for technical quality applies everywhere, since governments buy food, medical supplies, computers, and many items where factors other than price are critically important. This same concern applies to the procurement of services.

The ability-to-perform qualification is especially important. Too often, even with all the safeguards, government agencies have found their contractors unable to perform satisfactorily. They therefore usually scrutinize proposals most carefully for evidence of the proposer's ability to perform. That makes this evidence a most important element in your proposals and sometimes the essential key to success.

Specifications

Many people believe that the biggest problem in doing business with the government is the difficulty of meeting government specifications. The fact is, even military specifications—really the main source of that complaint—are far less onerous today than they once were. Ironically enough, when it comes to most negotiated procurements, the lack of specifications is often a problem. When the government cannot furnish detailed specifications, the contract must be negotiated, rather than awarded to a lowest bidder. In this situation, the government needs your recommendation and asks you to furnish the specifications in proposing a project to satisfy the need. If the government could furnish detailed specifications, it would be less costly and more efficient all around to invite sealed bids rather than proposals.

Sometimes this inability to furnish specifications is inherent in the nature of the requirement, as when the need is for an R&D project or for pure research and fact finding. But it may also be a reflection of the lack of suitably specialized knowledge or skills on the part of the client. And, in at least some cases, the client knows how the job can be or is usually done, but wants to examine as many innovative ideas as possible before deciding which is the best.

This results in two kinds of competition: There is the typical and classic price competition of the familiar sealed bid; but there is also the quality or technical competition embodied in the request for proposals and subsequent technical evaluation. There are some variants—hybrids—but all are based on these two competitive parameters, with technical factors increasingly reflected in the criteria for evaluation and selection. Hence, the importance of proposals: For clients, it is the role of proposals in helping to select capable consultants. For consultants, it is the importance of knowledge and skills necessary to writing successful proposals. More and more procurements by clients in private and public sectors require studies and recommendations; the competition is growing. Consequently, of the two ways governments buy most goods and services—via sealed bids and via proposals—you will almost always find it necessary to write proposals to win contracts. In recognition of this truth, an entire chapter is dedicated to the subject of proposals later in this book.

Special Cases

There are some special cases, such as small purchases—up to $25,000 each in the federal system, somewhat less at state and local levels—for which there are special, simplified procedures. There are also provisions for emergencies, when the agency's need is urgent and there is not enough time for the usual procurement procedures. Too, some procurements are set aside for small businesses, meaning that only small businesses as defined by the Small Business Administration are permitted to compete. These and other aspects of public purchasing are covered by regulations.

Procurement Regulations

There were once three sets of procurement regulations for the military, the civilian agencies, and a special set for NASA, plus thousands of bulletins and memoranda having the effect of regulations. It has all (or nearly all) been combined, merged, revised, and reduced to a single set, the Federal Acquisition Regulations (FAR), which, in turn, was modified by additional procurement legislation, such as the Competition in Contracting Act. The superabundance of regulations tends to nullify control and order: With so many regulations to resort to and choose from, a determined procurement official can usually discover regulations that authorize or appear to authorize almost anything he or she wants to do, even if it means stretching the law a bit. However, although there are exceptions, there are a few basic principles embodied in the federal regulations and reflected in the regulations of state and local governments. First, the principal provisions of regulations covering sealed bids (also known as advertised or formally advertised procurements):

- Bids must be delivered to the place specified by the time specified. Late bids must be rejected.
- Sealed bids are opened publicly. Anyone may attend and witness the bids being opened and read aloud. The contracting official scans each bid for compliance with the regulations.
- Awards are made to the lowest qualified bidder in each case. (This is not done at the bid opening, but only after the contracting official has reviewed each bid and verified compliance with regulations and qualifications of the bidder—that the bidder has not been barred or suspended from bidding.)

Compare this with the basics of what the government now officially calls procurement by competitive proposals (formerly referred to as negotiated procurement):

- Proposals must be delivered as specified by the time specified. Late proposals are to be rejected.
- Cost information must be provided in a separate proposal, and may not be given in the main (technical) proposal.
- Technical evaluation must be made of each proposal by some objective rating scheme, which must be described to the proposers, along with the impact of cost figures in evaluation, as part of the information in the solicitation.
- The government is free to negotiate with proposers after proposal evaluation, and may require supplements, presentations, or other additional inputs before reaching a decision.

Government representatives may opt to visit your premises to verify that you have the facilities and resources to perform. This can be extended to include a pre-award audit to confirm the acceptability of your accounting system and/or your financial stability. (This is not often done for small contracts, however.)

Appeals and Protests

You are always free to appeal or protest an award decision. It is usually of little use to do so in a sealed-bid procurement, since the rules are so simple and clear, unless you wish to argue that the low bid should have been disqualified or unless you have had your own bid disqualified. (It is difficult to disqualify a sealed bid unless the bidder has failed to sign the bid or made some other gross error.) On the other hand, protests of award decisions based on competitive proposals are common, and sometimes they are successful.

The procedure is quite simple because it is an administrative appeal, not an action at law. To protest a competitive proposal, simply write to the contracting official or, in the case of the federal government, to the Comptroller General of the United States, who is also head of the General Accounting Office (GAO). The letter may be informal and should set forth the basis of your complaint. This action, regardless of how it turns out, in no way compromises you or your further actions. You can even go ahead and sue in the courts, if you wish to. (Some large organizations protest quite routinely and sue occasionally.)

Many pages document government procurement policies, procedures, and controls, but it is not necessary to become a guardhouse lawyer, to do business with the governments. You should, however, know the general policies and procedures.

Types of Contracts

Government contracts are usually of only two basic types: fixed price and cost reimbursement, although there are many variants and hybrids of these. Just as contracting officials prefer sealed-bid purchasing whenever possible, they also usually prefer fixed-price contracts. But that is not always possible because of the many uncertainties, such as the following:

- *Indefinite quantities.* The government often does not know how many or how much of something will be needed. This is especially in case when someone is awarded an annual supply contract for goods or services. The contract fixes the rate(s) and the period for which they are to apply, but leaves the total open.
- *Research and development.* R&D is almost impossible to predict or estimate with any certainty.
- *Surveys and studies.* The rational is the same as for R&D.
- *Phased projects,* in which each phase is evaluated before deciding on the next one.

Cost-reimbursement contracts are, therefore, of the well-known cost-plus fee, time-and-material, basic-ordering-agreement, call, task-order, and labor-hour types. These are all similar because all are indefinite quantities.

The government also uses purchase orders, which are a specialized form of contract, for small purchases—not more than $25,000 in the federal system, and with lower ceilings in most state and local governments. Technically, a purchase order is a contract, but it is a far simpler way of handling the paperwork of contracting.

Purchase orders may be used to contract for individual tasks, under the Small Purchases Act and the procurement regulations that apply to small purchases, but they may also be used to authorize each individual task under an annual contract with a consultant.

MARKET RESEARCH

It has been said that the biggest difficulty in selling to the government is finding the doors. Although the government market is highly competitive in general, there are many cases in which there is little or no competition. That is especially so for small purchases made with simplified procedures. In the small-purchases milieu, advertising of a procurement is limited; for a large class of small purchases, even that limited amount of advertising is now required. Ergo, finding the doors means finding, bidding/negotiating, and winning contracts that won't be formally advertised or before they are advertised. It is possible to do a good bit of government contracting this way.

Aside from that, there are provisions for noncompetitive procurement when the normal time requirement for awarding a contract competitively cannot be tolerated or when what is required can be gotten from only one source—a proprietary item that is unique—or an unsolicited proposal that has been accepted. (These are sole sources or selected source procurements.)

Making a Start: Studying the Federal Marketplace

Most of us find those doors gradually, as we spend time in marketing to the government and become acquainted with government organizations and the individuals in them. It is possible to begin by the traditional knocking on doors or cold calls on government offices. (They are listed in your local telephone directory under *U.S., Government of.*) Probably the best initial research is done at your own desk with the *Commerce Business Daily* (CBD), however, studying the federal government market. Most state and local governments tend to emulate it, so the federal market and procurement system is a good model.

Studying the announcements (synopses of current requirements and opportunities), you can become familiar with the federal agencies and what they buy. You can send for many of the solicitation packages and study them. Study also the awards section, wherein you will learn of contracts awarded, which is also valuable market intelligence.

You can order the paper copy of the CBD from the Government Printing Office (GPO), who prints it, or from the Department of Commerce, who is the publisher. It is mailed to you daily, but the postal service being what it is, it is a rare issue of the CBD that reached you before it is from three days to an entire week old. Fortunately, there is an alternative, one that brings you the CBD on the day of its publication. The CBD is not available in an online edition, called CBD Online, from several sources (online databases will be identified later in these pages). If you have a personal computer and a modem, you can arrange to get this edition easily.

Once you begin to perceive which agencies are likely to be your best prospects, you can begin to file copies of Standard Form 129, Application for Bidders List. You need to file a copy of this form with the contracting office of each agency with whom you wish to do business. This form tells the contracting officer what solicitations are likely to be of interest to and bring responses from you. You will then be listed on each agency's bidders list and receive many solicitations—invitations to bid or propose—without asking specifically for them.

You can also visit contracting offices periodically and ask about current requirements. You will be given the opportunity to examine file copies of current solicitations. In fact, the larger procurement offices often have a separate room, a bid room, with copies of current solicitations posted on a bulletin board.

There are at least two other measures you can take to familiarize yourself with the federal system. The Small Business Administration (SBA) operates approximately 90 offices in the United States, so it is likely that there is one listed in your telephone directory. A visit will put you in contact with someone who can help you. Even a telephone call will bring you some useful literature.

Even more helpful is a visit to one of the 13 Business Service Centers operated by the General Services Administration (GSA) in Boston, New York, Philadelphia, Washington, Atlanta, Chicago, Kansas City (MO), Houston, Fort Worth, Denver, Los Angeles, San Francisco, and Seattle. These centers are operated expressly to help businesspeople learn how to do business with the federal government.

With all these facilities and resources available, there is little reason to neglect the huge federal market for consulting services.

Following Up in State and Local Markets

State and local government markets, taken together, are about twice the size of the federal government market. Individually, however, each is relative small. Hence, none do quite as elaborate a job in organizing their procurement systems and aiding prospective suppliers in learning how to participate. Still, most do emulate the federal system, and the parallels are there.

State Governments

Each state government has, in the state capital, a central purchasing and supply office. This may be an independent entity, or it may be an office within an organization, such as the state's finance office or administrative agency. In Georgia, for example, the Division of Purchasing and Supplies is in the Department of Administrative Services, as it is in Idaho, Indiana, Louisiana, Montana, and several others. The purchasing office is in the finance or accounting agency in Kentucky, Maine, and Mississippi, but it is a separate division in Massachusetts, New York, and Texas.

Such differences are superficial, for there are many commonalities among all or nearly all state purchasing and supply offices:

- All urge prospective suppliers to visit their offices personally and become acquainted with the several buyers, the requirements, and the procedures.
- All have some form of required registration or bidders' list application, which prospective suppliers are urged to complete and submit.
- Many supply lists of all purchasing office personnel, including buyers and what each buys.

- Many have technical specialists (as the federal government does) for the approval or negotiation of contracts for computer equipment, supplies, and services.
- All award annual supply contracts for items that are commodities—goods and services they buy regularly throughout the year.
- Most delegate to the various other agencies throughout the state that purchasing which is peculiar to the other agencies' needs, such as consulting services.
- Most permit local governments to utilize state supply contracts to buy goods/services the local government needs.
- All have some kind of provision for small purchases and noncompetitive purchases, as established by statute.
- Most will supply you by mail, upon request, a brochure of some kind, explaining their system and governing statutes, often accompanied by a thick document listing/identifying their supply groups (often closely resembling and sometimes identical with the federal listings) and names of various commodities—lists of what they buy regularly in goods and services—and forms for you to complete to get on the state's bidders lists and qualify as an approved supplier.
- Some will also supply a lengthy list of state agencies—hospitals, mental institutions, prisons, museums, departments, administrations, commissions, and many others—often with the names of administrators who do independent purchasing for those organizations.
- Most advertise their requirements and bid opportunities in a local newspaper, generally in the classified columns under the heading Bids and Proposals. (For major procurements, they sometimes use display advertising in the financial/business pages of the newspaper, as in Figure 11.1.)

Special Considerations

State governments, like the federal government, have their own socioeconomic programs. These include, in some states, preferential treatment for in-state bidders. In practical terms, this usually means that an in-state bidder gets a 5-point edge in technical-proposal evaluation or gets the award when he or she is equivalent technically and/or in cost with an out-of-state bidder. This may mean a slight edge for you when pursuing contracts in your own state.

Many states emulate the federal government with other aids such as loan and loan-guarantee programs, set-aside procurements for small businesses and for minority-owned firms, and counseling for small businesses.

Local Governments

We have, even at the local levels, a great deal more government than is readily apparent. Most of what has been said for state purchasing offices is equally true for the purchasing offices of local governments. A personal visit to the seat of government—

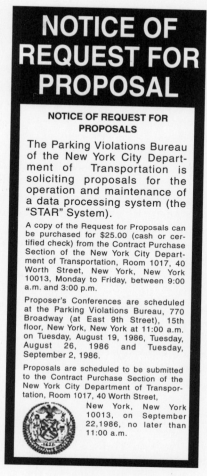

Figure 11.1   Solicitation advertised in newspaper.

county seat, town hall, or city hall—is always a good first step. The larger local governments often have purchasing organizations, descriptive literature, lists of supply groups, and procedures that rival those of the federal government and larger state governments, and they also often have an array of local agencies and institutions far more extensive than you may have dreamed. The list of local-government agencies in Washington, D.C., alone proved long, almost as long as the lengthy list of Massachusetts state agencies.

For your purposes, it is those many other agencies—that myriad of public institutions and government bureaus—who are most likely to become your clients. Here are just a few of the types of other agencies you are likely to encounter:

Hospitals	Library systems
Halfway houses	Departments of housing
Transit authorities	Child protective services
Equal opportunity offices	Economic development administrations
Port authorities	Health services
Offices of human rights	Public roads bureaus
Consumer protection agencies	Tax collection offices
Environmental control offices	Prisons
Boards of education	Special commissions of many kinds

These are the bureaus and agencies most likely to need consulting services. In most cases, however, you must be registered with the government's central purchasing authority before anyone in that government can do business with you. In some cases, purchasing authority can be delegated to the other agencies, but in many cases the other agency may select you but have the central purchasing organization do the actual contracting with you. In such cases, you must market to those other agencies, but still handle all administrative and contracting matters with the central purchasing office.

SUBCONTRACTING AND OTHER SPECIAL MARKETING APPROACHES

None of the contracting organizations, not even the supercorporations, do everything themselves. Most, especially the larger organizations, find it necessary to subcontract a great deal of the work. A major procurement to a large corporation—General Motors, Boeing, IBM, GE, or any other—can easily result in 200 or 300 subcontracts. Thus, subcontracting to the winners of government contracts alone represents a great deal of opportunity for you. It is itself a multibillion dollar market.

One place to learn of these subcontracting opportunities is in the CBD. Most issues include an awards section, which lists the contracts awarded recently. Each of these notices offers a synopsis of the work contracted for, the size of the contract (in dollars), the agency for whom the work is to be done, and the winner of the contract, usually with an address included.

Occasionally the winner of a large prime contract will ask for and get permission from the government to advertise for subcontractors in the pages of the CBD. You should therefore be alert for such notices in relevant categories.

Often the prime contractor who is seeking subcontractors will invite bids and request proposals, just as the government does. In fact, the terms of major contracts often clearly imply or even specify a requirement to do so when letting subcontracts. It is therefore a good idea to prepare and circulate capability brochures (these will be discussed in the chapter on proposals) to all organizations who appear likely to let subcontracts for services such as you offer.

On the other hand, you may wish to offer your services to contenders for contracts before awards are made—as soon as you learn of the request for proposals (or even earlier than that!). Many organizations pursue contracts for which they are not fully staffed. Because they lack some of the key personnel needed to conduct the proposed program, they need to include in their proposals the resumes and services of expert consultants to support the program. You can thus be assured of a subcontract if the organization manages to win. (But it is a good idea to have a written agreement with the primary organization to that effect, since you do not have the leverage of being the prime contractor.)

You may wish to permit more than one contender for a given contract to include your resume and promise of availability to support the program. This is not unethical if all parties are aware that your resume will appear in competing proposals and do not object.

As an alternative, you can co-bid with someone else, where the two of you are a far stronger contended for the contract than either of you alone. Usually this is still a prime contractor and subcontractor presentation, but you both participate in writing the proposal. (You must decide which of you should be the prime contractor and which the subcontractor, and this ought to be decided solely on the basis of what combination makes you the stronger contender.)

FORMS

There are two federal forms you should recognize. (Most state and local governments use quite similar forms.) One is the Standard Form 33 (Figure 11.2). This is the form for both sealed bid invitations and proposal requests, either of which may be checked off. The other is Standard Form 129 (Figure 11.3) Application for Bidder's List.

SOLICITATION, OFFER AND AWARD	1. THIS CONTRACT IS A RATED ORDER UNDER DPAS (15 CFR 700)		RATING		PAGE	OF	PAGES

2. CONTRACT NUMBER	3. SOLICITATION NUMBER	4. TYPE OF SOLICITATION	5. DATE ISSUED	6. REQUISITION/PURCHASE NUMBER
		☐ SEALED BID (IFB) ☐ NEGOTIATED (RFP)		

7. ISSUED BY	CODE	8. ADDRESS OFFER TO *(If other than Item 7)*

NOTE: In sealed bid solicitations "offer" and "offeror" mean "bid" and "bidder".

SOLICITATION

9. Sealed offers in original and _____ copies for furnishing the supplies or services in the Schedule will be received at the place specified in Item 8, or if handcarried, in the depository located in _____ until _____ local time _____

(Hour) *(Date)*

CAUTION - LATE Submissions, Modifications, and Withdrawals: See Section L, Provision No. 52.214-7 or 52.215-1. All offers are subject to all terms and conditions contained in this solicitation.

10. FOR INFORMATION CALL:	A. NAME	B. TELEPHONE *(NO COLLECT CALLS)*			C. E-MAIL ADDRESS
		AREA CODE	NUMBER	EXT.	

11. TABLE OF CONTENTS

(X)	SEC.	DESCRIPTION	PAGE(S)	(X)	SEC.	DESCRIPTION	PAGE(S)
		PART I - THE SCHEDULE				PART II - CONTRACT CLAUSES	
	A	SOLICITATION/CONTRACT FORM			I	CONTRACT CLAUSES	
	B	SUPPLIES OR SERVICES AND PRICES/COSTS				PART III - LIST OF DOCUMENTS, EXHIBITS AND OTHER ATTACH.	
	C	DESCRIPTION/SPECS./WORK STATEMENT			J	LIST OF ATTACHMENTS	
	D	PACKAGING AND MARKING				PART IV - REPRESENTATIONS AND INSTRUCTIONS	
	E	INSPECTION AND ACCEPTANCE			K	REPRESENTATIONS, CERTIFICATIONS AND OTHER STATEMENTS OF OFFERORS	
	F	DELIVERIES OR PERFORMANCE					
	G	CONTRACT ADMINISTRATION DATA			L	INSTRS., CONDS., AND NOTICES TO OFFERORS	
	H	SPECIAL CONTRACT REQUIREMENTS			M	EVALUATION FACTORS FOR AWARD	

OFFER *(Must be fully completed by offeror)*

NOTE: Item 12 does not apply if the solicitation includes the provisions at 52.214-16, Minimum Bid Acceptance Period.

12. In compliance with the above, the undersigned agrees, if this offer is accepted within _____ calendar days *(60 calendar days unless a different period is inserted by the offeror)* from the date for receipt of offers specified above, to furnish any or all items upon which prices are offered at the price set opposite each item, delivered at the designated point(s), within the time specified in the schedule.

13. DISCOUNT FOR PROMPT PAYMENT *(See Section I, Clause No. 52.232-8)*	10 CALENDAR DAYS (%)	20 CALENDAR DAYS (%)	30 CALENDAR DAYS (%)	CALENDAR DAYS (%)

14. ACKNOWLEDGMENT OF AMENDMENTS *(The offeror acknowledges receipt of amendments to the SOLICITATION for offerors and related documents numbered and dated)*:	AMENDMENT NO.	DATE	AMENDMENT NO.	DATE

15A. NAME AND ADDRESS OF OFFEROR	CODE	FACILITY	16. NAME AND TITLE OF PERSON AUTHORIZED TO SIGN OFFER *(Type or print)*

15B. TELEPHONE NUMBER			15C. CHECK IF REMITTANCE ADDRESS IS ☐ DIFFERENT FROM ABOVE - ENTER SUCH ADDRESS IN SCHEDULE.	17. SIGNATURE	18. OFFER DATE
AREA CODE	NUMBER	EXT.			

AWARD *(To be completed by Government)*

19. ACCEPTED AS TO ITEMS NUMBERED	20. AMOUNT	21. ACCOUNTING AND APPROPRIATION

22. AUTHORITY FOR USING OTHER THAN FULL AND OPEN COMPETITION: ☐ 10 U.S.C. 2304(c) ( ) ☐ 41 U.S.C. 253(c) ( )	23. SUBMIT INVOICES TO ADDRESS SHOWN IN *(4 copies unless otherwise specified)*	ITEM

24. ADMINISTERED BY *(If other than Item 7)*	CODE	25. PAYMENT WILL BE MADE BY	CODE

26. NAME OF CONTRACTING OFFICER *(Type or print)*	27. UNITED STATES OF AMERICA *(Signature of Contracting Officer)*	28. AWARD DATE

IMPORTANT - Award will be made on this Form, or on Standard Form 26, or by other authorized official written notice.

AUTHORIZED FOR LOCAL REPRODUCTION
Previous edition is unusable

STANDARD FORM 33 (REV. 9-97)
Prescribed by GSA - FAR (48 CFR) 53.214(c)

Figure 11.2 Standard Form 33.

SOLICITATION MAILING LIST APPLICATION	1. TYPE OF APPLICATION ☐ INITIAL ☐ REVISION	2. DATE	OMB No.: **9000-0002** Expires: 10/31/97

NOTE: Please complete all items on this form. Insert N/A in items not applicable. See reverse for instruction.

Public reporting burden for this collection of information is estimated to average .58 hours per response, including the time for reviewing instructions, searching existing data sources, gathering and maintaining the data needed, and completing and reviewing the collection of information. Send comments regarding this burden estimate or any other aspect of this collection of information, including suggestions for reducing this burden, to the FAR Secretariat (MVR), Federal Acquisition Policy Division, GSA, Washington, DC 20405.

3. SUBMIT TO

a. FEDERAL AGENCY'S NAME

b. STREET ADDRESS

c. CITY | d. STATE | e. ZIP CODE

4. APPLICANT

a. NAME

b. STREET ADDRESS | c. COUNTY

d. CITY | e. STATE | e. ZIP CODE

5. TYPE OF ORGANIZATION *(Check one)*
☐ INDIVIDUAL
☐ NON-PROFIT ORGANIZATION
☐ PARTNERSHIP
☐ CORPORATION, INCORPORATED UNDER THE LAWS OF THE STATE OF:

6. ADDRESS TO WHICH SOLICITATIONS ARE TO BE MAILED *(If different than Item 4)*
a. STREET ADDRESS | b. COUNTY
c. CITY | d. STATE | e. ZIP CODE

7. NAMES OF OFFICERS, OWNERS, OR PARTNERS

a. PRESIDENT | b. VICE PRESIDENT | c. SECRETARY

d. TREASURER | e. OWNERS OR PARTNERS

8. AFFILIATES OF APPLICANT

NAME	LOCATION	NATURE OF AFFILIATION

9. PERSONS AUTHORIZED TO SIGN OFFERS AND CONTRACTS IN YOUR NAME *(Indicate if agent)*

NAME	OFFICIAL CAPACITY	TELEPHONE NUMBER	
		AREA CODE	NUMBER

10. IDENTIFY EQUIPMENT, SUPPLIES, AND/OR SERVICES ON WHICH YOU DESIRE TO MAKE AN OFFER *(See attached Federal Agency's supplemental listing and instruction, if any)*

11a. SIZE OF BUSINESS *(See defintions on reverse)* ☐ SMALL BUSINESS *(If checked, complete Items 11B and 11C)* ☐ OTHER THAN SMALL BUSINESS	11b. AVERAGE NUMBER OF EMPLOYEES *(Including affiliates)* FOR FOUR PRECEDING CALENDAR QUARTERS	11c. AVERAGE ANNUAL SALES OR RECEIPTS FOR PRECEDING THREE FISCAL YEARS $

12. TYPE OF OWNERSHIP *(See definitions on reverse)* *(Not applicable for other than small businesses)* ☐ DISADVANTAGED BUSINESS ☐ WOMAN-OWNED BUSINESS	13. TYPE OF BUSINESS *(See definitions on reverse)* ☐ MANUFACTURER OR PRODUCER ☐ SERVICE ESTABLISHMENT ☐ CONSTRUCTION CONCERN ☐ RESEARCH AND DEVELOPMENT ☐ SURPLUS DEALER

14. DUNS NO. *(If available)*	15. HOW LONG IN PRESENT BUSINESS?

16. FLOOR SPACE *(Square Feet/M²)* a. MANUFACTURING	b. WAREHOUSE	**17. NET WORTH** a. DATE	b. AMOUNT $

18. SECURITY CLEARANCE *(If applicable, check highest clearance authorized)*

FOR	TOP SECRET	SECRET	CONFIDENTIAL	c. NAMES OF AGENCIES GRANTING SECURITY CLEARANCES	d. DATES GRANTED
a. KEY PERSONNEL					
b. PLANT ONLY					

The information supplied herein *(including all pages attached)* is correct and neither the applicant nor any person *(or concern)* in any connection with the applicant as a principal or officer, so far as is known, is now debarred or otherwise declared ineligible by any agency of the Federal Government from making offers for furnishing materials, supplies, or services to the Government or any agency thereof.

19a. NAME OF PERSON AUTHORIZED TO SIGN *(Type or print)*	20. SIGNATURE	21. DATE SIGNED
19b. TITLE OF PERSON AUTHORIZED TO SIGN *(Type or print)*		

AUTHORIZED FOR LOCAL REPRODUCTION
Previous edition not usable

STANDARD FORM 129 (REV. 12-96)
Prescribed by GSA - FAR (48 CFR) 53.214(e)

Figure 11.3 Application for Bidder's List.

12 | Proposal Writing: A Vital Art

It is true enough, in general, that the best proposal writers win the contracts because they appear *to be the best qualified contenders. But the meaning of best proposal can be misleading here if you take it to mean the proposal reflecting the greatest literary skill. There is more to creating the best proposal than writing skills.*

THE EVOLUTION OF MODERN PROPOSAL PRACTICE

The word *proposal* once referred to what was little more than a list of what was offered, the prices, and the terms of sale. A printed brochure or two might be enclosed, and perhaps some boilerplate material—a standard form or two.

Given the increasing complexity of projects (especially those that are at least in part based on technological solutions and require more than one department's involvement with the client, or if the project is cross-functional), decisions on which firm to award a contract to are based on a vendor's ability to provide *both* technical expertise and functional competence, as well as managerial or project management expertise. Additionally, in some instances, a project may be "put out to bid" (that is, proposals are requested from multiple consultants or suppliers) where the client company is unsure of how best to proceed or a solution is not yet known. In this instance, the client is soliciting the insight and guidance of outsiders to create, test, or assemble a concept to address a need.

The government and many larger businesses have buying policies that mandate competitive bidding and the collection and analysis of proposals from potential consultants. In their attempt to be as objective as possible in their decision to award consulting projects, they have established methods for weighting and assessing consultant responses to requests for proposals. One important criterion in judging proposals is the cost or fees section for services provided. However, that is only one element and is not always the most important one. While pricing must be competitive, and must demonstrate "value" to the client, other factors can sway a decision toward one supplier over another (service, reputation, speed, experience, creativity, etc.).

176

WHAT PROPOSALS CALL FOR

Unwritten, perhaps, but clearly expressed between the lines of a request for proposals, may be any of the following messages:

- Here is our problem, with its symptoms and, as far as we know, an accurate definition of the problem. This is everything we know about it and can tell you. We want help. What would you suggest? (Describe your detailed plan.)
- Here is a concept that has appeared in the literature. Is it feasible? Can it be developed into a useful methodology? How would you proceed? What kind of results would you project?
- Here is an idea that has been put forth for a new kind of information system. How would you develop this into a working prototype?
- Here is a need (addressing one of our weaknesses, address an opportunity, deflect a competitive threat, or other). Give us your best ideas for developing a counter or solution.

By such means, the raw idea of a laser is developed into working models and practical devices that ultimately find applications in medicine and industry, as well as in military channels. Radar, computers, infrared devices, and others are similarly developed through contracted programs. But it is not only equipment that is so developed. Many systems for improvements in safety, efficiency, training, and human betterment in industry, the professions, and society at large are born this way also.

The modern proposal is the instrument for choosing the best qualified contractor and/or the qualified contractor with the most attractive and most persuasive ideas for the project. It is the principal means by which we present our credentials and ideas, and by which the client evaluates those credentials and ideas and makes a choice.

In this chapter, the guidelines for writing proposals are applicable and appropriate for responding to requests for proposals (RFPs) issued by the American government, by private-sector organizations, and by foreign governments, and foreign privately-held organizations, who often refer to an RFP as a *tender,* but who have responded well to the type of proposals described here.

WHY PROPOSALS ARE REQUESTED

The rationale underlying RFPs has been explained; they are calls for help because the client does not know how to solve the problem (in many cases cannot even identify it), needs additional resources, or wants to study and evaluate different ideas and approached before selecting one. (And in the case of governments, there is the additional reason that the law requires competitive proposals.) There is also the consideration that the client needs something on which to base an evaluation of the contenders for the contract and judge the suitability of each. RFPs are signposts to success in writing proposals because they tell you what the client requires. They will guide you if you read them carefully and accurately. They resolve into the basic merits of your plan or proposed program and your qualifications as a consultant and contractor, but each of those breaks down into separate categories, too.

THE ELEMENTS OF THE RFP

The typical RFP has four major elements:

1. An introductory letter, information on when proposals are due, where they are to be delivered, who to call with questions, what kind of contract is planned, and other information, such as announcement of a preproposal conference.
2. Proposal instructions, including a specification of what information is to be in the proposal, how proposals are to be evaluated (if it is a government RFP), sometimes a dictated proposal format, sometimes forms to be used for cost estimates, and other such material.
3. Standard boilerplate information about the requesting organization, purchasing policies and regulations, contract terms, invoicing, and other administrative data.
4. A statement of work, describing the client's problem or need, symptoms, objectives, and other such orientation. Theoretically, this is a specification, a complete and detailed description. In fact, it is often far less than complete, for any of many possible reasons. But it is what you must respond to and address.

THE RESPONSE

When submitting your response to an RFP, remember that in many instances, this will be the document that the evaluators within the client will use to assess your "fit" and competence for the project, therefore, make sure to answer the needs as presented and adhere to the RFP's request for information to be presented according to the established order. This is not the time to be overly creative in format or organization. The following lists suggest some basic considerations and questions the client will be concerned with in reading your proposal:

Request

Summary of situation/what is the "need."

SWOTs (Strengths, Weaknesses, Opportunities, and Threats).

Why the need is best addressed by an outsider versus internal resources.

Proposed Plan

Is it what we want—what we are looking for?

Is it practical?

Does it appear workable?

Is it likely to produce success—the results we want?

The Proposer

Are you capable—do you have the skills and resources to carry out the plan?

Are you dependable—do you have a track record of making good and coming through in your projects?

Remember, it is the client's perception that matters, and that perception is (presumably) the consequence of your proposal; the client is influenced by your proposal and how convincing you were in selling your plan and capabilities.

KINDS OF INFORMATION AN RFP ASKS FOR

To determine which consultant has the best ideas (proposes what appears to be the best program) and best qualifications, most RFPs ask your proposal to provide these kinds of information:

- An analysis and discussion of the requirement, demonstrating your full understanding of the need and your capability for designing and carrying out a completely responsive program.
- A preliminary program design or approach, with sufficient explanation to demonstrate its suitability.
- A specific proposed program, with adequate details of staffing, organization, schedules, end products, interim products, procedures, management, quality control, schedules, and whatever else you deem important enough to merit discussion. (These vary with different requirements, naturally.) Cost estimates must often be presented in great detail.
- Your qualifications to carry out the proposed program successfully. This includes knowledge, skills, facilities, and any resources normally required for such a program as you propose.
- The record of your verifiable relevant experience in similar project for other clients, naming those clients and demonstrating your dependability as a contractor, as well as evidence of your skills.

WHAT IS A PROPOSAL?

I have already answered the question *What is a proposal?* from the client's viewpoint. There are significant differences when this question is addressed from the consultant's viewpoint.

First of all, there are questions of scope and size, questions of the physical format of the proposals, and the amount of effort required to produce them. Many consultants choose not to pursue business opportunities requiring RFPs because they consider the proposal requirements too onerous and proposal writing too expensive. Whether the rewards are or are not worthwhile depends on your personal view, especially on how you feel about writing—many professionals truly hate to write—and how badly you need sales.

The size of the required proposal usually depends on the size of the project. Small projects suitable for the independent consultant, which in today's economy are probably roughly in the range of $5,000 to $25,000, usually require only simple, informal proposals, actually letters of several pages in which the proposal is embodied. These are often called *letter proposals.* Even when formal proposals are required, they tend to be fairly small (unless you are in pursuit of the larger projects of perhaps $100,000 or more). Typically, for the small to medium projects an independent consultant is likely to pursue, a formal proposal will run about 25 to 50 pages, although many are far longer.

Before deciding that you will or will not write proposals in quest of contracts, you ought to consider a few points:

- With only an occasional exception, there is just one winner in a proposal competition. Winning second place is only slighter better than being in last place, although there are sometimes advantages to being close.
- It is not enough to show that you can do a good job or as good a job as anyone else. You must prove yourself and your plan better than all the others.
- The client is unlikely to perceive that your approach, plan, and qualifications are superior to the rest, and won't make the effort to do so, even if he or she has all the technical know-how. You must explain why and how they are superior; in other words, you must *sell* yourself and the program you propose.
- The short answer to the question of what a proposal is, from your viewpoint as the seller, is this: A proposal is a *sales presentation.* It cannot succeed unless it sells.

This is why proposal writing—*successful* proposal writing—is not so dependent on writing skills as it is on marketing skills. A proposal is a written presentation, and even great marketing skill won't rescue a badly written proposal, but the writing must implement a winning marketing strategy.

PROPOSAL SCENARIOS

Here are some of the typical situations that lead to proposal writing and also often influence the nature of your response:

- The most common situation is probably the one in which the client has identified a need and decided to seek help from an outside specialist. Presumably, an award will go to the writer of the best proposal. This is a kind of self-fulfilling prophecy because the proposal that wins is, ergo, the best proposal! Still, there is at least one exception to this: When the need is not too pressing and none of the proposals submitted are very good, the procurement is canceled. So it is not always possible to win by being the best of a bad lot.

- Some RFPs are inspired unintentionally by consultants working with the client: The consultant suggests something intended to promote more work for himself or herself, but the client decides to solicit competitive proposals despite the fact that the original idea was yours.
- In many cases, there is the happier situation where it is possible for you to suggest something to a client or prospective client that elicits an invitation to submit a sole-source proposal, one for which there are to be no competitive proposals. This may come about because the client has complete faith in you and does not wish to consider anyone else, or it may be the consequences of your offering a proprietary and unique idea or product (for example, a special computer program or some special and unique knowledge).
- Finally, you may offer an unsolicited proposal as a result of some knowledge of a client's needs or as a normal follow-up of a sales lead, usually as a voluntary act, with or without advising the client that you are planning to do so. (The client may or may not ask for something on paper to study and/or pass on to others in the organization.)

WHO MUST YOU SELL?

That last item makes an important and often neglected point: You may have to sell to more than one person in the client organization. You may have sold to the individual with whom you have had direct contact, but that individual may be required (or may prefer) to review the matter with others and get approval. In many cases, the individual wants to retain you or select you as a contractor, but needs your help in selling the idea within the organization.

In this situation, the proposal becomes all-important, even though you believe you are in already because the individual you spoke to was enthusiastic and assured you of his or her support and desire to retain you. But that individual may need your help in getting approval.

You must always operate on the assumption that there are others who must be sold, especially when you are submitting a proposal. More often than not, even when there is no formalized committee-type of proposal review (as there normally is in government), a number of people will review proposals, whether sole-source or competitive, and pass judgment on them, and those judgments will have an influence on the buying decision.

I have often been asked for something on paper by executives in both private-sector and government organizations. Sometimes the individual needs help or, at least, written backup to sell the idea upstairs, but there are other reasons too. When the client writes a purchase request or order, he or she must write a purchase description or specification of some kind. Given that many people have a great distaste for writing; that the client is not in nearly as good a position as you are to describe what the purchase is; that the client may be embarrassed to admit that he or she cannot write the description on what is needed without your help; and that it is always sound marketing strategy to make yourself as easy as possible to do business with, you will be wise to develop and document that purchase description in a proposal of some sort and be at pains to make it as easy as possible for the client to identify and transcribe the description or statement. (Never underestimate the power of convenience as a motivator for clients to sign.)

I have never found a sales situation in which a proposal, especially a written one, was not a good tool. Nor have I ever found a situation in which the proposal should not have been a sales presentation in every sense of that term. Verbal proposals are effective in selling situations where you might normally expect to close the sale on the spot—in one-call sales situations—but the verbal proposal is only the opening shot in most selling situations. You need to follow up a verbal presentation with a written one, one that is a permanent record for clients to review, study, discuss, evaluate, and consider at length. But a proposal also offers you the opportunity to develop your presentation at length, with careful study and consideration. That is one of its chief advantages: A written proposal allows you time to plan, draft, reconsider, edit, rewrite, and polish until you are satisfied that the presentation is everything you want it to be.

Remember always that you are in one of two selling situations: selling against competition (to a client who wants to buy but has to decide from whom to buy), or selling against almost automatic reluctance of many kinds:

- Reluctance to turn to outside sources for help.
- Reluctance to break a pattern and do something different.
- Reluctance to do something finally about a familiar old problem.
- Reluctance to battle internal resistance to contracting out.
- Reluctance to admit (even to themselves) that there is a problem.
- Reluctance to spend the money.

PUBLIC- VERSUS PRIVATE-SECTOR PROPOSALS

The most significant difference between public- and private-sector procurement (the respective proposal requirements and strategic considerations) is that private-sector clients may do pretty much as they please, whereas public-sector clients are bound by public laws governing purchasing.

The consequence of this is not trivial. In many ways, it affects what you must do in writing a proposal. When you respond to a government RFP, you can often enjoy an edge by being aware of the statutes and taking advantage of them. The objective is not to win recognition of your eloquence but to win the contract, and the award is for what you say, not how you say it—marketing strategy, not literary polish.

That is not the only difference between the two proposal situations. Another important difference is that in the private sector there is a strong tendency to accept you at face value—to accept that you are a competent professional. The assumption is that, since you are in the business and competing for the contract, you must be capable in that field. Government clients, on the other hand, generally require that you provide information to prove your competence and qualifications to bid on and to be considered for the contract. This is at least partially a consequence of the legal requirement to evaluate each proposal objectively. It also reflects some bad experience the government has had with contractors who were not competent and whose work had to be done over. Even worse, it reflects some bad experiences with contractors whose work affected important matters such as safety or performance of critical military systems. So you may expect that RFPs issues by government agencies will require evidence of your qualifications and capabilities, technical and otherwise. There is a growing tendency in the private sector to emulate government proposal practices in all respects, including this, so there are two schools of thought; (1) submit your proposal with this information regardless of whether it was requested (the rationale being that more information will, at worst, be ignored, and may serve to tip the balance in your favor) or (2) do not submit this information because sending information that was not expressly requested is more likely to result in more opportunities to discount the proposal and raise objections to it where none existed previously (the rationale possibly being that if it was important, it would be asked for, if it is not—the only outcomes are a neutral one or negative one). Include it at your discretion, but be forewarned that it is not universally suggested to do so by those consultants who have "snatched defeat from the clutches of victory!"

Still another important difference is that all but the smallest government contracts tend to demand a complete cost/price analysis, and that analysis requires you to reveal all your cost factors, direct and indirect. (Reluctance to reveal such proprietary and confidential information to anyone, including government agencies, is one reason some consultants do not pursue government contracts.)

Still another difference is the risk in revealing your program strategy. It is not unprecedented for unscrupulous individuals in the private sector to appropriate the plans and confidential information you reveal in your proposal and use this information for their own ends, thus victimizing you by what amounts to simple theft. (This has happened to me on at least two occasions that I know of, and it is a legitimate concern of many consultants.) This is a serious problem, and the risk should be taken into account in proposing to any organization, particularly in the private-sector. (The risk of such treachery is much smaller when proposing to a government agency.)

By far the most significant difference between the two kinds of proposal situations, however, is the one referred to at the beginning of this discussion, that private-sector clients may do pretty much as they please in their purchasing, whereas government-sector clients usually have legal restraints that compel them to evaluate each proposal along a variety of significant parameters, and they are required to give you some intimation as to what those factors are.

THE EVALUATION SYSTEM

Federal procurement regulations require an objective rating system to be used to evaluate and assign to each technical proposal a figure of merit representing its respective technical quality. (Costs must usually be supplied in a separate proposal, withheld from those evaluating the proposals until they have completed their technical evaluations.)

The resulting evaluation schemes vary widely from one agency to another and even from one procurement to another. Sometimes the RFP reveals and explains the evaluation criteria in elaborate detail, while in other cases the explanation is sketchy. Following are two typical examples:

Example 1: The following are the criteria on which technical proposals will be evaluated. Item (a) has twice the value of Item (b), which has one-half the value of Item (c).

Item (a): Understand and approach.

Item (b): Qualifications of proposed staff.

Item (c): Qualifications of the organization.

Award will be made to that proposer whose proposal is deemed to be in the best interests of the government, costs and other factors considered.

Example 2: Evaluation criteria are as follows:

(a) Understanding of the problem:	0 to 5 points
(b) Practicality of approach:	0 to 10 points
(c) Evidence of realistic anticipation of problems and planning for contingencies:	0 to 10 points
(d) Proposed management and organization:	0 to 10 points
(e) Qualifications of proposed staff:	0 to 25 points
(f) Qualifications of organization:	0 to 25 points
(g) Resources offered:	0 to 15 points
Maximum possible score:	100 points

When greater detail is provided, the criteria listed (as in the second example) are further detailed by subordinate items reflecting the analysis of each.

The Cost Factor

Note that little mention is made of costs in these examples, except that it will be considered. This method lays the foundation for the agency to defeat the purpose of the evaluation requirement because it leaves a final decision to the judgment of the officials making the procurement. There is, however, an appeal or protest process for seeking redress against unfair or illegal procurement practices, a subject that merits a separate discussion.

There are other ways in which the cost factor is taken into account. In many cases, costs are simply included in the list of criterion items as a specific, weighted factor added to the technical score. Presumably, the proposer with the lowest cost is awarded the maximum number of points, while the one with the highest cost earns zero points. But, as proposers, we are not entitled to know exactly how the evaluation is made.

Thee is also a method that links cost with technical considerations, dividing the dollars by the technical points to arrive at a cost per technical point. Presumably this results in award to the proposer with the greatest value—lowest price per technical point. For this to be viable, the client must first screen all proposals and eliminate the technically unacceptable, regardless of price. Elimination of unacceptable proposals, regardless of other considerations, is a common practice, although there are a few exceptions (contracting officers who believe that every proposer is entitled to a chance to revise his or her proposal and make it acceptable).

The Inevitability of Comparative Evaluation

The listing of evaluation criteria with specific weights suggest that the proposals are to be measured against absolute standards. This is virtually impossible. Take that 0 to 25 points listed for qualifications of the staff proposed. Would that mean that the perfect staff would merit an award of 25 points? That the client will attempt to judge how near to or far from perfect each proposed staff is? Or does it mean that the proposal with the staff adjudged *best* qualified earns the most points, perhaps the full 25?

The latter is unavoidably the method for choosing, and it means that the evaluation *must* be comparative. Your staff and all your other qualifications will go through two evaluations: One will screen for general acceptability, and the second will rank it on each criterion. No evaluation scheme can be entirely objective; human judgment is inevitably involved. Therefore, you must do whatever you can to influence that judgment in your favor by employing every element of sales and marketing strategy available to you. And do not lose sight of the fact that while the private-sector client can be as unfair as he or she wished when selecting a proposer for award, government clients are well aware that you have appeals from unjust decisions, and so they are not always free to make awards on the basis of friendship or personal preference, but are often compelled to make awards they would prefer not to make. Your sparkling personality, friendships, and charisma may help a bit, usually indirectly, but they are rarely decisive factors overall.

THE PROTEST PROCESS

If you wish to protest a decision made by a private-sector company, remember that they are not required to share their criteria with you and do not necessarily have to make decisions on any objective criteria, so the protest will *rarely* work (and may actually serve to remove you from further consideration for future RFPs). Should you wish to protest a government issued RFP, your chances of having a decision overturned are still small, but there is at least a process for it.

Protests may be lodged with either the contacting official responsible for the procurement contract in question or the comptroller general of the United States, who is head of the General Accounting Office (GAO), a branch of Congress. A staff of lawyers and others work there, devoting their full time to resolving protests. But you do not require a lawyer to register a protest. A simple letter, setting forth the facts as you see them, is sufficient to start the ball rolling. If the protest involves computers, computer software, and related matters, the protest must normally be made to the Contract Board of Appeals of the General Services Administration, which has jurisdiction in those cases.

The protest is an administrative appeal, not a legal action, and so in no way substitutes for a lawsuit or compromises a future lawsuit. That is, you are not legally bound by the protest and its decision, should you choose to sue the government—something major corporations and others do fairly often.

People who are not familiar with the process believe the protest is a measure to pursue after losing in the competition. Consequently, most protests are made after an announcement of the award. That, unfortunately, is the worst possible time to lodge the protest. Even if you win, it is likely that you will win nothing. Three possible consequences may snatch the victory from you:

1. The project is already well underway, and the decision is that, even if the award were improper, canceling and re-awarding it would cost the government too much money.
2. The decision is that the award was defective, but you have not demonstrated that it was you who should have won, and competing again for the contract would be prohibitive.
3. The agency decides to cancel the procurement entirely, possibly to recompete it at some future time.

You may protest any element of the procurement process at any time if you believe that something is improper—defective is the term used officially—in the process. For example, a client of mine protested successfully that the requirement did not permit enough time to write a proper proposal, forcing the agency to extend the closing date. Another client protested successfully that the evaluation scheme had built-in anomalies so that the award violated the scheme specified, forcing cancellation. And another, in quite a large procurement, protested successfully that the winning proposal had been delivered and accepted some minutes after the deadline, and managed to have the contract canceled and re-awarded to him, to the embarrassment of the agency.

A great many protests *do not* succeed. Many fail because they offer specious and irrelevant arguments and should not have been made at all. A common argument is that the protester offered a lower price, which is rarely a valid argument. One protester who used that argument had submitted a proposal that had been rejected as technically unacceptable, and so could not have won anything in any case. Another complained that the price was so low, that the winner would lose money on the contract. (The contracting official advised that it was not against the law to lose money.)

It is legitimate to challenge (protest) just about anything you believe improper or unfair about a government procurement. The apparent impropriety or unfairness may prove to be no impropriety at all—it may be the result of a simple mistake—or it may be an effort to wire the procurement for some favored consultant. That is, of course, illegal, and probably not quite as prevalent a practice as many think, but there is no denying that it does happen, and it should be challenged whenever it appears to deny you a fair opportunity to pursue government business.

Signs to Watch For

There are several ways in which a procurement can be rigged to give a favored consultant an advantage. These devices are usually rather transparent and suggest strongly that an effort is being made to wire the procurement. Be alert for these things as possible indicators of such an effort:

- The closing date is so near the date of announcement as to virtually preclude anyone not *already prepared to respond* to get a decent proposal together in time.
- The specification of what is required as qualifying characteristics is unreasonable vis-à-vis what is necessary to get the job done.
- The specification of what is to be done is excessively vague and thus extremely difficult to respond to—that is, it makes it ridiculously easy for the agency to declare your proposal nonresponsive and thus disqualify it.
- The statement of work or specification of what is required is so excessively and unnecessarily tailored that it restricts free and open competition.

None of this is intended to suggest that such practices are commonplace or that the system is not basically fair and honest; it is. But circumstances lead to these situations, no matter how innocently, and you are entitled to relief from them. That is the purpose of the protest process.

SOLE-SOURCE PROCUREMENT

Procurement regulations provide for sole-source procurement, generally under one of three conditions:

1. The need is urgent and for some reason (such as the typically late enactment of an appropriation bill by Congress or an unanticipated emergency), there is simply no time for the typical three- to six-months procurement process.
2. The requirement is for a proprietary product, service, or experience of some sort that is unique and unavailable elsewhere.
3. The procurement implements a contract resulting from an unsolicited proposal. (This is tantamount to contracting for a proprietary, since the idea is a proprietary one, and sometimes a proprietary product is involved as well.)

Unfortunately, not all sole-source procurements are justified. Many are announced in the CBD (claiming that the announcement is for information purposes only, whatever that may mean), with the alleged justification that the favored consultant has some special qualification, such as that cited in the second or third of the preceding examples (most often the second one). This favored consultant is alleged then to offer the government a more efficient program than would be possible with another contractor. To add insult to injury, that special, unique experience was often acquired in a current or recently concluded contract with the same agency!

Again, this may be legitimate, but there is evidence, often cited by the GAO in their reports, that many agencies make sole-source procurements that are not justified, often simply to speed up the process. (Sole-source procurement is a much faster process than is competitive procurement.)

You may use the protest process to challenge such procurement intentions and demand the right to compete if you believe that you can do the work and do it as efficiently as anyone else.

What Happens Next

Your protest results in a request by GAO for copies of all documents involved—the RFP, the winning proposal, your proposal, and others, along with a statement from the contracting official, responding to your complaint. While GAO studies these, you can respond to the contracting official's statement and he or she to your response. GAO may then issue its decision, although the process may be iterative and progress through several cycles until a GAO decision.

In most cases, that is the end of the process. However, you still have the right to sue in a federal court, if you choose to.

PROPOSAL FORMATS AND RATIONALES

Some RFPs mandate a specific format for the proposals requested, and even a format for staff resumes. Most list, describe, discuss, and even specify the information required, often in great detail, but do not specify a format, leaving that to you. A recommended four-section general format that has proved highly satisfactory for and readily adaptable to most proposal requirements is offered here, with a rational and explanation of each section, following a general explanation and rationale.

General Discussion/Rationale

Not surprisingly, the recommended proposal format is based on the general premises that (a) the client is asking for help with a problem, (b) it is a sales presentation and must use sound sales tactics, and, perhaps most important of all, (c) it must have a single strategy as its major thrust.

That latter consideration is all important. Bear in mind that a proposal saying, "Me, too: I can do the job as well as anyone," rarely wins. To win, it is necessary to stand out, to be superior to other proposals in some decisive manner.

FORMAT AND GENERAL RATIONALE

The following format has been successful in winning many millions of dollars worth of contracts—well over $360 million in government contracts alone. It consists of four main elements, with other elements included if and as necessary. It offers information in a logical flow, but still implements the promise-and-proof sales strategy. It also provides the seedbed for major technical/program strategy, discussed later. It is offered as a format for a formal, bound proposal, but the format is easily adapted to informal letter proposals.

The four main sections and ancillary elements (when needed) are these:

- Front matter
- Section/chapter I: Introduction
- Section/chapter II: Discussion
- Section/chapter III: Proposed program
- Section/chapter IV: Experience and qualifications
- Appendices and exhibits.

The chapter titles are generic. More imaginative titles, selected to reflect the client's needs, are recommended—urged. These will make it clear that the proposal was custom written for the client and not boilerplate taken off the shelf. That is not the only reason for devising specifically appropriate, rather than generic titles: The proposal is a sales presentation and ought to sell at all opportunities; each headline and caption is a special opportunity.

Front Matter

Formal proposals include front matter—a title page, a table of contents, and an executive summary. The latter is a kind of abstract, but it is used by most proposal writers to highlight the major selling points of the proposal. An informal, letter proposal would not usually include front matter; because it is a short and informal proposal, the advisability of using an abstract is questionable. The effect of an abstract can be easily achieved in a normal letter format through sensible organization, for example, the inverted pyramid of journalism, in which the entire story is summarized in the lead, with expansion following.

It is generally useful to incorporate into any table of contents a list of figures and a list of tables.

A typical title page is shown in Figure 12.1, Figure 12.2 illustrates a typical table of contents. Figure 12.3 demonstrates how a brief letter proposal might be organized according to the principles advocated here.

Chapter I: Introduction

The first chapter is divided into two sections: "About the Offeror," an introduction to who and what you are, with a very brief précis of your interest and qualifications, noting details to be detailed later; and "About the Requirement," an appreciation of preliminary analysis, validating your understanding of the requirement and laying the foundation for your approach, strategy, and whatever else is to follow.

A PROPOSAL
to the

AMERICAN SOY BEAN COMPANY

to train 500 Bean Counters in Quality Control Procedures

Prepared by

JCI Associates, Ltd

Consultantsville, California

January 22, 1999

Copyright 1999 by JCI Associates, Ltd.

Figure 12.1   Title page of formal proposal.

Chapter II: Discussion

The first chapter was a prelude to this chapter and should have set the stage for it. Here you explore the client's problem in depth. Demonstrate full understanding of the requirement and all that it implies (possibly defining it even more accurately than the client does); show technical experience, knowledge, skill, and creative imagination. Show that you have analyzed the problem thoroughly, identified all alternatives and possibilities, and identified the optimum approach, which you now present, with the rationale.

Sales Training Proposal Table of Contents

Section Number	Section Name	Page Number
Chapters		
1	Client Background	1
2	Statement of Opportunity	3
3	Project Objective	4
4	Approach	4
5	Methods and Techniques	5
6	Project Timeline	7
7	Consulting Fees	8
8	Payment Schedule	9
9	Project Staffing	10
10	Consultant Strengths	12

List of Figures

Figure Number	Title	Page Number
1	Client Revenue	Appendix 1
2	Client Market Share	Appendix 2
3	Opportunity Size	Appendix 3

Lists of Tables

Table Number	Title	Page Number
2.1	Opportunity Size	Appendix 4
2.2	Competitive Environment	Appendix 5
4.1	Approach Phases	Appendix 6
5.1	Methods and Techniques	Appendix 7
5.2	Method Comparisons	Appendix 8
6.1	Timeline Graph	Appendix 9
8.1	Payment Schedule	Appendix 10

Figure 12.2   Format for table of contents.

Make your technical sales arguments, implementing your strategy. You may have to educate the client, explaining your analyses, reasoning, conclusions, and plans for delivering all the benefits, especially those around which you have built your main strategy. Explain how you will meet the impossible schedule, reduce the costs, maximize the probability of success, eliminate the possibilities of failure, and bring to reality whatever it is you have promised or the client has demanded. Parade the benefits derived from your plan—especially the unique benefits that would not result from others' plans. Prove that point here and in the chapters yet to come. But this one chapter must end in a clear presentation of your approach, laying the groundwork for the next chapter.

This chapter of your proposal is the promise. The next one is the proof.

HERMAN HOLTZ

P.O. Box 1731   Wheaton, MD 20915-1731

301 649-2499   Fax 301 649-5745

CompuServe 71640,563

June 29, 1999

John W. Herr
Vice-President
American Soy Bean Company
99881 Process Avenue
Soy Mash, Pa 17765   Ref: QC Training Proposal

Dear Mr. Herr:

It gives me great pleasure to offer my assistance in helping you to reduce the number of rejects on your production lines while increasing customer satisfaction with your products. Our research, carried out since our recent meeting and discussion at the convention in New York City, bears out the correctness of your judgment: I agree completely that training in quality-control procedures is the proper avenue to improvement.

I visited your plant, as you suggested, and interviewed several of your employees, using a structured interview that I developed some years ago in carrying out a preliminary task analysis for a similar program for the Acme Paintbrush Corporation. That program, I am proud to report, produced a 14-percent increase in net production, reducing line rejects by 11 percent. Subsequent reports reflected a 27-percent drop in returns.

I am sure that we can do at least as well for you. Of course, while I will use the general approach that was so effective for Acme Paintbrush, I will develop a program designed especially for your company.

Full details are offered in the following pages for study by your staff and yourself.

(over please)

Figure 12.3   First page of an informal, letter proposal.

Chapter III: Proposed Program

This chapter is the proposal per se, the specifics of what, when, where, how, and how much you propose. Everything before has been prologue, everything after, epilogue. You show exactly how you will implement the strategy promised in the chapter just concluded.

In this chapter, pull the curtain back and reveal the details. No theory or philosophy here; just the bare facts When? (Schedules.) Who? (Proposed staffing.) How much? (Quantification of effort and/or products, if any.) How? (Management plans and procedures.)

You need a chart or two. (Charts are generally far more effective than text and even more effective than tables, in many cases.) An organization chart, if there will be associates working with you. A functional flow chart showing phases of work and major functions. A milestone chart illustrating the schedule. A chart or table matching major phases and functions with labor hours required for them.

The second chapter made promises. This one must offer proofs. (A few more proofs appear in the final chapter.)

Chapter IV: Experience and Qualifications

I usually include the staff resumes in the third chapter, although they can be fitted into this fourth chapter easily enough. While the staff resumes provide evidence of the qualifications of the individuals proposed to staff the project, this fourth chapter offers evidence of the organization's qualifications.

That can be tricky when you are operating as an independent consultant and a one-person enterprise—that is, you bid for relatively small projects and you are the entire staff, except for possible clerical and administrative support. But in many cases, especially when responding to a formal RFP with a formal proposal, you must comply and respond as though you were a larger organization. Thus, you offer your resume as an individual, covering formal education and all relevant experience, wherever it was gained, but you also offer your resume with accounts of your projects, as an independent consultant, experience in providing services to your own clients (rather than to an employer's clients, that is). Much of the information will be the same in each application, but the orientation will be different in each case.

That is not the only information that should be included. Include here an account of all facilities and resources that relate in some way to your consulting enterprise generally and/or to the proposed program. That might include your offices and equipment, for example, computers, copying and reproduction machines, photographic equipment, laboratory facilities, a library, photo files, and/or access to any relevant resources.

Back Matter

In some cases, it is necessary to include one or more appendices and an exhibit or two. An appendix is a proper resource when you have material that you believe will be of interest to some readers, but not to all, such as the complete text of a document or a drawing you refer to in your proposal. An exhibit, on the other hand, is often included when several copies of the proposal are called for, but only one copy of some supporting item—a set of slides or a sample of the product of some earlier project, for example— is available. When using an exhibit, advise all readers that such an exhibit exists, although it is not an integral part of the proposal itself, so they are alerted to seek it out.

THE NECESSARY IMPACT

As must any sales presentation, a proposal must have great impact if it is to do its job well. And if it is to have that hard-hitting quality, it must have a certain aura and deliver a clear sense of certain qualities. These are subtle emanations, but they can show that you are in charge of the situation, and know that you are. The client can sense these qualities:

- *Total competence.* The reader must sense your power as a consultant who brings complete technical and professional competence to the job.
- *Dependability.* The reader must feel that you are completely reliable, and will never fail to carry the job through to a successful conclusion.
- *Accuracy.* The proposal must convey the sense that you are absolutely precise and accurate in every action and in every step you take.

The keys to accomplishing this effect have already been provided, but a brief review is in order:

- *Specificity and detail.* One can generalize about any subject, so generalizations have little impact. A presentation that cites specific facts and details, particularly quantified data, is much more likely to impress a reader and be credible. (Credibility is all-important.)
- *Startling statistics.* Study your facts and proposition quantitatively to see what impressive numbers you can develop—total person-hours of directly relevant experience, number of pages of training material you have written or directed writing of, but especially numbers that relate directly to what you can do for the client. (In my case, I am able to point to an impressive total dollar amount of contracts resulting from my proposals.) If numbers are startling enough, see if you can work them into your introduction as an attention-getter.
- *Clear and unambiguous language.* Avoid euphemisms; you are not in the diplomatic corps. Use stark language, in good taste, but words that are straight from the shoulder and cannot be misunderstood or brushed aside.
- *Quiet confidence.* Hype is equal to protesting too much. It sounds defensive, as though you are trying to compensate for weakness. The absence of adjectives and superlatives, the conspicuous lack of bombast, and the use of a quiet reportorial tone convey strength. (Achieve emphasis and command attention through other methods presented here and elsewhere.)
- *Take-charge attitude/approach.* Most clients want a take-charge type of consultant, one who will relieve them of worry and tedious, time-consuming involvement. Make it clear that you know exactly what to do—present highly detailed plans—and be sure that your explanations, descriptions, and rationales reflect confidence in what you propose. Caution: Be careful; it is possible to overdo this, to suggest that you might run off with the bit in your teeth. Make it clear that you will remain under the client's control.

- *Thorough response.* A consultant on annual contract in Arizona had been renewed year after year for four years. He got careless because he and the client knew each other so well. The contractor turned in a causal proposal for a fifth-year renewal and lost out to an aggressive competitor principally because of a lack of attention to detail in the incumbent's proposal.

STRATEGY AND ITS EVOLUTION

Over the course of my long career, I have become convinced that successful proposals are most often those based on specific, well-thought-out strategies. Again and again, I have seen the dark-horse proposer, one that neither client or competitors had heard of before, upset the cart and win because he or she had an effective strategy that was implemented well. All marketing and sales effort ought to be based on specific strategy, but proposals especially because they are usually custom projects with only a single buyer. There are no percentages—probabilities—to play here, as there are in mass marketing. It's all or nothing in most cases; multiple-award programs are the exception. And even then, the number of awards is usually limited; only a first-class proposal can win.

Read the Client as Well as the RFP

In the typical situation, you must read between the lines of the RFP, where the client is pleading, "Yes, do explain your approach and program to me carefully, but don't stop there; sell to me, too; show me why I must select you as my consultant." Again and again, I have heard neophytes at proposal writing mutter to themselves as they pore over the RFP, "I wonder what they really want." They believe that some kind of guessing game is involved, and that the client will award a contract to the best guesser. They have trouble grasping that the client is often not at all sure of what is needed and wants help in identifying the problem, as well as in solving it.

If that is the case, it is by chance, not by design. It may well be a case of "Eureka!" in which the client reads a given proposal and reacts, "That's it! That's what I need!" That can happen when the client is able to describe only symptoms or unhappy results of some kind, and a consultant has been clever enough or, more likely, worked hard enough to infer the real problem. It is more likely, however, that the symptoms described are not that hard to analyze to determine that (1) they point to a recognizable problem or (2) the correct approach is to institute a two-phase program, in which the first phase is devoted to problem definition. But there is an approach to devising strategies by first analyzing the initial situation, which is usually one of the following:

- The client has a good and probably accurate understanding/definition of the problem/need.
- The client all but concedes that what is described are probably only symptoms, and the consultant will have to define the true problem and respond to it.

- The client claims or professes to know what the problem or requirement is, but is probably mistaken; you must discriminate between what the client thinks is the problem and what it really is.

Understand What a Problem Really Is

Not every RFP calls for services to solve a problem that the client cannot solve. Often, the client knows exactly how to solve the problem but lacks the wherewithal. The need may be for supplemental staff for a short time, access to laboratory services, field workers, or other ancillary support. In such a case, best may mean least costly. Depending on the client's orientation, best may also mean swifter response to the need (often the client needs help yesterday); ability/willingness to respond under adverse conditions, such as an impossible schedule; most-qualified individuals to be supplied; most cooperative attitude; most dependable support; best understanding of the need; or other factor not readily apparent.

Preliminary analysis to develop a sensible and specific strategy should, then, consider these factors:

- What appears to be the best (fastest, most efficient, most dependable, least expensive, most risk-free) way to do the job?
- What prejudices/special concerns/worries does the client appear to have, if any, about how to do the job best?
- What appears to be most important to the client? (Cost? Schedule? Technical approach? Qualifications of staff? Qualifications of organization? Working relationship? Other?)
- Do these factors relate to each other? If so, how? (Incompatibilities? Can they be resolved? How? Or are they mutually supportive, lend each other strength? If so, how?)

Actually, the main strategic areas to consider are cost and program or technical matters. Even so, the two are often related; if you offer lower cost, you should show how your proposed program makes cost savings possible while meeting the clients' requirements. While there are important areas of secondary consideration, the major strategic thrust is almost always in the proposed program plans and bears on factors such as these:

Cost	Risk of failure
Schedule	Staff qualifications/credentials
Reliability	Organization's qualifications/credentials

Evolution of the Strategic Base: Key Questions

The choice of factors on which to base your strategy is not random. It should be based on several considerations, the first and more important of which is usually the client's own perception of need or problem, which you may or may not agree with. But that must be tempered by related considerations, represented by questions like these:

- Is the client correct in assumptions of problems and/or needs—that is, do you agree with the client's definition of the problem (and possibly of the solution)?
- Do you have some firm conviction about how to define the real problem, or do you merely suspect that the client does not understand his or her problem—that is, that some work will be required to determine what the problem is before a reliable approach to its solution can be formulated?
- Has the client mandated in the RFP some defined set of services and method of operation to which he or she appears bound?
- If the client all but mandates (strongly recommends or even suggests) a method/service/approach that is workable, is it the best one—most appropriate, most efficient, most likely to achieve the stated goals?
- Is the client's definition so far off-base that it is impossible or would be risky to proceed without (a) an initial problem definition phase or (b) redefining the problem as it ought to be redefined?
- How firmly does the client appear to cling to his or her notion—would it be risky (to sales success) to confront the client directly about this in your proposal?
- Are there other problems the client fails to foresee (possibly naive, in fact, about the difficulties) or are there special problems of meeting requirements that are extraordinarily difficult, such as an impossible schedule?
- Does the client appear to be conscious of and/or especially concerned with some aspect of the problem such as meeting a schedule date, getting the job done at lowest possible cost, probability of eventual success, or other?

Making Lemonade

In time, you come across most of these situations, and each is both a problem and an opportunity. Some of the answers may pose a difficult sales problem for you; they may define whether or not you have an immediate problem of how to structure your approach without running head on into a client's bias or accepting a task that will be exceedingly difficult, perhaps impossible, as it is presented by the client. It is not at all unusual for a client to have a completely wrong idea about (1) what the problem is and (2) the best way to solve it. There is a great deal of truth in the adage that you can't win an argument with a customer. Still, it is essential that you recognize this common problem for several reasons, of which your professional integrity (and reputation) is the first one: You should feel honor bound to be honest with the client. A second excellent reason is that you may paint yourself into a corner if you go along with a false premise and thereby win the contract! That may hand you the problem of doing things entirely differently than you had originally proposed. You would then have to face the client and confess error and naivete, at the least. Those are negative factors. But there is this positive factor: Such problems are the seedbeds for successful strategies. They are opportunities, for you can make lemonade out of these lemons!

There are strategies for all the listed situations. But you will have to judge which is the right strategy for the occasion. There are clients who are willing to have you say plainly to them, "The approach you suggest is not the best one possible and will add unnecessary cost," or "The approach described is out of date and less efficient than the modern method." But even with those clients, it is better to put it like this: "There is an approach possible that will reduce the costs," or "A recently developed method promises greater efficiency."

That is normal diplomacy—differing with the client without challenging or appearing to attack. But the possible strategic implication goes deeper. There is the matter of what many professional proposal writers call the worry item. That refers to whatever appears to be of greatest concern to the client—cost, meeting the schedule, risk of failure, control of the project, the consultant's capability, the consultant's dependability, or other. Proposal success lies often in identifying that worry item accurately and focusing the proposal on it:

- If an extraordinarily rapid turnaround time is required, you must focus on the schedule and how you propose to meet it without fail. That is, the promise is that you will meet the schedule unfailingly—the client is assured of that— and the proof is your planned program and all the rationale you develop to show why your plan must and most assuredly will produce the result you promise.
- Build your program plan around a method for accommodating the client's chief worry item (and if there are several, decide which is the chief one and concentrate on it without neglecting the others), and be sure that the proposal dramatizes that suitably. That is, you should discuss those concerns, disguising them as concerns you have about the program, if the client has not openly expressed or admitted them. And you should explore them in depth and develop the chief worry item as a major consideration in the project.

Finding the Worry Item

It is not always easy to identify the client's worry item. Sometimes you must read between the lines of what the client has written or said, or even resort to other methods for gathering marketing intelligence. Even that is not always fruitful because the client may be reluctant to admit to any special concerns or may indeed have no special concerns! In that case, your course is clear. You must decide what ought to be a major worry item, one that, in your judgment, the client will agree on, once it is pointed out, and go on as though you had detected that concern. In short, help the client acquire a worry item! (Many successful marketing campaigns are based on analogous approaches.)

Remember, the creation of FUDs (fear, uncertainty, and doubt) is often a path to securing the contract, as the client/prospect wishes to eliminate or reduce those conditions and wants to avoid being viewed negatively by others.

Other Strategies

We have been discussing the master strategy or the capture strategy, as some refer to it. That is the main strategy expected to sway the client and be decisive in the award decision. And we have operated on the premise that the proposed program design is the critical area around which the strategy should be built. Normally, this is true. But there are other strategic areas and supporting strategies to be considered too. They are usually supporting areas, each requiring its own strategic approach, for none are unimportant. They might even be the critical areas and so become the master strategies. In any case, they merit careful consideration.

The cost strategy, for one, might, under some circumstances, easily become the major strategy. How will you organize and present your costs? How will you justify them? How will you demonstrate the value of what you are delivering for your price?

There is also the competitive strategy. How will you position yourself vis-à-vis your competitors? How will you manage to outshine them, appear superior? In some cases, this might become the capture strategy.

Finally, there is the presentation strategy. How will you present your proposal itself so that it has major impact and supports your master strategy?

A few suggestions to help you devise useful strategies follow.

Cost Strategy

In discussing costs, talk value and be clear about value offered. Try to quantify and pro rate what you offer across the total budget to demonstrate the value. Provide as much detail as possible in describing what you propose to deliver. That makes you appear more forthcoming and honest than competitors who are vague about what they will deliver for the dollars; thus the costs you quote seem far more palatable. But it also subtly suggests to the client the possibility of negotiation and prepares the ground by listing all the items that might be negotiable.

There is a special case you may run into: Some RFPs are so vague that pricing the proposal appears impossible. That is, the client has furnished no basis for you to estimate either time or material required to do the job. Given this situation, there is an almost automatic tendency to go back to the client and ask for clarification. Traditionally, that was usually a mistake for several reasons. For one, the client may not be pleased with this approach. Many clients think they have given you ample information, no matter how unclear their RFPs actually are. For another, you are throwing away an excellent opportunity to steer things your way, to develop a winning strategy. Contemporary thought is that when provided with opportunity to ask questions (some RFPs include a public opportunity for questions open to all respondents to preclude any one vendor from having an unfair advantage having their questions answered without other vendors having the opportunity to hear the response, or to ask their own questions)— take it! Even if your competition hears the answers to your questions, you still assume a lead by demonstrating to the evaluators that you understand the issues. (Remember, the decision is still a human effort and every chance you have to impress them is worth taking.) This chance is not always available, but when it is, it serves to refine your response and solidify your presence in the eyes of the client.

There are some consultants who believe that if the RFP has failed to provide proper specifications, the client may be implying, if not explicitly stating, that your recommendation is solicited. Provide that recommendation. Decide what is necessary to get the job done and meet the goals, and draw up the specifications—the quantification, as well as the qualification, of what you propose. That is what you price.

They maintain that this gives you several advantages, in addition to solving the problem: (1) It is a highly credible presentation because you are supplying the specifications. You are the true expert. (2) You are in control telling the client just what ought to be done. (3) On both counts, you are ahead of competitors. (4) This puts you in control of costs to a large degree. There is no special risk as long as you do quantify everything carefully.

There is one other advantage in this situation: You can offer the client options, inasmuch as the client has not offered a clear specification, and that is often a most powerful strategy. Some consultants believe that if there is opportunity for clarity to be offered, why continue to muddle in the dark hoping to please the evaluators? It is the belief of people that subscribe to asking questions, that you can eliminate potential protests over ambiguous direction, "fixed" RFPs, or other errors in the process. There is no right or wrong answer to this and it will be up to each individual consultant to determine his or her own level of tolerance for ambiguity in responding to RFPs.

Competitive Strategy

Don't refer to competitors directly at any time; however, it is perfectly legitimate when you know that you are in a competitive situation to address this problem indirectly. You can include a discussion of what is needed to do this job effectively and meet all goals, schedules—whatever is relevant. In this discussion, list whatever is appropriate—experience, physical facilities, access to other specialists, willingness to burn the midnight oil, and other factors. The mere fact of your pointing these things out—and especially of competitors failing to (they usually do not think to do so) is often highly effective.

Also stress heavily anything you can offer that is unique or unusual, and be sure to point that out. That scores for you—and against your competitors—in the client's mind. (Is marketing a mind game? It certainly is!)

Presentation Strategy

Your proposal is a presentation, as noted, and should be prepared carefully, even if it is an informal, letter proposal, to reflect professionalism and unblushing desire to make a good impression. In this area, do's and don'ts are appropriate:

- Do have your proposal typed neatly on standard-sized white bond paper (or any other light, near-white shade). You can use your regular letterhead if it is white or light cream color. Don't use dark papers; they are too hard on the eyes.
- Use *black* ink. Colored ink my get attention, but it's only momentary, and many people find colored type distracting. Be distinctive, but not bizarre.

- Preferably use a 12-point type in an easy-to-read font (many word processing applications allow for a range of fonts or type styles. This is not the time to get fancy or cute. Stick with one font type and use it for both headlines and body text). It is recommended that you leave generous margins for two reasons: (1) ease of reading (whether to double space the copy or not is personal preference; no clear standard exists if not specifically called for or stated in the RFP.) and (2) to allow evaluators room to write comments or to ask questions of themselves to follow up on in the evaluation.
- Use a simple report cover. You can get them in most office-supply stores, they are inexpensive, and they add to the impact.
- Use illustrations—simple line drawings, possibly photographs.
- Be careful about spelling, grammar, and such details. Professionals should not be careless with language.
- If you have a computer and a good printer, you can add a few flourishes, such as oversize captions and headlines. You may also find your desktop computer convenient for generating a few simple illustrations—charts and graphs—to lend impact to your proposal. You may even be able to provide well-drawn pictorials.
- Be aware that if you submit anything from a color printer or include colored graphs/charts/photos in the RFP response (as opposed to an exhibit), that it *may* be copied in black and white for distribution to others within the evaluation team. Therefore, you may want to test how well the colors copy in black and white to determine if they are distinguishable in shades of gray.

Should Questions Be Asked?

One point of view is despite the fact that many RFPs are sketchy and inspire more questions than answers, it is risky to ask the client to clarify or elaborate on a proposal request. One undesirable result is that you may inspire the client to send out additional information to your competitors. Another is that the client may withdraw the request entirely and cancel the procurement. You are usually better off to decide what the answers should be and bid on that basis (e.g., proposing the specifications), observing the precautions counseled earlier.

Other enlightened consultants believe that failure to ask questions is tantamount to playing the child's game of Pin the Tail on the Donkey by trying to guess what the proposal should accomplish without relevant clues. Even if it means the client delays making a decision, some consultants maintain that they have acted properly by protecting that client's best interest and that it will ultimately play in their favor when the decision is reached.

Don't Be Vague

Some consultants believe that if the RFP was vague, it is okay for the proposals to be vague. The result is disaster. Be specific, following the guides provided here. Many veteran proposal writers far prefer the vague RFP because it affords a much better chance of winning than does the crystal-clear one for several reasons: Reduced competition (many will drop out when the RFP is vague and thus difficult to respond to); the opportunity to outshine your competitors by being clear and specific, where they are vague and rambling; and being able to propose a project on your own terms.

Don't Start Writing too Soon

The rush to paper—starting to write before reaching a complete understanding of the client's need and, especially, before clearly formulating an approach and a strategy— is a common mistake that leads to poor proposals. Time is usually limited in proposal writing, and while it is almost an absolute rule that good writing results only from rewriting, it is usually an economy in proposal writing to try to get it right the first time; there is rarely time for a complete rewrite.

Do Rewrite as Much as Possible

Although the compressed schedules in proposal writing usually make it impossible to do a complete rewrite, at least do a thorough edit to ensure correct spelling and usage, and to polish the presentation as much as possible.

FUNCTIONAL FLOWCHARTS

People outside the technological fields have difficulty with functional flowcharts; yet, they are among the simplest ways to present and understand a process in which successive steps are required.

A chart depicting a relatively simple process may be considered to be a graphic version of a written procedure. Consider, for example, a cookbook explanation of how to make a plain omelet. The instructions might be written thus:

1. Heat butter in pan.
2. Beat two eggs in a bowl.
3. Pour eggs into pan.
4. Brown and fold omelet.
5. Remove when done and serve.

Graphically, as a flowchart, the process would be as in Figure 12.4.

The instructions might have directed the reader to beat the eggs while the butter was warming in the pan. Graphically, that would be shown as in Figure 12.5. That figure shows a phase or time relationship between the first two functions, to point out that they are or can be concurrent; this is often important in demonstrating how you plan to conduct the project and, especially, how you might meet a difficult schedule.

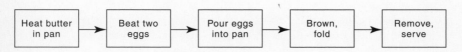

Figure 12.4   Simple flowchart.

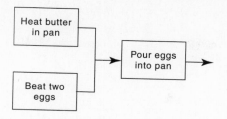

Figure 12.5 Flowchart showing phase relationships.

As processes become more complex, explaining them in words alone becomes increasingly difficult, and graphic aids grow more and more useful. On the other hand, it is sometimes more expedient to show only the major steps, as in Figure 12.6, when the intervening steps are obvious. You have to be the judge of the right level at which to present and explain your plan.

These figures are highly simplified. In practice, the processes are rarely that simple and straightforward. The processes are often iterative, as shown in the next figure, Figure 12.7. This figure illustrates a most useful idea in proposal writing: Develop a functional flowchart based entirely on the RFP, as a first step, and then refine it before you begin to write. This is a method I have found effective in developing successful proposals for rather large projects. If you do a thorough and accurate job of translating the RFP into a flowchart—usually a preliminary, rough-draft flowchart—you have accomplished a great deal:

1. You have your project design before you in a graphic form, one that enables you to study it effectively, perceive interrelationships among the functions, uncover anomalies, and perceive potential problems.
2. You have an almost ideal presentation tool; clients value graphic presentations because a flowchart makes it easier to grasp the logic of the project. Moreover, less text—less reading—is required, a boon to busy executives.
3. The ability to envision the project in this manner says a great deal about your ability to handle the project. It demonstrates your understanding, while it helps the reader understand your logic. The milestone chart (see Figure 12.8) is another aid to this.
4. Many of your writing problems are solved, since you now write to the flowchart. It's your road map, on the one hand, and greatly reduces the volume of words you need, on the other hand.

Figure 12.6 Simplified flowchart.

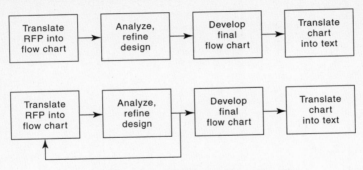

Figure 12.7   Proposal process showing iteration.

The Logic of the Flowchart

Flowcharts have a definite logic to them, and the logic is itself one of the keys to creating flowcharts (Figure 12.9). If you ask why to the notations in each box, the next box to your right ought to furnish an answer. Going in the opposite direction, you may ask how, and the box to the left ought to answer that. In Figure 12.9, you survey labor-surplus industrial areas to develop long-range economic forecasts, and you do that to prepare definitive recommendations, the objective of the project.

This enables you to check the validity of your flowchart, but it goes further because it helps you develop the chart in the first place. Sometimes you will be able to translate the client's statement of work in the RFP directly into a chart, but often the RFP is simply not that definitive. In that case, you may have little to go on other than the required end product or result. If, as hypothesized in Figure 12.9, the RFP asks you to develop a set of economic recommendations vis-à-vis the unemployment problem in labor-surplus industrial areas but gives you hardly a clue as to how you are to proceed, you might ask yourself how. That is, you might inscribe prepare

PROJECT SCHEDULE

Time in Months	0	1	2	3	4	5	6	7	8	9	10
Task Analysis	▬										
Preliminary Plan	▬										
Review			▬								
Revision				▬							
Field research				▬							
Interviews					▬						
Draft lesson plans					▬▬						
Tryouts							▬▬				
Analysis of tryout results								▬▬			
Final revisions and turnover									▬▬▬		

Figure 12.8   Example of milestone chart.

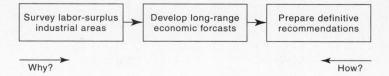

Figure 12.9   Logic of the flowchart.

definitive recommendations in a box on the right-hand edge of a blank sheet and ask yourself what should go into a box to its immediate left. That is the beginning of the process in many cases, and it is where you can outshine your competitors.

A FEW ODDS AND ENDS

A few consultants groan, inwardly at least, when they are requested to write a proposal. Some groan simply because they hate to write; others for other reasons: They are sure that it is a waste of time; they fear that the client is trying to pick their brains without paying for the privilege; they believe that only those who have fixed things in advance win proposal contests; and they often resent being asked to write a proposal, considering it an unreasonable demand and an imposition.

This is a short-sighted attitude. The RFP ought to be considered an invitation to bid, and a privilege. It is an opportunity to present your ideas, rather than your personality—it doesn't matter here whether you are a six-foot elegant dresser with a winning smile and overpowering personal charisma or a five-foot-six meek type with thick eyeglasses. Your ideas and presentation speak for you here, not your persona.

Many clients will include RFPs when trying to decide between multiple vendors that have been part of an ongoing sales process that included demonstrations of competence, discussions on approaches, and so on. When submitting proposals to the private sector in this scenario (and when possible, even to the public sector if it evolves this way in your selling effort and you are not responding to a blind RFP), the proposal should be a summary of agreements to that point—either through the RFP process of having the client organization state what those agreements are from their perspective, or in the more common case of a private sector company that has created an RFP and allowed further discussions to occur on the requirements, through the sales process. There should not be "surprises" in the RFP response that have not been addressed previously. There may be examples of creative approaches, unique applications, and other techniques. However, there should not be an instance where the client is caught unaware of an approach, method, or cost to be utilized in this scenario, because it was not mentioned immediately.

It is wise to grasp every opportunity possible to submit proposals, even when they are not requested. Always put your offer on paper. Give the prospect something to study and digest, something to remember you by even if you don't close this one. In the end, it will pay off.

13 | The Initial Meeting with the New Client or Prospect

The key to successful consulting is understanding the problem, and that means learning to listen, as well as to think. At the same time, you must also be businesslike and professional.

RULE NUMBER 1: HAVE A CLEAR UNDERSTANDING FROM THE BEGINNING

It's easy to have misunderstandings with clients and prospective clients. Many problems with clients arise out of misunderstandings. Probably a great many sales failures—losing the sale that you thought was certain—also arise from misunderstanding. More accurately, it is usually the lack of a clear understanding that results in problems.

The problem may arise early in the process, even in that first meeting, when the prospective client and you are trying to size each other up, but you are trying to avoid doing or saying anything that may have a negative effect on the sale.

We will assume that this is a first meeting with a prospective new client. There are many circumstances under which the first meeting might take place. By first meeting, however, I do not refer to a casual introduction or handshake at some function. I refer to a serious business contact during which you have a discussion in pursuit of new business. Probably the other party is sizing you up as a source of needed help, just as you are trying to assess the possibility of new business. Occasionally, it may be a situation where the prospect/client is not even "in the market" for a solution to a problem they have because (1) they are unaware that a problem exists, or that they are losing "traction" competitively (remember, FUDs), or (2) they know they have a problem, but were unaware that a solution existed to resolve it until you happened to make the business contact's acquaintance.

The origin of the meeting may have been a casual introduction at a convention or business club luncheon. But now you are seeking to ascertain the prospect's needs and the possibility of a sale. You are asking questions, seeking to get a fix on the need or problem, while the prospect is making conversation that may be intended to pick your brain to solve that problem.

You are well aware that most sales, except minor ones, are firmed up only after an initial meeting and a follow-up. This is inherent because consulting, by its nature, must involve guiding, counseling, advising, and doing service. Even in the extended meaning of consulting as a professional-temporary support service, face-to-face sales presentations and negotiations are normally a preliminary to a contract. The question often arises, especially if this is a meeting in your or the other's office: Is that other party now a client or still only a prospect? That is, are you on chargeable time—chargeable to the client—or is this still pure marketing activity and therefore chargeable only to your own overhead account? It is necessary to establish a clear understanding with the new client as early as possible to avoid serious differences later.

There are no easy answers to this question of who is paying for your time in the initial session. You must either have a fixed policy or you must judge each case individually. I get frequent letters and telephone calls from people who want to buy my lunch while they explore what lies under the increasingly sparse cover on my head. Most have no intention of paying for my time, information, and counsel; they haven't even considered it, and they think a good lunch is an ample fee for being permitted to pick my brain for an hour or two.

Once I indulged such outrageous presumption (if it is that, instead of true ignorance) in the hope of eventual assignments. I found it to be a losing game in terms of dollars. Several thousand dollars worth of free time produced perhaps one thousand dollars worth of paid time—occasionally. Not always. Too often, lunch was the only fee I ever earned from these encounters. They were hardly worthwhile. Still, occasionally one of those lunches resulted in a worthwhile assignment or even a series of assignments from a good client. Too, not everyone is insensitive to the issue: Occasionally a prospect who invites me to lunch makes it clear, before I have brought the subject up, that he or she is not trying to get something for nothing, but is willing to pay for my time, information, and/or advice, as well as for the lunch.

Many authors and lecturers on the subject of consulting promise to teach you how to avoid giving away free information, suggesting that you lock your tongue up as though it guarded the gold of Fort Knox. I think that is a bit extreme. If we face the facts squarely, we must acknowledge that it is not possible to avoid giving away at least a few samples of our skills and knowledge. It is naive to believe that anyone is going to retain you without having had some firsthand evidence of what you offer as a consultant. This does not mean, however, that everyone who invites you to lunch is entitled to pick your brain and get some free consulting, or even intends to do that. Quite the contrary, the invitation is usually quite innocent, and the other party is not trying to victimize you. But that does not change the picture: You can't afford very much free consulting, but you must judge for yourself what is free consulting and what is necessary marketing. While you must be ruled primarily by your judgment of each case, you should decide in advance whether you are willing to invest your time as a marketing expenditure or will bill for time spent in conversation over a luncheon table.

You might assess the gamble—the possibilities of substantial work resulting from the meeting. Is the prospect a substantial organization with many needs that match the services you offer or someone unlikely to offer any but a small commitment? Assess and estimate the possible reward in deciding how much to gamble on your investment (in time). (That is part of what is known technically as *qualifying* the prospect.)

You may fear that, if you insist on being paid for your time despite the invitation to lunch, you will lose the potential contract. That is a false fear. Anyone who is offended by this—assuming, of course, that you have made your point tactfully—is almost certainly a poor prospect for business. You will lose nothing by turning such prospects away. To the best of my knowledge, I have never lost a client or a contract by being businesslike and requiring my clients to be equally businesslike. Quite the contrary, this tends far more to inspire the prospect's trust and confidence. It establishes the business relationship on a sounder basis than if you were completely pliable and allowed yourself to be used badly. You must require respect for yourself as a businessperson, as well as respect for yourself as a professional expert and consultant, if you are to place your practice on a sound footing.

My own inclination is regard first calls and initial discussions as a marketing expense. For what it may be worth to you, here is my own policy in this regard:

- I will give anyone a few minutes on the telephone. If the caller asks specific questions, obviously with no intention to retain me, I answer the questions as best I can, pointing out that I can't detail my answers very well under the circumstances, and I end the conversation within a reasonable time—10 minutes, perhaps. When the occasion seems to suggest that the caller might become a client, I will mention that I am available on a regular consulting basis.
- I may agree to lunch if the caller assures me that he plans to retain someone—in other words, if I may regard the occasion as a legitimate sales call or presentation. I normally make no charge for a sales call/presentation/initial discussion if it is local and I think there is a serious prospect for business.
- I charge for my time and expenses for a first call/discussion if I must travel a distance and use up a day or most of a day in the process. I make that clear in advance, but I also make it clear that I will earn my fee by providing the guidance the client seeks, even if he or she does not pursue the relationship beyond that first day. When it seems advisable, I may offer the alternative of a proposal, if the prospect will furnish me enough information about his or her need.

RULE NUMBER 2: BE A DIGNIFIED PROFESSIONAL—ALWAYS

It is commonly said, and it may appear so to you, that what you are selling is your time. Don't be misled. Time is not the commodity you sell; time is a measure of quantity, used to plan your work and determine your fee. You may think that you are selling information, and perhaps you are, in a way, but even that is not highly significant.

For this important discussion, let us not forget that you are also selling a promise—what you promise to do for the client. What you are asking of a client is, usually, trust; that is not given to you, a stranger, easily and certainly not automatically, merely because you are a consultant. It is your image that inspires or fails to inspire trust. So, in a much deeper sense, you are selling your image as a competent and expert advisor, a total professional who can and will make good on the promise. (Strictly speaking, you sell the promise, and your image is part of the proof.) This is what you must persuade clients to perceive. (Advertising people sometimes refer to this molding of the prospect's perception as *positioning*.) It is the client's perception of you that has everything to do with your success or failure as a consultant. Still, moderation—striking a proper balance between extremes—is essential. On the one hand, it is necessary to establish and maintain an air of dignity, if you are to be taken seriously. On the other hand, taken too far this can make you appear cold, imperious, a stuffed shirt, or a pompous ass, all of which are equally deadly.

Professional dignity, image, decorum, stature—all pertinent terms—are not easy to define precisely, let alone prescribe by formula. You must not be aloof and cold, but you can be congenial, amiable, and even amusing, without losing dignity; it is not necessary to be somber. You can even be "laid back." Others should find it easy to talk to you and relax in discussion with you. It is helpful to be able to put others at ease. Clients and prospective clients are more receptive when they are relaxed.

It is important to remember that the prospect/client has a huge stake in your success. More than likely, the client's promotional opportunity, bonus, or other strong evaluative criteria will be tied to the project's impact on the organization. While consulting is an intangible in many ways (that is to say, it is not easily broken down into very discrete outputs that can be objectively weighed and measured), the commitment a client makes to the consultant when engaging him/her is predicated on a belief that the consultant will deliver on the promise of X (whatever the project is to provide).

The best determinant of future success is often perceived to be previous successful experience. That is why so much attention is paid to your resume and references. In lieu of that (or at times, to supplement that and confirm a prospective client's perceptions), a client may assess a consultant on the image projected. Despite the difficulty in defining the professional image or prescribing a formula for creating it, it is possible to offer a few guidelines to help achieve it:

- *Dress conservatively.* One consultant I knew was referred to by associates as Gypsy Jim, more for his typically green jacket, yellow slacks, and red shoes than for his itinerant working style. (As a result, he was not taken very seriously by even his associates, let alone his clients.) You need not go to the extreme of what was once the traditional business uniform—dark suit, dark tie, black shoes, and white shirt—but do dress in good contemporary taste.
- *Don't try to be Jerry Seinfeld.* Especially, if you must be a humorist, do not relate ethnic, chauvinistic, or racy jokes. (If someone must be the butt of your

humor, make it yourself.) But do be amiable, smile easily and frequently, and be witty at your own expense.

- *Keep your mind open.* If you are dogmatic by nature, work at overcoming that characteristic; it is essential that you manage to have an open mind, demonstrating that while you are knowledgeable, you are also always ready to consider dissenting views.
- *Keep calm and modulate your voice.* Carrying on conversation in a loud voice, getting excited, appearing anxious, trying too hard, bragging, showing signs of temper, or appearing other than cool and confident is coming on too strong. On the other hand, don't be excessively self-deprecating or modest; you must manage to give yourself credit for what you are and can do—for the real quality of what you offer—but without the obvious hype.
- *Be enthusiastic.* A consultant that does not have passion for what they recommend or their ability to contribute to the client's situation is not going to be highly regarded (or frequently hired). Much of what a prospect is looking for is someone who is able to transfer enthusiasm and zeal for the project to the organization. A milquetoast consultant is not likely to be very successful in convincing people who are skeptical to begin with that her suggested solution will meet the objectives. This is especially critical if the situation is one that internal resources tried to resolve and were unable to on their own.

RULE NUMBER 3: SELL WITHOUT THE HYPE

Marketing may be the most important thing you do in sustaining the long-term viability of your practice. Take your foot off of the marketing accelerator, and your practice will falter quickly as current projects conclude and none are "in the pipeline" to replace them. And selling—actually getting the contract—is the final act of marketing. It is far easier to win the contract when the marketing has been carried out effectively; the main goals of marketing include getting good leads and positioning yourself properly, but it is still necessary to sell effectively.

The subject of selling—positioning yourself—is an objective of this entire chapter. The subject of the right tone to adopt in selling merits more extensive treatment. This will be covered later in discussing proposal writing, but a few significant reminders are offered here. In an effort to "play bigger than one really is" or to try to impress a client, many consultants have "oversold" their backgrounds, capabilities, or projected impact of a consulting assignment. Clients are exposed to vendors, suppliers, consultants, salespeople, shamans, and a whole host of others promising results with thin proof of their competence. Therefore, it is suggested that every consultant and would-be consultant memorize the following don'ts:

1. Don't use hyperbole, such as millions, when you really are referring to several dozen or even to several hundred cases; unprecedented, when that is not literally true; nor magnificent, and other such verbal, Madison-Avenue and Hollywood-type hand grenades. Most people will lose faith in everything

you say, even allowing for rhetorical excess, once you have uttered obvious and gross exaggerations such as these.

2. Don't use superlatives such as most, greatest, largest, latest, or other such terms, unless you can support them with evidence. Like hyperbole, they are dismissed out of hand by most people as flights of fancy with no basis in fact, and they thus cast doubt on your entire presentation.

3. Don't rely on adjectives and adverbs at all (with the exceptions noted in the following discussion). Bertrand Russell remarked that faith is what we turn to when we have no evidence, and it seems that extravagant modifiers and hype are what we turn to when we have no facts. Or so it appears to the sophisticated prospect.

The do's are even more important than the don'ts. Here are three of those:

1. Do stick to nouns and verbs—the purveyors of fact—as much as possible.

2. Do make reports, rather than claims. (Sticking to nouns and verbs all but forces you to furnish reports, rather than claims.)

3. Do quantify as much as possible, especially when you have impressive numbers to offer. (I refer to these as startling statistics, when I find some I can use in a proposal or other marketing presentation.)

The Difference between Bragging and Reporting

For the client to want to listen to your "report" (as just mentioned), the client must perceive that you understand what his situation is, and that you have earned the right to share a solution suggestion (one that you may have implemented elsewhere that has immediate relevance to the client's situation). If the consultant has *not* proven that there is understanding of the situation, then the client will have no interest in pursuing the relationship and offering the project to him. Even if the consultant *could* have offered assistance, the client must perceive that the consultant is someone that can help. Once that has been established, the consultant should stick to "reporting" and not making unsubstantiated claims. The difference is not a subtle one by any means, and the difference in effect—in impact—is enormous. Here are two hypothetical statements you might make, verbally or in writing:

Example 1: When I design your systems and write your programs, Mrs. Murray, you can be sure that they will be many, many times more efficient than anything you now have, and will save you lots of time and money.

Example 2: Mrs. Murray, Charley Sugrue, the comptroller of Western Lumber Products, said that I reduced the run time of their accounting and inventory programs by more than 12 percent and saved them over $32,000 last year in computer time alone. I have his letter saying this, if you would like to see it.

The difference between the two examples is obvious. Example 1 is brag, a claim of something. Will the prospect buy it? Maybe. It's a promise, but there is no evidence offered. Anyone can make such a statement; it doesn't cost a thing to make a vague and general claim, does it? But the prospect is likely to perceive the truth that it is a claim with no supporting evidence or proof offered. (In fact, the clear implication is like that of the deadliest two words in the language: "Trust me.")

Example 2 is also a claim, in a sense, but it does not appear to be brag because it is specific and quantified. It names a client, furnishes what appear to be facts, names the individual, and offers to present the absolute proof. The prospect can call Charley Sugrue for verification, of course, but almost surely will not because he or she knows that you would not make that claim if you could not back it up.

That makes your statement a report, rather than a claim. A claim may make what purports to be a recital of fact, but lack of evidence and sweeping generalizations, with their inevitable hype, stamp the claim for what it is. A report, on the other hand, has no need for hype because it has strength from being able to state the facts. And in marketing, the facts are whatever the client accepts as facts. So the factors affecting the client's reactions to your statement are not only your citation of a client and the client's statement, but the fact that you supplied figures and did not round them off. Had you said "almost 15 percent" and/or "over $30,000," the numbers would have been less authentic sounding and, hence, less persuasive and convincing.

In the final analysis, it is a report because the client will accept it as factual. For practical purposes, that is all that is necessary.

In summation, to make credible presentations, sales or otherwise, you must have the facts at hand and cite those facts in such a way that their truth appears indisputable. Even so, the truth is not automatically accepted if it is not sold or presented in such a manner (with evidence and, preferably, details) that it is perceived and accepted as truth. (Unfortunately, the converse is true: Just as truth can be rejected when presented poorly, lies are often accepted as truth when they are presented so as to appear true.)

SELLING IS CONSULTING

It is true that the key to selling effectively lies in being a consultant to the prospect, no matter what it is that you are selling. You should be selling help of some sort, the solution to a client's problem, whether that problem is a sticky technical matter that the client does not understand (let alone know how to cope with) or some uncomplicated matter, such as a staff shortage or executive stress. The right mental set, the mental set that produces sales success, focuses on helping the prospect solve the problem, not on the sale per se. Show the prospect how to solve the problem through what you sell, and you have a sale. This has worked for me again and again, when I probed to uncover the worry items—what were troubling the prospect most at the moment—that my services could respond to effectively, and it worked for me when I went knocking on government agency doors in Washington, D.C.

Here is an example: I once called on the Occupational Safety and Health Administration of the Department of Labor, marketing my services as a contract writer and consultant. After meeting and chatting with people in various offices, I met a gentleman responsible for training people in subjects related to occupational health. After a pleasant exchange and brief period of getting acquainted, I began probing into the problems this executive was having. I soon learned that he was charged with developing a syllabus and curriculum to be handed over to various institutions of learning who would train occupational health technicians. The problem was that this gentleman did not know how to implement the project. He had a student manual and instructor's guide that a large company had produced for him under contract, but he had no idea of how to use these to satisfy his program. We talked about the problem, and I suggested, in general terms, what had to be done to put these manuals to work. I offered to furnish a detailed plan in an informal proposal. He invited me to do just that, and I went home to my office and wrote a simple letter proposal of a few pages. I submitted it to him, and within less than three weeks, I had a contract (more literally, a purchase order, in this case) to do the work.

Every contract is won on the merits of the client perceiving that the consultant has a satisfactory solution that is a fair and equitable exchange for the fee charged. Put another way, it is a high-value solution. That does *not* mean it is the *best* solution available. There may be options that may better meet a need, but are too time consuming, too expensive, or too risky. The consultant who provides a solution that meets the need within the parameters that the client is comfortable with (timing, cost, support, etc.), is the consultant that will be awarded with the assignment.

Underpinning the consultant's ability to create the appropriate solution is the discovery process that the consultant will have implemented to uncover what the client's tolerances are for solution definition and value.

The Significant Difference

The difference between offering "consulting" as a means to secure product sales (as is often seen when information systems salespeople make a call on a prospect) and offering consulting as the service to be purchased is often difficult to discern. Salespeople offering consulting assistance as an entry to selling their products are often biased and predisposed to solutions including their products within them. Consultants allegedly wear the mantle of objectivity and are advocates for the client and not any one particular manufacturer in making a solution recommendation. Still, at the margins, the differences may not be all that significant in the end result that the client sees if the consultant has not proven value to the client.

Consultants should never take credit for solving a problem that the client is encountering and never sell the promise to do so. The consultant is *not* responsible for the problem and, therefore, cannot be responsible for the solution. The client owns the problem and must own the solution. The consultant can offer ways to remedy it, or processes to follow to minimize its impact. However, the consultant who promises to solve a problem for a client runs the risk of buying him or herself a lawsuit when it does not happen as promised. The consultant is not responsible for how the client chooses to implement a solution recommendation, the consultant does not have control over the personnel selected to manage the project, and the consultant cannot respond to business challenges on behalf of the client. As mentioned before, a wise consultant will conduct some research on the client company that includes understanding the kind of work the company does; the kinds of people who are to be trained in terms of skill level, experience, job expectations, and so on; the company's experience in working with consultants; and in the discipline that he is to consult in, among other due diligence kinds of background necessary to provide comprehensive consultation.

As soon as the consultant is tasked with the above by the client, he has lost objectivity and is no longer consulting to the client, but is performing in a self-serving manner that is outside the bounds of consulting and is consistent with being an employee of that firm. Aside from the ethical considerations that this creates, it is also damaging to the credibility of that consultant (what is your motivation and what is the benefit you will derive from implementing the solution this way, are questions that are bound to be asked).

The salesperson offering to consult as a bridge to a product sale is under no such restriction and may choose to selectively suggest those elements of a solution that are most advantageous to the product offering being touted. It is assumed and expected that a product salesperson will offer a solution that uses a product manufactured by the company represented.

This also raises the issue of whether consultants should be aligned with particular manufacturers or products and should seek to include them in solutions offered to clients. While many do this, it is only appropriate that full disclosure be provided to the client, so that an informed decision can be made on the merits of the solution recommendation. This insidious phenomenon has occurred with increasing frequency in the Big 5 Accounting firms. Once the auditing business is established, the consulting arm of the firm would walk in and offer services that were not covered by the auditing division, but were not necessarily in the client's best interests to pursue (a recent book, *Soldier of Fortune 500* by Steve Romaine, Prometheus Books, 2002, addresses this issue from an insider's viewpoint). The incestuous nature of consulting and complex information systems is rife with such stories.

The Notion of Selling Benefits

You can't study selling very long before you discover the conventional wisdom of selling benefits, as in selling sex appeal, rather than lipstick, and security, rather than insurance. To sell products and services in vast quantities is a much different marketing problem than selling consulting services. The benefits promised must be generalized to fit almost everyone's hopes and aspirations—to be beautiful, to be loved, to be successful, to be secure, and otherwise to satisfy such basic needs. This approach does not work well in selling your services as a consultant because it asks the prospect to make his or her problems—especially the worry items—fit the general aspiration. It asks your prospect to perceive the generalized benefits you promise as specific to his or her situation. It is, in a sense, asking the prospect to sell him- or herself, and it works about as well as you might suppose—only occasionally. Consulting is a custom service. For the benefits approach to work in selling consulting, you must customize the benefits promise in terms of the prospect's individual need, showing the linkage.

This means that you are always a consultant. It is necessary to understand and do preliminary analysis of the prospective client's need if you are to offer an attractive presentation. Every good salesperson is a consultant. It's an integral part of the selling function.

The Consulting Steps in Selling

You cannot afford to make as exhaustive and detailed an analysis in a free marketing consultation as you would in a paid-for consultation. In a free consultation, you are actually paying, as a marketing expense and part of your overhead, the cost of doing business. This is therefore a kind of bobtailed consultation, one in which you should do enough to win the sale, but no more. The scale of the consulting effort is different, but the specific steps and goal are not essentially different than they are in your normal consulting role. They address the same objectives:

- Identify the prospect's overall goal/desires, perception of problem(s), and apparent symptoms. Don't stop at just the corporate level goals (efficiency, accuracy, ROI, etc.), but probe for what is in it for the client contact (promotion, getting the boss off of my back, bonus, etc.). Very often, those motivators are as important, or more so, than the more obvious objectives of the company. It may also lead you to determine solutions that are more targeted to the real objectives and accomplish the goal differently than you at first assumed you would.
- Make a reasoned analysis of these factors to define the problem properly.
- Synthesize an approach to solution through services you offer.
- Formulate a sales presentation to implement your solution and explain it— sell it—to the prospective client.

The idea is to do sufficient analysis to enable you to synthesize a highly specific presentation, as opposed to a vague and general one. Only detailed and specific presentations, whether oral or written, are truly convincing and persuasive. Anyone can generalize, but offering detail is evidence of true competence, and it is the detail that renders a presentation convincing and persuasive.

When I offer this idea of supplying detail to audiences, it almost always provokes questions reflecting a fear of giving one's expertise away free of charge. And when I point out that everyone in every business finds it necessary to give out samples occasionally, the next question is almost invariably, "How much should I give away?"

A proper and sensible answer is, "Just enough to close the sale." But how much is that? There is no practical way to measure. There are some client-prospects who need only the mere suggestion of an approach, and they can take it from there and solve their own problems (at your expense). There are others who can be led to the very brink of solution and still not be able to handle the problem without retaining you at your regular rates.

This means that you must size the prospect up, as he or she is sizing you up, to decide how much is necessary to sell the job without giving the store away. Generally speaking, it is far better to err on the side of giving a bit more than necessary than of giving too little. But perhaps a specific example will illustrate more effectively.

In my activities helping clients develop proposals, I may be asked to help analyze the requirement and suggest a basic strategy, participate in writing the proposal, lead the client's proposal team, or even write the entire proposal myself. I have done all of these. But in the discussion with the prospective client, before I am actually hired, before I am on billable time, the client may be probing for my ideas on proper strategy. To avoid giving away that which I have to sell, while still keeping the prospective client interested, I might find it necessary to say something to my client like this:

> It appears to me that your customer here is greatly concerned with costs, yet fearful that the contractor might sacrifice quality for economy. I believe that I can work out a strategy for you to keep your costs low while ensuring that quality will not suffer. I believe that I would need some estimate of [hours or days, as appropriate] to develop this for you.

If the prospect tries to push me beyond this observation, which might itself be an indication that this prospect is trying to get something for nothing, I would be deliberately vague and general, pleading that I need more time to work out the answers. I thus make it clear to the prospect, as tactfully as I can, that I will offer nothing more unless I am retained. In the meanwhile, I now concentrate on closing the sale.

This case is not necessarily typical. If your own services are more highly specialized than mine—if you are a specialist in some exotic computer field, for example—you may be able to give away quite a bit more that will still be of little value to the prospect without your specific services. Only you can make that judgment. But you should consider the problem and the alternatives.

PRICING PROBLEMS

At some point, the subject of price will inevitably arise. More often than not, pricing or, in many cases, the way the question of price is handled, becomes the most critical problem in the sales presentation; too often it becomes the make-or-break point, unless you take special steps to prevent that from happening. But there are many indications of what is happening and what the prospect is thinking that are revealed in connection with pricing.

Conventional wisdom about selling holds that it is usually a grave mistake to volunteer the price when making a sales presentation. It is wise to wait until the prospect asks what the price is. And the advantage in doing this is not only psychological but is a practical indication of the prospect's serious interest. Presumably the prospect has now found you and what you propose technically acceptable, and so is ready to move on to the subject of price.

Conventional sales wisdom also holds that it is a mistake to quote a price, even when the prospect asks for it, before you are ready to quote. You must have the prospect sold on the proposition before you throw the cold water of price on it. A premature quote or an evasion not handled properly can easily be the death knell of the sale.

Earlier we stated that the consultant must establish what the prospect/client perceives to be the "value" of the solution. Asking a prospect, "What would the value be to your company/you to have this problem resolved?" is not at all inappropriate. A prospect may have a problem, may even be aware of it, but has no intention of paying to have it solved. No amount of salespersonship will accomplish that. Or, a prospect may say, the problem currently costs my company $1 million a year; if I could resolve it for $500,000 this year and prevent us from spending the $1 million each subsequent year, I would consider that a real bargain. Knowing how a prospect would answer that question can steer you toward an appropriate price should the question of cost come up in the discussion. The reason why price discussions cause early deaths of potential project discussions is because the consultant has not done due diligence to uncover the true value of the solution and, therefore, is selling against expectations that were never identified.

Some prospects ask price almost immediately, even before the briefest discussion of their needs and what you can do to satisfy them. Such prospects are generally price shopping. This means that they have a clear idea of what is needed (or think they know exactly what they need) and are seeking the lowest-cost help available. Or, it may mean a tight budget so that the prospect does not want to spend time in serious discussion before learning if you are affordable. (Sometimes these are prospects who cannot afford consulting services but are desperately seeking someone who might want the job enough to work for a microscopic fee.)

Some prospects appear to be not seriously interested in the details of what you propose, or they may have lost interest somewhere along the way but are tolerating you and your presentation out of courtesy. You are probably wasting your time here unless you can find a way to strike a nerve.

Serious prospects hear you out, ask pointed questions about what you propose, and then ask the price. That is the indication of serious interest and that is often the point at which you win or lose the contract.

The Significance of the Pricing Problem

The problem of the salesperson who talks too much is well known; there are many stories of sellers who unsold prospects after they had sold them because they didn't know when to stop talking. More literally, the salesperson did not sense that the prospect was ready to become the customer; it was time to stop selling and close.

It is not always easy to sense that moment to close. The greatest salespeople have an instinct for sensing that moment, or they have trained themselves to estimate it almost unconsciously. It is possible, however, to sense that moment by relying on specific indicators that the prospect is about ready to accept your offer. (And your presentation should be an offer, not a plea.) One of those indicators is the query as to price. Only a seriously interested prospect is going to ask you how much (with a few exceptions, as noted). When this happens, you are at a critical juncture, when you may make or break the sale by your response to "How much will this cost me, Mr/Ms Consultant?" There is an immediate second question when a prospect asks you to quote a price. Are you ready to quote the price yet? Or is it too soon? And if it is too soon, how do you delay quoting a price without offending the prospect by avoiding an answer?

When Is Too Soon in Quoting Price?

If the inquiry about price is a indication of serious interest and possibly time to make the first close, you must ask yourself if you are ready to make that close. A premature close can turn the prospect off and lose the sale immediately.

There was a time when sales trainers would implore the salesperson that you should not close until you have completed your basic sales presentation, explaining your promise and presenting the necessary evidence to back it up and/or until you have some sound reason to believe that the prospect is about ready to agree to the contract you propose. There are occasional exceptions to this, admittedly, such as when a prospect is presold on you by virtue of earlier experience or personal recommendation or otherwise gives good evidence of a readiness to sign up without further discussion. The signs are usually rather obvious in such cases. Far more common is the case of the prospect asking the price before you have finished your presentation and before you are ready to close. More progressive salespeople/consultants/sales trainers now agree that when the prospect wants a price quote, you provide it and don't make them wait for it until you are through with your presentation (just a minute, Ms. Prospect, I am not ready to sell this to you yet. I created these 45 pages of presentation and by gum, you are going to see each and every one of them!). If you have correctly assessed the situation and developed the value equation with the client, you are ready to close when the client asks you to close. For those of you who feel that you need the presentation to more fully develop the value of the proposed solution, my advice to you is, "You won't be presenting *anything* if you haven't established what the prospect views as a fair solution/cost equation."

To be fair, if you are still in the data acquisition stage and have not fully scoped out the project, then it truly is too early to provide a quote. (You do not know what you are quoting on yet, and need additional insight before you can accurately provide a price quote back to the client.) Here are a few dialogues that suggest tactful methods used successfully by many consultants for fielding the how-much query:

Prospect: Tell me, how much will all this cost me?

Answer 1: Frankly, I don't know yet, and it would be unfair to you for me to make a guess at this point. I need to discuss this with you just a bit more before I can make a reliable estimate. But I will give you that estimate as soon as possible.

Answer 2: I can make a rough guess now, if you want me to, but it would probably be on the high side because I need to gather some more information. If we can postpone that for a few minutes, I can give you a more sensible answer to your question.

Answer 3: There are several options possible, and we need to discuss these before I can give you a sensible estimate.

Answer 4: I can price this on a total, fixed-price basis or open-ended on a day or hourly rate. If I can put off answering your question for a little while longer, I'll be able to suggest the pricing base most favorable to you.

Prospect: Well, can you tell me what your rates are?

Answer 1: Certainly. When I give you that estimate, I will also explain the rates and how I arrive at the estimate.

Answer 2: My assignments and contracts vary a great deal and affect my overhead differently. Therefore, my accountant has set up a whole rate structure for me, with different day rates for short-term or casual assignments than for long-term contracts, with a daily rate and an hourly rate, and with a base for estimating assignments on a fixed-price basis. I don't mind quoting and explaining these to you now, but I don't think that will be very helpful here because I don't know yet which would be suitable in your case.

Answer 3: Sure, here are my basic rates (quoting them), but that doesn't really tell you anything because it is the final cost, not the rates, that matters.

Answer 4: Sure. My rate is $XX a day. But you should know that I don't count the hours in a day, and the day rate applies to 12-hour days, as it does to 8-hour days. It also applies to weekends and holidays, when it is necessary to work them. My accountant calculated the rate to cover all that without charging premiums and doing a lot of extra record-keeping and bookkeeping. In the long run, I cost you less because I don't have all that extra bookkeeping of hourly time records, and you don't have to worry about overtime and other premium time. And, anyway, in the end it isn't the rate that counts but the total cost.

There are still other options possible. Some consultants believe, for example, that the quotation of an hourly rate—$62.50 an hour—is more palatable to most prospects than a daily-rate quotation such as $500 a day. Others prefer to charge a relatively low hourly rate, but they charge substantial premiums for overtime, weekend, and holiday effort. And some prefer not to quote verbally at all, but promise a follow-up written proposal and quotation. To accomplish this, they use wording such as you have just read in the dialogues, but plead that they need time to do some research and calculations in their own offices. This course may be dictated by an actual need for more time and research or for me to double-check everything and be sure that the figures are right; but many consultants follow this practice for psychological reasons. For any but small jobs or jobs on which you can't quote anything but an hourly or daily rate, it may be advantageous from the viewpoint of sales psychology to dramatize the importance of the proposed program by asking for time to study it carefully before committing yourself to a firm estimate. In addition to that, however, it is a businesslike thing to do and displays a willingness to put your offer and commitment in writing, again with probable beneficial fallout psychologically.

There are several advantages in putting your offer in writing, to submitting a written proposal, even a brief and informal one, and you should seek and welcome every opportunity to do so.

Some consultants have sliding scales or invent rates, even varying overhead rates arbitrarily for each prospective contract, as they think necessary. While I think this an unwise practice generally, I myself once offered special, lower rates to minority-owned enterprises that were struggling to get established.

What is not unwise, however, is to consider pricing the assignment based on value received by the client and not on hours invested by the consultant. Hours are a commodity that everyone can provide, and by virtue of the free market, there will always be someone willing to offer a lower hourly rate. Providing value, however, is less likely to be usurped by a competitor if the consultant establishes the link between services offered and value received. The other problem with offering hourly rates is that it encourages the client to want an accounting of time spent on the project and leads to potential conflicts. In most instances, the client really is focused on the value received and does not care if it took an hour or a month's work to achieve. This is also reinforcement for the idea of establishing the value of the project upfront, so that the discussion does not deteriorate into one of "hours of work." There are instances where a client will equate work output with hours invested to accomplish that output. Where possible, raise the dialogue to one of results and not methods or means to the end. A client who refuses to pay for results and only will pay for services on an hourly basis is either locked into a payment schedule that does not recognize the difference between effort and outcome, or does not have enough of a vision of the solution to effectively understand your proposal. This does occur at times when a competing consultant has established the parameters for a proposal or RFP. By focusing on the component elements, the consultant, and therefore the client, hopes to eliminate any competitors unable to match the expectations on a line-by-line basis. I have walked away from these situations and refused to participate. At times, I have been called back to repropose because the host company demands that there be at least three competitive bids and my refusal to bid has put that in jeopardy. While still a long shot to win the business, I have been able to change the parameters a time or two to at least level the competitive field.

WHERE TO CONDUCT INITIAL MEETINGS

Although your first contact with a new prospect may be casual, the first serious meeting—the one at which you will make a presentation and try to make a sale or start the ball rolling toward an eventual sale—must be planned. Theoretically, when you are trying to make a sale, you call on the prospect at his or her own office. Prospects may suggest calling on you, although you should normally assume that you will call on the prospect and plan to do so unless the prospect suggests some other arrangement. Such a suggestion often results when the prospect is from out of town and expects to be in your city on some near date.

If your office is in your home and you find it impracticable to conduct business meetings there, there are alternatives. Perhaps the most obvious is to meet for lunch. Many business relationships begin with a lunch.

Two questions arise in this connection: (1) Is it proper to have a drink and/or smoke at lunch with a new prospective client whose standards and mores you do not know? (2) Who should pay for lunch?

There is another problem in connection with that question of a drink at lunch. The first drink often leads to a second one, and perhaps even a third; even the first one may loosen your tongue or, even worse, tangle it. That is a serious hazard to consider.

You can never be wrong for *not* drinking at lunch. In contemporary business circles, you run the greater risk by ordering a drink than by not. The idea of power lunches including multiple drinks has become outmoded and few still abide by it.

Today the question about smoking is similar and equally important. The issue has become a highly charged one; many people become emotional about it. As many restaurants have decided or been forced by local law not to permit smoking, some smokers will light up outside the restaurant or in the car as they continue the discussion started at lunch. In general, it is best not to smoke in the presence of a nonsmoker, and not even to ask the other's permission to smoke. The query is unfair, for it is difficult and embarrassing to object, and the other person may agree to your smoking but silently resent having been all but forced to assent. Unless the prospect lights a cigarette, you do well to avoid both the subject and the smoking.

The question of who pays for lunch is a bit stickier, but the right course to follow is this: The individual issuing the invitation for lunch normally expects to pay for it, regardless of the business relationship between the two of you. If the prospect has invited you to lunch or suggests it, it is unwise to put up a struggle for the check. For one thing, some individuals can be offended by your refusal to permit them to pay, especially if they suggested lunch. For another, it suggests some lack of good taste or good grasp of proper protocol on your part. You should know how to accept the situation gracefully and with courteous thanks. Make the gesture, especially if it was you who extended the invitation, but don't get into an extended struggle over it. It should not be that big a deal, in any case, and you harm your image by making it appear that you think it is.

THINGS TO SETTLE AT THE FIRST MEETING

One thing that causes much trouble later, after a contract has been signed and the project is underway, is the failure to have achieved a complete and specific understanding with your prospect and soon-to-be new client. Distressingly often, consultants undertake assignments with only a vague understanding of what they are to achieve (and sometimes of what the price is to be), confident that they will somehow muddle through.

Clients are equally guilty in agreeing to projects with less than perfect understanding of the agreement made. Even having a written contract or letter of agreement is of little help if it does not include a clear specification or statement of work.

The problem is usually due to the normal difficulty in developing a highly specific statement of work. The client often has difficulty defining the problem clearly, while the consultant, eager for the contract, is reluctant to press too hard for details of what he or she (the consultant) must do. Although this is often a problem even when formal proposals must be drawn up and submitted, it is even more commonly a problem when the agreement and negotiations leading to a contract are informal and based entirely on verbal understandings and agreements.

Asking the client for their vision of what would be an acceptable solution upfront, what the value is for them of such a solution will go a long way toward clarifying the expectations. Even in the event that the client does not have a clear understanding of what the project will entail, the dialogue that these questions elicit can help the consultant guide or direct the prospect toward a clear vision of the solution (the one that the consultant, through acquired wisdom, experience, and overall savvy has been able to identify).

FOLLOW-UP

Some first meetings wind up in commitments or agreements, but many others turn out to be exploratory and inconclusive. Unless you do something specific and positive to prevent that dead end, you will have wasted your time and energy. In short, the first meeting should never be permitted to end without preparation and planning of the next step. Often, that first meeting exploratory and fated to end inconclusively unless you do something to avoid that eventuality. It is essential that every first meeting end with a definitely planned follow-up of some sort. That may be a written proposal, a firm commitment for lunch, a formal presentation (what some have called a "dog-and-pony" show), or other definite commitment calculated to move the action forward—progress toward a sale. It is up to you to plan and prepare for a follow-up. Otherwise, it is almost foregone that nothing will result from the first meeting.

Negotiations,
Fees, and Contracts

Consulting is a business as well as a way to practice a profession, and you must never lose sight of that if you are to survive in your practice. Be businesslike always, and if being businesslike costs you a client or a contract, it is almost certain that the client or contract was not worth winning.

FEES, COSTS, AND PROFITS

Should you ever fill out one of the federal government's forms for estimating costs, you may be puzzled by the next-to-last line—one step above the famed bottom line—that says fee or profit. Obviously, the government considers the two terms interchangeably synonymous.

In consulting, fee and profit are not synonymous at all. The fee is what you charge, usually by the hour or day, for your services, from which you hope to realize a profit. The fees are your total income from your consulting (although you may have income from other sources that may or may not be directly related to your consulting). Your salary (I hope you pay yourself an adequate salary) and all other expenses must be paid out of this income before you can enjoy a profit. Although you collect fees for your services, you do not always enjoy a profit, as sad experience will demonstrate now and then. Depending on the organizational structure chosen when establishing your consulting practice, you may be "legally" an employee of your own one-person firm, or you may be a "Managing Partner" of a Limited Liability Corporation (LLC), in which case you are not paid a salary per se but take a distribution of the company's income as your share of the ownership. In any case, whether your income is derived from a salary or a distribution of corporate funds, it behooves you to ensure that your consulting practice's income covers the business' necessities and expenses *plus* your personal needs that are separate and distinct from the business.

Charging an hourly or daily fee is the conventional, classic practice in consulting. But there are exceptions, many exceptions. One major reason for the exceptions is that often consulting work is not identified as such, but is labeled otherwise. So many programs are exploratory, awarded and undertaken with no clear idea of how much effort or time will be required, that in some cases the client feels the need to make special contractual arrangements.

In the case of federal agencies, who undertak̶ ̶ ̶ ̶ ̶ ̶ ̶ ̶ ̶ ̶ ̶
ects, and other open-ended programs, the inclinat̶ ̶ ̶ ̶ ̶ ̶ ̶ ̶ ̶
contracts that permit the government to audit the ̶ ̶ ̶ ̶ ̶ ̶ ̶
a large one. At the least, except for small contracts, t̶ ̶ ̶ ̶ ̶ ̶ ̶ ̶
sis of estimated costs that will reveal all elements of ̶ ̶ ̶ ̶ ̶ ̶ ̶ ̶s. Because
of this requirement alone—that you open your books—̶ ̶ ̶ ̶ ̶ ̶sultants do not wish
to do business with the government.

This is not to say that the government never pays consultants on a fee basis. In
fact, the government hires many consultants and is a major and even sole source of income for many consultants. Unfortunately, however, most agencies have an archaic
and unrealistic view of what a competent consultant is worth today because they try to
equate hourly or daily consulting rates with hourly or daily earnings of government
employees, an unrealistic scale against which to measure. An experience of my own a
number of years ago illustrates the logical absurdities in some bureaucratic thinking:

The Region III office of what was at that time (circa 1978) the Commerce Department's Office of Minority Business Enterprise (OMBE) hired me to conduct a half-day
seminar for their contractors in Wilmington, Delaware. My letter proposal quoted
$300 plus expenses. The agency agreed, I conducted the seminar, and I was duly paid.
End of the story? Not quite.

Some three months later, the headquarters office of OMBE asked me to present a
similar half-day seminar to their staff in Washington. Again I wrote a letter proposal
describing the seminar and quoting $300. (No expenses involved this time, since my
offices were then in Washington.) This office balked, objecting that their maximum
daily rate for consulting was $150. (In their generosity, they offered to pay me the
full-day rate for my half-day presentation!)

My response was that I would amend my proposal to accommodate their problem, and I did so. I made a rather minor change to the proposal and modified the cost
presentation to read as follows:

Preparation for seminar presentation:	$150
Presentation of seminar:	150
Total cost:	$300

The agency had no problem at all with this. They accepted it immediately, and I
presented the seminar.

There is a moral here: How you present a proposition may be more important
than what you propose. That is often true, and it is important to understand the other
person's problem and work to solve it. In the case of the OMBE office, the problem
was an archaic and unrealistic internal policy, not the cost of my services. When I
solved their problem, I solved my own.

When selling to the government or to any large bureaucratic organization (and
most large organizations tend to become bureaucratic), you are likely to run up against
such problems as these, stemming from what appear to be inflexible rules. Generally,
the rules are not that inflexible; instead, the individuals are fearful of deviating from

usual practice, making exceptions, or asking someone in higher authority to approve an exceptional procedure.

STANDARD RATES

There are no standard rates for consultants. The very nature of consulting all but mandates that each consultant has a unique worth, determined by a number of factors. But there are typical rates. Witness another of my own experiences in the days when I maintained a suite of offices in downtown Washington, D.C.

A stranger who had gotten my name from some publicity about my work dropped into my office unannounced one afternoon and introduced himself. He represented a prominent company and was visiting Washington from Atlanta, where his company was headquartered. He was seeking a consultant to help his company in their pursuit of a government contract. He had barely finished his brief introduction and accepted my invitation to have a seat when he demanded to know what my daily rate was.

This was an immediate tip-off. When a prospect wants to know the price before discussing his or her need and inquiring into what you can promise to accomplish and what your credentials are, you are almost surely wasting your time in further conversation. Experience shows that you can do business with such a client only by lowering your rates to less than break-even, and that such clients are almost always impossible to deal with.

Well aware of this as a result of many earlier experiences, I was more than willing to end the interview immediately and get back to my work. I quietly quoted him $500 per day plus expenses, if required. His response was prompt: "You fellows must have a union. Everybody charges $500 a day in this town."

It wouldn't have mattered if I had quoted $300 or $5,000. I did not expect or want to hear from this gentleman again, nor did I. There is no profit and certainly no future in being the cheapest guy in town. The point, however, is that he did encounter a number of consultants who all charged $500 a day or thereabouts. And most able consultants at that time, according to a poll by the late Howard L. Shenson, a trainer of consultants, reported daily fees close to that figure.

Today, the average daily rate is probably considerably in excess of that—$1,000 to $3,000 per day is not unusual—although there are still many consultants charging fees on the more modes scale of approximately $800 per day. That is probably a bottom figure, however, for an able and well-established consultant.

Unless your circumstances are unusual or you are now only starting your practice and want to get yourself established by charging modest rates in the beginning, you will be well advised to make $800 per day your minimum. A bit of analysis will show why that is a realistic bottom rate. Let's look at some figures.

As a specialized expert (and the assumption in this book is that you are "expert" in the content of your consulting area) in your field, you are probably entitled to, in today's economy, earn at least $100,000 a year. Expertise level and experience may greatly influence that target. That provides you with a solidly middle-class earning in most urban areas of the United States, without causing you to scrimp and save to

would send it to $9,948. You would thus have to persuade the client to pay you $995 a day to cover all your costs and provide a profit. And again, this is based on your being satisfied with a $75,000 salary. For every incremental amount above that, the numbers escalate proportionately. The effect of an increase in the overhead rate is not linear; it snowballs. Each dollar you pay yourself at 50 percent overhead (in the example used here) is billed to the client at $2.23; at 150 percent overhead, each dollar you pay yourself results in $3.38 on the bottom line.

This presents a dual problem. On the one hand, your escalating costs compel you to ask for larger fees, and on the other hand, they restrict your earnings. Ergo, it is important in every enterprise to control and minimize overhead.

High overhead is a serious problem when dealing with government agencies, too, especially when you are required to supply detailed cost analyses, as exemplified in Figure 14.1. This is an example of a Standard Government Cost Form, and it follows the general format of the example given here, although it is more detailed, providing for a G&A figure and consulting fees as a separate item of direct cost. (Should you bid with someone else as a potential subcontractor, an estimate of the cost of your services would appear here.) The reverse side of Figure 14.1 provides space to add explanatory detail. Because the government agencies buy so much from the private sector, government procurement officials are usually aware of typical overhead rates in various industries and are sensitive to any they consider to be unduly high. To them, a high overhead rate suggests an inefficient contractor.

Provisional Overhead

The explanation of overhead given here was derived, as stated, on the premise that you or your accountant had a full year's figures to study in determining what overhead rate you had actually experienced in your practice. This—an experienced overhead rate—is often referred to a historical overhead. There are circumstances, however, under which you will not have or will not be able to use an historical overhead rate. (For example, you may not yet have a full year's experience and records to review, or you may have good reason to believe that your current and future overhead will be substantially different than your historical rate.) In such a case, you are compelled to resort to an estimated overhead rate, often referred to as a provisional overhead. The adjective *provisional* means that, while you may bill the client on the basis of that estimated overhead rate, after the contract is over you may have to make an adjustment on the basis of the true overhead during the life of the contract, as determined by a post-contract audit. In the case of government contracts, a post-contract audit would rarely take place on contracts less than $100,000, and a rather small number of those are audited unless there is reason to believe that a substantial adjustment is necessary. On the other hand, a government client may decided that a pre-award audit is necessary and may therefore want to know the basis for your provisional overhead estimate, as well as some other details. It is all bureaucratic necessity, but usually not difficult to live with.

The discussion on overhead rates and costs as a determinant of fees can be overcome when a project can be stated in terms of value received by the client. Selling consulting services to the government, by necessity, requires much more of a "commodity

CONTRACT PRICING SUMMARY (RESEARCH AND DEVELOPMENT)			Office of Management and Budget Approval No. 29-R018Y		
This form is for use when (*i*) submission of cost or pricing data (see FPR 1-3.807-3) is required and (*ii*) substitution for the Optional Form 59 is authorized by the contracting officer.			PAGE NO.	NO. OF PAGES	
NAME OF OFFEROR		SUPPLIES AND/OR SERVICES TO BE FURNISHED			
HOME OFFICE ADDRESS					
DIVISION(S) AND LOCATION(S) WHERE WORK IS TO BE PERFORMED		TOTAL AMOUNT OF PROPOSAL		GOVT. SOLICITATION NO.	

DETAIL DESCRIPTION OF COST ELEMENTS					
1. DIRECT MATERIAL (*Itemize on Exhibit A*)			EST COST ($)	TOTAL EST COST	REFERENCE
a. PURCHASED PARTS					
b. SUBCONTRACTED ITEMS					
c. OTHER -- (1) RAW MATERIAL					
(2) YOUR STANDARD COMMERCIAL ITEMS					
(3) INTERDIVISIONAL TRANSFERS (*At other than cost*)					
TOTAL DIRECT MATERIAL					
2. MATERIAL OVERHEAD (Rate %*$ base =)					
3. DIRECT LABOR (*Specify*)	ESTIMATED HOURS	RATE/ HOUR	EST COST ($)		
TOTAL DIRECT LABOR					
4. LABOR OVERHEAD (*Specify Department or Cost Center*)	OH RATE	* BASE =	EST COST ($)		
TOTAL LABOR OVERHEAD					
5. SPECIAL TESTING (*Including field work at Government installations*)			EST COST ($)		
TOTAL SPECIAL TESTING					
6. SPECIAL EQUIPMENT (*If direct charge*) (*Itemize on Exhibit A*)					
7. TRAVEL (*If direct charge*) (*Give details on attached Schedule*)			EST COST ($)		
a. TRANSPORTATION					
b. PER DIEM OR SUBSISTENCE					
TOTAL TRAVEL					
8. CONSULTANTS (*Identify - purpose - rate*)			EST COST ($)		
TOTAL CONSULTANTS					
9. OTHER DIRECT COSTS (*Itemize on Exhibit A*)					
10.	*TOTAL DIRECT COST AND OVERHEAD*				
11. GENERAL AND ADMINISTRATIVE EXPENSE (Rate of cost element Nos.)					
12. ROYALTIES					
13	*TOTAL ESTIMATED COST*				
14. FEE OR PROFIT					
15.	*TOTAL ESTIMATED COST AND FEE OR PROFIT*				

Figure 14.1   Standard government cost form.

This proposal is submitted for use in connection with and in response to *(Describe RFP, etc.)*

and reflects our best estimates as of this date, in accordance with the Instructions to Offerors and the Footnotes which follow.

TYPE NAME AND TITLE	SIGNATURE
NAME OF FIRM	DATE OF SUBMISSION

EXHIBIT A--SUPPORTING SCHEDULE *(Specify. If more space is needed, use reverse)*

COST EL NO.	ITEM DESCRIPTION *(See footnote 5)*	EST COST ($)

I. HAS ANY EXECUTIVE AGENCY OF THE UNITED STATES GOVERNMENT PERFORMED ANY REVIEW OF YOUR ACCOUNTS OR RECORDS IN CONNECTION WITH ANY OTHER GOVERNMENT PRIME CONTRACT OR SUBCONTRACT WITHIN THE PAST TWELVE MONTHS?
____YES ____ NO *(If yes, identify below.)*

NAME AND ADDRESS OF REVIEWING OFFICE AND INDIVIDUAL DHHS Audit Agency, 1200 Main Tower Bldg., Dallas, TX 75202	TELEPHONE NUMBER/EXTENSION (214) 767-3261

II. WILL YOU REQUIRE ANY GOVERNMENT PROPERTY IN THE PERFORMANCE OF THIS PROPOSED CONTRACT?
____ YES ___ NO *(If yes, identify on reverse or separate page)*

III. DO YOU REQUIRE GOVERNMENT CONTRACT FINANCING TO PERFORM THIS PROPOSED CONTRACT?
____ YES ____ NO *(If yes, identify.):* ___ADVANCED PAYMENTS ___PROGRESS PAYMENTS OR ___GUARANTEED LOANS

IV. DO YOU NOW HOLD ANY CONTRACT *(Or, do you have any independently financed (IR&D) projects)* FOR THE SAME OR SIMILAR WORK CALLED FOR BY THIS PROPOSED CONTRACT?
____ YES ____ NO *(If yes, identify.):*

V. DOES THIS COST SUMMARY CONFORM WITH THE COST PRINCIPLES SET FORTH IN AGENCY REGULATIONS?
____ YES ____ NO *(If no, explain on reverse or separate page)*

Figure 14.1   Reverse side of standard government cost form (Continued).

sale" mind-set in many instances due to the restrictive nature of the contractual obligations of a governmental agency. Should your consulting services lend themselves to governmental targets, it is essential that you understand the parameters of their process for evaluating and assessing proposals.

PRIVATE-SECTOR PARALLELS

That huge market (over $600 billion annually) represented by federal, state, and local government purchases of goods and services has had a profound effect on the economy generally and even on the purchasing practices of private business. For one thing, almost all government contracts of size result in subcontracts. As this book is being written, the government has contracted with huge defense industry manufacturers and contractors to conduct the War on Terrorism (Haliburton, Sikorsky, and EDS among them), each of which has turned to smaller niche consulting concerns to provide support to the larger contract winner. Subcontracts have become so important a source of income for small business that the federal government has established special offices to aid small business in winning subcontracts. Another effect of today's huge government markets, especially that of the federal government, is on the shaping of procurement methods practiced by private-sector corporations. There has thus developed a tendency in the private sector to emulate government procurement practices.

This is not entirely a matter of choice. Government clients are well aware that their prime contractors will have to subcontract portions of the work so that, in effect, the prime contractor is acting as surrogate for the government, spending government dollars in subcontracts to carry out government programs. The government often extends the principles of open competition and equal opportunity by providing in prime contracts a requirement to award subcontracts on the basis of competition. The private sector, therefore, tends to emulate the government systems as the simplest way to comply with such contractual requirements. Ergo, the ascendancy in recent years of bids and proposals as procurement methods in the private sector, even when government contracts are not involved. Therefore, even if you never pursue government business, either directly as a prime contractor or indirectly as a subcontractor, you may eventually find yourself facing similar requirements in bidding or proposing. Moreover, the written proposal has proved itself an effective marketing tool, even when the client has not specifically called for it; the ability to develop a good proposal should therefore be on your must list in any case.

GOVERNMENT CONTRACT NEGOTIATION

The federal Standard Form 33 (Figure 11.2) is itself a contract when signed by the two parties, you and the client's authorized official, although it usually includes other documents—work statements, items descriptions, bids, and/or proposals—by reference. In the case of small contracts based on sealed bids, there is no further action or follow-up, normally, because the award is made to the lowest bidder. There simply are no negotiations of any kind; they are reserved to competitive proposals, which are the bidding instruments for negotiated procurement. Even in the case of the latter procurements, quite often there are no follow-up actions after proposal openings and evaluations, other than simple signing of the form by the procurement official, thereby accepting your proposal as submitted and establishing a contract on that basis. Even when there is a follow-up, in the case of a small contract, it will usually be nothing more formal than a telephone call from the contracting officer to verify your readiness to proceed and accept a contract based on your proposal.

There are exceptions. In some cases, even when the contract is a relatively small one, the contracting officer will call, write, or wire, inviting you to submit a best and final offer. This is an effort to elicit a best price from you, and presumably (but not necessarily) is asked of each proposer deemed equally qualified to be awarded the contract. The contract is subsequently awarded, presumably (but again not necessarily) to the lowest bidder among those invited to submit a best and final offer.

For small contracts, this is usually the extent of the negotiation, if it is done at all. But in the case of larger contracts, the request for best and final offers is almost automatic, and even that is not necessarily the extent of the negotiation. There may be discussions with the client's staff and procurement officials, and these may become quite extensive in some cases, concerned with technical details of performance and programs, as well as costs.

PRIVATE-SECTOR CONTRACT FORMS

Again and again. I have had corroboration from other independent consultants of the hazard in presenting a client with an excessively legalistic contract form for a relatively small contract. In my own case, a $26,000 contract with the American Red Cross was scuttled by the introduction of excessive legalese. After submitting a proposal, discussing it with the client's training director (it was a training-development program), and reaching technical agreement and agreement on cost, we were invited to meet and negotiate the contract. Alas, our corporation's marketing director, for reasons that were a mystery to the rest of us, decided that he had to have our corporate attorney present. The client became alarmed that we felt a need for legal representation to conclude what were to be little more than formalities on a relatively small contract, and terminated our relationship at once. Failing to learn from this experience, our marketing director proceeded to draw up a statement of standard contract terms that would be boilerplate copy for all contracts. These were so legalistic as to scuttle many other contract negotiations and present us with a problem in negotiating all future contracts.

Hubert Bermont, a successful independent consultant of many years' experience and publisher of *The Consultant's Library* series, agrees. He believes that asking any client to sign a formal contract for a small consulting assignment is risky because it usually alarms the client. Today, most of us are conscious of an exhortation to sign nothing without reading it carefully. We are also suspicious of the mysterious and often arcane phraseology of lawyers and legal forms—torts, habeas corpus, flagrante delicto, and other Latin words. Even when we do read a contract with great care, we are usually unsure of what it actually says! (And too many courts and trials have demonstrated that even the lawyers, as well as the rest of us, are often wrong in what they/we think the contract said.) So it is not surprising that even in normal times, but especially in these litigious times, clients become alarmed by multipage, Latin-laden contracts for small and simple programs.

Even the U.S. government has forsaken those wherefores, whereases, and party of the second part terms in contracts and now executes them in simple, everyday English (or, at least, what passes for simple, everyday English in the government bureaucracy).

None of this is to say that there should not be a distinct understanding between you and your client, or that the understanding should not be recorded in some manner. It is to say only that the understanding should not be recorded as thick documents with blue binders and numerous signatures. They should be simple letter agreements, at most; most of my own assignments are on the basis of verbal contracts, reached after informal and friendly discussion (which has often followed an exchange of letters inquiring into my services and availability and my response, listing my offer and simple terms) and a handshake. (Such correspondence becomes an important part of the documentation and should be filed.)

Perhaps that is because I do my best to keep the set of terms as straightforward and simple as possible. I make clear that I charge a substantial daily rate, which I stipulate, but I do not charge overtime or premium time rates. I recommend what I believe to be the best courses of action, but I do whatever my client decides to have me do. And I do those things to the best of my ability. I do not flail at windmills; I urge whatever I think is best for my client, but I recognize the client's right to act contrary to my counsel. I cannot guarantee any particular outcome, of course; I can guarantee only my best efforts. Therefore, the only things to reach specific agreement on are costs—my fees and expenses—and length of commitment or estimate of time required to achieve the desired result. I may sometimes furnish a not-to-exceed estimate or guarantee completion within some specific time frame. In that case, that information must be in the agreement too.

Your own terms and stipulations are likely to be different than mine, and they ought to be whatever is fair and proper for you and your own clients. Whatever they are—if, for example, you charge premium overtime—draw them up as standard terms, stated as simply and as clearly as possible, and include them in any agreement you sign with a client or in response to a request for quotation. At most, you will normally require only a simple letter of agreement—probably a single page—and in many cases you will not require even that.

WHAT IS A CONTRACT?

The consultant accepting an assignment from a client has entered into a contract with that client as soon as the two of them reach agreement. A contract is not a piece of paper; it is an agreement. A lawyer might stipulate the legal need for related considerations, but the essence is the agreement and mutuality of purpose. Thus, the agreement between the consultant and the client is a contract, even if it is only verbal.

Verbal contracts are perfectly valid and binding. Human memories are faulty, however, especially if and when a dispute about the contract terms—what was agreed to—arises. It is therefore wise to record the contract by specifying its terms on paper.

It is also advantageous to record the contract in this manner because the act of writing the terms out compels the parties to think things through in advance, covering details that might easily have been overlooked had the agreement been verbal only and reached only via informal conversation.

Things that often merit inclusion in a contract are:

- Date that the project is to commence.
- Date or event that will conclude the contract (as of December, 2005 or Upon Delivery of Findings Report).
- Payment terms (when payment will occur, how much the fees will be, what is included in the fee and what is not, etc.).
- Project scope (the project will include A, B, and C).
- Upon occasion, for longer term contracts, milestones, and "go/no-go" steps if appropriate. This provides *both* you and the client a chance to reassess if the original plan is working out as planned and mutually decide if the project is still viable.

Things to avoid putting into a contract:

- Promises of results (i.e., sales will increase 50 percent).
- Deadlines based on circumstances outside of your control (don't commit to interviewing 15 people, if you are not assured that they will be available before your deadline of project delivery).
- Overly legalistic or boilerplate language that you yourself do not fully understand, but "have borrowed" from some other source. If you are questioned on it, you may not be able to explain it (assuming the client gives you the chance to explain it before deciding to use someone else who is easier to do business with).

POTENTIAL HAZARDS

The principal hazard in failing to have a written contract is the possibility of disputes over the specific terms agreed to. There is also a hazard of quite another kind: That is the possibility, a very real possibility, experience demonstrates, of losing the sale by alarming your client with an excessively formal written contract of many pages, with seals, witnesses, and other legal formalities. Clients tend to find such documents formidable—even forbidding—and they often shrink at such extremes, especially when the project is not especially large.

Take special note here: The real contract is the *understanding and agreement* between you and the client. Unless that exists and is a sincere understanding and agreement, one that each of you intends to honor fully, the most elaborate and formal document will not be effective. Unless you are satisfied that the client understands the agreement and fully intends to carry out his or her end of it faithfully, go no further: The business relationship is most likely to be an unhappy and unsuccessful one. On the other hand, when there is mutual understanding and sincerity, a simple written agreement will serve as well as the most formal and elaborate one.

ALTERNATIVES TO FORMAL DOCUMENTS

This discussion is not in the context of the major, multimillion dollar project, where we would expect detailed specifications, letters, and multi-page contracts negotiated by the parties and drawn up by their attorneys. This discussion is entirely in the context of the relatively small projects for which the independent consultant normally contracts.

The middle ground between the major project and the minor task requires that you document what is to be done in an informal contract or agreement of some sort; there are several ways to accomplish this. In some cases, the client issues a purchase order, which is itself an informal contract, even if you do not sign it; the fact that you accept it and begin work is normally evidence of agreement. (Some clients do ask that you sign and return a copy of the purchase order to signify your acceptance of it.)

In other cases, the client issues a Letter of Intent (or acceptance) of your written or verbal proposal. Often the client sends you two copies of such a letter, asking you to sign one copy and return it for the client's record.

Finally—if the client does not produce a purchase order or some other paper signifying a contractual obligation—it is wise for you to produce your own informal contract.

With the advent of the Internet and use of e-mail for business correspondence, some consultants have begun to use e-mail letters for their Agreement Letters in place of hardcopy mailed letters on letterhead. This is perfectly acceptable for *most* business dealings (remember, based on the previous section, contracts between consenting parties rarely run afoul of the agreements established and, therefore, don't usually wind up in dispute). There are some companies that will not accept e-mail proposals, letters of agreements, or other formal business relationship correspondence because it lacks an official signature (though there are now e-mail signatures available, they are not universally accepted by all clients). The best counsel that can be offered is to inquire with your client on that company's perspective on using e-mail for that purpose and then cooperating with their policy. There is no sense in trying to play attorney with them and convince them otherwise; if they prefer hardcopy letters of agreement, then use that approach.

THE INFORMAL CONTRACT OR LETTER OF AGREEMENT

It is probably best not to use the word *contract* (that word itself can scare off a client), but call it a *Letter of Agreement* or, simply, *Agreement*. A suggested agreement form appears as Figure 14.2. It would appear on your own letterhead, of course, unless the client prefers to have it on his or her letterhead. (I have found that some do prefer it.) In that case, simply create an electronic file with the agreement either completed or with blanks left for the client to fill in with data as appropriate.

AGREEMENT

Client: _____

_____
     (Name & address)

Client
contact: _____
      (Name of individual)

Services to be provided or relevant specifications/proposal, if applicable:

_____

_____

_____

Reports/presentations: _____

On client's premises [ ]   *On consultant's premises* [ ]

Other or special arrangements: _____

Beginning date: _____ *Target completion date:* _____

Fees: $_____ *per* _____ No. _____ *Total est. fee/cost:* $_____
   (hr/day/other)   (hr/day other)

Other costs: $_____ (for: _____)

Advance retainer: $_____ *Terms for balance:* _____

_____

Notes, remarks, special provisions, if any: _____

_____

_____

_____

For_____ (consultant) For_____ (client)
  (type/print)   (type/print)

_____ (signed) _____ (signed)

_____ (date) _____ (date)

Figure 14.2   Simple letter of agreement.

If possible, keep this to one page in the interests of simplicity and informality. (If you fear that this agreement is too simple to furnish you full legal protection, bear in mind the injunction expressed earlier: No agreement or contract document, however detailed, however long, or however many seals, signatures, and flourishes it contains, is worth the paper it is on if the parties have not executed it in good faith.) The most elaborate contracts are violated and contested in the courts every day. Aside from that, you can always add your own boilerplate, as noted in the next paragraph.

Although most of the items in the form offered here as a model are probably self-explanatory, some discussion and explanation of others are in order. First of all, the form is generalized and suggests the major points such an agreement should specify. You should modify it to suit any special needs or considerations by deletions, additions, or changes, or incorporate your own boilerplate about your normal terms and conditions. Give each of these items careful consideration. Also, in the event the client prefers to have the agreement executed on his or her own letterhead, some of the items may require rewording to be appropriate. For example, if the agreement is on the client's letterhead, the first line should be changed to identify the consultant, rather than the client, and the same consideration applies to the signature blocks at the bottom of the form.

The item "No. _____" may appear cryptic. It calls for the number of units upon which billing is based—hours, days, and so on. That is followed by the rate of billing for each unit and the total fee. (If this is based on an estimate of the time required, that should be indicated.) If you are using a project fee approach, or any other nonhours worked basis for the fee, you would not use this field and would not include it on the agreement.

Any anticipated extra costs—travel, telephone tolls, printing—must be covered also, if applicable. They can be noted under the block provided for notes, remarks, or special provisions, if lengthy explanation is required.

Aside from that, you may wish to consider the implications of some other blocks, especially the one suggesting an advance retainer. You may or may not consider this applicable in your own case. If your practice is such that you re always paid in advance, the wording should reflect the receipt of the total fees. If you are being engaged by a major corporation, especially if the project is short-term and must be initiated at once, it may be unnecessary and impractical to demand an advance retainer. If you are retained by an individual or small organization of whom you know little, requiring an advance retainer (I suggest one-third of the estimated total cost) is a wise practice. It will almost surely save you from a few problems, as it has me. It is a good way to validate or qualify such a client, for one thing. But it is also good fiscal policy to ensure that you do not wait interminably for payment; instead, you get a substantial retainer and set forth clearly defined terms for the balance due.

My practice in such situations has been to require a second one-third of the total at the approximate midpoint of the project, and the final payment on completion. Where the project is long-term or of indefinite term, you may wish to set forth a system of progress payments on some regular basis, such as every two weeks, every thirty days, or at defined and identifiable milestones. In some instances, as noted previously, you may wish to reassess the progress of the project at the time of these milestones and determine if the project is still worth pursuing. In essence, you and the client determine if it still makes sense to continue, this is sometimes referred to as "go/no go" step. You can, of course, add a second page, if it is necessary to describe the agreement in greater detail or if your client wishes more detail, but clients are usually more inclined to keep the agreement as simple as possible, and that has been a prime consideration in designing this model.

One further point: If the client has supplied a detailed work description (specification of what is to be done) and/or if you have supplied a detailed proposal of what you offer to do and the project is based on your mutual acceptance of either or both of these documents, the letter of agreement should cite and identify this/these document(s) and indicate that this/these constitute the details (the clauses or what lawyers tend to identify as the schedule) of the contract. In that case, the letter agreement need merely add any details not covered in those other documents and bear your mutual signatures. That incorporates the other document into the contract by reference and greatly simplifies the final process.

Unlike some private-sector clients, the government client recognizes your right to be paid with reasonable promptness and is likely to be apologetic about any delay. Here, the largest advantage to you is the statutory protection and preference you can enjoy, especially as a small business, when dealing with the government. For one thing, the law says clearly that as a small business you are entitled to receive progress payments, whereas a large company might be expected to wait until the project is completed before submitting a bill. It is common practice on ongoing contracts to submit invoices each month, and in most cases contracting officers will accept and process invoices from small businesses as frequently as every other week. So you can see that there is no reason to be bashful about demanding payment without unreasonable delay, nor need you be hesitant about stipulating your need for progress payments.

ANNUAL RETAINERS

I have used the term retainer to mean an advance payment or deposit made at the outset of a consulting contract. This I consider to be a must in certain cases, as I indicated, although there is no harm in asking for it in the case of large and well-known corporation. Even the large corporation officials understand your cash-flow needs (they have them too!) and will accommodate you. (Federal procurement regulations make provision for advance payments too, but this is rarely exercised and is reserved to unusual circumstances.)

The term retainer has another meaning, as applied to an entirely different situation, although it is still an advance payment. There are some cases where clients use consulting services frequently but irregularly—unpredictably, that is. To ensure that their chosen consultants will be available to them when needed, they sometimes place their consultants on a retainer basis, paying in advance for guaranteed availability and services if and as needed.

This is usually under an annual agreement in which the client pays the consultant some fixed monthly sum, in return for which the consultant guarantees his or her immediate availability when called. If services are not used in any given month, the payments accrue as a credit until the client does call for services, whereupon the client may use the equivalent in services, at regular rates, with normal billing for any services beyond the amount standing to the client's credit. If there is any credit left at the end of the year, it is wiped out and the agreement renewed with a fresh start. That is, is the client has paid the consultant $200 a month for 12 months, and used $3,500 worth of services, the client pays the additional $1,100. On the other hand, if the client has used only $1,000 during the year, the consultant keeps the $1,400 difference because the slate is wiped clean at the end of the contract year.

It is in your interest, should you enter into such an arrangement, to key the monthly figure to whatever amount of time you expect the client to require of you each year. But you must also ask yourself what it is worth to you to guarantee your availability to a given client no matter when he or she calls. It is certainly a comfort to have some guaranteed income, but it may become a stone around your neck if you do not think it out carefully.

NEGOTIATING TIPS, TACTICS, AND GAMBITS

In any negotiation, no matter with whom, the other party is trying to psych you out, and you are trying to do the same to the other party. Each of you is trying to read the other's intent, willingness to yield on certain matters, and bottom lines. You want to determine the maximum price and/or other benefits you can win, while the client wants to know what is the best deal that can be struck with you.

As the seller, you probably believe that the other party, as the buyer, has a great advantage in the bargaining session. You are forced to compete with others, and it's all or nothing: you win or you lose. But the client can't lose because he or she can buy from someone else if your terms are not acceptable. And, presumably, the client already knows everybody's asking price, while you are playing a guessing game.

But you may be entirely wrong in that pessimistic assessment. The thing you need most here is information. It's easy to be a brilliant negotiator if you know that you are the low bidder or that the client is not seriously considering anyone else for the project. So you ask questions and make conversation in the hope that the client will let some information slip out to help you judge how close you are to the goal and how you compare in costs and quality with your competitors. You want to know how hard you can press and how stubbornly you can hold out without losing the contract.

The most reliable source of information on how the client feels and thinks about all the relevant matters—price, program, you, and your competitors—is the client. I am constantly surprised at how many people resort to devious means for getting information rather than trying straightforward ways, such as asking direct questions. In trying to determine how the client really feels about the price or what importance he or she attaches to reducing the price, such questions as the following have often produced the information I needed:

"Mrs. Client, I know that the project plan I have proposed is fairly elaborate and sophisticated, possibly beyond what you believe you need. Are there provisions in my plan that you feel you do not need so that we can cut them back and reduce costs or beef up other areas?"

Even an evasive response to this question can be quite helpful, and sometimes the frankness with which the client answers tells you everything you need to know—how highly the client rates you and your plan, whether you need to find a way to reduce costs, or other valuable input. Moreover, the client who truly favors you as the prospective consultant will try to hand you the information you need to win the contract.

If you have used the strategy of pricing a basic model and offering several options, the situation is tailor-made for inviting the client to discuss the various options or to ask you questions about them.

An alternative approach is to invite the client to review the major features of your proposed plan with you, and ask questions as you go.

I have known cases where the client has said something such as, "Mr. Consultant, I think your plan is fine and your personal reputation is excellent, but frankly I find your costs far too high."

The proper response is not an argument that your prices are right, but a question along these lines: "Mr. Prospective Client, may I ask you what in my proposal you feel is unnecessary and that we can cut from it to reduce the cost?" The idea in this instance is *never* to drop price without getting a concession back (otherwise, your pricing appears to be designed to gouge the client and has no "real" value basis).

Regardless of the answer, your objective is to get into a discussion of the value you are offering; if the client tells you effectively that you are prescribing a limousine when a tin lizzie is needed, review your plan step by step to see what can be taken out.

You may find, as I have so often, that in the end the client does not want to give up anything offered and convinces himself (or herself) that your plan is the right one and your price is right for it. It is amazing how often, with the Socratic method (asking the right question), you can permit the client to do your final selling and closing for you!

On the other hand, if you do find it necessary to reduce your price, it is unwise to do so arbitrarily. That suggests that you either priced the program higher than necessary in the first place or you are desperate for the contract. It adds to your general credibility to negotiate any price cuts by asking the client to give up something, no matter how small the sacrifice might be. Perhaps the client will chuckle inwardly at his or her shrewd bargaining in getting a significant price reduction in exchange for a minor sacrifice. That's fine; the client ought to be satisfied. What you employed here is a legitimate bargaining tactic; it not only solves a problem, but it encourages the client to believe he or she is making strides toward a favorable contract with you.

In one case where I was negotiating a contract for services to a small company, the client made what I refer to as the usual proposition because it has been offered me so often: My payment, the client proposed, would be some lucrative portion—a subcontract—of the contract I would help the client win. I politely but firmly made it clear that I do not work on speculation or contingency. (Some bitter experiences are responsible for my making that a firm policy.) The client was evidently prepared for that response because he almost immediately proposed that I accept part of my fee in cash and part as a subcontract. I took time to appear to consider it, and then agreed reluctantly and proceeded to negotiate the cash payment and the size and nature of the subcontract. But I insisted on a cash payment that would satisfy my normal fee requirements. The client was pleased with his competent negotiating strategy, and we concluded the agreement.

I was not disappointed: I never got the subcontract. (I did not expect it.) But we were both satisfied, so it was a fair bargain.

In one instance, a client came back to me after I had proposed a project and fee schedule and wanted to "get more" for the same price (additional consulting for the price charged). In that situation, I was actually able to negotiate for the increased scope *and* for the corresponding increase on fees. (I did offer a discounted rate based on the larger project scope, but still raised my price to reflect additional work to be done as part of the contract.)

You should recognize that a successful negotiation is one in which each party is satisfied, one in which each party believes that he or she got what he or she wanted. No contract and no negotiation are of any value if either party emerges feeling victimized.

The enemies of successful negotiation are greed, the intention to outwit and take advantage of the other party, and the ego trip of believing yourself more clever than the other party. To win at the negotiating table, try earnestly to make a fair bargain, an agreement in which both you and the client get what you want in a fair exchange, and to respect the other's intelligence. This does not mean that you should not employ sound bargaining and negotiating tactics or that you should reveal your own hand. You may plant throwaway items in your technical proposal and/or proposed budget, items that you are prepared to bargain away. That's a common negotiating tactic, and you may expect the client to make some early demands that he or she is prepared to yield on eventually, as you approach agreement. Remember, however, that you probably are bargaining against what your competitors have proposed, rather than against the client's notion of what the program should contain or cost. Using throwaway items is so commonly used, however, that it is effective only if you follow certain principles and practices in using them:

1. Do not employ obviously useless or meaningless costs as your gambits. That is underestimating your client, even showing contempt for his or her judgment.
2. Design your program full scale, the way you would prefer to see it done. Then study it to determine what could be cut out, if required, while still achieving the main objective.
3. Determine the costs of those items to see how much you can reduce costs overall by eliminating them.

Those are your proper bargaining chips. They are not trivial. They are useful to the design, but they can be eliminated without endangering the program overall in its main purpose.

When you feel that you must cut costs to win the job, use this information and negotiating strategy. Don't wait for the client to insist on cuts. Explain how costs can be cut with some predetermined sacrifices, admitting frankly that you analyzed and designed the program especially so that you could, finally, tailor it to the client's wishes if cost-cutting became necessary. This frank admission and the explanation of your farsightedness will help you at the negotiating table. Be sure that the client understands that you pledge three conditions:

1. A specific cost reduction.
2. Achievement of the main objective.
3. A sacrifice of some sort.

15 | Consulting Processes and Procedures

In this chapter, you will find three essential rules for success in building and conducting your independent practice. These are probably the most important ideas in this book.

THE ART OF LISTENING

Listening must be a lost art if we judge by the many training programs offered to teach us how to listen. We apparently hear less and less of what others are saying. Perhaps this is due to the growing cacophony in which most of us live today, especially the chatter of children; the blather of radio and TV talk shows, game shows, and loud commercials; ear-shattering rock music; the omnipresent roar of traffic; and other sounds of our modern civilization. Whether in office, automobile, home, on the street, or almost anywhere else, we are besieged by sound; true quiet is increasingly rare.

These aural assaults force us to learn how to shut them out and reject the distraction. We have learned to filter the olio of sounds unconsciously and strain the unwanted out, to quote the late Isaac Asimov. Unfortunately, the unwanted is often not unimportant or unnecessary; quite the opposite, it is often what we ought to hear. So ingrained and automatic is this filtering reflex, that we truly fail to hear what others are saying, even when it is very much in our interest to hear clearly.

That isn't the only factor that interferes with our hearing. Pressure is a factor, pressure to get many other things done simultaneously, and the pressure of competitors for our attention. We often try to speed things up, to skim what others are saying, as we might skim a report or magazine article, trying to detect and draw out the essence, while rejecting the rest. And so we often miss important details in our efforts to speed listen and leap to conclusions, usually wrong ones. We even make preemptive judgments, deciding arbitrarily what to accept and what to reject—making summary judgments of what is valid and what is not valid. Given the premium that is placed on responding faster, doing more with less, and accomplishing things in "real-time," it is not surprising that we often rely on key phrases, words, or comments and then "fill in the blanks" based on our perception of what we are hearing, or expect to hear, and not at all on what we actually hear.

Some of us go to the opposite extreme and decide that we haven't time to weigh things, and so we make judgments, often wrong ones, based on nothing more than impatience, the need and desire to get on to other things.

And finally, especially when we are trying to close a sale or win an argument, we spend our listening time thinking about what we want to say next to continue the prior exchange, and so we tend to miss what the other is saying.

THE ART OF LISTENING PART 2

Perhaps we should not be focused on hearing at all, since the ability to detect or discern sound is of less consequence to us then the ability to process, focus on, and respond to the messages we are receiving. What is truly critical is our ability to grasp what others are saying (and what they are not). Many of us believe that we are listening, and perhaps we are, but too often we are not as actively involved in the process as we need to be as consultants. What we hear is what we anticipated hearing back, or what we have a predisposed bias toward, and we react on that basis.

Listening is an active exercise (as opposed to passive receiving) that does not come naturally to many of us. Especially when we are "experts" in our chosen field, it is all the more difficult to withhold judgment and truly listen to what is said and evaluate it as if it was the first time we are hearing it before we respond.

Listening Is Not Passive

In consulting, listening must be neither passive nor unilateral. To listen, truly listen, to what prospects, clients, and others are saying, you must assume an active role, prompting, asking questions, signifying understanding, indicating a need to repeat or elaborate some word or phrase, and otherwise responding. Listening is two-way, inter-communication. Your initial part in the exchange is quiet listening and hearing, but you can hardly expect the client to judge what you need to know; you must guide the client with occasional questions and prompting.

Listening Depends on Your Role

Listening is not the same in all cases. It varies according to the role of the moment—according, that is, to your needs at the moment. Listening, when you are meeting and talking to a prospective client for the first time, is one thing; listening, when you have won the contract and are listening to the individual who is now your client, is quite another thing. In the first instance, you are listening for that which will enable you to win the contract. You need to understand the prospect's problem or need in enough detail to devise a program in at least outline form, but you also need to hear a great deal more information that will enable you to devise the sales strategy to win the contract.

Listening as a Salesperson

We consultants are professionals, and we must maintain our dignity as professionals. Nevertheless, we must also be salesmen and saleswomen in our profession, and it is not beneath our dignity to do our own selling. The irony in this is that sales professionals agree that the most successful salesperson is in effect a consultant to his or her prospect—who counsels and guides by showing how the product or service offered will solve the prospect's problem and provide valuable benefits. Salespeople are thus constantly enjoined by sales managers to be consultants to their prospects. Therefore, selling ought to come naturally to professional consultants; you need only apply the consulting technique to the sales situation. It is almost unforgivable for a consultant to be a poor salesperson!

Thus, listening as a salesperson is listening as a consultant, but as a consultant interested primarily at the moment in making a sale. That must be paramount. Nor is it cynical to reason this way; you cannot help the client until he or she is your client—until you have made the sale. You need to learn certain things to make this a reality, however, and so you must not only listen and hear, you must also respond and participate to promote or provoke the utterance of that which you need most to hear.

It is a platitude among sales professionals that one of the most self-defeating actions of salespeople is talking too long, talking when they ought to be writing—the order, that is. They fail to sense the prospect's readiness to buy (and there are methods for testing to detect that readiness, if the salesperson is unable to sense or estimate it) and go on prattling until they unsell the prospect.

A second sin of selling is failing to listen—talking when they should be listening. Quite often, that is an even worse sin, for it not only tends to offend and even alienate prospects, but it often blocks out information you need to close the sale. Be careful always to yield the floor to a prospect who wants to say something. Ask the right questions, respond as necessary, but be brief and encourage the prospect to talk, for the prospect will tell you how to sell him or her and win the contract if you listen carefully. You can and will learn while you are listening (if you pay attention), but you can learn nothing if you are talking instead of listening. It is fair to say that the art of listening is the art of learning.

Listen to and encourage the prospect to discuss these items before making a consulting recommendation:

- The essential problem or need, in as much detail as possible.
- The prospect's own notions, if any, about how to effect a solution.
- Whether the client's need calls for special problem-solving skills—that is, painstaking analysis of symptoms to synthesize a solution—or simply services for professional and specialized work, but work that is nevertheless more or less routine.
- Any specific constraints or related requirements, such as limitations of cost, time, or other factors.
- The intent of the prospect—whether firmly committed to retention of someone to help (and, if so, how soon), merely exploring the possibility of retaining

someone, or merely making conversation and trying, perhaps, to pick your brains with no intention of retaining you or anyone else.

- Whether funds are available.
- Whether the individual to whom you are speaking has the authority to retain you or, if not, who has, whose approval is needed, what the process is, and/or whatever else you can learn regarding approval and award requirements.
- What the solution would be worth to the client if it was to fix the problem identified.
- What has the client tried to do to date to address the problem? Was it successful? Why or why not?

On the basis of answers to these and related questions, you can estimate or perhaps even determine firmly whether you have a serious prospect for a contract or are wasting your time. Most of these items—those designed to determine whether there is a serious prospect of winning a contract—are known also by sales professionals as *qualifying the prospect*. Let's explore some of these items in greater depth.

The Essential Problem or Need

Many of us refer to the well-known situation of people who offer solutions for which there are no known problems. It is true enough that some consultants have favorite programs or processes, and they do work enthusiastically at trying to force-fit every prospective client's problems to one of their off-the-shelf solutions. Some even believe invariably that the client's systems are hopeless and that he or she, the consultant, must design and install entirely new ones. Still, there are prospective clients who are no less biased and shortsighted in identifying and describing their own needs. Some attempt their own diagnoses, despite having called you in as a consultant expert; then they all but demand that you confirm their diagnosis, which is sometimes far off the mark (or even a total non sequitur), making it clear that they consider you to be a charlatan if you fail to confirm their findings. They appear to be embarrassed to call on a specialist for help and are apparently trying to place you in the role of lowly assistant, carrying out orders mindlessly, perhaps to soothe their own egos or perhaps to try to be heroes in their own organizations. Often they will assure you that they called you in only because they simply don't have the time to solve the problem themselves.

From a sales viewpoint, the smart thing is to go along with this prospect's ploy; to embarrass him or her is almost surely to lose the sale entirely. Even so, you still need to know what the real need is if you are to respond intelligently. For example, a government General Services Administration client, who was responsible for preparing public information to document changes in the forms and procedures to procure A&E (architect and engineer) services, called on me for support and told me that he had already written the necessary brochure and manual. All he wanted me to do was to edit them and prepare them for the Government Printing Office, who would publish them. I agreed to do the job, but asked to see the manuscripts before I rendered an estimate. As I feared, they needed extensive rewriting and reorganization. Rather than risk embarrassing—and thus offending—this executive, however, I observed that the manuscripts needed a rather heavy edit to be made into first-class products, and I assumed that he wanted nothing less than first-class products as reflections of his work. There was no way he could object to that argument. I priced the job for rewriting, although the purchase order called for editing, and we were both satisfied.

Another problem you may run into in identifying the need is the tendency of some clients to surround the statement of need with a jungle of gratuitous remarks and speculations. (This can reflect the client's misunderstanding of the problem, but often it is a case of the client trying to fatten his/her part, to enhance his or her own importance.) The result is that it is not always easy to determine what the real problem is or, even then, to distinguish it from all the secondary problems you must respond to if you are to satisfy the client and win the contract. The following is an example.

The U.S. Army Corps of Engineers at Fort Belvoir, Virginia, called for proposals to provide support of their night-vision laboratory projects in developing infrared (night-vision) equipment by supplying a number of engineering services. It appeared clear from the Corps' description (statement of work) that the principal need perceived by the Corps was for value-engineering services, with some reverse-engineering services also required. (Value-engineering would seek design and/or manufacturing improvements and cost reductions in equipment products, while reverse engineering would update engineering drawings to reflect all changes made in equipment products.) It was thus necessary to write a proposal oriented primarily to and stressing capabilities in value-engineering services, with reverse-engineering services only incidental, and in fact the proposal was evaluated on this basis. But in practice, the project proved later to require almost entirely reverse-engineering services, with virtually no value-engineering services required.

Regardless of how things are documented in a contract or proposal, the true problem definition must be mutually understood by both parties the same way. The words chosen to describe that agreement (edit versus rewrite, reverse versus value-added) are secondary to how the words are understood between consultant and client. This raises the issue of knowing when there is agreement and when there is perceived agreement, but in fact, there is not. That is why there is as much emphasis there as on ensuring the problem is defined well.

The Prospect's Own Notions

Often enough, even the client who openly admits the need to bring in a specialist as a consultant is stubborn about his or her own prejudices as to what needs doing and how it ought to be done. Some clients describe the requirement in such detail, even furnishing outlines and block diagrams, as to create a virtual blueprint. This is a direct contradiction of the logical concept under which competitive proposals are requested. That ought to be a quest for the best ideas, and proposers ought to be encouraged to offer their best ideas. Too often, the client's bias denies him or her access to those best ideas, while it handicaps proposers seriously. It handicaps you in two ways: One, it tends to mislead you by directing your attention to the client's biased notions and diagnoses instead of providing objective information and encouraging creative thinking;

two, it all but bludgeons you into agreeing with what may very well be a totally wrong concept and approach.

You must approach this kind of situation with great caution. An eyeball-to-eyeball confrontation with the client over what should be done or how it should be done will certainly not help. But you can't agree to utilize a plan that will not produce the desired results or, at best, would be far less than the most effective or most efficient way to do the job.

A first step is to try to determine whether you have all the information you need to make a qualified judgment about the requirement. You must review critically the information supplied and make at least a preliminary judgment to determine the need for asking questions and probing for more details.

You want also to know whether the client is truly biased about how the work is to be done or is merely trying to be helpful. That is, you need to determine whether the client is open-minded and willing to consider other approaches than the one he or she appears to mandate, while avoiding a direct confrontation.

In my own experience, both sides generally lose in such confrontations. Positions become polarized, compelling each party to save face by finding justification for his or her position, no matter how illogical the justification may be. The right approach, generally, is to suggest a possible difference of opinion in a nonthreatening way, while carefully structuring the situation so as to avoid any necessity for immediate decision or immediate resolution. Give the other party a generous allowance of time to ponder and adjust to possible change. It permits that pondering and adjustment to take place without the stress of direct confrontation. This is always a good alternative to confrontation.

The method is based on being careful to avoid the appearance of attacking the client's plan. One way is to drop the merest hint that you have not yet bought the client's plan but are still open-minded by some ploy as this: "Well, that seems to me to be an excellent way to go at this, but since we are in an early talking stage and I haven't yet had time to become familiar with the details, why don't we discuss the specific approach later?"

Even if the client wishes to pursue the matter at once, you can employ this philosophy by objective discussion, rational and unemotional arguments, and reactions conditioned to those of the client. If the client appears to feel a need to defend his or her original position, your objective is still to avoid polarization and give the client ample time to think about and adjust to your ideas. Surprisingly often, the most determined opposition to your arguments or, for that matter, to any change, melts away when the other party is given time to adjust to new ideas and allowed to save face. It is almost always a grave mistake to press for an immediate decision when you and the client differ on important matters.

On the other hand, in a formal, written proposal situation, you won't usually have the opportunity to do this. You will be compelled to respond directly to a written request and statement of work (as in the case of the value-engineering services project cited here). You are not entirely without recourse, even so. You can always submit questions asking about the acceptability of exceptions and alternatives to the work statement or specifications. When properly posed, your questions often lead to a written modification of the original statement of work or even to a pre-proposal conference where the entire proposed program can be discussed freely.

Expressed Need versus True Need

As much as we would like to believe that the main function of a consultant is to use his or her knowledge, skills, and wisdom to troubleshoot, analyze, and solve difficult problems, the majority of consulting assignments do not require solving any but routine problems. For the most part, the services required are the provision of appropriate skills and knowledge to conduct a survey, design a system, perform a study, write a report, plan a project, evaluate data, determine a need, make a presentation, develop a program, and/or otherwise supply services to carry out missions that are usually more or less routine for the consultant, even when they are by nature creative services of some kind.

This is not to say that solving a specific problem is not the main objective of retaining the consultant. When the U.S. Postal Service found it necessary to update the rate data manual used by those responsible for using common carrier services in transporting the mail, they discovered that the resident expert who had always done this work had retired and was not willing to come out of retirement even as a consultant to update the manual. They therefore went in quest of an outside consultant. It was not a particularly difficult task technically—it would have been pure routine for the former employee—but it represented a problem to be solved, as well as the legwork necessary to get it done. (Nor did either client or consultant have a realistic view of how difficult the task would be technically.)

It turned out to be far less a problem than either the client or the consultant had originally anticipated. Both expected a relatively extensive overhaul and rewriting of the original manual, but research demonstrated quickly that rates had changed little since publication of the prior edition, and only a few pages required updating.

Clients err in both directions in their perceptions of what is needed. In some cases, they grossly overestimate the difficulty of the task and the qualifications—knowledge, skills, experience, and/or other resources—needed, while in others they fail completely to understand the true difficulties or qualifications necessary for the assignment. But they also sometimes fail to understand what the job is, as in (again) the case of the Fort Belvoir Corps of Engineers Night Vision Laboratory and their confusion between their need for value-engineering and that for reverse-engineering services.

Partly because of this, but also because they sometimes are unable to draw the proper conclusions from the symptoms, clients often fail to describe the true problem. In the case of the U.S. Postal Service rate manual, the client thought that special knowledge of the common carrier systems and their rates was necessary to get the job done. The consultant, who was not an expert in common carrier systems or their rates but was experienced in research and data gathering, also thought at first that a great deal of painstaking research would be needed. It turned out, however, that the data needed was readily available and could be gathered in only a couple of days. Learning this, the consultant was able to assess the need accurately and submit an appropriate bid for the task.

Clients have made such gross errors as calling for the development of written materials to give to people who are functionally illiterate, but usually it is not this easy to judge whether the stated problem is the true problem. It generally requires a bit of analysis to make the judgment, but it is essential that you make that judgment before committing yourself.

There is one exception to this, especially in contracting with government agencies: If your proposal and contract make it abundantly clear that the detailed specifications to which you agree and commit yourself are those listed by the client in the proposal request and its statement of work, you are protected contractually. By identifying the specific section of the RFP you are addressing (and aligning your responses), you make it easier for the reader or evaluator within the client to assess how well your proposal addresses the stated need. If the needs are determined to be other than what was stated, you have protected your ability to re-propose by virtue of how well you understood the original request and were prepared to address it (and, if necessary, consult with a lawyer as to what type of language is appropriate). If it becomes necessary to make changes later because the original specifications or description of the requirement prove faulty, you can then support a claim for a change in scope or specifications and contract an amendment to the price.

Specific Restraints and/or Related Requirements

Because of the inherent nature of consulting services and the arrangements under which consultants are often retained—on an hourly or daily rate for indeterminate periods, that is—you need to know whether there are any special constraints or requirements (such as a cost ceiling or not-to-exceed figure) established in advance. But there are other special constraints and requirement that you may encounter and should be alert for, such as the following:

- Requirements that the contract and work be reviewed and approved by higher authority, a list of individuals, or—even worse—a committee. Review committees, especially when they are large, can be endless trouble unless they are under the control of a decisive leader. A lengthy list of individual reviewers can be equally troublesome. *Recommendation:* Find out about this in advance, ask whether approval must be unanimous, ask what the procedure is when there is serious disagreement or deadlock, and what is your protection against arbitrariness.
- Progress reports. These can slow you down considerably, especially when the requirement calls for formal review and approval of these reports, which often leads to special meetings, with attendant demands on your time. *Recommendation:* Try to get as much information about this as possible in advance. Otherwise, if formal progress reports are required, factor estimated time for these into your schedule and price.

- Government-type cost analyses, cost revelations, and pre- and post-award audit requirements. Many people object to making such disclosures and therefore don't do business with government agencies or major government contractors who impose such requirements. *Recommendation:* If you feel this way, now is the time to find out if there are such requirements. *Note:* These are not usually imposed on small contracts—those under $25,000—but you should check and make sure.
- Turnkey requirements. These require you to install the system you design, get it running smoothly, and then train the client's staff to run it before turning over the key. Sometimes clients forget to mention that this is expected. *Recommendation:* Be absolutely sure that you know exactly what you are to deliver and protect yourself by documenting it accurately, as noted earlier.

The Prospect's Intent

The question is whether the prospect truly intends to do business, is on a fishing trip, merely curious, or wasting your time for some other reason. This was referred to earlier, in explaining that prospects must be qualified to assure yourself that they have the funding or the authority to negotiate and make a deal for your services—to bind their organization, in short. It is important enough a matter to justify another reference here to the need to determine whether the prospect's intent is serious or whether he or she is even able to do business with you. Save your time by investigating this as early in the game as possible by asking such questions as whether funds are currently available, whether the program has been budgeted yet, who must sign off on the program, and other questions that do not appear to challenge the authority or the integrity of the prospect yet elicit the information you need. If the prospect furnishes only evasive answers or declines to respond at all, you may easily judge the answer.

This does not always mean abandoning a prospect who, in turns out, has no authority to contract or negotiate with you. Even a prospect such as this may be the key to business via some indirect means and should therefore be carefully cultivated, rather than written off. Such a prospect may easily be a rich source of information about the organization, its needs, its hierarchy, and other intelligence valuable for marketing purposes. Such a prospect may also be the conduit for meeting someone who does have the authority to buy and can be persuaded to do business with you. And, in some cases, even the prospect who does not have buying authority can sell or help you sell your ideas to others in the organization. (I found this to be particularly significant in government agencies, but it is true for all organizations, especially the large and bureaucratic ones.)

VALUE OF SOLUTION

Very often, a prospect will share with you that they have identified a problem, or you may encounter a situation where you are able to build a need within the prospect that you perceive is worth pursuing. However, the prospect may not have quantified that need or come up with the priority or urgency to resolve that need. By asking that a value be assigned to a need being resolved, you can assess whether this is a problem that the client will be inclined to solve, or if it is one of many things to be tackled, "when I have the time" (and therefore, not likely to ever become critical enough to get proper time and attention, or resources against it).

In a related way, asking if the client has attempted to solve the problem to date, and if so, what the result of the attempt was (and why they perceive it was not successful) will also let you know if the client has a genuine interest in seeing the issue resolved and, if so, how urgently they want it to be completed. A prospect that has put no energy into the resolution of the problem to date, is more than likely uninterested and will be more inclined to allow the project to flounder until such time as some event (a boss demanding a response, a competitive threat, etc.) precipitates a change in motivation.

LISTENING AS A HIRED CONSULTANT

Now that you have listened carefully and heard all you needed to hear to close the sale and win the contract, it is time to begin listening as a consultant—on chargeable time at whatever hourly or daily rates you have contracted for (on a fixed price or project fee basis, if that is the case). Now you are listening not for the information you need to win the contract, but for the information you need to carry it out successfully and efficiently. It's a different proposition, although there are some points of commonality.

Just as you must discriminate, in the marketing phase, between the problem/need defined and the true problem/need, when the two are not identical, you must now discriminate between the correct solution to the problem and the client's desired solution when—again—these are not the same. In each case, you must recognize that you have two requirements to satisfy, and you must somehow satisfy both in each case.

One problem you encounter all too often in both listening and hearing situations is that clients cannot discriminate between problems and their symptoms. Those who are not trained problem solvers tend to confuse the two. One of my own clients told me that he was not winning enough government contracts. I agreed that this was a serious problem for someone whose business was government contracting per se. But, I felt compelled to tell him, the lack of success in winning contracts was the problem only in his upper-management perspective; in my own firing-line, in-the-trenches perspective, that was a symptom of some problem. But what problem?

- Poor proposal writing?
- Poor estimating?
- Addressing the wrong market segment?
- Failing to keep in touch with requirements?
- Overreaching for markets in which he did not qualify?
- Poor track record—past performance?
- Poor past contract administration?
- Overpricing?

Even this analysis is only a first step, for the initial problem identification itself yields to a similar analysis in which the problem identified must then be regarded as a symptom to be analyzed. Suppose the first analysis results in a judgment that the problem is poor proposal writing. What are the true possible causes or problems?

- Poor program design?
- Weak (poorly written) staff resumes?
- Weak (poorly written) organization credentials?
- Unpersuasive, unconvincing writing?
- Unimpressive/unimaginative presentations?
- Poor/lack of effective graphics?
- Poor/lack of strategies?

Each of these may be analyzed in similar fashion. Poor program design, for example, may be due to any of many factors, including these:

- Unorganized proposal efforts.
- Inexperienced staff used to write.
- Poor technical (design) capabilities of staff.
- Cursory and imperfect analysis of client wants.
- Hasty and casual design efforts.

Each of the series consists of identifying the symptoms, some obvious and others that must be identified by troubleshooting, testing each as a hypothesis to decide whether it is a valid symptom or an irrelevant factor, and deciding for each symptom remaining as a relevant factor whether it is a cause or an effect. (Effects are not of interest here; only causes are.)

Note that each of the series becomes more sharply focused on possible solutions. In fact, the series of analyses should continue until final solutions are suggested.

The series ends only when you have isolated and properly identified the problem. One of the techniques used as part of the Quality Improvement Process efforts of the late 1980s and early 1990s, an outgrowth of the Dr. Edward Deming's initiatives, is worth borrowing in this instance: the "five whys." Simply stated, before determining what to address or "fix," you need to ask why it is occurring five times (so at each subsequent layer of detail you can uncover the cause of a situation and prevent prematurely solving a symptom instead of the root problem). An example may help demonstrate the power of this technique:

Prospect: My salesforce needs training on handling objections.

Consultant: Why do you think they need that help?

Prospect: We are losing sales to the competition.

Consultant: Why is the competition able to close sales better than your salesforce?

Prospect: Customers tell me that my competitors are better at addressing their needs. I am sure that my folks need help in pointing out that our product can do the same things the competition can do.

Consultant: Why do your sales people fail at not overcoming objections now?

Prospect: They don't have the time to spend with their accounts, they have to close the sale quickly and get to their next call.

Consultant: Why can't they devote the time necessary?

Prospect: Their territories are so large, and we mandate that they must call on every client at least once a quarter, so they can't afford to spend hours with one customer without writing up a sale.

Consultant: So the problem is not overcoming objections then, it is better territory management, right?

As you can see from this exchange, the consultant did not jump too early on the project presented. Rather, the need was explored and ultimately, had this consultant delivered on the initial request, the outcome would likely not have made a bit of difference in this situation. The salesforce was not likely to practice the new skills, because that would have led to even longer times in front of the prospect or client and they still did not perceive that would be time well spent. The needed project was in managing territories and not in overcoming objections at all. Proper definition of the problem points to the possible solutions. The final step is to select that solution best suited to your own situation. The three ideas arrived at in this example are basic; in the actual situation, you might opt for something slightly different, but it would embody one of these general ideas. (Most problems have more than one practicable solution; you must decide which is most appropriate for your own case.)

In this case, the next stage of analysis will be the critical one. All the possibilities listed begin to point to these choices:

- Create a proposal department or at least hire a proposal manager.
- Retain consultants to lead proposal efforts.
- Send someone (the marketing manager?) to proposal-writing training seminars.

The client will have to decide which of the alternative solutions is appropriate, but you might be asked to make recommendations. In such cases, you must conduct still another analysis to determine which is most efficient, most effective, most practical, and/or most acceptable to the client. But that is a completely separate matter, which might involve other factors, such as company policies and goals. And in this case, there is a special problem: How could a consultant recommend the hiring of consultants as a solution? It would be necessary here to develop a complete set of pro and con facts for each alternative and ask the client to make the decision.

A BASIC APPROACH TO ALL ANALYSIS: FUNCTION

Analysis is the separation of something into its constituent parts to determine what it is made of, how it is made, and how it all functions together (qualitative analysis). A quantitative analysis would determine the amounts of the various components and other data of size and proportion. Here, we are concerned primarily with qualitative analysis, although we might have occasion to perform quantitative analysis too. In most of our work, we are more likely to conduct analysis not as an end in itself but as a means to an end—as a means to synthesis, synthesis of a solution.

To put this another way and in a more relevant perspective, we pursue analytical methods as the means to uncover causes, so that we truly understand the problem, and this enables us to pursue synthesis as a means to create a remedy or solution.

The key to analysis of most things, whether we are analyzing a physical device, an organization, a management system, or anything else, is function. While the item being analyzed is subjected to an identification of all its component parts, each of these parts is identified also as a function. This analysis separates all component functions of the item, and then sorts them into their various function, which must also be identified as a first order of business in the analysis. This is the basis for that discipline known as *value management* (also known as *value analysis* and *value engineering*), and describes generally what has come to be known also as *systems analysis.* The basic methods can be a valuable asset to you in both your role as a marketer and as a practicing consultant. That's because it is an orderly and systematic way of analyzing things, whether you are analyzing a client's requirements in the preparation of a proposal and development of a capture strategy for it or analyzing systems, problems, needs, and even jobs or other items as a consultant. (Analyzing positions or position titles in an organization, using the value methods, is quite enlightening and can be particularly valuable to you as a consultant. Try it and see if you still think a secretary ought to file, type, and make coffee.)

This is not intended to be and does not purport to be a definitive course in value analysis or its derivatives. That would go far beyond your needs. But it does borrow from that basic discipline and adapts what it borrows to your interests as an independent consultant.

What It Does versus What It Is

The value method requires that we shed one of our human fallacies: Most of us tend to consider only what something—an object, practice, procedure, or system of any kind—is. But if you wish to get a truer perspective into the worth and essential nature of anything, you must consider not only what it is—and consider even that primarily for purposes of identification only—but what it does—its function. That is the essential item in value analysis, the item from which all else stems and all benefits become possible.

The problem with judging something by what it is lies in the fact that the answer to "What is it?" is only a name, and all too often a name that does not tell us with any accuracy what a thing does but, on the contrary, misleads us. Take a wristwatch, for example, and ask what it is. The answer is, of course, a watch. What does a watch do? The answer you get too often to this question is that it tells time. But a watch does not tell time at all; people do that. A watch *indicates* time. You can see already that the name does not even suggest what a watch does. The conventional watch has a pair of hands that indicate the time. Many modern watches now use digital readouts as indicators. So both types of watches indicate the time, but the digital watch has many advantages over the old style (often referred to as a "dial or analog" watch to distinguish it from the digital type). For one thing, even the least expensive digital watches tend to be more accurate and less prone to needing repairs because they are entirely electronic and thus have no moving parts.

So, if they are superior in some ways, why do people spend more—much, much more—for analog watches in preference to digital watches?

They do so because a wristwatch is more than a device to indicate the time of day. That is its main function, a utilitarian function, but it has a second function. For some people, a watch is also a piece of jewelry, with great esteem value, and analog watches offer a greater artistic opportunity to designers. Those who value a watch as jewelry will tend to purchase the analog watch.

The value analyst would consider the primary function of a watch to be the practical or utilitarian one, defined as indicates time, while its esteem value (if it is a watch that is also regarded as jewelry) is defined perhaps as gives pleasure—a secondary function.

A value analyst would go at the initial analysis in an organized fashion, to get answers to several questions:

1. What is it?
2. What does it do?
3. What else would do that?
4. What else does it do?
5. What else would do that?
6. What does it cost?

To ensure objectivity, clarity, and commitment, answers must be rigidly disciplined as only verb and noun; modifiers of all kinds are banned. Hence, primary answers are indicates time, gives pleasure. The question "What else does it do?" forces you to look at other (secondary) functions, which may be of several kinds:

- Supportive of and necessary to accomplish the primary or main function.
- Supportive of but not necessary to the main function.
- Additional to and valuable or desirable function.
- Additional to but not particularly useful or valuable function.

I carry a tiny clasp knife on my key ring to open packages and serve other such chores. It has also a screwdriver, nail file, and bottle opener attachment. I have no use for those extra gadgets; they add undesired weight, bulk, and cost to the knife, and I would have preferred one without these features, but I had no choice; mine was the only such knife I could find. (Other people might find those additional items useful and desirable, of course.) Inevitably, the worth of secondary functions not essential to the primary function becomes a matter of subjective judgment, varying with individual interests.

Answering that question "What is it?" is usually easy; you need only name the item. Answering "What does it do?" is not always easy. In fact, it is sometimes rather difficult. Take that little key-chain pocket knife, for example: What does it do?

I am tempted to respond "opens packages," but that is wrong. It is I, not the knife, opening the packages. Moreover, someone else may use it for different tasks. We need to offer a simple but universally true definition, probably one that uses cuts as the verb—cuts software, perhaps, since certainly this knife would not cut anything very hard.

Some people may use the knife for things other than cutting, but the definition ought to address the intended purpose of the item.

Without belaboring the point, the idea is to identify function(s) objectively. By this means you can determine not only how well anything performs its function(s), but also how well the function or functions serve or contribute to the overall need.

Take the humble paper clip as an example. Undoubtedly it is a great invention as proved by the fact that it has existed without significant change for so long and no other temporary binder of papers has become a serious rival. One secondary (support) function was added to some paper clips in the form of serrations to add gripping power, but the idea has not really caught on because it has added nothing very significant to the function; by far the majority of paper clips are plain vanilla, as they have been since the beginning.

The reason for the paper clip's success is that it is simple; most great ideas are. In fact, it has become an article of faith with me, at least, that any fool can find a complicated solution to any problem; genius lies in finding the simple solution. It appears to be almost a natural law that unnecessarily complicated systems die early deaths, replaced by simpler systems that achieve the same results. Too often we humans are tempted to make a Swiss army knife of everything we do, burdening our products and systems with unnecessary additions that do not contribute to the main mission and even detract from it. The simpler system is almost invariably the pure system, the one that single-mindedly pursues a clearly perceived and clearly defined main objective and permits no distractions. Early radios, for example, had several dials—as many as four to six—that had to be manipulated to tune each receiving circuit to the frequency of the desired station. But Edwin H. Armstrong put an end to all of that with his invention, the superheterodyne, which simplified tuning by converting all desired signals to a single frequency for which all but the basic circuits were tuned in advance. Nor has anyone improved on the superheterodyne since; it is still the basic design of all radio and TV receiving equipment. And that is another hallmark of the right design or solution: It is usually extremely difficult to improve upon.

The functional analysis referred to here is an organized, procedural discipline. Therefore it has rules. Following are several that are most helpful.

Rule No. 1: Verb-Noun Rule

The verb-noun rule has been mentioned earlier. It requires the use of a single verb and noun to define a function. No modifiers—adverbs and adjectives—are permitted, although sometimes a compound noun is necessary. Its purpose is to enforce clear and unequivocal thinking, as well as comment. You must decide, without the hedging of adverbs and adjectives, what function, intended functions, and/or needs or purposes are. Too often in our everyday lives, we use euphemisms, hyperbole, and modifiers to dodge the issue, qualify our positions, avoid clear comment, and otherwise shrink from a firm position. That won't work in problem solving. If you fail to define the problem clearly, you are not likely to reach a solution, and you can't define the problem without having a good understanding of the need. You must learn to ask what and why and settle only for clear and unequivocal answers.

For example, in one consulting organization, the manager was plagued by the frequent return of his invoices by his customers, who asked that the invoices be corrected. Somehow and somewhere in the accounting system, error was creeping in.

Analyzing the system, in search of the problem—not the solution, for the problem was not yet identified—the manager found a system in which raw figures were collected on a worksheet, then transferred to the invoice. Well aware of the need to identify functions, the manager asked the accountant what the function of the worksheet was. He was told that labor charges from employee time cards and other charges from suppliers' invoices were collected and posted on the worksheet before being transferred to the invoice.

"Why?" asked the manager.

"That's a standard system for this kind of operation," replied the accountant.

"What do you do with the figures on the worksheet?" asked the manager.

"Transfer them to the invoice," replied the accountant.

"But why do you need the worksheet?" asked the manager. "Why can't you post the numbers directly on the invoice, since this is a cost-plus contract that requires us to show all the costs and burdens in detail?" (He had already discovered that the mistakes were being made in the final transfer of figures from the worksheet to the invoices.)

The accountant shrugged, while he also looked somewhat incredulous at the question. "It's a standard system," he protested. "Everybody does it this way."

The manager eliminated the problem by eliminating the worksheet, which was unnecessary since there was no processing or reorganization of the figures, but only a simple transfer. All the worksheet added to the system was a greater opportunity to make mistakes.

Quite aside from eliminating the problem, consider the labor saved by the solution. The increase in efficiency alone justified the change. And note again the simplicity of the solution—they simplify the system, that is, by subtracting from it, rather than by adding to it. Bear that in mind as you study problems: Frequently the problem is the result of some unnecessary element(s) in the system, and simple surgery is the most direct and best solution. That is, in technical terms, elements performing secondary functions that appear to be supportive of and necessary to the primary function are often not only unnecessary but actually harmful. So the questions "What is it?" and "What does it do?" often lead to "Do we need it?" and "Does it contribute?"

The opposite is also sometimes true. An engineering services firm employing thousands of people nationally in over 40 small offices ran the weekly payroll for all workers on a large IBM mainframe computer in its New York City headquarters. Yet, when summer vacation rolled around, the home office had to ask each branch office manager to determine how much vacation time each employee had earned. They had failed to arrange for the computer to keep track of this most basic element of a master payroll record.

The true cause of this is a common problem which many who have worked for large and bureaucratic organization encounter: The home-office/corporate-offices staff are sure that only they are alert and aware and all others—especially those provincials out in the field offices—are naive boobs. The corporate sages therefore tend to make decisions for the bucolic boobs without consulting them, with predictable results.

In fact, those unfortunates in the filed offices are favored with thick bundles of 11- × 24-inch computer printouts every week or two, which reach their maximum usefulness in the cold months when they can be used to kindle fireplace logs. (There is evidently an unwritten law mandating that anyone possessing a mainframe computer must generate, print, and distribute an unending stream of ponderous bundles of data-laden paper that no one knows what to do with.) Or they are bombarded with demands from home offices for reports of various kinds, often presenting information the home office already has or should have.

These and many other irrational acts in organizations result from the failure to do reasoned analysis, especially the failure to identify the need and primary function required, and to do so in that simple and objective verb-noun discipline that forces commitment and clear thinking—uncomplicated thinking.

Rule No. 2: Agree on the Need

Sometimes we hear someone blame a dispute or a failure on a breakdown in communications. That's a partial truth in many cases: Two people didn't understand each other. But in a great many cases, the misunderstanding goes beyond that and is really a failure to reach agreement.

Failure to reach agreement with a client on the true need means that you are pursuing a goal that may be the right goal, as far as you are concerned (in your opinion), but is probably the wrong goal, as far as the client is concerned (in the client's opinion). There are many reasons for such failures to reach agreement with a client on just what the need is, including at least these:

- The reluctance to dispute the client for fear of losing the contract; you hope you can muddle through somehow without having to confront the problem of a client who is grossly misguided as to what his or her true need is.
- A client who is less than clear in explaining his or her own ideas and thoughts so that you are not even aware that you are in disagreement.

- A client who has been totally noncommittal and unresponsive to your proposal so that you have (or think you have) good reason to believe that you have persuaded the client to your view and that you are now in agreement (but this is not so).
- Your own failure to make your thoughts clear so that you mistakenly believe that the client understands and agrees with your diagnosis and proposed project.
- Your common failure to think things out and express the need in that simple verb-noun definition.
- Meeting a need of a person who is involved in the process, but not a different need of the person contracting for your services (on occasion, a senior executive and subordinates will have identified needs that are at odds with each other, or you have not sufficiently uncovered one of their needs until the project is nearing completion).

It is not necessary to provoke a direct confrontation to reach agreement—and to ensure that you do understand each other. If you find yourself in disagreement with the client or, at least, have not yet reached agreement, working through the first few steps of the value analysis will often help. (If it does not, avoid confrontation and pursue the negotiating tactic advocated earlier of expressing arguments and proposing to shelve further discussion for a few days.)

The formal process in value analysis, than, is to pose and seek answers to this series of questions:

- What is it? (Descriptive, functional name)
- What does it do? (Main function)
- What else does it do? (Secondary functions)
- What does it cost?
- What else would do it? (The same main function with at least equal quality, reliability, and efficiency)
- What would that cost?
- Who (in the organization or outside of the organization) uses it? Is anyone dependent on its existence to do their job?
- When do they use it? What triggers its use?

This is a series of questions that compels you to organize your analysis and synthesis along unemotional, logical lines. (The same series of questions may be proposed for each element or component performing a secondary function of some kind.) Used by engineers, this kind of analysis has led to many design and manufacturing simplifications that reduce costs and, in many cases, produce a better product at the same time. (The discipline was born as a result of World War II, when it was discovered that substitute materials, whose use was forced by wartime shortages, often were better and cheaper than the original materials.)

The method is not confined in its purpose to saving money. The method may be used to conserve energy, time, materials, or other resources. The questions are modified to direct the analysis properly. "What would that cost?" may become "How long would that take?" for example. When the Environmental Protection Agency found itself in difficulties getting its program to improve water-treatment facilities completed within the time schedule mandated when Congress authorized the program, the agency called on value-engineering consultants to work on the problem. (Specifically, the agency was to award $10 billion in grants to communities, but it was taking up to two years to approve applications by the communities.) The team of three consultants tracked the problem down through the analysis of each element required to process each application, and found that the problem lay in the communities' slowness in writing final engineering reports required by law to qualify for the grants. More precisely, the problem was that the engineers waited until their engineering studies were completely and totally finished before even contemplating the writing of their reports, which could have been more than half completed by the time the engineering studies were finished. Guidance in this solved the problem.

Value engineers have developed their own special block diagraming method to assist in the analysis and presentation of functional analyses. A simple example of this is shown in Figure 15.1, illustrating the logic of an ordinary mouse trap.

In this presentation, the overall goal or need is to eliminate mice, whereas the main function is kill mice. The distinction and the reason for it are important. The need is to get rid of mice, not necessarily by killing them, however. The device used and analyzed here is designed to kill mice. If another kind of device had been studied, the main function might have been defined as trap mice, but the need would have

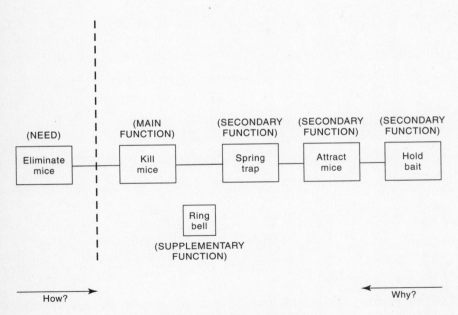

Figure 15.1   The mouse trap.

remained the same because the need has nothing to do with the method, while the main function has everything to do with the method. The *How* defines the relationship.

How to eliminate mice? By killing mice.

There are secondary functions necessary to accomplish the main function, but there is one that is only supplementary—ring bell—and not necessary to accomplish the main function.

Brainstorming

I have found brainstorming a useful way to reach agreement with clients, especially when my assignment requires me to work with, and often to lead, the client's own in-house experts. This is almost invariably a disparate ad hoc group who may not even know each other. They therefore require firm and positive leadership, and brainstorming fills the bill nicely in a great many cases.

The method was invented by advertising executive Alex Osborne, and the overall objective is to inspire a synergy of fresh, creative ideas through free association.

A brainstorming session is conducted in three major phases:

1. The group is assembled, with a leader, who lays out the rules—throw any and all ideas on the table, spin-off on others' ideas, offer twists on your own ideas, and be entirely uninhibited—but no ridiculing others and their ideas: All ideas are to be recorded and considered. The leader then throws out the basic question to be answered or the problem for which solutions are sought, encourages everyone to participate, and enforces the rules. Ideas are recorded on a blackboard or poster board where everyone can see them.
2. When the group runs out of fresh ideas, the next phase starts. Here ideas are evaluated and rejected, retained, modified, or combined with others.
3. Final evaluations and choices are made.

This is intended to be a group activity. Value-engineering teams use the discipline, as do many other teams; however, it is possible to do this on a solo basis, too. Again, the creative process involves three stages:

1. *Concentration.* Thinking intensively about the matter, seeking ideas consciously.
2. *Incubation.* Putting the matter out of your (conscious) mind, after you have exhausted all approaches consciously, and going on to other things. (This is turning it over to your subconscious mind.)
3. *Illumination (or inspiration).* This is when your subconscious mind provides an answer, as when you wake up one morning with the answer to something that has defied conscious solution or when a word or name that has eluded you suddenly pops into your head.

Whatever the means, you must somehow manage to reach a clear and mutually understood agreement with the client.

Rule No. 3: Written Agreements Must Be Specific

You must never sign an agreement that is not absolutely specific in what you agree to do; when you agree to do it or have it completed; what you agree to deliver and how much of it; how much you are to be paid; when you are to be paid; and all other such important details. Whatever the agreement, it must be absolutely specific, and that usually means that it must be quantitative, as well as qualitative. The failure to be specific is a major reason for problems. Remember, too, that when you write a proposal you are in effect proposing a contract, for your proposal will probably become the key part of the contract, incorporated in it by reference. You thus have time to think things out and decide exactly what you wish to have in the contract.

It is rare that some kind of deliverable item is not involved in a project, even a project calling for services. At the least, there is usually a requirement for a final report and often for a series of reports. That is the only physical evidence that the client can show for the money spent, so it often assumes a correspondingly large importance to the client.

In many cases, the client has no firm idea of how to specify requirements for the report(s), and so it is not a good idea to press for specifications. Instead, you should offer your own, making your won best guessimates.

Some consultants will resort to specifying the length and format of the final report as proof that they have completed the assignment appropriately. This is measuring the wrong things. The consultant was not hired to produce a report. Just as we saw in the earlier section, there are multiple ways to accomplish the *need* (and the report is just one of those main functions).

The deliverable should be defined by what it will include, address, cover, and allow the client to do with it and *not* by its heft or weight.

Any client who wants to stipulate the size of the report (number of pages, charts, etc.) is less interested in solving the problem and more interested in micro-managing the details and should cause you to reconsider how well you have identified the "true" purpose of the assignment. While the client wants assurances that you will perform as contracted and will proffer an appropriate effort on the client's behalf, any consultant that agrees to be assessed and evaluated by the pages in a report deserves a client that demands that.

What Should Be Spelled Out

There are no hard and fast rules as to what must be specified. In custom work, which most consultants do, each case is unique. But do specify everything that is going to cost you time or money, for you must be paid for your time and reimbursed for your expenses. You can't know in advance just what all those will amount to, so you must cover them in two ways: One, plan all the chores and functions and estimate the time and money you will have to spend on them—travel, tool calls, printing, writing, research, interviews, and whatever else you can anticipate; two, write general provisions specifying that you will be reimbursed in full for time and out-of-pocket costs for these items, being sure to list all the types of expenses you expect to incur. Some consultants prefer to add a fixed rate for expenses above their project fees. Their thinking is that rather than keep track of each small expense, and having to submit a receipt to prove purchase and worthiness of reimbursement, that it is just easier for all concerned to add 10 percent (or whatever they decide in concert with their client) to the total cost and not rebill the client for each expense individually.

Other consultants will charge an "administrative fee" for overseeing subcontractors contributions, collecting and documenting expenses, purchases made on behalf of the project, and so on. Here, too, it is determined prior to the first bill being sent to the client and is done under the guise of removing work from the client's hands to administer the petty tasks of the project and allow them to focus on the areas where their time and expertise are best applied. Not all clients will agree to these billing practices, and it tends to be the larger consulting firms that can command these kind of approaches more often than the smaller shops.

The estimated costs are a must for the fixed-price contract, because the client is obligated for only a specific total of dollars. Therefore, it is important that you estimate carefully, but it is also important to fix limits. Returning to our previous example, if you ignored the advice of not to specify the number of pages to include in the report, your client can now come back to you if you provide 85 pages instead of 100 and ask that additional effort be expended. (I suppose the reverse is also true, if you provide 100 as contracted for, the client can't demand 300 pages from you . . . but if you had correctly scoped the project's purpose up front with the client beforehand, this should not be an issue in the contracting stage when you can approach them as separate phases of the sales cycle. In any case, should you write 300 pages when you were contracted to write 100 pages, don't expect to get an additional fee for the extra work that rarely occurs.)

Cases of this type are not rare. Once, having prepared and delivered a training film and 50 copies of a manual, as required by contract, I was confronted with a demand for an additional 150 copies of the manual at no charge. Oddly enough, the demand did not come to me from the client, but from our own marketing vice president, who was relaying the client's request and who evidently shrank from telling the client that we would be glad to supply more copies but would have to charge for them. When I explained that I was not willing to have my department stand the loss (how easy for him to give away something for which someone else has to pay!), he indignantly demanded that I tell that to the client.

I did so. I had no difficulty explaining calmly to the client, an important manufacturer of cans and containers, that while we would be happy to supply a few extra copies—we had a few on hand—we would be forced to charge for as many as 150 copies. (We did, in fact, have to go back to the printer to produce another 150 copies.) There was no problem. (There rarely is when you are calm and businesslike.) The client was quite willing to pay for what he wanted. In fact, I doubt that the client had ever expected us to provide additional copies free of charge; almost certainly our employee had presumed that the client was seeking extra copies at our expense. I have never found being businesslike a problem or a handicap in doing business. Quite the contrary, most clients respect your right to be as businesslike as they are, and are astonished if you are not. This in not to say that I never found a client unwilling to take advantage of me if I permitted it—it has happened to me at the hands of individuals in supercorporations on two occasions—but those have been the exceptional cases. (I am sure that the two individuals were not reflecting their companies' policies, but action in what they thought to be their personal best interests.)

I tell new consultants to focus on the end result of the project and not to get caught up in the methods and procedures of it with client. When it is raining outside and you need to get from point A to point B, do you want a cab to come by and drive you, or do you want a blueprint drawing of Ford's latest innovation for transportation?

Verbal Understandings Are Important, Too

I have found it conductive to good relationships with a minimum of problems to be up front—open and honest from the beginning—with clients, while still trying to be diplomatic and tactful. (Admittedly, it is sometimes difficult to be both at the same time!)

I have not found many clients willing to retain me on a completely open basis—that is, sign a blank check for me by retaining me at a daily rate on an indefinite basis. Although such arrangements are made occasionally, as when an organization retains you as a technical/professional temporary, they are the exceptions. In most cased, the client wants some idea of what the entire commitment is likely to be. I therefore make it a practice to try to get enough detailed information about the requirement to enable me to arrive at a reasonable estimate of the cost and offer the client a not-to-exceed figure on that basis. I then try earnestly to live with my estimate. If the job runs slightly over, I absorb the difference normally, assuming that I underestimated the time required. If the job runs over due to the client adding work or to experience demonstrating that my estimate was based on inaccurate input from the client, I discuss amending our contract (or purchase order, which is a contract). I have rarely had a problem with this; most clients are reasonable if you have been careful to arrive at a clear understanding at the beginning. I work at making sure that the client understands exactly the basis for my not-to-exceed estimate. I do something to create that basis in writing—in a formal contract or purchase order, if we have one between us, or in a letter of understanding otherwise. However, it is equally important—perhaps even more important—that the client has been helped to understand that basis clearly in the beginning. The paper in the files is less than helpful if the client is not conscious of what it says and therefore feels victimized when you ask for an amendment to your agreement and more money.

In one case, for example, a client retained me to help prepare a proposal which was due only a week later. Obviously, I could not spend more than seven days on that task, and I agreed to do my level best to prepare a first-class proposal despite the time constraint. Near the end of the period, my client's customer allowed an extension of several days for the proposal, and we therefore raised our sights a bit on the task, so that I spent two additional days on it. My client agreed that this was a change and issued me a second purchase order to pay me for the extra two days. It took a little conversation—it was really only conversation and did not merit the term negotiation—and several days to reach agreement, but there was never a question about my right to be paid for the extra days.

Specifying Rates

The daily (or hourly) rate you charge includes the salary you pay yourself, the overhead, and a profit margin. Although there are some exceptions, for most of us the overhead is a major element of cost in our daily rate, often as much as 50 percent of that rate. And a major overhead item is our unbilled time, especially that time we spend in marketing, finding clients, and assignments.

That means that when we draw a long-term assignment—perhaps many weeks or even months of work without breaks or with only minimal unbilled time—our overhead costs plunge sharply during that period. Should we then favor the client who retains us for an extended period with a significantly lower rate reflecting that reduced overhead?

You are likely to encounter clients who will expect to bargain with you about your rates, especially when they can offer long-term assignments or promise a great deal of work for the future. (They understand the overhead problem too!) Should you agree to negotiate your basic rates in such circumstances?

There are some consultants who will not vary their rates under any circumstances. (In fact, many believe that it is beneath their professional dignity to bargain.) Some will bargain and negotiate, given special circumstances such as those hypothesized here. And there are those who will negotiate whenever things are slow and they feel a need to win an assignment, even at a reduced rate.

This is a matter of policy, and you must define it for yourself. But, if you do negotiate special rates with a client, be sure to have a clear understanding of what the rates are and for what duration they are effective. It's a good idea in this case to commit the special rates to writing via an agreement or contract of some kind, since they are an exception.

There are hazards in this arrangement. Suppose you agree to charge a special, reduced rate on the basis of a promise that you will be working a minimum of so many days per week or so many total days over the next three months. And suppose that most of the promised work does not materialize, and you are employed only sporadically for a day here and a day there. (Even with the best of intentions on the part of a client, this can and does happen. As Samuel Goldwyn was alleged to have said, "Verbal contracts are not worth the paper they are written on!")

For such cases, you must protect yourself with written guarantees, guarantees that you will be employed for some minimum number of days over the specified time period or paid your full rate if the promised volume of work fails to materialize. If the client refuses to enter into such an agreement, the refusal speaks for itself.

16 | Final Report, Presentations, and Other Products

Reports and other products are sometimes the most important aspect of the consulting project. They are always a reflection of you, the consultant—how well you perform and how effective your services are. They tend also to become permanent records and leave permanent impressions.

WRITTEN REPORTS: PRODUCTS OF THE CONSULTING PROJECT

Most consulting projects require the development and delivery of some physical product. In all but the most brief and informal projects, at least one written report is required, whether or not there are other products such as computer tapes, slides, manuals, procedural lists, or management plans. If the project is relatively large and/or long-term, and if the client is a large organization with multiple levels of management, you will often be required to submit progress reports, usually on a monthly basis, with a final report at the end of the project. The monthly progress reports, required in as many as 10 copies, permit various executives and, in some cases, technical specialists to monitor the project, judge how satisfactorily it is progressing, and learn of special problems, if any exist. (They may be an ad hoc oversight committee and/or may want to offer suggestions, as well as criticisms and general comments.) The executive who authorized or even inspired the project—and who may in that sense be the true client, despite the fact that your contract is with the organization—needs and desires constant awareness of the project in most of its details. He or she is responsible for the program, and may have to report on it and answer questions about it regularly at staff meetings. You may also have to arm your true client with informal memoranda and notes in preparation for those boardroom inquisitions!

With the speed of e-mail messaging and other electronic modes of communication come certain drawbacks. The ability to delay a client from seeing work in progress until you are ready to show it has been shortened because clients are more apt to ask for files and ask to have things widely distributed to others within the organization that way (you can't hide behind the time it takes to make copies when it is far faster to send a single copy of an electronic file). Additionally, clients may be more prone to ask the consultant to "just send the file" and not request that the consultant travel with the report to make a presentation to senior management. In this way, the consultant loses control of the project and runs the risk of recommendations being incompletely explained and worse, incorrectly implemented. Consultants would be wise to refrain from sharing final reports in any way but in person to ensure that it is correctly positioned and presented.

In the event that a client much prefers to receive material electronically and assures the consultant that it will be distributed to the appropriate parties and explained as needed, I suggest that you send only an executive outline of findings or results and copy all relevant decision makers and influencers you previously identified in your project preparation and through working on the project. I suggest a note be attached offering to explain the findings in a meeting, but that the material is such that it cannot stand on its own. Then, reinforce that the real value of the project is in the client's ability to leverage and use the material in a way that is meaningful and leads to positive action. In this way, you make sure that you do not allow the project to be taken from you by an internal agent at the last minute and that you are in direct communication with those who truly will be tasked with implementing the recommendations. Much of this can be avoided if the original proposal spelled out that the findings report will be delivered in person to ensure that it is appropriately explained and all questions are answered at that time. At all costs, I would not allow the report to go out without it being attached to my hand at the moment I pass it off to the client. If it is unavoidable, then the consultant need understand that they are relying on good fortune and luck to ensure that the hard work invested is properly analyzed and understood. Even if you are invited to visit the boardroom periodically to make a presentation and discuss the status and progress of your project, at least one of the staff is expected to be able to answer all questions and provide all information about the project.

General Nature and Content of Reports

In light of these considerations, the written reports must be more than boilerplate or window dressing. They must report accomplishment, problems, plans, and projections, and they must provide suitable transitions—bridges—to and from the prior report and the succeeding one. They must be entirely lucid—precise, logical, and to the point—informative, complete, and accurate. They must also be completely dignified and discreet, and, like proposals and similar writing (see Chapter 12), they must be factual in tone and style. That is, they must be objective, scrupulously avoiding hyperbole and extravagant superlatives; rhetoric excess is definitely out of place here. While the tone should be upbeat, reflecting confidence in the outcome of the project, reports must present the facts and avoid gilding them.

The best consultants will also include a single page, or perhaps two pages that very clearly spell out this information, and add "what steps to take" and "what the expected impact" will be if followed. This executive summary can be in bullet form and need not be elaborately explained (that is what the report does), but should be clear and action oriented as to the what, why, how of the situation and provide steps to take to reverse, leverage, or act on the original reason for the project.

Progress Reports

Progress reports are usually written in an unvarnished narrative format, reporting events in chronological order, generally in forward sequence—the order in which they occurred, although it is possible that occasionally a reverse chronology or even a totally different format may be necessary. Since the progress report is normally one of a continuing series, it should first present a link with the prior month's report, refreshing the reader's memory on the project status of that time as a baseline for the current report and a yardstick for measuring progress. The single most important consideration is progress and/or the lack of it and causes thereof. The report must identify specific problems encountered, what is being done to copy with them, and what the plan are for the month to come, especially with regard to the problems requiring solution.

A Common Mistake to Avoid

Only significant facts affecting progress belong in the progress report. Don't confuse *effort* with *accomplishment*. Effort that is fruitless might be mentioned in passing, but it is the problem and its solution, or plans for its eventual solution, that are important and should be described and discussed. Suppose that by extraordinary effort and clever improvisation you acquired difficult-to-get information that proved, unfortunately, worthless for your purposes. You have that all-too-human (and understandable) passion to tell the world. Don't. No matter how heroic or brilliant your effort, no matter how hard you worked, only success or impediments to success are significant. Cruelly, the typical client and the world at large do not care about the storms you met at sea; they want only to know whether you brought the ship home.

Organization and Formats

Information can be organized in a variety of ways, and each report or other presentation should use the most appropriate kind of organization. Here are some ways in which information can be organized:

- Chronological—order of occurrence.
- Historical—similar to chronological, but not necessarily in strict order of occurrence.
- Reverse chronological—tracing events back to origins or first causes.
- Order of importance—least to most important or vice versa.
- General to particular or vice versa.
- Syllogistic—beginning with premises and developing logical arguments.
- Deductive—stating principles and analyzing facts, relating them logically with principles listed.
- Inductive—examining facts and organizing them analytically for logical inference of governing principles.

Although chronological order is used most often for project reports, reports of any substantial size are generally broken down into a number of sections, and each section has its own organization, according to need. Some clients have their own, standard formats, and you may be asked to follow those. Even if the client does not have a standard or preferred format, it is a good policy to describe the format you propose and ask for approval. Following is a detailed explanation of a recommended and typical six-part format:

1. *Background information.* If this is a final report or the only report to be submitted, the first section is likely to recapitulate the overall objective of the project, the general strategy and principal functions, and other data which would bring the reader up to speed about the project. If this is merely one of a series of progress reports, the introduction need merely furnish a brief transition from the prior report and introduce the objective of this just-expired reporting period's effort.

2. A *narrative recounting* of all events of the reporting period or total project (as appropriate), usually in chronological order. If necessary, linkages to or transitions from the prior report may introduce the various elements of the reporting period's efforts.

3. *Problems encountered.* This should include complete accounts of the problems encountered and how they were overcome or solved (or plans for solving them in the next month). Usually includes follow-up report on projections made in prior report.

4. *Examination of results.* In some projects, such as studies and surveys, the data collected must be presented in full detail, discussed at length, and analyzed. This is generally syllogistic, may involve mathematical presentations, must show methodology of analysis and rationale for using methodology chosen, and should present results such as logical conclusions to be drawn or premises established for future investigation (next reporting period, perhaps).

5. *Plans for next month* (if progress report). Links from this report logically, projects problems anticipated and how they will be handled, and attempts to project next month's achievement as targeted goals. Must usually be specific about next month's goals.

6. As an alternative to (5), if this is a final report, this section will probably be one of *extending examination of results* on a total-project basis and extending conclusions drawn in (4) to final recommendations.

7. Include an Executive Summary that includes the original intent of the program, the likely ROI or value to the recommendation, and any critical information likely to either interfere with it happening, or contribute to it occurring.

The nature and objectives of each section dictate to a large extent how the information in it must be organized. Raw data, for example, may be presented in a straight chronological narrative; when data are to be examined and analyzed, they must be arrayed, grouped, and processed to facilitate manipulations and the detection of correlations and other relationships. Hence, the data may themselves dictate the organization necessary to achieve the goals of the report. It may be necessary to try several different organizations and reorganizations of the data to achieve this.

Syllogistic presentations are inescapable. The client wishes to know how you reached conclusions and on what basis you offer recommendations. Where you must explain a premise or principle upon which you based some of your work, it may be necessary to make an explanatory excursion, which will require a from-the-general-to-the-particular presentation or even a reverse-chronology of effect-cause to trace something back to its source or origin.

Project reports, then, tend to be both reportorial and, to at least some extent, speculative. Most have sections which ought to be confined strictly to factual reporting, while in other sections you may speculate—albeit with syllogistic logic—on the meaning of the facts presented earlier. Even here, it is necessary to be entirely objective in tone and method, and to offer no conclusions, recommendations, or even general opinions for which you cannot or do not demonstrate a logical chain of reasoning supported by demonstrated facts. That is absolutely vital to the overall credibility of your report, and it is essential that you preserve that credibility with scrupulous care. Once lost, such as through anything clearly and indisputably in error, credibility is difficult to regain. This does not refer to trivial errors, such as minor spelling or typographical errors, but to errors of fact or method. Having typographical errors or syntax mistakes will torpedo a presentation more quickly than you may imagine. The client may distrust the report and your findings because if you can't get spelling right, they wonder what else eluded you!

It is also relevant to mention that while software and word processors do come with grammar and spelling checkers, they are not infallible and should not be blindly trusted. The document must be proofread, preferably by someone other than the author if possible. It is still good practice to use the spell checker and grammar checkers contained within the word processing application (at minimum, it should be used to prompt you and force you to decide when to make an exception to their rules). Any consultant who does not use them is asking for trouble, but they are not sufficient on their own in guaranteeing error-free work.

You would prefer to have the client focus on your conclusions than on your spelling. Having to defend your hard work from attacks due to poor typing puts you at a disadvantage that is completely avoidable. Fending off client questions on your reputation and skills is challenging enough, and that is where you need to marshal your responses.

One common error is the assumption, perhaps an unconscious one, that the consultant's professional image and reputation are so impressive (or must be made to appear so impressive) that clients will accept anything he or she says on his or her authority alone. It may be true that some clients will accept your pronouncements as self-evident fact or even wisdom. But it is most hazardous to depend on this: You can never be sure that any given client is trusting enough to accept all your counsel without question or, perhaps even more significant, that your counsel will always prove wise. An inflated self-image may prove to be its own undoing.

It is not necessary to risk your reputation and image. In fact, it is quite easy to avoid the risk. I do so by always qualifying my advice, especially when it is called for and delivered under conditions of urgency, such as when a client calls in obvious distress, demanding an immediate judgment. I always explain my rationale—why I advocate whatever I do, often pointing out that under the circumstances I have not had the opportunity to ponder the problem at length or to consult any of my sources of information.

For example, a client called me from the opposite coast to ask my help with the U.S. Postal Service, which had denied him a second-class mailing permit for his newsletter and invited him to appeal. I probed with questions and then ventured an opinion, but I asked him to do nothing until I had time to verify my spontaneous opinion. I was sure I knew what the problem was, but I wanted to play safe by doing some checking. I spoke to a postal service official, after reviewing relevant regulations, and then offered my client final advice on how to straighten the matter out and get his permit. Had he acted on my early advice—he would probably have accepted my judgment without question, had I offered him assurances that my counsel was accurate—and failed to get his permit; I would have lost him as a client. Nothing was lost by asking him to wait a few days while I validated my opinion, and I reduced the risk of looking foolish and incompetent.

To preserve your reputation, make it a practice to think syllogistically—logically—whenever you are speaking or writing for the record or in formal counsel to a client. Remember that few things are entirely predictable and no one is infallible. Report objectively, and do not put yourself in a position where you may have to eat your words and lose face. For example, if a client asks me whether a federal contracting official will always bow to pressure from the General Accounting Office to allow protesters enough time to write a formal proposal, I can only answer that they should do so and that I have succeeded in persuading them to do so in the past, but I cannot guarantee that they will always do so. I must qualify my answer because I cannot guarantee that others will always do what they are supposed to do. If you and your client run into an exception to the rule—for instance, the contracting official defies the General Accounting Office—your credibility is undamaged because you were not dogmatic about your advice.

This runs counter to the principles and practices of some consultants, who believe that they must always hold their cards very closely and appear to be immutably wise or even omniscient. They fear that, if they are open, the client will learn too much and not depend on them in the future. They see this policy as one of self-preservation. And it is for that reason, also, that many professionals develop a jargon that is almost indecipherable to anyone outside the profession.

This is clearly evident in the use of Latin in medicine and law, for example, and in the distortion of word meanings to make jargon. Why does the insurance industry use the word premium to mean payment? Why do accountants say you are on a cash basis when you bill clients and expect to wait 30 or more days to get paid? And why does cost of sales mean, to an account, total cost of production, rather than cost of getting the order?

Consultants are no less guilty, even when we use mystical jargon in all innocence. I befuddled one correspondent by using the term *sign off* to mean approve. My client, thinking of radio broadcast jargon, interpreted the term to mean say good night and was annoyed with me for confusing him.

For this reason, avoid the use of jargon when communicating with anyone outside your industry, whether client or prospective client, unless you explain or interpret the jargon carefully.

I reject the idea that it is necessary to inhibit my clients form learning what I know and/or how I achieve my results so that they must become dependent on me. I could not admit, even to myself, being so insecure or fearful that I need secretiveness. Quite the contrary, I am eager to reveal what I know to my clients and so am entirely open with them. I turn this to my advantage by conducting many training seminars in government marketing and proposal writing, earning highly satisfactory fees for doing so!

Aside from that practical consideration, however, this is an ethical question too: Is not the client, who is paying you the fees you ask, entitled to know exactly what you are doing and how you are doing it—to complete disclosure? I think so, although others think otherwise (and are entitled to their own opinions). Aside from the fact that training seminars may constitute a substantial element of your practice and income (which we discuss in a later chapter), the fear that you may be giving away too much has little basis, in my own experience. Clients may be interested in learning something of your methodology and the rationale for it, but few want to do the work themselves. Quite the contrary, most want to call you back again if your work proves effective, and so regard you as a valuable resource. And, of course, clients may interpret evasions and other efforts to avoid disclosure as mistrust on your part, an infectious disease that leads the client to become mistrustful of you. That is hardly the relationship you want.

All of this adds up to the need for writing your reports and other presentations carefully and with clear communication aforethought—premeditated; it also points to the need for self-editing. Because you are an individual, probably a one-person enterprise, you will not have an editor on staff to review and edit what you have written. But that does not mean that what you write must go unedited. To achieve the lucidity essential to effective communication, you must accept as gospel a writer's cliché that all good writing is rewriting and that with only the rarest of possible exceptions is the first draft as good as it could be. (In fact, many professional writers rewrite repeatedly, producing a half-dozen or more drafts before deciding that they have achieved a final draft.) You must review your draft, edit it, and rewrite it as necessary.

Among the most important editorial considerations is this: Examine everything you have written in your first draft as a Devil's advocate by studying your draft for possible ambiguities: Can anything you've said be reasonably interpreted to mean anything other than what you intended? Are any of the words you used special terms or jargon? (If so, and if you must use those terms, have you provided their definitions?)

One tip on clarity in writing: Long sentences and big words are not as much the problem as are unusual words, words the average person is not familiar with. I once created a serious communication problem by using the word *epitome* in the draft of a manual. To my surprise, almost everyone involved in a dispute that arose concerning this word insisted that I had misused it, and there were many red faces when we were forced to turn to Webster's dictionary to resolve the matter. Worse, I had to discard this word, not because it was the wrong word—it was exactly right—but because readers might misunderstand what I had written, as so many fellow writers and editors had!

Level of Detail

Not unconnected with the matter of disclosure is the question of how detailed your reports should be. Unless the client has mandated detailed specification, the level of detail is dictated by your own judgment. Here are several factors to consider:

- *Objective of the project.* If the project's primary objective is some end-product, such as a manual, computer program, or inventory system, it is usually not necessary to go into painstaking detail but merely to report on progress, problems, and whatever else is necessary to define the amount of progress achieved, account for time and money spent, and otherwise keep the client informed. If, however, the project is aimed at making a study, carrying out a survey, or devising new methodology that the client is to use, the client will feel a need to have a great deal of detail formally documented.

- *The client's technical level.* If the client is a technical or professional specialist in the same field as you, he or she will probably want technical data, but will not require explanations and interpretations of the data. You can use the special idiom and shorthand that the jargon of your field affords you. Be sure, however, that you can use such jargon and still communicate effectively with the client. In many fields, practitioners get so specialized that they develop an ultra-special jargon peculiar to their ultra-special niche. An electronics engineer specializing in communications equipment may use technical jargon that is cryptic to an electronics engineer specializing in test equipment or missile guidance systems. Different users of a given technical term may have different definitions or referents for the term and therefore mean different things by it. For an example, I was once at a social gathering discussing the implications of a particular approach to solving a problem. I used the shorthand "I/O" as in "From an I/O Perspective . . . (what I was referring to was Industrial/Organizational Psychology)." What the others heard me say (based on their experiences and use of that term) was Inboard/Outboard as in boat motors; Input/Output as in electronics; and still another thought I/O was a way of referring to film that was equally adept at taking photographs inside or outside. Jargon tends to evolve and change. For example, *byte* has a different meaning now, as used in personal computer technology, than it did when I first encountered it at IBM (where the term was born in connection with mainframe computers) in 1960.

- *Objective of the report itself.* Some reports are almost pure routine and are hardly glanced at, except to verify that they have been rendered and to see if there is anything unusual or special about them. But some reports are themselves the objective of the project and constitute the end-product. For example, I was once awarded a government contract to carry out a swift study and survey for an official who needed the report to validate his budget request. In another case, the report incorporated a model for a training program evaluation, and that model was the objective of and justification for the entire project. It was the model itself that the client wanted; the rest of the report was unimportant to her.

The Report as an Opportunity

There is at least one other consideration that justifies special discussion: That is the potential of the report for generating additional business. Many reports represent that potential or can be made to. Some excursive discussions are needed to sketch in the background and explain this fully. One relevant situation is illustrated by the following anecdote.

Some years ago, when I was the general manager of a technical-services organization, a government executive with whom I was acquainted approached me about an idea he had. He was sure that one of the major operations carried out by his agency could be done far less expensively by contracting the work out to a private firm, such as the one that employed me. His idea was to have me write an unsolicited proposal, which he believed he could get approved as the basis for a contract award.

I found the notion appealing, inasmuch as the contract would have been for a national network supplying some $15 million worth of auto parts annually to the agency's many vehicle maintenance facilities, and we spent a day together visiting some of those facilities and getting firsthand information. I then returned to my own office to study the matter at greater length.

I soon realized that the proposal would require extensive research and thus involve a large effort and be costly to write. This would be with no guarantees that a contract would actually result.

That prospect was unacceptable, and I so advised the official, who was an old client, as well as an acquaintance. I suggested a reasonable alternative: If he awarded us a small study contract, the resulting report would furnish him all the data he needed to publish a comprehensive statement of work and invite proposals from everyone, including my own firm. (I was willing to bid competitively, and preferred that to the risk already detailed here.)

This is quite proper, although a contractor who does such a study for a fee—under contract, that is—may be disqualified from bidding. It is not unprecedented, either, for many clients, especially government agencies, to retain consultants to assist them in soliciting proposals and even in evaluating proposals and selecting awardees.

Although this kind of consulting opportunity for new, expanded, or follow-on business may arise from or at the initiative of clients, it arises far more often from the initiative of the enterprising consultant who is always alert for opportunities. Writing a report and reviewing the situation overall, if you do so thoughtfully, ought to be an ideal situation for searching out opportunities for follow-on contracts, for you have become thoroughly familiar with the client's situation—the needs and problems of the client organization.

Report writing should therefore be regarded far more as an opportunity than as a chore. If you refer to item 6 of the suggested report format of a few pages ago, you will note that in a final report there is frequent opportunity to make recommendations. Where that—offering recommendations—is a logical and reasonable final step in the report, it is also the perfect opportunity to seek additional work. You should have been alert from the beginning to opportunities—been seeking opportunities for follow-on contracts—and the final element in your report is the place to begin selling. (At the same time, when carrying out a project for a department or division in a large organization, get acquainted with other potential clients in other departments or divisions of the organizations. These are among your best leads.)

VERBAL REPORTS AND PRESENTATIONS

In the course of many consulting contracts, you will make frequent, informal verbal reports, reports that are actually dialogues, in which the client asks questions and makes observations. This is often crucially important in achieving client satisfaction. It is also common for clients to request formal verbal reports and presentations, usually to an assembled group. Here, too, you will probably be asked questions and expected to engage in dialogue after you have first made a formal presentation.

The questions asked by listeners may be sincere inquiries, efforts to gain greater understanding or to make contributions to the project. But they may also be ploys by individuals—especially those who are relatively low-level staff—to gain attention and demonstrate their alertness, intelligence, perceptiveness, and other admirable traits to the senior executives in attendance. Many people sitting in on such presentations feel the need to express themselves for this and for other reasons, often selfish ones.

That's not all. Sometimes those present resent the introduction of consultants for one reason or another (some infer that the use of consultants impugns their own competence and credentials as in-house experts, for example), and intend to bring you down, if possible. Such individuals may pose deliberately antagonistic questions, by which they hope to discredit you, while gaining points for their own images at your cost.

You must therefore expect an audience that may be friendly and sympathetic, but also may be antagonistic and predatory. Be prepared to keep your sense of humor and pretend that you do not perceive the all-too-apparent barbs in some of the questions. You can deflect those barbs quite easily with a show of good humor.

As an example, I once undertook to develop, for the U.S. Postal Service Training and Development Institute (established when postal service became a government corporation), a model evaluation system to make a direct measure of training transfer— that qualitative and quantitative measure of actual improvements in job performance resulting directly from training programs. This was a pioneering effort; no one had made a serious attempt before to do this. Perhaps the training professionals were reluctant to test their theories on the anvil of practical results, but in any case it had not been done before. Moreover, I had been cautioned by those professionals reputed to be experts in the field that the task was impossible. (Training and education professionals in my own organization had actually used such dogmatic assertions to dissuade me from attempting the project. But those are fighting words to me; I think that the word impossible ought to be banished from the language!) In any case, I persisted and produced what I thought to be a respectable first effort to do something about this impossible task—to surmount what I sincerely believed to be a barrier of fear.

I did not know at the outset that there had been internal dissension in the postal service training organization; the PhD assigned to monitor our contract was opposed to the effort because she agreed that it was impossible to make such measures.

The rather large group—about 20 professionals, all specialists in training and education—that I faced were not all hostile, although several obviously were, but most of them were at least skeptical. They tended to believe the dogma about the difficulty of actually measuring training transfer and did not hesitate to attack the model. As a first effort, the model had to be based largely on arbitrary premises, and so it was vulnerable to polemic assaults. Still, we disarmed the critics largely by our smiling agreement with their skepticism and our frank admission that we had a Model T here, on which a great deal of improvement had yet to be developed and was not even possible until extensive testing and field tryouts had taken place. They had been prepared for pitched battles—for our arguments in defense of turf—not for complete understanding of their skepticism. At the same time, we—my own staff and I—could offer respectable foundations for our premises and projections, while we also confirmed that our own accomplishment represented only the first step of a long journey. We made it abundantly clear that we had no illusions about this.

Our sub-rosa champion, who was the driving force behind the project, was the head of the agency. Still, it would have been quite impolitic for him to have subdued critics by sheer authority of his position. It seemed rather obvious to me, therefore, that he asked for the unprecedented large-scale presentation to give all of us—the consultant and the staff critics—our day in court. I felt certain that he had his fingers crossed that we could defend our work adequately and silence the critics.

That raises an important point. As a consultant, you owe allegiance to the organization overall, in one sense, but you owe special allegiance to the individual who has been responsible for retaining you and who is, in a very real sense, your true client. In making reports and presentations, you are often really representing that individual and his or her own interests.

The yes, but—argument is effective (because it is not a challenge) in such situations and in selling generally. The conditions are similar: You cannot win arguments with clients because to win arguments is to lose sales—to lose clients, that is. Moreover, the more the other party defends an opinion or position, the more bitterly he or she resents any efforts to rebut or discredit that position. Logic is not effective against passion. If it is necessary to resist a client's will—and only absolute necessity should lead to such resistance—you must offer only passive resistance and as much agreement on major issues as possible.

On one occasion, an interviewer asked me if I could write a number in Boolean algebra. To have guffawed at this or even to have said something like, "Boolean algebra deals with logic, not with numbers," would have embarrassed the other. Instead, playing dumb and saying, "I'm afraid I don't know how to do that, but I can write you the Boolean equation for any logic circuit," saved the day. He knew immediately that he had made a gross error—he had only a vague idea of what Boolean algebra is—but since I gave no hint that I recognized his faux pas he was not distressed and the situation was not polarized. He merely shrugged, and we went on.

Preparation

Some people are fortunate enough to be able to speak well spontaneously—with little rehearsal—but even they must prepare to make a presentation. Smoothly professional presentations are rarely spontaneous. While the appearance of spontaneity is a desirable trait in a presentation, it is an illusion usually, resulting from careful preparation. This does not mean, however, that you should memorize a speech, for only a polished and experienced actor can make a memorized speech appear spontaneous. Instead, prepare to speak by knowing your subject thoroughly. Plan an organized sequence of information and arm yourself with a guide in the form of an outline or set of notes. (I prefer an outline, in classic outline format on one or more sheets of paper, but many speakers prefer an outline or notes on a numbered series of cards.)

One caveat worth being aware of is that there is a difference between "presenting" material, which is very transmission focused and "facilitating," which is more centered on helping others learn or understand the content. Depending on the specifics of the assignment, you may be called on to do either or both. Preparing for a facilitated discussion requires more planning and more awareness of how to ensure that the participants of the meeting understand and can use the information, as opposed to a presentation, which can be more of a "data dump" of all that you have uncovered, assessed, and synthesized.

The Importance of Visual Aids

Visual aids are enormously helpful in even brief presentations: They help your audience grasp the information quickly; they provide a change of pace and add interest; they lessen the reliance on your words alone and transfer attention from you to the visuals. In so doing, they relieve you of much of the pressure of a verbal presentation.

The question of what kinds of visual aids to use—of presumed effectiveness, that is—is often debated. You have, among the many possibilities, chalkboards, flip charts, graphics or presentation programs that permit computerized images to be projected onto a wall or screen (PowerPoint being among the most popular), posters, transparencies, slides, videocassettes, filmstrips, and movies, in about that order (ascending) of cost and complexity. Since you are not normally going to undertake truly massive projects, you are not likely to go to great expense in preparing visual aids such as movies or even sets of slides. In some cases, however, you may be able to use off-the-shelf films, videotapes, and slides; there are many large libraries of such materials, and it is often possible to rent visuals or even borrow them without charge. (Even then, you have the problem of equipment, which may or may not be readily available.) On the other hand, you can use chalkboards, flip charts, and posters, and freehand illustration is usually quite acceptable for all but the most formal presentations. But there is a backlash you need to be aware of: Using outdated technology can cast aspersions on your image as a leading industry source for current thinking or practices. Conversely, there is also a ground swell of frustration by clients against consultants who use their laptops for presentations incorrectly and bore those who endure the presentations. So if you choose to create presentations in PowerPoint or other electronic formats, be sure you are comfortable with the procedures involved, and that the client will be able to properly set up the room.

Computer Graphics and Desktop Publishing

Desktop publishing has become firmly established as ready-to-use software applications compel more and more users to integrate their use into their business communications. Now, laptops and even peripheral devices that simply plug into USB ports or serial ports on a resident computer within the client's site can store and present information that previously required either large numbers of pages, or having to carry an unwieldy desktop into the meeting. Furthermore, animation, video clips (.jpg, .mpeg, .mvi, files, etc.), and audio clips can all be incorporated into presentations (as well as "effects" such as fades, wipes, washes, etc. to transition between "pages" of data or presentation). The downside is that many users have become so enamored with the tools, that they have caused distractions within their presentations by calling attention to the sophisticated technological wizardry and away from the intended purpose of the presentation. With the pervasiveness of clipart and the ubiquity of MicroSoft Office™ as the foundation for much of the presentations, too many presentations have relied on "stock" art to enhance presentations. Focus instead on the originality and clarity of your ideas.

Handouts

Handouts—information in physical form, usually printed—are another aid in presentations. Some presenters like to hand out material piece by piece throughout the presentation, while others distribute the entire package at the beginning. Here, the personal computer and special graphics and desktop publishing programs are useful for generating this material.

You can use handouts in addition to or in place of posters and flip charts, since the effect is similar: Everyone can see graphically what is being discussed or referred to. In some cases, the handout is the most practical solution because the information is too voluminous for a poster or chalkboard presentation. Handouts offer another advantage: The attendees do not have to rely on memory or notes when they have handouts to carry away. Using handouts is also to your advantage in planting seeds for possible future business. Be sure that you and what you do are clearly identified in your handouts and that the handouts are worth keeping for future reference!

Depending on the software used to create the handouts, often there is the ability to put multiple images on one page, change from landscape to portrait orientations, or leave room for note taking within the page of presented material. There also is an opportunity for the consultant to leave narrative enhancements to the captured images that appear on the handout (drawing attention to a particular finding, explaining a result, or just further fleshing out a finding beyond what may be contained within the image itself). In this way, the consultant need not solely rely on his or her verbal explanations and the hope that the meeting participant actually understood the significance of a specific finding and took the appropriate notes on it.

OTHER PRODUCTS

Many consulting projects require the delivery of products other than reports and presentations. These may include manuals of various kinds, instructional materials, audiovisuals, program tapes, designs, drawings, specifications, administrative guidelines, or other final products.

There is a common hazard such requirements often invoke. Disputes can result from the failure to have clear understanding and agreement between you and your client when entering into the project. This is not a new topic—it has been mentioned before, especially with regard to proposal preparation—but it is such a common and serious hazard that it is worth stressing again. It not only causes problems vis-à-vis the immediate project but also sours relationships and compromises both the possibility of future business with this client and, sometimes, your own professional reputation.

The only sensible way to avoid this problem is to anticipate the probable need for an end-product and come to specific agreement on just what that end-product is to be. That means quantitative as well as qualitative definition. If you agree on a need for a manual as an end-product, for example, you must agree on what it is to cover, contain, provide, and so on. Anything less—anything undefined or left to chance—is an invitation to grief.

One of the common problems, even so, is the tendency to take what appears to be the easy way out, using such euphemisms as best commercial practice or good commercial quality, when trying to set standards of any kind. That kind of phraseology leads to disputes and lawsuits. Here is an example of one dispute arising from a client's unfamiliarity with standard practices and the common jargon of publication and printing:

In a contract to produce a multimedia training system, we stipulated each item to be delivered, and we specified that we would deliver camera-ready copy, a common enough phrase that I naively believed was well understood by all, including our client.

The client was greatly upset when he inspected the end-product, the camera-ready copy. He objected loudly and unremittingly to the paste-ups and spliced corrections, rejecting our protestations that these were all standard practices that met even the exacting standards of military organizations. He was unmoved until I persuaded him to call on any printers and have them inspect our camera-ready copy. Only when several printers assured him that the copy was completely acceptable and would produce clean printed pages, did he finally yield.

Perhaps this is an unusual case; admittedly, few clients are that difficult or that reluctant to learn what they ought to know. But it is not only clients who can be unreasonable. In one case, where the consulting firm was to conduct training operations on the client's premises, the consultant was authorized to sell to his own on-site project—billing the client ultimately, that is—up to $75,000 worth of his own training manuals at prices not to exceed those charged his most favored customer. The consultant organized a $75,000 project to develop and have manufactured such manuals, to be delivered to the on-site project, and billed the client $75,000 for the labor and related costs or producing the manuals.

The client refused to pay the bill, ruling it non-allowable under the terms of the contract. The contractor haggled and haggled, but the client was immovable on the subject, and the consultant was unable to understand why the item was not allowable. He thought the contract was clear enough, and even his attorney was unable to understand the client's argument.

Finally, the consultant brought in an expert to help. The expert, a consultant himself, spent only a few minutes studying the relevant clause in the contract.

"Here is the problem," the expert told his client. "You are billing your client for R&D—labor and materials to develop this set of manuals. But the client authorized sale of off-the-shelf, proprietary manuals at the best prices you offer anyone. He did not authorize the development of new, special manuals and won't pay for your R&D."

The solution was to set a retail price on the manuals, discount them properly, deliver them, and invoice the client for the books, less the discount—$75,000 worth. The client then paid the bill without a murmur!

The outside expert who came in and solved the problem did so entirely on the basis of interpreting the language of the relevant clause. He realized that the phrase identifying the maximum price to be charged could logically be applied only to proprietary manuals and so could not be interpreted to authorize R&D of special materials.

Pyrrhic Victories

You can also win Pyrrhic victories, victories in which you emerge a moral victor but lose far more than you win. One consulting firm who did so charged a federal agency approximately $50,000 to develop two manuals, a student manual and an instructor's manual, for a training program. They failed to provide administrative guidance in organizing a program to use these manuals, however, and when the agency protested that the manuals were of little use without such guidance, the consultant merely shrugged and pointed out that they had satisfied the contract. The agency had to bring in another consultant to develop a solution to use the two manuals. The first consultant won the argument but lost the goodwill of the client. Ironically, the original consultant could have easily negotiated a follow-on contract or amendment to the original contract, while retaining the client's goodwill, but he failed to perceive the opportunity.

While the original consultant was technically within his or her rights to wave the original contract at the client and claim scope change, you can see that the downside of doing so is enormous. The first consultant likely lost future business as a result of his or her shortsightedness in not anticipating this outcome. While the advocacy is not to do things for free because a client asks for it, this situation also points out that neither the client nor the consultant truly had a clear vision of what the project should have entailed from the beginning. The sale of the materials was insufficient to meet the true problem. The problem was in getting people to perform differently as a result of the training, and creating the manuals by itself does not accomplish that. This project should have included the "bridge" to administrative support and implementation guidance.

Report Writing Is Opportunity

Report writing can often represent great opportunity for additional sales. It offers opportunity not only to lay the groundwork for new marketing efforts but even to determine what new marketing efforts in initiate, largely because such reports are—or should be—highly introspective. Your interim or progress reports often focus on specific problems encountered and highlight them. The act of doing so should produce insights into possible new projects. Final reports offer even greater opportunity of this kind, since they review the entire project, from the original problem through all efforts to solve it.

Every project ought to be a learning experience, and it would be a rare contract in which the parties had complete insight in identifying and defining the end-products needed. Quite the contrary, the wise consultant does not delude himself or herself about this, but expects to learn what really should have been stipulated in the contract, if foresight had been as reliable as hindsight. Do this, and you are likely to find many new marketing opportunities.

The Hazard of Completion-Percentage Reports

Some accountants call for a particularly treacherous progress-reporting device by advocating the use of monthly estimates of the percentage of completion for each project. Theoretically, if all goes as it should, the percentage of completion tracks the percentage of dollars spent with fair correlation. Serious deviations from that—spending proceeding at a faster pace than completion, that is—is a danger signal. That is, if a given project is scheduled for six months and $30,000, every percentage point of progress (completion) should reflect approximately $300 of the budget expended.

Unfortunately, this rarely works out. Typically, the consultant is likely to report on a six-month contract along the following lines:

Month Number	Percentage Completed (%)	Remaining Effort (%)
1	10	90
2	25	75
3	45	55
4	65	35
5	70	30

The trend is this: The consultant tends to equate time and/or labor hours—percentage of effort, that is—with percentage of completion. But the accountant finds the two, money spent and progress made, proceeding along these lines:

Month Number	Completion Reported (%)	Budget Spent
1	10	$ 4,500 (15%)
2	25	9,500 (32%)
3	45	17,000 (57%)
4	65	25,750 (89%)
5	70	28,000 (93%)

What is happening here is obvious. The consultant begins to perceive, as time goes on, that early estimates of progress were optimistic. As the scheduled delivery date grows closer, the consultant begins to see just how optimistic those early estimates were. In the meanwhile, the accountant begins to see fiscal disaster building. In the early months, this does not appear to be a problem because the substantial budget expenditures are apparently balanced, at least roughly, by progress. But when the progress proved to be an illusion, it is too late to save the day.

The trap lies in trying to measure something by itself. The system is supposed to balance the budget against the progress, but it works only if progress is measured, not estimated, and measured by some objective means.

FINDING A MEASURING STICK

It is not easy to find an objective set of measures for most consulting projects. There are methods that do work, however, and in principle the way to set up an objective measuring system is this:

- Break the entire project down into as many distinct, observable or verifiable steps as possible, trying to make them at least roughly equivalent to each other in effort or size. Let us assume, for example, that you can identify 50 such steps or elements. (Try for 50 as a minimum.)
- Assign each a pro-rated percentage value. In this case (50 steps), each represents two percent of progress.

- Monitor each step or element continuously—once a week.
- Score progress each month by assigning values to each step or element and adding them up, along this scale:
  - Step not begun in 0 percentage.
  - Step begun but not completed is 1 percent.
  - Step completed is 2 percent.

These arbitrary measures—0, 1, or 2 percent—will tend to average each other out, very much along the lines of a series of approximations. The more elements you have, the greater the accuracy will be. Even if the accuracy is less than perfect, it is far, far better than the almost pure guesswork that typical percentage-completion methods involve, for it is based on measurement, not estimating, once the measures are established.

The other way to approach this issue is to recognize that equal increments of time within a project of multiple months do not always translate to equal proportions of progress on a project in a phased approach. For instance, if you are asked to build a new performance appraisal system for a client, your first few months may be spent observing and interviewing those impacted by the current and proposed performance appraisal process (managers, human resources department personnel, those to be evaluated, etc.). These are time-consuming steps, they may represent 80 percent of the time of the project with the remaining 20 percent of the time devoted to assessment of findings, recommending, and offering consultation on appropriate next steps. The latter may be accomplished in a much shorter time period, yet is not worth "less" than the upfront work required to allow that work to occur.

17 | Fees and Collections

We all pay for our education, especially the practical one.
Here are just a few ways to avoid that special consultant's
hazard of being tricked or duped into working for nothing.

CASH FLOW IS A PROBLEM FOR EVERYONE

In an earlier chapter, I discussed how the strength of a consulting practice requires constant and vigilant attention to the cash flow requirements of the business. I then revisited that discussion when we looked at fees, contracts, and negotiations. In this chapter, I focus in on how cash flow is governed by the actions of our fee collections.

As a result of some costly early experience, I require one-third of my total estimated fee upon agreeing to an assignment, another one-third at some identified and agree-upon midpoint, and the final one-third upon final delivery and acceptance. This has served me well in two major respects. For one thing, it has greatly helped my cash flow, a not-inconsequential consideration for the independent consultant dependent on the timely receipt of payments from clients. Most small independent consultants do not have the wherewithal to "subsidize" slow paying clients who extend the terms of their payment schedule. The consultant must closely monitor and track the payments owed. Equally important, the initial payment serves as earnest money—an indicator of the client's intentions to retain you and the ability to pay your fees. It is surprising—and expensive—to discover that many people, even some who appear to be in sound financial condition, will undertake an obligation they cannot honor later or perhaps do not intend to honor. Whichever the case, it costs too much to learn this lesson the hard way. This is a consideration primarily when dealing with clients who are small and unknown. If you do business with large and well-know corporations, this may be impractical, although it has not always proved so. And if you do business with federal government agencies, as I have often done, this may be impossible. Wherever it is applicable and practicable, however, it is prudent.

The cash-flow problem affects even large organizations, and is especially painful for independent entrepreneurs. Moreover, if you are charging your expenses to clients at your actual out-of-pocket costs—without markup—you are allowing them the cost-free use of your money, something you can hardly afford. To further complicate the situation, if you try to overcome the problem by discounting your paper—borrowing from the bank with your contracts and/or invoices as collateral or even assigning your receivables to the bank—you will probably find that this is not as easy in practice as it is in theory, despite the urging of many financial advisors. Banks are reluctant to lend to service businesses in general because service businesses usually have few tangible assets; bankers also appear to have difficulty understanding the nature of service enterprises and, especially, of labor inventory in a list of assets.

The problem of learning that you have been providing free services, however unintentionally, is no small problem to an independent consultant. It can be a hazard with a concealed and unpleasantly surprising dimension: Some who appear to be serious prospects will waste huge quantities of your time in preliminary discussions during which they milk you for information, if you permit, but never retain you. They are picking your brains, manipulating you into free consultation, at least insofar as advice and information are concerned. You may even be unwittingly encouraging them to do this by being too eager to furnish up-front information free of charge. But the other case is even more serious. A typical scenario follows.

You are invited to visit the client, who is situated in a well-furnished office suite in a modern building. Secretaries and others are busily engaged in tasks in the reception area and several other offices in the suite. You are favorably impressed with the businesslike atmosphere of what appears to be a successful company.

The well-dressed, affable client greets you cordially, invites you to sit in a comfortable chair, offers you coffee, and takes an adjoining chair. He smiles, calls you by first name tentatively—"George—may I call you George?"—assumes your consent and goes on, "We have lots of work here, and I can send a lot of business your way." And he is off on a discourse of what marvelous things await you as a result of meeting him.

Once you have reviewed the requirement, you can estimate the probable size of your fee, and you mention it as tactfully as you can, although the new client has not asked you about the cost. (This is itself a bad omen.) Because you've been warned, you ask, somewhat reluctantly—you don't want to offend this new client—about a retainer. "Sure thing," he assures you, "no problem. It will take a few days for the paperwork, of course. But in the meanwhile we have to get started right away."

This is further reason to delay starting a project until some written documentation is agreed on between you and client. Even if it is simply an e-mail that documents the agreement that you request be sent back to you with an authorization to undertake the project.

Maybe you will get that promised retainer. And maybe you will not. Maybe you will get evasions, excuses, and stalls until it dawns on you that you have absolutely no assurance that this client can or will pay the bill after you have done the work. In fact, it may be that the client owns absolutely nothing in the office except his briefcase. (I have known substantial office suites to be furnished entirely with rented furniture, fixtures, and equipment.) If you sued and won a judgment, you couldn't collect your money; it is much easier to win in court than to collect what you supposedly won.

WARNING FLAGS

Trouble overtakes the unwary. But how can you be wary unless you know what to be wary of? In the sincere hope that this will help you to avoid having to gain your practical business education the hard way, here are some signs that should alert you to possible trouble ahead.

Client Indifference to Cost

It is unnatural for any buyer under any circumstances, except possibly the most desperate ones, to be indifferent to cost. The client who asks you what your services are going to cost is revealing a serious interest in retaining you. Even if the client is asking your price to compare the cost with that of competitors, it still reflects acceptance of you as one of the consultants worthy of serious consideration. Most clients do not waste time discussing costs with a consultant who is, for any reason, unacceptable.

Conversely, the client who never bothers to ask the cost is usually uninterested, and you can adjust your actions accordingly. If you run into a client who shows definite desire to retain you but is uninterested in the costs, something is very wrong, in all probability. I would be alarmed by that. Clients who agree readily to my terms and do not even attempt to negotiate alarm me. Perhaps they do not worry about my charges because they have no intention of paying me!

One prospective client called me from California to discuss his need. We chatted a bit, and I suggested he mail me some of his material so I could discuss his need more intelligently. He did so, I studied it, and we talked again. He displayed great eagerness to get on with the job, and I waited with a growing sense of unease for him to raise the question of cost. (Good sales technique dictates waiting for the prospect to raise the question of how much.) When he did not, I raised it, and he assured me that cost was not an object; he would pay whatever was necessary.

That convinced me that we would not do business. But I played out the hand: I stipulated a retainer before going further.

I never heard from the gentleman again, which did not surprise me at all.

Beware the client who professes no interest in cost. Be sure to demand a substantial retainer before proceeding with such a client.

One of the techniques discussed earlier was to ask the prospect/client what the value of having a solution to the problem would be worth. If your prospect/client cannot provide you with some measure of worth or value, the project is not viable and *if* you are granted the project, your chances of ever being paid are dismally low.

Handshake Contracts

A written contract is not a guarantee of anything, nor is the purpose of a written contract to guarantee anything. Contracts are disputed in courts every day, a certain indicator that they guarantee nothing. Rather, the sole reason for a contract is to submit the agreement to writing in the hope that this will help you to avoid disputes later as to the intent of the two parties—what you and your client actually agreed to.

If either you or your client is not acting in good faith—does not mean to live up to what you agreed on verbally—no written contract is worth signing, and you should not be doing business together.

That does not mean that you should not have a written agreement with your client. A lengthy, legalese-Latin-ridden contract is likely to alarm a client and destroy your chances of doing business together, but a simple letter agreement is an excellent idea. It commits your agreement to writing and so relieves you of relying on your memory if you have disputes later on.

The actual signing of such a simple letter agreement is less important than is the willingness of the client to sign. That indicates the client's intent, which is far more important. The client who balks at signing a simple letter agreement has issued me a warning to beware, and I would then insist absolutely on a substantial advance payment in such a case if, indeed, I agreed to continue in the relationship at all. (The prognosis for the relationship is not encouraging in such a case.) But that isn't all of it either: The letter of agreement or confirmation is a useful marketing tool in many situations that might be rather difficult to handle otherwise. As stated previously, a simple letter of agreement or e-mail, essentially a boilerplate agreement that you tailor to fit the unique circumstances, is all that is being suggested here.

Handshake contracts can be treacherous. My suspicions are aroused by the hearty and bluff prospective client who assures me that his word is his bond and that all we need between us is a handshake to seal our agreement. I am especially put on guard immediately by the prospect who says, "Trust me." Those are two words that signal danger. When I have allowed clients to overcome my fears and persuade me to vary my policies I have usually regretted it.

I do not always insist on a written agreement. There are situations—old clients with whom you've done business in the past, for example, or situations where you have good reason to have no fears—where a handshake agreement is entirely acceptable. In fact I generally ask the client whether he or she will issue me a purchase order or prefers a letter of agreement. However, even this is not necessary in many cases. Large organizations such as many of those with whom I have done business usually issue purchase orders or letters of confirmation as a matter of course. It is usually the smaller organizations with whom you have to raise the point specifically. But the written agreement is useful in another way, especially in those sticky situations just described.

For example, when you find a client who shows no interest in the cost side of the problem, raising the question of a written agreement helps you tactfully introduce the question of advance payment as a retainer, midpoint payments, and other matters. Perhaps the individual with whom you are not talking is not truly authorized to commit the organization. Asking for a purchase order or letter brings that matter to a head and resolves it quickly.

Choosing a Midpoint

If you try to arrange a one-third advance retainer and one-third midpoint payment, you must define or identify a nominal midpoint. This is not always easy, important though it is. I try to set it at the point when I have completed the rough draft of a proposal and gotten the client's agreement that the draft is good.

That leaves me with some leverage: The client still needs me and my services to complete the job properly, and he has too much invested in me at this point to risk trying to finish the job without my services. It is important to set that midpoint, the point at which you are to be paid a second one-third of the total estimated fee, with that consideration in mind; it should be a point at which you have reached a significant milestone and yet a point at which the client still needs you to get the job finished properly. If you succeed in doing this, you are protected for at least two-thirds of your total fee.

If you have difficulty deciding on a midpoint, try identifying a series of milestones or objectives for the assignment overall. Then select one that comes as close as possible to these criteria:

- It occurs well after the beginning and before the end of the project. (It is a midpoint in a general, not literal, sense.)
- It represents a major step toward final achievement of the main goal of the assignment.
- It leaves you with adequate leverage—the client has a substantial investment in the project, still needs you, and would not be able to finish easily without you.

The points raised in Chapter 14 about comparing how the consultant versus the accountant looked at project progress is relevant here as well. The payment should coincide with a project milestone or timing that represents some project "anchor" or significant occurrence and not simply the midpoint based on time alone. The payment schedule chosen may contain lags *until* that point is reached, or may be amortized over a period of time so that when the milestone event is schedule to occur, payments align with contribution level or project progress.

Overtime

Some consultants charge a flat daily rate and do not count the hours. Others do count the hours and charge premium overtime rates when they work more than eight hours in a day or on weekends and holidays. Whichever you do, you should have a clear understanding with the client about it, and any written agreement between you ought to note this carefully.

This is based on structuring the fee on an hours worked basis and has fallen into disfavor as a method for billing clients within some consulting circles (which is not to say it is wrong or bad. Merely, it is not the preferred method of many consultants who prefer to use project or value-based fee structures).

Progress Payments

For some types of assignments, the division of the payments into thirds is not practicable. This is the case, for example, when you are retained on a long-term contract or one of indefinite duration, such as when you are virtually a contract employee, working on the client's premises.

That is not the only situation where the assignment may run into many months or even several years. It is impossible to estimate the total cost or to fix a midpoint in these cases, and you could hardly wait for many months to collect your fees. In such situations, you must arrange for regular progress payments, at least every month, although weekly or biweekly payments are more usual in such cases.

CREDIT CARD CONVENIENCE—AND INCONVENIENCE

We have become accustomed to using credit cards for our convenience in purchasing. With a credit card, you don't need to carry much cash or a checkbook; you can almost always use your bank credit card, even for major purchases. Most merchants—retailers, restaurants, motels, and other establishments, large and small—accept them without hesitation and without the occasional hassle that you must undergo to have your personal check accepted. (Visa and MasterCard are bank cards and are true credit cards: The card holder has a line of credit and can pay back on a schedule. Others— American Express—are charge cards, and charges against them must be settled in full each month.)

That is extremely convenient for you when you are buying something. It's also extremely convenient for the seller. It's quite a simple transaction for the merchant: He or she simply deposits the credit card slip as cash, and the account is credited immediately; no waiting to clear, as in the case of checks.

On an average, most retailers consummate from about 30 to 70 percent of their sales via credit cards, and in some businesses—especially the hospitality enterprises— the percentage approaches 100.

The credit card business has changed over the years. For one thing, nearly $1.5 trillion was spent in 20 billion transactions within the year 2000 according to Dolores S. Smith, director of Federal Reserve Board's Division of Consumer and Community Affairs in a recent appearance before the subcommittee on Financial Institutions and Consumer Credit of the Committee of Financial Services, House of Representatives (November 1, 2001). For another, it is almost totally electronic in its processing and does not require your signature on the form, thus enabling the expansion of buying by mail, telephone, and computer.

As an independent consultant, you may or may not need to accommodate your clients with credit card convenience. If your work is all on substantial projects for larger companies and corporations, it is not likely that any client will ask you to charge the work to a credit card. On the other hand, if you sell your services to private individuals, sell products (books, tapes, newsletters, seminars), or sell by mail, it is probable that your clients are going to want you to accept their credit cards in payment. And that is where you run into trouble. Recent advances in how home-based businesses, small businesses, and service businesses in general are viewed by banks and lending institutions have allowed for nearly every business to establish a credit card processing account. The advent of the Internet and sites such as www.ebay.com have fostered services such as PayPal or others to help the small business person or individual provide the ease of credit card payment to customers. Now, to be sure, the small business person may have to endure the cost of processing equipment for credit card transactions, and may not get the same level of volume discounts as a larger business may for each transaction processed. All of these issues aside, the establishment of *merchant accounts* (that is, businesses that are authorized to accept payment via credit card) is becoming the standard for nearly any business that seeks to accept payment through credit cards.

Should you encounter problems with your preferred bank of choice, there are banks who will approve you for merchant status if you persist. (One consultant told me that he got his merchant status 15 minutes after he stamped his foot.) Some banks may wish you to post a collateral account, perhaps a CD, to serve as a security bond. For the average independent consultant, $1,000 will satisfy the bank's uneasiness.

If you prefer to turn to some service to help you, it will cost you a consideration. Often that consideration includes buying a terminal, as mentioned earlier, for entering your credit card information and getting an approval of the charge. That is an expensive investment and an unnecessary one. A clear explanation of the pros and cons of the different approaches and suppliers of credit card processing can be found at http://www.noblehosts.com/guide/ecomm.merchants.htm.

Credit card accounts and merchant status are not without problems, such as chargebacks, when a client contests a charge and the bank withholds payment to you, pending settlement of the claim. This is one of the many problems the Association offers to help you solve. Problems or no, if you do business by mail and telephone and sell commodities of any sort, being without merchant status will cost you sales and client goodwill.

COLLECTIONS

If it is your good fortune to do business with clients with AAA credit ratings, you may never have a collection problem, although even those with AAA credit ratings can be agonizingly slow in paying their bills. I have been the victim of well-known large corporations whose bill-paying habits make even the federal government appear to be a fast payer. Fortunately, there are a few things you can do that usually help speed the process.

You must understand that large organizations become somewhat muscle-bound for a variety of reasons, only one of which is ponderous paperwork stemming from archaic procedures. Those procedures grow up over many layers of management, and the procedures in a large organization often become enormously detailed. But that is not the entire problem. One of the greatest problems is the indifference of workers who tend to become bureaucratic in any large organization. The essence of bureaucracy is that the means is all-important, and the end must be sacrificed to the means when the two conflict. In short, if it is not by the book, it simply does not happen. There is one other typically bureaucratic problem: Only at he highest levels may anyone exercise initiative. (But at the highest levels, it is not necessary to exercise initiative!)

For example, if the procedure requires three copies of your invoice, but you have supplied only two, the invoice may never move from the in-basket to a payment schedule. Don't expect the clerk to make a copy or to call you; such things happen only rarely. (I once waited eight months for a bill to be paid because of such a problem, unaware that it had not been paid. It would probably never have paid had I not monitored my unpaid invoices.)

If you are doing business with a large organization, ask in advance exactly what you must do to get paid and follow the procedure. If at all possible—and it usually is—personally hand your invoice over to whomever you are dealing with. By knowing how the system works, you can track down problems of nonpayment much more rapidly. In any case, here is the typical series of steps when you are having trouble getting paid, including those unfortunate cases where you must start getting tough with a client who refuses to pay:

1. Normal billing: submittal of your regular invoice.
2. Statement of money due issued at regular intervals, usually first or fifteenth day of the month.
3. Courteous form collection letter requesting payment.
4. More insistent, less diplomatic letter.
5. Telephone inquiry, courteous but firm.
6. Severe letter, stipulating firm action, such as legal measures or collection agency, if bill is not paid soon.
7. Matter turned over to collection agency or lawyer.

You don't want to come to these latter situations, although if the client is resistant to paying, you've nothing to lose—you don't want to do business again with such a client. There are few such problems when you exercise the precautions suggested here. Still, you can never tell what will happen, even then. You may be the victim of another kind of depredation, such as in the following story.

A client came to my office and retained me to prepare a special sales brochure for him. We agreed on a price of $600, and he paid me $300 in advance as a retainer. I prepared several roughs, as I do in such assignments, and we reviewed them together, coming to agreement on which should be developed to its final stage. Shortly after that, the client advised me that he had sold his business and wanted to abort the brochure. I agreed reluctantly to settle for the money already paid, although I had already done about three-quarters of the work. But the client demanded a refund of the advance retainer! When I refused, he sued me in small claims court. The case lasted about 10 minutes, the judge advising the gentleman that he was lucky to get off for one-half the total fee, under the circumstances. (He, not I, had breached the contract.) Still, the whole affair cost me most of a day sitting in the courtroom waiting for my case to be called, so I was a loser after all, despite being the victor in the case.

As a good general rule, avoid all litigation, and even all legal expedients, if possible. Even when it is you who are doing the collecting, you may win a Pyrrhic victory or, at best, a limited one. If you turn the matter over to a collection agency or retain a lawyer and sue, it is going to cost you one-third or more of whatever is collected for you, and often that is less than the full amount. And in civil court, the court cannot and will not try to collect for you, even when you win. The court awards you a judgment, which is a hunting license.

Judgments

When you sue and a judge or jury finds for you—enters judgment for you against the defendant—it does not mean that the defendant will then pay you the money you have won, for you have won a legal battle, but not the war for your money. Probably a well-established firm will pay, but you may be up against a defendant who will refuse to pay even then, and may think that he or she is judgment proof. In other words, the defendant thinks he or she had his or her assets so well hidden or protected by legal dodges that you will not be able to seize the funds and/or property. (I have reluctantly allowed some legal debts to go uncollected because I knew that I could win a judgment but would be unlikely to be able to satisfy it, and in some cases I settle for far less than the total amount for the same reason.) It is better to take any steps possible to minimize the probability of having collection problems.

Credit Ratings

You can subscribe to a credit rating service, of course, and get a rating on a client with whom you wish to do business. There are two problems with that: You are likely to find that some of your clients or prospective clients have no ratings established. You may find also that a client who enjoys a good credit rating is a slow or reluctant payer of bills or one who makes a practice of contesting every bill—especially bills for services—and regularly bullies vendors into settling for less than the full amount. Again, getting a retainer in advance is a far better credit rating than any reported by any agency or bureau.

Mechanic's Lien

In general, the law provides that a mechanic (using that term rather loosely), may hold property that he has repaired pending payment of your bill. If you fail or refuse to pay, he may take measures leading to selling your property to satisfy the bill.

You could conceivably be in the position of the mechanic, with the client's property—for example, a computer program you have been working on—in your possession. This does not give you the right to seize a client's property, however, or to reclaim property that you have returned to the client. You need to consult a lawyer about the specific case.

One way to minimize your exposure is to get partial payments, either through the milestones, and/or an upfront advance so that problems are either identified early on and less work is completed on behalf of a client that will not pay—or in the worst case, the money owed represents a small amount of the total fee and is "easier" to write-off for you without undue hardship to your financial position. Obviously, when possible, you would prefer to resolve issues without the involvement of the courts, and you are best served to deal with the client in as professional a manner as possible to avoid any potential ill feelings or backlash from the client discussing their opinions of you with other potential clients.

COLLECTING FROM GOVERNMENT CLIENTS

A common complaint about doing business with government agencies is that the government takes too long to pay its bills. That complaint has finally resulted in legislation designed to compel federal agencies to pay more promptly. How well it has succeeded is questionable, for the typical delays in being paid by government agencies are not the type of ills corrected by legislation. (Unfortunately, the solons on Capitol Hill know only two solutions to all problems: Pass a new law and/or start a new costly program.)

The Prompt Payment Act has helped a bit, but delays in payment are almost invariably the result of typical bureaucracy—any bureaucracy. Unfortunately, legislation does not cure that disease. On the other hand, there are direct measures that do produce results. Only once, in all my years of dealing with the bureaucracy, have I failed to get reasonably prompt payment. But it was always because I took direct action when payment was not forthcoming within a reasonable period—20 to 30 days. I *prevented* the delay from becoming a problem.

In fact, I have found it easier to collect from the government than from private-sector organizations. All it normally takes is follow-up—telephone calls in which I insist on learning where my invoice is at the moment and why it has not been processed for payment. I have invariably found bureaucratic sloth at work; my invoice is still gathering dust in someone's in-basket because they wanted my invoice in triplicate or quadruplicate, rather than in duplicate; they have lost the invoice somewhere in the chain; there was some petty detail out of order. A little outrage, sometimes a duplicate invoice sent directly to some individual, or other action usually produces results—a check in the mail—within days.

The cure for the disease is this, if you do business with the government (or with private enterprise for that matter): (1) ask what the payment procedure is—who is in the chain of approval and what are the several steps before the check is cut, what information must be included in the invoice, how many copies of your invoice are required, how long should the process take normally; (2) go back to the individuals in that chain if you do not get your check within normal processing time and start asking blunt questions. This procedure usually produces results. In two exceptional cases, I still managed to get paid with only an extra couple of weeks delay. Once, I was required to submit two additional copies of my invoice, and the government insisted on then paying me three times! In the other case, I had to write a letter of complaint to the agency head, whereupon I was finally paid.

One of the advantages of dealing with government agencies is the objectivity typical of the government as a client. You can be very blunt, indeed, when pursuing something such as overdue payment and not offend anyone. (Unfortunately, this is not always the case with private-sector clients.) The government client recognizes your right to be paid with reasonable promptness and is likely to be apologetic about the delay. The largest advantage to you is the statutory protection and preference you can enjoy, especially as a small business, when dealing with the government. For one thing, the law says rather clearly that as a small business you are entitled to receive progress payments, whereas a large company might be expected to wait until the project is completed before submitting a bill. It is fairly common practice on ongoing contracts to submit your invoices each month, and in most cases contracting officers will accept and process invoices from small businesses as frequently as every other week. There is no reason to be bashful about demanding payment without unreasonable delay, or hesitant about stipulating your need for progress payments.

18 | Skills You Need: Making Presentations

An inherent anomaly of consulting is that clients want your services as a specialist; yet, as an independent practitioner, you must rely on yourself for all the ancillary skills and functions, which then requires you to be a generalist!

CONSULTING: BUSINESS OR PROFESSION?

Is consulting a business or a profession? The question may have more than a bit of significance academically and may, in fact, ultimately have a decisive effect on your standing, influence, and even income. Meanwhile, we who are engaged in consulting as independents must face realities: We are engaged in both a profession and business. We provide highly specialized professional services to clients, but we also provide business services—marketing, accounting, invoicing, and the management and administration common to all business enterprises. Nor is that the whole story. The complexities of independent consulting go well beyond that.

I refer to three sets of skills: technical, managerial/administrative, and entrepreneurial. In some respects, the entrepreneurial skills are even more significant than the others, for you embark on an entrepreneurial adventure when you set out as an independent consultant. Your entrepreneurmanship is going to be the principal influence and probably the deciding factor in the future of your venture.

Thus, you must be the master of all three sets of services. Survival as an independent consultant depends as much on your managerial/administrative skills and your entrepreneurial vision as it does on your technical and professional skills. Even that does not fully explain the necessity for and interrelationships of these sets of skills: You must have not only the managerial/administrative skills to deliver your services, but also the skills necessary to conceive, organize, and operate those ancillary functions that broaden your income base adequately. You will recall that the failure to establish and build up a broad enough range of income-producing activity is one of the chief causes of failure in independent consulting; this applies to all the skills. Writing and public speaking, for example, are essential skills in delivering your basic services, but they are also important in adding profit centers—income—to your practice. Again and again, we find enterprising independent consultants who have built successful practices and expanded them into even larger and more ambitious ventures. A few examples follow.

Dr. Alan Weiss may hold the current title of "The Consultant's Consultant" in many people's eyes with his series of books, speeches, and his own practice, Summit Consulting Group, Inc. Dr. Weiss has extended a practice focused on client consultation to include working with Kennedy Publications (publishers of the magazine, *Consulting*) on consulting to consultants. His series of books under the Ultimate Consulting Series title for Jossey-Bass/Pfeiffer is highly regarded by many experienced as well as neophyte consultants.

Dr. Jeffrey Lant, a Cambridge, Massachusetts, consultant, has written and published so many thick tomes on the how-to of consulting that it is difficult to believe he has time left for consulting itself, although he is active as a speaker and in related activities. (He is his own publisher, as JLA Publications.)

Hubert Bermont, a Sarasota, Florida, book-publishing consultant, spends most of his time today running his association, The American Consultants' League, in addition to publishing *The Consultant's Library*, which he established a few years ago after the success of his own seminal books on the art and business of consulting.

One of the areas that is of high interest with many consultants and that provides additional income based on presentations is to run *Share Groups*. In these sessions, customers, prospects, and industry professionals are called together (either for a membership fee or not) and share approaches to common problems, hear from thought leaders in the field, or are exposed to ideas from customers or suppliers that all attendees either have in common or would have an interest in hearing about in building their own businesses. These sessions allow the sponsoring consultant to position himself or herself as a value-added provider to the attendees (at the same time it provides opportunity to have the consultant identify potential projects or areas of interest/concern to the attendees).

PUBLIC SPEAKING

A great many people shrink from writing as an unpleasant or difficult task. Even more shrink from public speaking, many in absolute fear of it. Even the most experienced and highly respected executives, professionals, and other accomplished and successful individuals are often terror-stricken at the thought of facing an audience. For that matter, even professional speakers and performers often confess to fear and nervousness every time they mount the platform; they must somehow drive themselves each time to once again face an audience. So you may or may not get used to it. That is, you may or may not get completely over your fear of facing a room full of people intent on your words, gestures, and facial expressions, although most people do get over the fear. You can learn to live with the fear, however, and overcome it each time to become a good public speaker.

THE NOTION OF BORN SPEAKERS

You may have the notion that there are born speakers, as there are born salespeople or born artists. If there are any, they are in rare supply; the most gifted speakers have usually worked hard to learn to speak well and appear to be completely at ease. Probably the notion of the born speaker arises from the fact that some individuals are blessed with naturally good voices for public speaking—strong, resonant, clear, and pleasant. Yet some quite successful public speakers have voices that are not inherently well-suited to speaking. One prominent broadcaster, Barbara Walters, is probably best known for her ability to persuade public figures to allow her to interview them, but she has a reedy, shrill voice and a pronounced lisp. Dave Yoho, a successful professional speaker with a marvelous speaking voice, struggled to overcome his speech defects as a youngster; nor has stuttering prevented broadcaster John Stossell from becoming successful. Key points to be aware of:

- The corollary of the basic truth that successful public speakers *learn* to speak well is that anyone can learn the art; even natural handicaps do not prevent the determined individual from becoming successful on the platform.
- Actually, the key to overcoming fear of speaking lies in first identifying the basis of the fear. If you fear appearing foolish, take steps to ensure that you have something to say (so many people mount the platform and have nothing to say) and that you are well prepared to say it—that you know your material and how you will present it. That does not mean a memorized speech, however; that is the most difficult thing to deliver without anesthetizing your audience. It does mean knowing your material, and you should carry cue cards or an outline listing your main objectives and key points, arranged in logical order—with a beginning, middle, and end—that leads to your main point, so that you do not lose your way. (I still do this, despite having presented my material again and again.) You will almost always do far better speaking extemporaneously with such aids than you would reading a written speech or reciting from memory.
- Be enthusiastic and don't be afraid to show that enthusiasm; it's contagious, and it compensates for many things that might be lacking, such as the professional polish that comes only with years of experience on the dais. (Corollary: Avoid any subject about which you are unable to be enthusiastic.)
- Make sure that you are dressed properly; the best insurance here is to be conservative; you can never go wrong that way. Wear quiet, conventional clothes, with a minimum of jewelry. Some attendees will focus and comment on a speaker's wardrobe whether they did or did not like the words and messages they heard. There are also those who will seize gleefully on anything they can find to criticize.
- Don't try to be a comedian. David Letterman makes it look easy only because he is so accomplished after so many years. Trying to emulate him is likely to bring you a great deal more grief than acclaim. Just be you.
- Have a proper feeling for and attitude toward your audience. They are not your enemies. Quite the contrary, they want you to succeed. (If you fail, you will be a bore, so wanting you to succeed is in their own interest!) Ergo, don't be afraid to gesture freely, smile, scowl, pause, shout, whisper, and otherwise act out your material. That, which manifests your enthusiasm, is the

real secret of being a smash hit on the platform. You are a performer, or you should be, and your audience wants to be diverted as much as they want to be informed. Even not having a great deal to say will be forgiven if you are a sufficiently forceful or entertaining speaker who can energize an audience.

PLANNING THE PRESENTATION

Despite the Murphy's Law stating that anything that can go wrong will do so—or perhaps in support of that oft-quoted law—it appears to be only the disasters that happen spontaneously. Calamities need no help to bring them about; the gods are only too eager to visit them upon you, and they show no sign of requiring anyone's assistance in the process.

On the other hand, events that are much to be desired seem to become reality only when we somehow make them come about—when we plan, organize, prepare, and even then take as many precautions as possible.

Find out how well lit the area where you will be presenting will be during the presentation. If it is a lights-out dark area in order to permit videos, projected images, slides, and so on to be viewed by audience members, you may wish to bring a small light to illuminate your notes. If there is a podium, you may wish to place a glass of water on it just in case you start to cough, or find your mouth going dry in the middle of your presentation (if you can avoid standing and presenting from behind the podium, it is advisable to do so). The more you can interact with your participants, walk among them, and remove barriers between you and them, the more likely you are to be well received. Of course, if you are "tethered" to the podium due to the size of the room, necessity to advance your presentation slides or computer presentation, make sure you remain animated and make plenty of eye contact with your audience.

This applies in full measure to making presentations. Whether you write out your presentation in full text, memorize it, use notes, carry an outline, or use a set of cue cards, it is the act of preparation, regardless of the means and methods you prefer, that matters and is effective in making things go right.

I do not use the same method for each situation. That is partly because I do not always deliver the same material, and quite naturally I need more planning, preparation, and guidance material for a new presentation or one that I have not delivered often. In the case of presentations I give frequently, I need only the sketchiest of notes to ensure that I do not, in my enthusiasm, forget to make key points. On the other hand, I have sometimes prepared a full lecture guide for myself when I am breaking in an entirely new presentation.

That's a good plan if you are new to speaking. If you get so nervous that you forget everything your notes were supposed to remind you of, you can at least read your presentation. That's better than stumbling along aimlessly. Some public speakers—Franklin D. Roosevelt, for one—could read a text well, as can many professional performers and public officials. Of course, they have usually invested time in rehearsing carefully; some even make notations on paper of where and when to pause, make gestures, whisper, shout, smile, and otherwise supplement and dramatize the material. But if you are enthusiastic about your subject, you will probably not need such clues.

True enthusiasm causes you to forget about yourself and your anxieties, and you make gestures and inflections unconsciously. That is by far the most effective way to make any presentation, but planning is still necessary.

Goals and Objectives

Presentations, written or oral, fall into certain broad categories, defined by a general goal or theme, such as one of the following:

- How to solve a problem.
- How something works.
- How something came about—history, causes, origins.
- New developments in a given field of interest.
- How to do something.
- Arguments for or against something.
- Reporting on a project, new developments, new views.
- Organizing a group or an effort.
- Leading a discussion.
- Offering a demonstration.
- Introducing another speaker.
- Presenting an award.
- Warming up an audience.

Aside from these general goals, which reflect only broad categories, you need to have a specific objective or set of objectives when you plan a presentation. When I offer a seminar on marketing to the federal government, for example, my general goal is to teach my audience both the basic philosophy of marketing successfully to government agencies and the art of preparing bids and proposals, the key instruments for winning government contracts. But I also have many specific objectives outlined, each of them a milestone along the road leading to the achievement of the broad goals. (This is how I visualize the relationship of objectives to goals—the objectives representing an orderly sequence of steps defining the path that leads to the goal.)

The Beginning

You must somehow let your audience know what your goal is and how you will approach the subject generally. And you should do so as early in the presentation as possible. The introduction should make that clear. For example, when I present a seminar on proposal writing, I start by defining what a proposal is in such a way as to make the general philosophy and theme of the seminar apparent. I make it clear that a proposal is a sales presentation, and that we will keep that definition clearly and unequivocally in mind. I state that the chief ingredient of success in a proposal is sales strategy, and that excellent writing skill helps greatly, but only if effective sales strategies and techniques are present. I also make it clear that we are going to talk about winning and whatever is required for that.

Not very many minutes into the presentation, my listeners know, in general but clearly characterized, what my goals and themes are. There will be no confusion about where we are headed.

Other presenters will enumerate the objectives demonstrably for audience members (first, I will talk about . . . , then, we will discuss . . . , finally, I will respond to questions, etc.). Given that the participants do not have a road map to follow as you speak in many instances (sometimes this is the case even if you have provided a handout), it is helpful to be very clear as to what your topic is, what you will cover (and by inference, what you will not cover or what is outside the parameters or scope of this presentation), and what you anticipate the outcome of the presentation to be.

An Opening

None of this is to say that you *must* launch abruptly into a "This is what I am going to talk about" opener. For one thing, an oral presentation benefits from an opening attention-getter just as a written presentation does. Many performers and professional speakers therefore open with something humorous or novel. That does more than get attention. It also assures your listeners that you are not going to be dull and so creates a receptive mood, which is a decided asset to you as a speaker.

It is not necessary to be a comedian; you do not have to tell jokes to get attention and set the mood. There are other ways to be interesting:

- Ask a key question, one that addresses the heart of your presentation. It can be a rhetorical question, one that you are going to answer yourself, such as "What is a proposal? Let's think about that for a few minutes."
- Ask a question that you wish attendees to respond to with their ideas. You may have to smile reassuringly and urge them a bit, but inducing their responses can be an effective way of arousing interest and setting the stage for your presentation. (I often ask for volunteers to describe their businesses or their jobs.)
- Start your presentation with an amusing or novel anecdote. Do a little advance research and try to come up with such an anecdote or two.
- Use startling statistics as an opening. Did you know, for example, that there are 79,913 governments in the United States, according to the U.S. Census Bureau? Or that nearly one-third of all our citizens receive some form of federal assistance?
- Use the unexpected, perhaps a startling fact. Did you know, for example, that making sales to the government is the easy part; the hard part is finding the right doors, behind which government officials are waiting eagerly to buy your goods and services?
- Reveal or promise to reveal insider—little known—information about your subject, especially information that has been deliberately kept secret.
- Reveal or promise to reveal the very latest information on the subject, information too recent to have reached conventional channels.

- Open with an apparent anomaly, such as this: Charles Kettering knew as well as other engineers that the self-starter for automobiles was an impossibility. But when Ransome Olds, original builder of the Oldsmobile, hired him, Kettering knew that he was going to find a way to invent the impossible.
- Use a gimmick, a device that can be quite effective in the right hands and used properly, but be careful; it can backfire. If you place a wrapped package or strange object on a table with deliberate and great care before you begin to speak and then ignore it during the early stages of your presentation, you'll arouse a great deal of curiosity. But you must not wait too long to reveal what it is, for the distraction can weaken your presentation if it goes on too long. The gimmick must also be related directly to your presentation or your audience will feel tricked, and they will not like that.

The opener must lead smoothly into your theme, to which you now proceed. That's the introduction, a preview of what is to come with a few items defined in advance with the hope of avoiding confusion later. In a sense, the introduction gives your listeners a road map, telling them what you promise to do or reveal and giving an idea of your overall theme.

The Middle

Now that you have prepped your audience by previewing your presentation, it is time to get down to business and deliver on the promise made in your introduction. The level of detail and often the kinds of details here vary, according to what you are trying to accomplish, amount of time you have, and the scope overall of the subject. In my own case, I would focus on bids and federal supply schedules, rather than on proposals, if I were addressing a group of suppliers who would rarely be required to write proposals in competing for government business; I would focus on special programs for minority-owned ventures if I were addressing a group of minority businesspeople. So the body of my presentation, and even the introduction, in many cases, would include both generalized information about government procurement and specialized information relating to the special interests of my audience. When I prepare a presentation, I make it a point to learn as much as possible about the audience I will address. I ask questions of whoever is arranging my appearance, and I collect annual reports, brochures, and other literature about the organization.

It is far more useful and interesting to your audience if you talk to them in terms of their direct and immediate interests rather than in the abstract. I could use generalized examples to illustrate what I am explaining. But that would compel the listener to translate that into his or her own need and application. A large part of the appeal of your address lies in making connections for your listeners. I don't use an example from a successful engineering proposal when I am speaking to a group engaged in developing training programs, for example; instead, I find training-program examples.

My public speaking engagements are almost always how-to presentations, while yours are likely to be something else. But the principle is the same: Do what is necessary to learn the direct interests of your audience, then relate your presentation to those interests as much as possible.

Ending

In come respects, closing your presentation is similar to opening it because the conventional close summarizes and reinforces your key point or points. A great deal depends, however, on what kind of presentation you have been making. A logical argument for or against something is generally ended by summing up the facts presented and offering the conclusion. An emotional argument is ended by an exhortation that iterates the primary pro or con positions. A how-to is often ended by inviting questions from the audience. Whatever the case, it is proper to thank your audience for their attention and patience, and if they choose to applaud, thank them again when the applause subsides.

A FEW PRESENTATION PRINCIPLES

Language is a first consideration in all presentations, whether written or oral. Unless you are understood clearly—unless the message received is the same as the message sent—your presentation cannot be a complete success.

Fortunately, with today's communications—telephone, radio, TV, and Internet for both voice and data—and today's travel—we travel freely, quickly, and often all over the country—regional differences in our language are fewer than they once were. If you are a native of Philadelphia, you must try to remember that in Chicago you must ask for a sweet roll when you want a coffee cake, or a danish. Pop becomes a soda in New York, and a tonic in Boston. And if you are in some place where hardly anyone is a native, such as Miami, the complications multiply considerably.

These are minor difficulties compared with the general uses and misuses of English in America. Ours is a remarkably rich language, at least partly due to extensive borrowing from other languages; there are probably about one million words in the language, divided into two roughly equal halves—general words and technical terms. On the other hand, the size of the average individual's vocabulary ranges roughly between 12,000 and 15,000 words, with 20,000 words considered to be a large vocabulary. (It is not at all unusual, however, for individuals to have vocabularies of less than 10,000 words.) Some scholars, writers, and others have vocabularies ranging to 40,000 words and even above that. These are unusually large vocabularies, and these learned individuals must avoid more than one-half their vocabularies in writing and speaking if they want to be understood by the average reader or listener.

Most of us have two vocabularies, our speaking/hearing vocabulary and our reading vocabulary. Our reading vocabulary is normally larger than our speaking vocabulary; you should keep that in mind and be especially careful when preparing an oral presentation.

Possessing an unusually large vocabulary is not a disadvantage or handicap—unless you permit it to be one. A large vocabulary is, first of all, a marvelous tool for reasoning. (We use both words and images in our thought processes.) It is also a marvelous tool for organizing information, whether to be presented orally or in writing. You should prepare the draft of your presentation with whatever words come to mind as most appropriate, most definitive, and most suitable generally, without regard to your prospective reader's or listener's vocabulary. When you edit and revise your draft into the final document, you can eliminate all those big words—the terms that are more likely to prevent communication than to further it—remembering that most people can handle more words in reading than in listening because of their greater reading vocabulary and because they can reread and ponder over written material to infer meaning from context.

In both cases, during editing and revision processes, try to find and use the simplest possible words and terms, and try to eliminate all unnecessary phrases. Here, to illustrate, are just a few examples, the original words or terms in the left-hand column, and suggested replacements in the right-hand column:

in order to	to
comprise	contain, include
epitome	essence, representative
mendacious	lying, untruthful
luminous	glowing
for the purpose of	to, for
utilize	use

Avoid cliches, words and phrases that have been so overused that they have gone completely stale and are considered bad writing. Some of them are also grammatically incorrect (point in time is redundant, since point means the same thing). Here are just a few of those:

bottom line	point in time
along these lines	cutting edge
fallout	few and far between
goes without saying	in-depth
richly rewarding	matter of course
safe to say	all in all
state of the art	spin-off
mind over matter	be that as it may

Be careful to use words correctly. Just a little carelessness—not even ignorance, but just absent-mindedness—can produce ludicrous and embarrassing results. One technical writer, for example, referred to the duplicity of the circuits when he meant duplication or redundancy, and assignation when he meant assignment. Keep a good dictionary at hand and use it whenever you are not absolutely sure that the word you are using is the right one. Keep a basic grammar text at hand, too, for swift reference when you are not absolutely sure about your constructions. (Even better, avail yourself of the services of a professional editor if at all possible. It will save your time and help you produce a thoroughly professional result.)

Understanding versus Belief

Most of us believe that which we understand, and we therefore try to persuade others by what we consider rational explanations and arguments. We find it frustrating when others stubbornly refuse to believe our conclusions, and we often say in exasperation, "Look, you don't understand this," perhaps without realizing how right we are. Belief and understanding are so closely related that it is by no means clear which follows which. We have seen photographs of Earth from thousands of miles in space and can perceive the globular shape, but most of us never doubted that Earth and other celestial bodies are globular in shape. We took it on faith as an accepted premise. Yet, there are flat-earth proponents who interpret those photographs as showing merely that Earth is a flat disk; they refuse to believe that Earth is globular and so they do not understand the photographs and all the other evidence of Earth's shape. They do not even understand (believe) those physical laws that compel bodies to be globular because they could not spin on their axes, be balanced between and among many gravitational fields, and be otherwise than globular.

Even in conventional logic and argument, the conclusions reached—ergo, understanding—must stem from acceptance of (belief in) the premises.

There is much that we can verify with our own senses, but there is much that we cannot verify; we validate our understandings of what we cannot see, hear, smell, taste, or touch by the logic of authority. We accept certain things as fact because we accept the authority of those who present it—teachers, scientists, and clergy, for example—or we accept because it is common belief, accepted by almost everyone, apparently, and so must be correct.

The importance of this cannot be lost when thinking about how your presentation will be received by the audience members. Some will have a predisposition toward believing what you present on no stronger basis than you "must" know what you are talking about, since you are the speaker chosen. Others will perceive your positions to be erroneous on equally tenuous reasoning: You can't possibly know what you are talking about, because your position does not agree with theirs. Regardless of which situation you find yourself in, understanding the motivation of the audience, their backgrounds, experiences, and so on will allow you to present more effectively by addressing those perceptions directly in your presentation.

Communication Is Really Persuasion

It seems clear that belief must come first, and that it is difficult to define the line between belief and understanding. If we wish to communicate clearly, we must understand the are of convincing others—inspiring their confidence and persuading them to believe as we do. In short, to write—communicate—effectively, you must be persuasive first, logical second. Yes, most people want logical explanations—rationales—to support what they wish to believe, but they will reject logic contrary to whatever they wish passionately to believe. Only persuasive techniques stand any chance of overcoming bias.

On the other hand, most people are strongly biased about only a few things, and even those are often predictable. It is predictable, for example, that a factory worker, a truck driver, a stevedore, and many other workers will almost surely be biased in favor of labor unions because their personal interests are at stake; it is in their interests—or at least they perceive it to be in their interests—to be so biased. But they are probably not strongly biased about most other things, and are willing to listen or read and be convinced—persuaded, that is.

The basis of all persuasion is to make the other party perceive it as in his or her interest to believe you, to *want* to believe you. Many people will believe extravagant promises if you furnish enough supporting data as evidence or proof and if your presentation is attractive enough—if they want to believe you because you've made a hit with them.

That latter factor is not trivial. If an audience finds you offensive in any way—and that applies to your written presentations, as well as to those you deliver personally—they tend to reject what you say. I have witnessed quite excellent speakers with good material strike out with audiences because they came across as arrogant, sneering, boorish, or otherwise offensive. One man overdid his use of the first person, for example, which made him appear boastful and vain. Another came across as smug and condescending. Even if you do not appear offensive, failing to gain respect has the same devastating effect; one speaker was so deliberate and measured that he appeared to be hesitant and fearful, out of his depth on the platform.

That is one reason that efforts to be a comedian are so dangerous. Any humor that makes a class or type of person the butt of the humor by denigration is dangerous. Even expert comedians are on dangerous ground when the laugh is at the expense of any identifiable group or kind of person—ethnic, religious, political, or other. A humorous anecdote about your own mother can bring down on your head the wrath of those who think you are insulting mothers generally.

Presumably you can tell funny stories about some mythical stranger or relative who isn't representative of anyone else, but the hazard still exists. If you must try for laughs, avoid making anyone except yourself the butt of your humor. I occasionally relate humorous stories, but the joke is always on me. I'm the expert who got to be that way by making all the stupid mistakes, and I gleefully relate a few of my most humorous blunders. I often tell audiences about how contracts are sometimes wired for favored bidders, but to demonstrate that this is not foolproof, I admit that I managed to lose a contract that was wired for me, and I explain how.

A story of this type has a positive effect. It tends to make you likable because you admit your human weaknesses and are not ashamed to laugh at yourself. How can anyone hate a guy who makes jokes about his own stupidity?

A Few Do's and Don'ts

Here are a few things you should and should not do when you are facing an audience:

- Don't display nervous habits such as fidgeting, pulling an ear lobe, playing with keys, drumming your fingers on the lectern, or other such little habits. Aside from what they can do to your image generally, they can become distracting and irritating to an audience.
- Don't slouch, lean against the wall, or show other signs of boredom or weariness.
- Don't try to explain with words alone. Make use of a blackboard, posters, slides, transparencies, models, handouts, or whatever other aids are suitable and available. They are a stress-relieving change of pace for your audience, as well as for you.
- When the presentation is to last for hours and the choice is yours, make your audience more comfortable by using a classroom style—chairs at tables—instead of theater style—rows of chairs. (Remember to give breaks, too.)
- While you may be totally engaged in the material being presented and can maintain a frenetic pace for long periods of time due to your passion and enthusiasm for the topic, be aware that asking adults to remain seated for more than 90 minutes at a time without a bathroom break or chance to stand up and at minimum stretch their legs or change positions is an invitation to people losing focus and "checking out" on you and your presentation.
- Meet people's eyes as you speak, but do not focus on anyone in particular or dwell on one individual for long (despite some bad advice to the contrary). To do so is to make that individual uneasy and to mystify and possibly offend others.
- Don't try to speak in public as you do in private. (That is also bad advice often given by those who ought to know better.) Most of us speak disjointedly in casual conversation, often with such interjections as, "Y'know," "uhhhh," "uh-huh," and sentence fragments. Those are taboo in public speaking. Remember the repeated advice about leaving the comedy to the professionals of comedy.
- Show your respect and affection for your audience. They want you to succeed in being a good speaker. Relax, smile, and enjoy talking with a roomful of friendly people.
- Learn how to stop when you are finished. Stick to your schedule. Don't allow the one-hour lecture to become two hours. Let the audience know that you have finished, ask for questions if appropriate, and thank them. (If you are given applause, it may be because you have stopped, but it is still appreciation!)

You will be pleasantly surprised at how soon you will begin to feel comfortable on the dais and actually enjoy being there and talking to those who came to hear what you have to say.

19 | Skills You Need: Writing

The ability to write well is perhaps even more important and more frequently needed in your work as an independent consultant than the ability to speak publicly and make presentations.

WRITING SKILLS FOR THE CONSULTANT

We use the word *presentation* to refer to an address delivered vocally. But we also make many presentations in writing, although we may not use that term when referring to written accounts. Most of what has been said about public speaking in the previous chapter applies to or has its counterpart in writing. You may be able to avoid or at least minimize making formal presentations from the speaker's platform, but you will have to write a great deal in pursuing your consulting career, unless you are an atypical consultant. In fact, hardly anyone in the business world today can avoid the necessity for writing frequently. The information explosion and paper explosion are not something that happened to someone else; they happened to you and me, and they continue to happen and to have pronounced effects and influence on what we do. We must not underestimate the enduring role of paper as the principal medium, either. Computers have had an enormous impact on our world and on how we do things. Still, despite the proliferation of computers and the vast archives of information stored in computer media—tapes and disks, primarily—paper archives continue to grow. Advances that have put computers on desks in almost every office today are at least partially responsible for the swelling in paper records. Our knowledge is advancing exponentially in every field—even the meaning of well educated has grown dramatically—and it is all transcribed somewhere on paper. Millions of words processors are spewing out reports, manuals, proposals, specifications, books, texts, seminar programs, lecture guides, and countless other records and manuscripts written to record, to report, to inform, to document, to educate, and to train. If anything, computers have accelerated the growth of information on paper.

With the acceptance and use of the Internet as a medium for conducting business communications (be it e-mail, web sites, electronic bulletin boards, chat rooms,

307

etc.), the "paperless society" that was anticipated has not materialized. People print out the electronic messages and either respond to it, save it for future reference, file it, or in some other way create a hardcopy version. The "paperless" benefit we had all hoped to see from using electronic means of communication has not yet occurred.

Written versus Spoken

Despite modern technological advances and the pervasiveness of computers and electronic means of communication, the "currency" is still the written word (albeit in a different form now, it is now electronically transmitted instead of printed on paper and distributed via mail). When compared to the spoken word, the written word has many advantages and is a more powerful tool for most consultants to master.

Greater Efficiency

One immediate advantage of the written word is this: A vocal presentation reaches a limited audience, even if repeated a number of times and broadcast electronically, and even then it is transitory, whereas written words and drawings can be reviewed and studied repeatedly and indefinitely. (Tape recordings of oral presentations are sometimes made to preserve the presentations, but they lack the visual elements of the original session.) There is no limit to the number of people who can be reached by a written presentation, and no limit to how often one can review the material.

Even the information archives that exist on computer disks and tapes suffer by comparison; they are useless for practical purposes of transmitting information to people until projected on screen, e-mailed to another, or printed out on paper. The written word is still the most efficient way to disseminate information, as well as to record it, study it, and use it.

Details and Precision

Written accounts must be as accurate and precise as possible, even more so than formal vocal presentations. The written account is a permanent and unchanging record. Misstatements and inaccuracies in a written account will return again and again to haunt you, whereas they are forgiven and often even unnoticed in an oral presentation. This is especially true of a formal written record, such as a technical manual, progress report, or textbook. Readers expect find gross inaccuracies in newspaper accounts, for example, given the nature of newspaper data gathering and writing, and they forgive these. They are far less forgiving of errors or lack of precision in the permanent medium of the printed page.

These details were not of special importance in earlier chapters, when we discussed the writing of informal documents such as press releases and newsletters, which were adjuncts to your main activity of direct consulting services. In the next few pages, however, we are going to discuss formal applications of writing skills to consulting activities. This becomes most important for two immediate reasons: In many cases, writing is an integral part of the consulting service itself, and it therefore seriously and substantively affects the quality and effectiveness of that service. But there is also the matter of the kind of impression made on the client by your writing—the effect on your professional image, that is. That has great significance and affects the probability that clients will recommend you to others. To quite a large degree, your client will judge your professionalism and competence by what and how you write as much as by what you say and how you handle yourself in fact-to-face exchanges or by the actual results of your work. (In many cases those results are not easy to assess qualitatively or quantitatively, and you are therefore necessarily judged by other, more subjective standards.)

This does not mean that you must be an accomplished master of polished and elegant phrases, but it does mean that you must construct well-organized writing to produce documents that accomplish your purposes accurately and efficiently—writing and documents that are thoroughly professional, that is.

You must master the basics of usage and, even more critical, you must know how to organize a written presentation of each type. Here are two reasons for stressing this latter point:

1. Most of us who are natives of the United States or another English-speaking country and have achieved at least a high-school education are reasonably familiar with the basics of English usage, and we can easily consult dictionaries and other references if in doubt. The finer points of usage are rarely a serious problem. We can also turn to a skilled editor for help, which is a good idea in any case. (Most of my own writing is sifted through the screen of professional editors, to its betterment.)

2. Editing can correct weaknesses in usage—spelling, grammar, punctuation—but it cannot help defects in basic planning and execution—concepts, organization, and construction. That requires rewriting, not editing. Not even heavy editing will salvage poorly planned or poorly executed writing. Therefore, the emphasis here is on those subjects, rather than on usage. Incidentally, it is not necessary for most purposes to keep a separate text on usage at hand; many good dictionaries include excellent front matter and back matter on usage and related subjects, features that are usually adequate to help you. *The American College Dictionary* (Random House) includes such material, as do *Webster's New Collegiate Dictionary* (G. & C. Merriam Company), *Webster's New World Dictionary* (Simon & Schuster), and the *New Comprehensive International Dictionary* (Funk & Wagnall). Incidentally, disputes over which is the best dictionary seem to rage constantly (whatever best means), so I keep more than one dictionary at hand and often consult several when I am in doubt. The Funk & Wagnall's volume, by the way, is an unabridged dictionary, where you can find information not in the smaller dictionaries. For that reason, it is an excellent idea to have an unabridged dictionary in your office, although it certainly does not have to be the same one I have; there are other excellent ones readily available, including the classic Webster's version.

Concept and Initial Planning

Every activity has a purpose or objective. The problem often is that we do not think out precisely what that purpose is. We sometimes undertake activities with the knowledge (or even merely the impression) that we are expected or required to undertake the activity, but without knowing why we must do so. In short, we sometimes do not think out what we are doing or why.

That is a common difficulty. If a client requires you to write a report—or even if you have yourself proposed to do so because you know that such reports are standard practice expected in consulting projects of the type you undertake—but you do not know precisely the uses to which such a report is put, it is not at all surprising that you are unable to plan it well.

Even so, and even if you do know the purpose of the report, it is necessary to know what planning well means. And that involves remembering who your client— or, at least, your patron—is. To understand the significance of that, we must digress for a moment to consider an important problem most of us face in marketing our services: the fear of consultants.

The Fear of Consultants

Perhaps it has never occurred to you that many employees of organizations actually fear consultants. Or perhaps you have sensed hostility from employees on the client's premises but never realized that the hostility was the result of fear.

This serious marketing problem faces every consultant. When management hires a consultant, management is perceived to be implying to any fearful employees that the staff needs help or are less than totally competent. This may not be the case at all; management may have made a determination that with limited resources to accomplish multiple priorities, the internal staff is better suited to handle other tasks, and the task that is being outsourced to the consultant is the objective that can most easily be bought from another, while the other tasks require someone with insider experience and knowledge. The sales manager may feel threatened by a consultant who can help train a sales force for higher productivity. The comptroller is not fond of the idea of retaining a consultant in financial management, nor is the production manager happy about an outsider coming in to help organize or improve inventory control. That fear extends to all departments, and many executives and others are almost automatically hostile to the idea of hiring consultants, insisting stubbornly that the consultants cannot supply anything that they, the employees, do not already provide. Understanding this problem and its causes helps explain the following rationale.

Clients and Patrons or *True* Clients

Whether you do business with large or small organizations, you need to remind yourself of who your true client is. The nominal client is the organization itself, of course, whether small or large. With a major corporation, you are usually dealing with some discrete portion of the organization, such as a department or division. Whether you won the contract as a total stranger through competitive bidding or had a patron in the organization—someone who helped you win the contract—you may owe loyalty to some individual whom you should regard as the true client. In fact, it is usually the individual you support directly who is the true client, and it would be wise to regard that person as your patron. That must be a consideration in conceiving the proper goals and objectives in all written submittals you make; that is, you must consider the interests and concerns of that individual. Even beyond loyalty to the patron or true client, there is the matter of preserving your own interests by doing everything you can to prove that you are not a threat to any individual on the staff and that you actually enhance that individual's image in his or her own organization.

For example, there is always the temptation, when writing a report, to maximize your own role and the magnitude of your achievements as a consultant to the organization. But you will be a far more judicious consultant if you are self-effacing and maximize the importance of your patron. When the head of marketing in one company retained me to help with a proposal, he was my patron and my client, and my job was to be his alter ego, doing a fine job that would reflect credit on him. And when an engineer in the same firm was assigned to develop a proposal later and arranged to have a purchase order issued to me for services, he became my client, and I gave him the best proposal I could and made sure that he saw, reviewed, and approved all copy before it went to management for review and approval. (Interestingly enough, that engineer had been involved in the earlier proposal and had given me the greatest amount of difficulty in that project, but apparently he was impressed enough to bring me back to help with the proposal assigned to him; he was much easier to work with the second time.)

Consider then, in the initial stages of planning any writing, both the nominal purpose of the document and how that may affect your client and your relationship with your client. Even a client on whom your services have been imposed against his or her wishes can be won over if you are wise enough in your writing, as well as in your face-to-face relationships, to do everything possible to further that client's interests.

The only caveat to this advice is that you not do something on behalf of the patron that you believe to be outside the best interests of your business (commit an act that is dubious or even criminal), or is not of benefit to the organization. While there is much that is admittedly gray as to where each of us may draw the line between what is consistent with our understanding of the Hippocratic Oath of "First, Do No Harm" and performing services for a patron that call that into question, you are implored to behave in a manner consistent with your role as an ethical consultant being paid for your objective counsel, and the expectation that you subscribe to a standard of professionalism that overrides the immediate benefit of acting in a discordant way with those principles.

The Deliverable Item

Every consulting project has a deliverable item. And in virtually every consulting project, a tangible deliverable item is required. In some cases, however, the tangible deliverable item is itself the entire purpose or goal of the project, while in other cases the deliverable item is intangible—usually a service—but a required tangible item represents that deliverable.

In most of my own consulting projects, a definite tangible product is required, which is itself the purpose of the project: a proposal. On the other hand, I sometimes deliver training seminars, and the presentation of the seminar—my lecturing on the subject—is the deliverable item. But the client requires something tangible, too, something that justifies the cost. (In industry, as in government, executives must always be prepared to exhibit what the organization got for the money; hence, the need for tangible items for files.) In the case of my custom seminars, I provide a substantial seminar manual. It is useful for the authorizing executive's official files and for reference and refreshment by those who attended the session. (Occasionally I am required simply to study something and render an opinion, which I do, but I always substantiate it in writing for the record—the client's files.)

As in my own case, a computer consultant will most likely be asked to produce and deliver a specific program, in which case there will be at least two deliverable items: the program itself, probably as a tape, and the documentation, probably in both disk and hard copy.

In many cases, such as one in which I assisted an EPA contractor evaluate municipal water-treatment grants, the value-engineering assistance was the deliverable service, but the client required a written report as a tangible item to file (if not to use) to document and justify the project.

In other cases, as one in which I assisted the U.S. Postal Service Training and Development Institute update a transportation-rate manual, the deliverable item was a manual (or, more precisely, an updated manual).

Most consulting projects thus require writing something as the final deliverable item or as representative of it. Long-term projects often require interim written products, such as progress reports or drafts of final reports.

Purposes, Real and Nominal

Some suggestions as to true purposes of written documents have been offered already: Organization executives and staff specialists must be able to document their expenditures and so justify them when and if they are audited. They usually require some fileable tangible—reports, manuals, or other paper—for the purpose, and (as in government bureaucracies) the reports and other documents may have no other purpose or utility. On the other hand, the written product may be itself the purpose of the project. That would be the case with proposals, manuals, computer programs, specifications, training programs, and custom-developed systems for inventory, purchasing, accounting, and other functions. Sometimes that written item is both a backup for the executive who authorized the project and a functional item.

Important Truths

Writers and others engaged full-time and professionally in editorial functions have their own sets of platitudes. Several of those platitudes reflect the philosophy that good writing is invariably rewriting—that is, that the really good first draft is by far the rare exception.

That is one of the distinguishing features of the truly professional writer or, at least, the professional attitude toward writing: Professional writers operate on the premise that everything must undergo at least one complete cycle of the draft/edit/rewrite phases (and many writers go through several or even many such cycles). The belief that one can write well in a first draft is usually the hallmark of the novice and, unfortunately, a novice who does not write well. Admittedly, there are rare exceptions, but it is overly optimistic to expect to be one of those exceptions.

Editing, as used here, refers to editing by a person other than the writer, preferably a fully qualified and experienced professional editor. Careful writers do a great deal of editing of their own copy—self-editing—and rewriting before the editor sees the first draft. But it is difficult to be objective about your own copy. So self-editing is highly desirable and ought to be done by every writer, but it does not take the place of full-scale, formal editing by another.

Conventional wisdom holds that good editing reduces the bulk of the draft manuscript by about one-third—that is, that most writers overwrite in their first drafts, and one of the functions of a good editor is to tighten up the manuscript, filtering out redundancies, irrelevant details, and excess verbiage.

In actuality, overwriting is a good practice and is often encouraged, although with the proviso that it must be followed by conscientious editing. It is a good practice because it permits both writer and editor to study the material and decide, in a second look, what to keep and what to discard. Writers do well to get it all down on paper and decide later what is most important, most useful, and most effective in meeting the goals and objectives.

There are many writers who do write tight first drafts. Usually, when that is the case, it is because they have done scrupulous self-editing and already eliminated what is obviously superfluous, extraneous, or trivial.

In self-editing, a writer comes to appreciate word processing. The processes of editing, rewriting, and even extensive reorganization and revision are so facilitated by word processing that I often wonder how it was ever possible to produce a serious work without this marvelous tool. What computers and word processors (which are software programs, not hardware) do in automating certain repetitive and tedious chores is insignificant when compared with these much greater capabilities and contributions. The widespread practice of using typists to enter handwritten or typed manuscript is almost tragic in its underuse of the tool. Writers must work at the keyboard to gain the true benefits of word processing, which can improve the very quality of writing. Nor is the common excuse of some that they are not trained typists a valid one. I and many others turn out a stream of books and other manuscripts with two fingers! (More thoughts on computer usage appear in a later chapter.)

Good writers understand that writing is not confined to words alone, but includes all relevant aids to communicating to the reader. That is, necessary illustrations are the writer's responsibility, for a good writer does not illustrate his or her words, but uses whatever is the most effective and/or most efficient medium for conveying the message. The writer must decide where illustrations are necessary—where words alone cannot do the job or, at least, cannot do it as well as an illustration—and conceive or find suitable illustrations, make sketches, or otherwise define the need to a specialist, such as a photographer or artist. (Illustrations include photographs, line drawings, renderings, charts, graphs, and even tables.) In self-editing, the writer ought to keep in mind whether additional illustrations would be helpful. One more point about illustrations. Good illustrations do not merely *supplement* extensive and tedious text passages; they *replace* such difficult to write and difficult to read text. If an illustration cannot displace its own weight in words, it is not a good illustration; it does not do the job. The quality of an illustration is in inverse proportion to the amount of text required to explain it; the best illustrations require little supporting text. You should use that as a yardstick in evaluating or appraising illustrations.

Writing, then, is an all-inclusive word that involves far more than writing per se. In fact, writing itself is probably not more than one-third of the total effort and is, in many cases, a smaller portion of the total than even that. There is also planning, research, illustrating, editing, and, in most of the situations we are contemplating, production to be considered. Moreover, much of it is iterative. Even with a well-thought-out and detailed plan, initial research may turn up information that compels you to revise your plan, or you may have to do research before you can even begin serious planning.

Steps in the Development

The development of any written instrument follows a logical progression, beginning with need or purpose: What do you wish the written instrument to be or do? That can be any of a wide variety of things, including (but not restricted to) the following:

- Log the project chronologically and logically.
- Justify the effort and its cost.
- Guide future researchers.
- Provide useful information derived.
- Report specific advances.
- Provide how-to guidance.
- Provide reference data.
- Inform stockholders.
- Inform the public.
- Provide input for a prospectus.
- Study a problem.

That is a first step in defining what you must do, and only a first step. You must actually progress through the development of an entire hierarchy of definitions before you can actually develop a manuscript. You must also identify clearly both your overall goal (train, advise, argue, document, etc.) and product (manual, proposal, report, etc.). That done, you must develop a working plan, preferably in outline format, to include the following main items:

- Set of objectives.
- Content outline.
- Format.
- Illustrations.
- Schedule.

The schedule should include projected times or dates for at least the following items:

- Start.
- Draft completion.
- Review of first draft.
- Revision, rewrites.
- Second review.
- Final reviews.
- Production and delivery.

Execution

Writing itself can be easy or difficult, depending primarily on how thorough and detailed the basic research and the planning have been. The more thorough and well thought out the planning—especially the research—the easier it is to stitch all the information together coherently. On the other hand, if you have not thought things out and planned thoroughly, and especially if you have not researched your subject thoroughly, you may be forced to do a great deal of improvising and patching. This is likely to affect continuity and make it difficult to produce an acceptable final product without extensive editing and revision. In short, time spent in thorough planning and preparation usually saves more time later than it consumes itself, while it also helps you produce a better product. In fact, good preparation is an antidote for that stubborn resistance to and fear of writing that characterize so many people. The true difficulty in writing (and almost certainly the most common cause of bad writing) is lack of preparation. That includes the failure to do the things just outlined here, but it applies even in the case of someone writing on a subject in which he or she is already expert—that is, developing a manuscript for which the writer requires little or no research. Even in such cases, too often the writer is overconfident ant and neglects to think the project through. Again and again in leading writing groups, I have found that bad writing was not due to any basic inability of the writer to use the language effectively, but was due to the failure to know what he or she wanted to say; the writer had simply neglected to think about the subject and identify a goal and a set of objectives. Even having a general outline of required coverage and specification does not help if you do not think the subject through completely. It is quite easy to deceive yourself into believing that you know the subject so well that you do not have to waste time in research or planning. Wishful thinking makes it easy to persuade ourselves of things that are not so. Sometimes we even lure ourselves into believing that the ability to memorize and recite certain facts or to use certain jargon demonstrates understanding and mastery of the subject.

A reasonable test of proof of understanding is the ability to explain the concept in lay language to someone else, someone who is totally inexpert and unfamiliar with the subject. Perhaps it is necessary to use jargon to demonstrate that you are a professional and an expert, but do be sure that the use of the jargon is incidental and not central in the manuscript, and be especially careful that knowledge of the jargon is not essential for understanding the document.

In technical fields, jargon is thick and mystifying even to those who work with it every day. (For example, once an unexpected failure of a computer program resulted in a dump of data; now the program crashes, and who knows what it will do next year. Improvisations in radio years ago were referred to as haywire wiring and outboard circuits; in computer software, at least in software for personal computers, improvisations are kludges. But certain other changes or modifications to programs are known as patches.)

There is a tendency in many cases to explain things by labeling them with such terms, which are not necessarily definitive even to those in the technical field, let alone to others. In fact, another test of true understanding is the ability to translate that jargon accurately into everyday English and into concepts that anyone can understand. That is the job of the writer and the main goal of the document, in many cases.

Don't be misled by advice to use short sentences and short words, either, for many short words are uncommon words, and being short does not make them any easier to understand. Tell the average individual that the earth is an oblate spheroid; it is not likely that you will paint an accurate image, for not many people know just what those words mean. Tell them, rather, that the earth is a globe, but slightly flattened at the top and bottom—at the poles—something like an orange, and they will get the picture.

Use the ability to translate jargon and concepts as a yardstick by which to measure your own readiness to begin writing. If you can't make the translation easily, your understanding is probably less than perfect. Try doing a little more basic research into the subject and think it out a bit more. You are likely to discover that you did not know the subject as well as you thought. (I am skeptical when I hear someone say, "I understand it, but I can't explain it," or, "You wouldn't be able to understand this.")

In cases where the publication is small and informal—perhaps a proposal of only a few pages—there is no occasion for all the formal paperwork of developing book plans, outlines, schedules, and research plans. Most of that can be done mentally and spontaneously. But that, too—thinking the matter through thoroughly—is planning and preparation and is as important for the small writing project as for the large one.

Many professional writers think on paper. They start writing down ideas, notions, and bits of knowledge almost at random, thinking the organization of the product out en route and often in the process discovering gaps that need to be researched and filled. Ultimately, they reorganize and rewrite all the material. The writer who works this way is developing an introduction, while thinking the thing out generally and planning the rest of the work.

That introduction is known as a lead, and the process is working from a lead. It is a perfectly legitimate way of working for those who prefer it, although it is effective for only relatively short pieces; it would be extremely difficult to do that for a lengthy manual or book. Even with detailed outlines prepared in advance as guides in starting a new book, I have written leads of as much as 50 pages and then discarded them completely because I decided I was on the wrong track. That's not easy to do. In fact, it is quite painful. But it is the kind of discipline you must have if you are to turn out quality writing.

I use that method—planning and outlining primarily in my head and writing from a lead—for short pieces, and I combine methods for longer ones, such as books and manuals. That is, I plan a book by developing a formal outline and planning the content, chapter by chapter and subject by subject, along with general ideas for illustrations. But I work from a lead to develop each chapter, although I am guided generally by the original outline.

This method is probably not good for those to whom writing is a difficult or distasteful chore. It takes a long time to learn to work that way and to be comfortable and effective with it, and it is most appropriate for the professional writer because it means a great deal of self-editing and rewriting. If you go through careful and painstaking formal planning and preparation, on the other hand, you will surely minimize the amount of writing and rewriting you must do later.

Reading Level

It may surprise you to learn that relatively few people read with great facility above the eighth-grade level, which writing style is well represented by the popular and enormously successful (on a world-wide scale, in fact) *Reader's Digest* magazine. You can do much worse than emulate *Reader's Digest* style, and many do emulate it to the best of their abilities. If you succeed in emulating that style faithfully, you need not worry about your reader's general reading level; you can hardly go wrong.

On the other hand, as a consultant you are probably working in some specialized or highly technical areas, and so cannot avoid the use of jargon entirely. It is important to know to whom you are writing and to judge accurately your reader's probable knowledge of the jargon. That means discriminating effectively between the general jargon of the field, which most people in the field know, and the special jargon that requires explanation.

For example, if you are writing to individuals knowledgeable in electronics technology, you can probably use such terms as positive feedback, resonance, and impedance without explanation, but it would be wise to provide good clues to meaning when you use such special terms as Chebyshev effect or Butterworth filter. If you are writing to lay people, even those most common electronic terms must be explained, if it is, indeed, necessary to use them at all.

In general, follow this rule: It is not the writer's responsibility to understand what you write; it is your responsibility to see to it that you can be easily understood. One wise editor of my early experience went further than this. He said that it is not enough to write so that you can be understood; you must write so that you cannot be misunderstood.

Along the lines of this philosophy, I try to review my own copy while asking myself whether it can be interpreted ambiguously—whether it can be reasonably interpreted to have more than one meaning. If so, it must be changed. I do not knowingly permit my writing to be ambiguous.

Before we leave this point, it is necessary to point out a fact that may not be apparent at first blush. While you may be creating the report for the eyes of the technical expert, in many instances, that same document may be (likely will be) passed to someone else (a manager, or executive) who has generalist knowledge of what is being discussed, but is nowhere near as proficient as the recognized technical expert for whom the report was originally written. Therefore, it is a good idea to spell out acronyms fully (at least the first time), explain concepts that may be jargon (the expert will read through that without complaint, but the novice will appreciate it and even more importantly, understand it).

Outlining

References to many kinds of outlines may be found, but I know of only two kinds that have any true significance: an outline of what you intend to write about and an outline of what you intend to write. The difference between these two appears to elude a great many people, so it is worth spending time on the subject here. In fact, examples are probably the best way to illustrate the difference. Following is an example of the first type of outline, followed by an example of the second type. The subject is a symptom diagnosis of a malfunctioning TV receiver.

Type One: What You Will Write About

1. Visual and aural inspection of picture and sound.
   (a) Video symptoms.
   (b) Audio symptoms
   (c) Raster.
   (d) White noise.
2. Functional checks.
   (a) Front panel controls.
   (b) Real panel controls.

Type Two: What You Will Write

1. Visual/aural inspection, picture and sound.
   (a) Raster present? Video information present?
   (b) Audio present? If not, white noise present?

    (c)   Conclusion as to probable trouble indicated by symptoms—high-voltage problems, loss of video, loss of sync pulses, loss of input RF, other.

2.   Functional checks.

    (a)   Rotate brightness control: response? significance?

    (b)   Rotate contrast control: response? significance?

    (c)   Rotate volume control: response? significance?

    (d)   Rotate automatic gain control (agc): response? significance?

    (e)   Conclusions from above (probable cause) and/or logical next trouble-check.

Note: Use one or more logic trees to illustrate trouble-shooting rationale and analyses.

The difference between these two outlines is apparent. In fact, the second outline could be even more detailed and often is (I would make it so), but the point should be clear now. The first outline may serve in an early stage of planning, but you are not ready to proceed to writing a first draft until you have developed an outline of at least the second level of detail. It is foolish to believe that you are ready to write before you have reached that stage of planning and preparation.

You may have to do extensive research to produce an outline equal in level of detail to the second model here. But that is a positive effect: It indicates that you were not ready to begin writing before that research.

It is therefore a good idea to develop the first outline, as long as you recognize it as a preliminary step, exploratory planning.

Organization

Writing is a flow process; there is a logical progression of ideas and information. There is, in fact, a natural or at least a logical order to all materials, whether or not it is immediately apparent. If it is not immediately apparent, the writer may have failed to make a firm determination of who the reader is to be. Consider the outline just presented, for example: Is it apparent for whom this is intended? Is it part of a training program for electronic technicians? A do-it-yourself program for householders? An orientation for students? Of course, none of that is apparent, but obviously the translation of the outline into text would be different for each case.

Identifying Readers

You need to know who your readers are—students, lay people, technicians, or other; how little or how much they already know about the subject; and, finally, why they want the information—what they will do with it. It is not enough to say that they are clients, that is, for your readers must be defined in terms that you can translate into guidelines. This information enables you to judge how technical or nontechnical your explanations are to be—whether you get into all the technical rationale of the circuitry, in this case, or stick to handyman generalities.

Logical Charting

Once you have a firmly established and well-defined goal, you can turn to a simple block diagram—a flow chart—for direct help in thinking out the intermediate objectives that will lead you logically to the goal. Such a diagram is a generalized outline in graphic or chart form, and it is an excellent first step in outlining. Actually, it precedes outlining, since it helps you think out the problem and organize the basic phases and functions logically.

Designers of computer programs tend to draw their charts vertically, from top to bottom, while designers of equipment tend to draw charts horizontally, from left to right (the way we read). I favor the second method, but you can use either. Whichever method you use, begin with the one thing you know (or should know) for sure, the final block, which represents the overall goal.

In this case, I will assume that the publication is going to teach handyman-TV service to the nontechnical person, and my goal is to enable the reader to do what is stated in the box below:

Make
simple
repairs

That established, I can begin to perceive the objectives necessary—the progression of things the reader must learn to do in order to reach that goal of making simple repairs. The obvious major steps in the process are these:

- Observe symptoms.
- Analyze symptoms.
- Reach conclusion (diagnose).
- Verify diagnosis.
- Make repair.

There is a preliminary objective: The reader must gain an understanding of the basics of TV operation, enough at least to understand the simplified procedures presented. So my set of objectives is to teach the reader how to do the things illustrated in the logical block drawing:

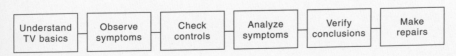

Check controls is added because that is part of observing and analyzing symptoms. Actually, many more details will be added in the full outline because each of these is a major topic that must be expanded. The outline must explain the implementation of each of these items, in fact.

Rarely is any outline or chart developed in one pass. Both generally go through several rough-draft and revision stages before the writer becomes satisfied with the result. These are the stages in which to do the bulk of your thinking, drafting, rethinking, and revision—long before you attempt to do serious writing. The more you do here, the less editing, rewriting, and polishing you will have to do later and the better the result will be. The chief advantages of charting your thoughts as an early or even initial step are twofold. First, doing so compels you to think out the steps and the sequence. It is amazing how easily we can ramble on in writing and deceive ourselves into believing that we have said something when we have actually evaded saying anything significant because it is too difficult to think things through in language. Words are abstractions, of course, and for some uses, such as this one, far from the best tools. But charting, even with blocks containing those abstract symbols (words), evasion becomes difficult, as visualization becomes easier. Secondly, once even a primitive chart is sketched it is much easier to perceive the logical flow in chart form than in text form, and thus the process of developing the full chart and subsequent detailed working outline is greatly facilitated. (Writing is itself a flow process, remember.) An excellent technique is to print the logical blocks on 3 × 5 inch cards and lay them out on a table, where they can be shuffled around, seeking the most logical and effective flow. Cards may be added, if and as necessary.

Actually there is a third benefit: The chart itself usually becomes an asset you can use directly or via adaptation as an illustration in the written presentation, thereby simplifying the writing chore further.

You can easily verify the logic and validate your diagram by reading through the drawing in either direction. Reading from left to right, the boxes reveal the why of the flow. And a feedback loop is provided from *check controls* to *observe symptoms* because checking the controls provides some of the symptomatic information. Even this drawing is overly simple, and many more blocks could be added as guidelines to the development of the working outline, which should be much more detailed than the diagram. The outline ought to answer the how of each block and of each transition from one block to the next. If it does not do so, you probably ought to add blocks or otherwise revise the chart to rectify the deficiency. In this manner, you can use the why and how questions to help in developing the chart, as well as in validating it and generating the working outline.

Functional Divisions

Organization means separating the document into functional sections or groupings and presenting them in a consistently logical sequence. The actual designation of such sections varies, largely as a consequence of the total size and nature of the end-product. If the end-product is to be a book-sized document—let us say 100 or more pages, to set a minimum limit—it is almost inevitable that it will be divided into chapters, whether they are or are not called chapters, each titled in a manner that identifies the focus of the chapter. If the simple drawing shown is to define the coverage of a book-sized product (admittedly, if that is the case, the drawing is too primitive to be anything but a very early approximation of coverage), each block might identify the focus of a separate chapter, or perhaps even more than one chapter. On the other hand, if the drawing describes what is to be only a relatively brief report, article, or chapter of a book, each division would normally be identified and introduced by a headline.

Thus, the divisions would be physically different, but functionally they would have the same needs and treatment; each division (subject) would require an introduction at its beginning and a transition to the next division at the end, matters we'll take up later in this chapter.

RESEARCH AND DATA GATHERING

The quality of the research is often the key factor in the quality—and success—of the written product, and the quality of the research is determined by several factors, especially its completeness. There is the need for accuracy and selection of the most important material, but even these are linked closely to the completeness of the research, for that is the key to selecting the best data. And best is usually the information sought out and selected according to these guidelines:

- The information that is most germane to your overall goal and the objectives you have established as the itinerary for reaching the targeted goal.
- The information that appears to be most complete and most accurate or most reliable.
- The information that appears to be most up-to-date.
- The information that provides you, as a writer, the greatest opportunities for drama, excitement, or other interest-arousing prospects. (And do not assume that because you are writing a business paper or article it must be dull!)

One clue to when your research is complete or nearly so comes when your digging turns up little that is new—when the resulting information has become repetitious. This is also a tool for judging accuracy: If most accounts agree, what you have is accurate. But if there is serious disagreement among the sources, you are wise to search for ways to validate one source or the other.

Despite all this, you must still rely largely on your own judgment, even when you have drawn information from official records. Court records, for example, may be legal truths, but they are still reflections of claims and opinions, and certainly not always factual.

Sources of Information

The biggest problem today is not how to find information—we live in an age of super-abundance of information—but how to process it: compile organize, filter, analyze, and otherwise assimilate and utilize it sensibly and efficiently. Among the many sources most readily available, are the following:

- Internet/Web. There is much available electronically, some from original sources, some from commentators, experts, or critics, and while it is plentiful, it is not always accurate. Be sure to confirm or check facts taken from web-based sources.
- Public libraries.
- Newspapers. (Libraries usually have microfiche copies of old ones, and actual copies of recent ones, but newspaper morgues—in-house libraries, that is—will often allow access to their files of back issues.)
- Other libraries. (Many government agencies, universities, civic nonprofit organizations, and even large corporations will allow you access to their files.)
- Public-information offices (also known as public-affairs offices and by other names) of all those organizations.
- Government agencies generally, especially those of the federal government.
- Publications of the U.S. Government Printing Office (GPO). (Usually you can quote directly from these and use illustrations and other material from them because most GPO publications are in the public domain; anyone can use the material in them. But there are exceptions: Some government publications include copyrighted material, for which permission to use has been granted the government. That permission does not extend to anyone else, so you must make sure that what you use is, indeed, in public domain.)
- Press clipping services. (These search many newspapers and other print media daily, clipping items on subjects you name, charging a fee for each clipping.)
- Public databases you can access via your personal computer and modem. These have recently become a particularly rich source, and some can even help select the specific data you seek. (In one case, I carried out a complete research job for a client by having a database service search their files via computer, and send me the data via our telephone and modem link. I then needed merely to edit and print out the data to complete the task.)
- Historical societies.
- Foreign embassies, consulates, and tourism bureaus.

Guidance in seeking out some of the offices and organizations suggested here is offered later in this book, but the library and the telephone directory are always a great help. For example, if the information you want is industrial or technological, you may be able to get what you need from industrial or business firms. Moreover, you may even get reproducible materials—news releases, specification sheets, tables, charts, and photographs, for example—with permission to use these directly. You normally must promise attribution—a line acknowledging the source and identifying the product or process. You should obtain written permission to use the material—a release form.

Some organizations and individuals, particularly in cases where you seek permission to quote directly from copyrighted material, will require you to specify exactly what you wish to quote; they may even demand the right to review your manuscript and approve or disapprove of your use. And some require payment, especially if the quotation is a lengthy one. I refuse to give the copyright owner the right to edit and approve or disapprove my work, so I generally drop the matter when that degree of control is demanded. I find a way to get along without the material.

Some organizations will include a letter granting permission to use their material (and in the case of news releases and accompanying material, such as photographs, formal release is not necessary because the permission to reproduce is implicit), but it is more practical to supply a release form of your own. I use a rather simple one, shown in Figure 19.1. It has served me well enough in most cases, and rarely have I found it necessary to use anything more elaborate. (I do, however, send a courteous letter of request making clear that I will use the material objectively and will be scrupulously fair if I find it necessary to make a critical comment. But I try to avoid the necessity for criticism, since I generally use materials to exemplify good practice, rather than to recommend for or against.)

THE DRAFT

The focus in this chapter is on usage and writing practices, although summarily so because it was never my purpose to teach the basics of grammar, punctuation, spelling, and other such subjects. But contrary to what other writers and lecturers on the subject appear to suggest, expert knowledge of grammar, punctuation, spelling, rhetoric, and other mechanics are not writing any more than the ability to use a hammer and saw are cabinet-making or even carpentry. They are the tools of writing, and you must have a reasonable mastery of them, but that mastery, no matter how great, will not of itself make you a writer. Moreover, you must have a good dictionary, and you should have a good grammar text at hand if you are not completely at ease in matters of usage. What is more useful here than a brush up in usage is a discourse on some practical problems

---

RELEASE

Permission is hereby granted to Herman Holtz and his publishers to reproduce, cite, comment on, and/or quote briefly from material supplied herewith, with the understanding that full attribution will be made.

_____   _____
(Typed/printed name/title)   (Signature)

_____   _____
(Company/division)   (Date)

Figure 19.1   Simple release form.

in writing. Before embarking on a discussion of these, a general caution about writing a draft is very much in order.

Even if you do everything recommended here as thorough planning and preparation, expect to write a rough draft as a first step following outlining. Thorough planning greatly reduces the amount of revision you must subsequently do, but it does not eliminate the need for a first draft. At the same time, don't fall into another trap for inexperienced writers: That is the trap of being careless in writing the first draft, reasoning that, "It's only a draft, so I can fix things later." Experience reveals that far too many carelessly conceived drafts never do get fixed, but haunt the writers for a long time. The more care you exercise with the draft, the fewer changes you will have to make later and the less danger you will risk that something wrong will appear in the final document. With the convenience of word processing to induce me to more self-editing and revision than ever before, only a small proportion of what I finally print out now has to be rewritten later, even after scrupulous editing by my publishers. It's a simple case of maximum prevention, resulting in minimum need for cure.

Introduction

Every subject and every functional division must be introduced, whether with a sentence, a paragraph, a chapter, or an entire volume. With a paragraph, the introduction is the first sentence, usually referred to as the topic sentence.

Introduction, as applied to writing, is not a mysterious term, nor is it jargon. In fact, it is simplicity itself. It means telling the reader what you are going to discuss or reveal. Check some of the paragraphs in front of you and verify that: Each one starts with a sentence that telegraphs what is to come, directly or indirectly. The rest of the paragraph is about that topic, and that topic only; when you have said all you have to say about that topic, end the paragraph and introduce the next one. Glance back (or forward) at the paragraphs here and see whether or not each paragraph was introduced with a sentence that telegraphed what the paragraph was about.

The same philosophy applies to the chapter, if you have chapters. The opening paragraph ought to introduce the chapter in the same way. Check the opening paragraphs of the chapters in this book and see if that is not so.

Transitions

Introductions to new material and new subjects, whether they are presented in new paragraphs or new chapters, are actually made or at least strongly suggested in the preceding paragraph or chapter. That is known as a transition, although some writers refer to it as a bridge, with rather accurate imagery. It is, quite simple, a clear clue to what is to come, so that the new paragraph or subject is not a surprise. (Surprising the reader is not proper in expository writing.)

Somehow, writing effective transitions appears to be a difficult chore for many writers, and the ability to write smooth transitions is one characteristic of the accomplished writer. Perhaps writing transitions is more art than science—one develops an almost instinctual sensitivity to the need for smooth transitions and the ability to create them (even expository writing itself is probably far more art than science)—but there are a few tips that will help anyone create effective transitions.

One tip is to use key words as transitional links. That is, introduce a key word or topic at the end of a paragraph, then use that same key word in introducing the next paragraph. Note, for example, the word tip ending the last paragraph and introducing this one and the following one.

Another tip is to telegraph the next theme or subject, even if you do not use a key word to do so, for theme is very much a part of writing anything. My theme is this section of this chapter, for example, was that the mechanics of English-language usage are the tools of writing, but not the art of writing, and becoming letter perfect in all those rules will not, of itself, make you a writer.

I did not set out to prove that idea, but offered it as a theory, asking you to accept it on my authority as an experienced professional writer. And here, in this paragraph, I deliberately avoided using that word *theme* in making this transition because I wanted to demonstrate another means for making smooth transitions: I used another word—idea—instead of theme, knowing that you would have no trouble following the train of thought.

There are many cases where you are concluding a discussion and preparing to set forth on an entirely different topic. This calls for a transition, although of a different kind. In such a case, you must let the reader know that you are making a change. In some cases, you need only an appropriate transitional word or phrase such as *however, on the other hand,* or *in comparison.* In other cases, such as when you are concluding a chapter and preparing to take up a quite different and not directly related subject, you might require an entire concluding paragraph to prepare the way for the introductory paragraph of the new chapter. But, again, the final paragraph or paragraphs will be of that however and on the other hand philosophy.

There are other methods for achieving good transitions, but all are based on the same idea: Guide the reader to the new subject by linking it directly to the subject you have just summarized or alert the reader to the new subject or theme and provide an introductory orientation to it.

Readability

Readability means different things to different readers. Many people mean understandability when they use the term, but there are no really good, scientific measures, despite many efforts to create standards.

One measure often used is grade level, with the *Reader's Digest* a de facto standard of an eighth-grade level suitable for everything except certain scientific and technical materials. Other ideas about readability concern the length and complexity of sentences and words, with some writers insisting that to be highly readable the words should never have more than two or three syllables.

The problem with all of these standards and guides is that there are too many exceptions. For example, there are many difficult or uncommon words that are short, while there are many common, easily understood words that are relatively long—more than two or three syllables. Ted, for example, is a short, one-syllable word, but few people (other than crossword-puzzle fans and possibly farmers) know the word. On the other hand, most readers would have no trouble with the polysyllabic managerial or insomnia. Semanticists can account for this quite easily in technical terms, explaining the existence or absence of suitable referents on the part of the reader. And because of this, systems designed to help writers determine the grade level of writing must include vocabulary lists.

As a practical matter, you must judge which are common words, easily understood by most readers, and which are uncommon, not so easily understood by the average reader—provided that you, as the writer, have a good idea of who the average reader is and what he or she is likely to understand easily. (And provided, also, that there is such an entity as an average reader, an idea that is not necessarily a reflection of fact, given that humans represent an infinitely variable sample.)

All of this applies to sentences and their length also. Contrary to some of what has been written on the subject, long sentences are not necessarily difficult, nor short sentences easy to understand. Stops in a sentence—full stops, such as semicolons and dashes—are as effective as periods in permitting the reader to pause and digest what he or she has read so far, but even short pauses, such as commas, are helpful. The important thing is not the total length of the sentence, but the organization of information. If a sentence has one central idea, and the information is presented in a logical sequence, readers are not likely to have trouble with it. Readers have trouble with sentences that are guilty of one or more of these sins:

- Tries to present more than one central idea.
- Fails to get to the point.
- Fails to make a clear and unequivocal statement.
- Uses an irrational or illogical order of presentations.
- Evades the issue by using euphemisms.
- Works hard at saying nothing.

On the other hand, readability also refers to other aspects of written and printed materials, including format and related matters. Here are some tips to make your writing more highly readable in these respects:

- Solid, unbroken blocks of text are formidable and may demand the reader to retain large amounts of data before reaching a summary or conclusion. Keep paragraphs reasonably short and summarize key points often.
- Use bulleted or otherwise listed items to make points.
- Don't rely on text alone, especially when you want your reader to perceive an image. Even for presenting and explaining abstractions and broad concepts, analogies and drawings help. Readability is not concerned with words alone, but with total communication.

Imagery

Illustrations are not necessarily drawings or photographs—not necessarily graphics, that is; they can be verbal illustrations, imagery, or images drawn by words. Similes—as strong as an ox—and metaphors—a bear of a man—are two common types of imagery used to help readers (and listeners, in the case of oral presentations) grasp the concept. But simple word descriptions that help the reader or listener understand readily are also imagery.

In using imagery, it is important to use comparisons that the reader is likely to be familiar with. It does not help to call something as complex as a tracking equation when the reader or listener is not likely to have any idea what a tracking equation is, much less how complex it is. The thing to which you refer as a simile or metaphor, or even as a simple comparison, must be commonplace and easily understood—recognized—by readers and listeners if it is to be effective.

Do-It-Yourself Artwork

It is often not necessary to turn to professional illustrators for artwork. Most art-supply stores and office stationers can help you with templates, transfer (decal) type, drawing symbols, and clipart. Moreover, many desktop publishing programs include clipart and related capabilities to help you. Do-it-yourself illustrations are a reality.

Level of Detail

The amount of detail you include should depend, logically, on two things: the reader's need—and that should equate with the goals and objectives you are addressing in writing the material—and the reader's ability to absorb, appreciate, and utilize the detail.

Most technical publications offer readers far more detail than they need or can use, often more than they can understand, in fact. As a writer, you do not need to report everything you know about the subject. Make an objective evaluation of what the reader needs and can use, and restrict yourself to that. If you conclude that your reader needs technical detail but is not trained in even the rudiments of the technology concerned, there are still ways to provide a limited and almost painless education in the salient facts by providing tactful explanations as you go.

One problem, however, is that you often have a mixed audience or readership. Some are technical/professionals, while others are lay people. It is necessary to present the information so that both understand, and yet the technical/professional readers must not feel that they are being talked down to. Consider the following ways of explaining a multiplexed interface as an example of achieving this goal:

- The interface is multiplexed, permitting the equipment to carry on concurrent exchanges of information with several dozen sources and destinations.

- The interface is multiplexed, sampling each of several dozen inputs at 50-microsecond intervals in turn so that, for practical purposes, several dozen transmissions are received concurrently.
- The interface is characterized by multiplexing or ability to handle a number of inputs and outputs in such rapid succession that they appear virtually simultaneous.
- The interface has a multiplex characteristic (ability to handle a number of inputs and outputs in such rapid succession as to appear to be simultaneous).

These are in a descending order of technical detail or an ascending order of technical explanation. Anyone can learn from this what multiplexing means, at least in a general sense. And yet no one should be offended, not even the knowledgeable engineer or technician.

Visual Elements

Many consultants and small businesses have been able to use digital cameras to supplement their presentations with visual examples or detail that would otherwise be difficult to communicate.

The ability to store many images on a hard drive of a computer and create your own "stock" of commonly used photos for business purposes have all but eliminated the use of slides or transparencies in many presentations given by consultants.

Another benefit to using any of the commonly available digital photo handling applications is that presentations can be dynamically altered as needed to suit unique client or prospect presentation needs without having to incur the cost of slide or transparency creation (one simply *cuts and pastes* the photo in a new location or alters it as necessary to suit the new use).

The fact that more businesses are using Internet connections that permit fast upload and download of graphic intensive files without bringing the entire process of reviewing the presentation to an electronic crawl has also facilitated the ability to edit, re-edit and respond to client feedback more flexibly and quickly in communicating ideas visually.

20 | Additional Profit Centers: Writing for Publication and Self-Publishing

Counseling clients on a one-to-one basis is not enough to constitute a successful practice. The successful independent consultant is, or should be, well rounded in counseling as a writer, publisher, lecturer, teacher, and leader.

CONSULTING MEANS DIFFERENT THINGS TO DIFFERENT CONSULTANTS

As do most enterprises, a consulting practice ultimately begins to assume a life of its own. In most cases, the venture evolves gradually into an enterprise the entrepreneur never visualized. Among the major consulting firms today, few started as consultants. Many began business life as accounting firms, a few as engineering firms, and others in other capacities. (May continue to operate in those original capacities, with consulting a separate division.)

It is not only large firms who so evolve; even independent entrepreneurial ventures are overtaken by change and diversification. As has been previously shared, many consultants branch out into areas that complement or supplement their original consulting services and offerings. Alan Weiss provides seminars to consultants or would-be consultants in addition to maintaining his own consulting practice, others have started publishing their own written materials as a product to increase their market reach, only to find that publishing became more than a sidelight to their practice and ultimately dwarfed their own consulting with clients in generating income. Many consultants have discovered that one of their clients will pull them in a direction that ultimately becomes the focus of their business from that point forward.

Despite this, all are still consultants, still counseling and guiding clients in their own ways and through their own media—often multimedia. In fact, many carry on all the activities concurrently, as different aspects of their consulting services, rather than acting as specialists in any one ancillary activity.

Sometimes consultants simply gravitate into these adjacent consulting specialties—for they are consulting services, despite their specialized natures. Sometimes the

330

movement or diversification is an accident, the result of circumstances. Often, however, the decision to make the move is deliberate, a business necessity or growth to establish a firmer base for the independent consulting practice. That latter case—diversifying to establish a firmer base for success as an independent consultant—is the main topic in this chapter.

WHAT ARE PROFIT CENTERS?

Many corporations organize and reorganize themselves into various departments or divisions, and these are not unique or single occurrences. They take place periodically in the life of an organization, as circumstances inspire or dictate changes. General Motors, for example, is organized into separate divisions, one for each brand name of automobile manufactured by the corporation, and each division is itself broken down into many departments.

There are many reasons for so structuring an organization. Different divisions often require entirely different talents, resources, marketing, and management. In more than a few cases, many divisions chronically lose money, while one or two divisions are so profitable that they carry the entire corporation. It helps to keep those losers identified as separate entities so that they can be turned around or turned off. The underlying thought, however, is always that each division is or should be a profit center, a producer of income for the central organization. Separating different kinds of activities into separate divisions facilitates managing them for profit.

The size of the organization has nothing to do with the philosophy of separate profit centers. A one-person enterprise can be so divided. Although all the several activities are consulting services and are integral to your practice overall, each is or should be regarded as an entity if you are to manage them well and derive maximum benefits. To do that, you should treat them in the following manner:

1. Establish each activity—newsletter, seminars, books—as a separate identifiable entity.
2. Set up separate accounting records so that you can track expenditures and income for each.
3. Operate each in such manner that all become mutually supporting in sales—a newsletter promotes seminars, seminars promote book sales, and so on.
4. Make the activities mutually supporting in costs also, sharing as many costs as possible, and reflect these shares in the accounting records of each.
5. Keep close track of the activities so that you can also estimate, perhaps even measure, the spinoffs—the benefit one derives from the other.

WHY OTHER PROFIT CENTERS?

There are several reasons for initiating additional profit centers:

1. Someone has suggested an idea that appeals to you (for example, "Why not start a newsletter?" or "That would make a good seminar"), or an unexpected

and unsolicited opportunity comes your way. (Herman wrote his first book for a commercial publisher as the result of a chance meeting. David proposed an article idea for a trade publication covering training and the editor asked if he would like to make it into a monthly column [and he cheerfully said, yes!]).

2. Market demand—individuals who are potential clients seeking you out with specific requests—for a seminar, a newsletter, a training program, a speech, or some other service inspires you to initiate an ancillary service.

3. You write or lecture for some reason, and you discover that you enjoy it, and it is profitable.

4. Another consultant approaches you with an idea to pursue an opportunity jointly and enter into a relationship where you cooperatively work together.

5. You need additional sources of income. (This is probably the most common seedbed of new and ancillary ventures.)

Every venture takes time to grow from its beginnings, to mature until it bears fruit; consulting is not an exception. Unless you are exceptionally fortunate, you are not likely to be profitable the first year of your practice, and probably not even in the second year. Conventional wisdom is that most new ventures take several years to begin earning modest profits.

This is almost surely true of consulting if you keep your practice based on a narrow one-on-one service at some fixed hourly or daily rate. There are two difficulties in surviving as an independent consultant, especially in the early years:

1. Consulting is typically a feast-or-famine enterprise. It's perverse, but that is the way it is: You get several opportunities all at once, but you can usually handle only one at a time and must decline the others. Despite your best efforts to market effectively, between those bonanzas of opportunity there are lengthy, hungry valleys of despair, in which you try in vain to win clients and assignments. Experienced consultants refer to the *Sell-Do* cycle to explain this phenomenon. When there is little or no business currently being transacted, the consultant pursues opportunities, makes sales calls, or networks more diligently. As soon as there is enough work to sustain the consultant for the time being, or the work consumes so much time as to not allow further selling efforts to occur, the consultant stops selling and goes into *production* or *project* mode. It is not until the existing projects are nearing completion, that the consultant once again realizes the need to fill the pipeline with additional projects (lest he be faced with long stretches of time without income). In some instances, the sales cycle may be sufficiently long that no new business can be signed and commenced and therefore payments received without there being a lag that unduly pinches cash reserves from the prior project.

2. Equally perverse, when you are in the early years of your practice, you simply cannot charge high enough rates in peak seasons to build up profits that will see you through lean times. You must do something to smooth the peaks and valleys of income. One way out of the dilemma is to develop

other, ancillary, sources of income—other profit centers. That is why we find independent consultants becoming writers, lecturers, publishers, and otherwise diversifying their services.

It is not unusual for young engineers to discover that engineering is less interesting, less fun, and/or less rewarding than they had imagined. The same is true for lawyers, doctors, architects, teachers, and others; many careers prove disappointing or uninteresting, and it is therefore not unusual for their practitioners to cast about in search of something else for which they are fitted and which has greater appeal.

THE COMMON DENOMINATOR

Consultants are specialists' specialists. They are specialists with rare and impressive records of achievement in their fields, outstanding talents and instincts, and possess a vast array of specialties. Consultancies have been founded and are based on an infinite variety of technical/professional fields and, more often, on very special niches in those fields. If there is any common denominator among the many consulting practices, it is that single characteristic of specialized knowledge—knowledge that is specialized in terms of both formal training and the unique knowledge that results from experience. The consultant is also the practitioner of a specialized skill based on his or her knowledge, experience, and often on special instinct or talent; the services provided to clients may include actual performance—application of those special skills. A computer consultant, for example, may have an unusual instinct for troubleshooting or programming. If the client uses computers but has no computer technical skills, the consultant's knowledge can solve a problem for the client only by actually doing the troubleshooting or programming. If the client is also a computer specialist (or has such specialists on staff), the consultant may serve the client effectively by the classic consulting service of studying the problem and advising the client—recommending a method or procedure to pursue.

That is application-oriented information—a counseling or advisory service that is the tradition of consulting. In many circumstances, however, the client requires information that covers a specialized field but is still presented as general information on the subject. That would be the difference, for example, between calling on a consultant to solve a specific problem in telemarketing and calling on one to train a staff in telemarketing techniques generally.

It is thus clear that consultants practice by utilizing their special knowledge in several ways, including these:

1. Counseling a client with regard to a specific problem or need (the classic and most basic consulting service).
2. Applying specific, specialized skills to do something for the client.
3. Providing general information—training—in some specialized field.

That last-named item opens the door to a variety of options for adding income-producing activities to broaden and solidify the base of your consulting practice.

Providing your knowledge, experience, and skills on a generalized basis can be implemented in two ways: writing and speaking, both of which can be applied in many ways to produce a number of profit centers.

WRITING FOR PROFIT

There are two avenues for earning income with your writing:

1. Writing for commercial publishers.
2. Publishing your own writing.

Which avenue you choose depends on your objectives and preferences. That is something of an oversimplification, however; there is a great deal more to be said and a great many avenues and byways to explore in even a brief treatment of the subject.

Writing for Publication by Others

Writing for publication by others is a low-risk effort, as far as financial investment is concerned, since the chief investment is time—your time. But writing for publication by others is by no means easy to do, if you wish to depend on freelance writing as a substantial source of income. It requires time and effort to study the markets thoroughly and to learn how to write in a manner that meets the requirements and standards of commercial publications. While it is not easy to do, there are many opportunities to write for publications (although, initially, you may have to volunteer or provide articles at no cost to the publication). The reason for publishing may be as simple as viewing it as *marketing* and not seeking direct compensation for your efforts, or you may perceive it to be a separate avenue of revenue generation (and with that, the resultant higher expectations of publications and editors that will demand concurrence to their standards before paying fees). Still, there are many consultants who do a considerable amount of profitable freelance writing, so a brief survey of the market is useful.

Writing for Periodicals

Many publishers of periodicals—newspapers, newsletters, and magazines—buy articles regularly. Each of these kinds of periodicals breaks down into a variety of types. In each case, there are two broad types of periodical, those addressed to the general public—the popular or general-interest types—and those addressed to readers with special interests. And even that latter class breaks down into two types, those addressing individual readers with appeals to avocational interests, such as collecting stamps or antiques, and the trade journal, addressed to businesspeople and professionals with information about their industries, businesses, or professions.

There are, for example, many magazines and tabloid newspapers in the trade-journal class; it would be difficult to find an industry, business, or profession that did not have at least one such journal, and in most cases there are several. Newsletters tend also to be addressed to vocational, avocational, and industrial/business/professional interests.

In sum, there is a vast array of periodicals, representing a proportionately great market for freelance writing. These are the general facts:

1. Daily, regular newspapers buy relatively little material from freelance writers. They do buy a number of feature stories, especially for Sunday supplements, and often these are expert pieces on technical subjects of interest to the public—diets, health, military positions of the nations, and others.

2. By far the best rates for freelance writing are paid by the publishers of the major newsstand periodicals—the most popular magazines—that is, those with the greatest circulation figures.

3. Not surprisingly, the most difficult magazines to sell to are those that pay the highest rates. That is partly the result of exacting demands by publishers and partly the result of intense competition, most of it from experienced professional freelancers.

4. Equally without surprise, the trade journals pay far less and are far easier to sell to than the popular magazines. Much of their material is bought from experts in various fields, such as yourself, who are not professional writers.

5. Many newsletters buy some of their material, but they pay in pennies per word; these publications can be a good training ground for you to break into this generally profitable field, but they are not a good market in themselves if you hope to earn a significant portion of your income from writing.

6. Many consultants view writing for "webzines" as an alternative to print publications (magazines or newsletters that are available through the Internet as either sites on their own, or as part of an opt-in option that the receiver of the webzine has requested to receive the electronic publication). The Internet also provides opportunity for posting on industry or other sites that have a bulletin board or place where subscribers can post questions, or discuss issues of importance among them. While not typically paid for, it does offer opportunities to write and communicate with a targeted population.

Writing for Syndicates

It is possible to write indirectly for periodicals by addressing your writing to syndicates. Most newspapers and some magazines get much of their material from syndicates. These are the middlemen of freelance writing, organizations who distribute the work of writers as brokers, on a commission basis; newspapers have come to depend on these brokers for most of their special features. For example, most newspaper columnists and cartoonists are syndicated nationally. The columnist sends his material to the syndicate, and the syndicate sends copies out to all the newspapers and magazines to which it has sold the column. The writer gets approximately one-half the revenue. (Commissions vary, according to circumstances, but they are much larger, in percentage terms, than those charged by literary agents. That is because syndicates do more work, including distribution of the material; the literary agent's work is largely done, once the sale is made, although the agent continues to earn commissions from the royalties and other, subsidiary earnings.)

Syndication offers the opportunity for substantial income if what you write proves popular, since syndicates generally sell the material on a non-exclusive basis. The buyer, usually a newspaper with only local circulation, has the right to the piece exclusively in its own distribution area, but not elsewhere. So the syndicate may sell the item to many newspapers, as long as none are directly competitive with each other—are not published in the same city or area.

Syndicates sell columns, crossword puzzles, quizzes, cartoon strips, and other continuing features, but they also sell many one-time pieces, so it is a market open for the single feature article also. Any article you might sell to a magazine is likely to be of interest to a syndicate. Most newspapers, however, do not like lengthy articles, except for their Sunday magazines, in those cases where the newspaper publishes one independently. (Syndicates furnish many Sunday supplements also.) They are more likely to want the shorter feature article of perhaps 1,000 to 2,000 words.

Writing for Book Publishers

Writing for commercial book publishers probably represents your best opportunity to write for profit through publication by others. It is not easy to succeed at this; you must met certain criteria to get your book published, much less to earn substantial income, including:

1. You must have something to say. That's a euphemism heard often among writers and editors in connection with writing. It is an indirect reference to the tons of manuscripts that do little but echo already well-known truths. What it really means is that to be worthy of publishing, the manuscript must offer something new, different, profound, insightful, and/or otherwise worthy of the cost of buying it and the time spent in reading it. A recapitulation of what has already been published, widely circulated, and commonly accepted is not something to say.
2. You must write in a style that is not only literate but conveys its meanings with sufficient clarity so that it does not require excessive editing before it can be set in type. (The style and language depend on the intended reader.)
3. It must have a wide enough appeal—potential readership—to be economically viable.

Of these requirements, the third is possibly the most critical, but that depends in large part on satisfying the publisher that you can meet the first requirement. And that requires a bit of independent discussion.

Bear in mind that the typical book publisher does not have an in-house expert on every subject. When a manuscript on a specialized subject is received and it appears to be literate enough and professional enough to merit serious consideration for publication, the publisher must seek an expert technical appraisal before going further. That is usually done by a consultant expert in the field, sought out and engaged by the publisher to validate or invalidate the manuscript as technically accurate and worth reading. Your manuscript, if it is rather technical, will have to pass that test.

Even then, there is no assurance your book will be profitable. That is a matter of imponderables, of chance. No one could have forseen or predicted that John Gray's *Men Are from Mars, Women Are from Venus* would have been a bestseller, for example. But that is true of most nonfiction best sellers. More than a few—and the temptation is to say most—nonfiction best sellers have been written by authors who were not professional writers, but who were specialists of one kind or another and who wrote books that somehow appealed to a great many people for reasons almost impossible even to guess at. (That is the nature of bestsellers; it is very much like a fad, such as hula hoops or pet rocks.)

Of course, there is the matter of your intended reader—for whom you wrote the book. The book without potential interest for the general public—one that is so specialized that it appeals to only a select group—has little chance of gaining a spot on the bestseller lists, although it may become a best seller within its genre. On the other hand, most popular best sellers are like novas: they flare briefly, then die rapidly. (There are occasional exceptions, bestsellers that remain on the list for many months, and even years.) Many books that sell more modestly—several thousand copies each year, rather than each week—go on selling at that more modest rate for many years, and are ultimately more profitable than the bestseller, paying royalties year after year and subject to less of a tax bite, as well.

But even this is speculation. By far the overwhelming majority of the 40 to 50,000 new books published annually are only modest successes, if they succeed at all; many sink without a trace shortly after publication and are seen thereafter only on the remainder tables. But this should not deter you, if you have something to say and believe that what you have to say merits a book.

Miscellaneous Writing for Others

There are several other ways to write for publication or related use by others. This is, generally, writing on a contract basis. Over the years, I have been paid flat fees many times to write about my special fields. These materials have included, for example, lecture guides, syllabi, manuals, storyboards and scripts for audiovisual presentations, brochures, and papers. Some were for seminars and lengthier training programs, others for publicity and public information generally. In one case, I ghosted a brochure on proposal writing for an association executive; his signature appeared on the cover as the author, while I was paid approximately $1,000 as the ghost author. In another case, I ghosted a brief course in consulting for a home-based mail order dealer. In most of the cases of such contract writing, however, I wrote anonymously: no one's name appeared as the author. I was simply paid a flat fee for my services, and the product appeared as the document of the organization. Kevin Coupe, self-proclaimed "Content

Guy" of www.morningnewsbeat.com (a web site that provides insight into the CPG and Retail industry) supplements his business with writing annual reports, presentations, and speeches for executives in the industry looking to become more progressive and leading edge in their corporate communication.

This can be highly profitable writing, especially with today's computers, which enable you to store, revise, and otherwise utilize basic information over and over. (I keep many archive files of basic data, charts, diagrams, tables, glossaries, and other materials I have developed, and I draw on these frequently in my writing. In many cases, I can use computer programs to prepare and print out camera-ready graphics, and I save those in files because it is easier to modify and adapt them to other uses than to start all over each time I need a chart or diagram.)

Rates of Pay

Writing, as an occupation in general, is not one of our higher-paid professions. Still, that general truism has not prevented a great many individuals from earning a great deal of money at the craft. You may very well be or become one of those exceptions. Rates paid by commercial publishers vary enormously, especially with periodicals and even for a given publisher and/or publication. So it is not possible to do more than give approximations and examples. Here, however, are a few basics about typical earnings of writers.

Newsletters generally pay from about $5 per item to 3 to 5 cents per word. Some trade journals pay as little as that also, but others may go to many times that amount. Many of the slick-paper trade magazines pay by the printed page, and generally range from about $75 to $150 per printed page. Top-rated popular magazines are more likely to pay from 25 cents to 50 cents per word, and even more in some cases. Newsprint publications—newspapers and tabloids—may pay by any of these methods and at any of these rates, often paying for news items by the column inch.

Book publishers generally pay royalties (although they occasionally buy a book outright), usually starting at 10 percent of the publisher's dollar receipts from sales of the book, and rising upward of 17 to 18 percent for highly sought properties, or if the book sells well enough. There may or may not be a cash advance against royalties, depending on several factors and circumstances.

Contract writing is an entirely different matter: You name your price, usually on the basis of your hourly rate and the estimated number of hours required for the job, and possibly following negotiations with the client. Such tasks in my personal experience have involved fees ranging from a few hundred dollars to $25,000 and even more.

Payment by periodicals is generally offered either on acceptance or on publication, with some offering to pay after publication. Unfortunately, none of these necessarily represent prompt payment or even the strict truth. Even those who claim to pay on acceptance often take a long time, and I have sometimes been forced to write a stern letter demanding payment. In one case, the publisher advised me that he must have an invoice from me before he could process payment. In another case, even that did not help, and I never was paid by that prosperous trade journal. I a suspect that some of these publications have a policy never to pay until pressed, and even then to take as much time as possible. On the other hand, I do not wish to malign honest publishers who do pay exactly as they promise. The problems have been exceptions, not the rule, in my own experience. I generally shun pay on publication periodicals, however, because they can take many, many months to publish, and sometimes never do. (And you have no way to check unless you happen to subscribe to and read the publication regularly.)

Tips on Selling to Periodicals

Remember always that you must slant or orient your article to fit the periodical. The requirements, rates of pay, and other details of most periodicals are reported regularly in monthly writers' magazines and annual writers' journals (see the chapter titled "The Reference File" for these), but only sample copies of the periodical can give you the full flavor of the publication's special slant. Refer to the writer's guides for specific information about how to get sample copies and how to get the guidelines to authors that many periodicals will send you on request if you send an SASE—self-addressed stamped envelope. The more closely you can match the periodical's own slant, the better your chance of selling the piece and the better the rate of pay you are likely to get. Sometimes you simply get a check, with an endorsement statement that conveys rights to the publisher; but often the editor calls you to make an offer and may make the offer conditional on certain requested or suggested changes to your manuscript. Often you receive a contract to complete and sign, certifying that the work you are offering is original, your property, not previously published, and conveying rights to publication.

The common mistake of beginners in this field is writing something and then offering it to totally inappropriate periodicals. Rarely will an editor buy something totally different from material he or she ordinarily uses. A magazine for industrial engineers would be unlikely to give a second thought to a manuscript offering tips on buying a CD ROM player unless the author had been able to establish some clear linkage between CD ROM players and industrial-engineering applications. Even then, the manuscript is on shaky ground at that journal.

Cold Turkey versus Proposals

It is not easy to anticipate an editor's probably interest. It is also impossible to know whether the editor has just bought or agreed to consider a competitive manuscript—one on the same subject. A perfectly good manuscript text and the quality of the writing. Only beginners send unsolicited manuscripts out to editors they do not know and have not talked to or corresponded with. The professionals research the market, list the most likely prospects for whatever they intend to write, and send those editors proposals, outlining their idea (before they invest time and money in writing) and asking for an expression of interest or even an assignment.

Sending a proposal is by far the wisest procedure, even when it leads to an "on-spec" agreement, rather than an assignment. An assignment means that the editor has ordered the article written for some agreed-upon price, and if the editor subsequently cancels the agreement and does not take the piece, you, the author, get a kill fee, usually one-third to one-half of the agreed price. On spec, however, means that the editor is speculating that you will produce an acceptable manuscript, and you are speculating that the editor will buy the article! It is a rare professional writer today who writes anything but proposals on spec.

It was once considered unethical to give a proposal to more than one editor at a time with any given idea, but that worked a hardship on the writer, given the slow pace at which editors respond. It is common practice to make multiple submissions, querying several editors at a time.

What Belongs in a Proposal

A proposal for an article need not be elaborate. A page or two—a single page with one or two enclosures, in fact—is generally adequate. Here are general instructions:

1. Explain your idea in summary form, preferably opening your proposal with the proposed lead of the article and following that with an outline or summary and explanation.
2. Demonstrate how the article is of relevance to the readership (demonstrate that you know what the readers of this publication want or need).
3. Avoid hyperbole—all adjectives, in fact. Explain and describe your idea; don't appraise or evaluate it. Let the editor do that.
4. Explain your credentials vis-à-vis the subject—where the expertise and information will come from. That may be your own expert credentials or other sources. (You may refer to an enclosure here if you have one that lists your credentials.)
5. Explain your credentials as a writer. If you have had other things published, cite them and furnish a few clips as samples. Again, that may be in an enclosure.
6. Estimate the proposed length of the article.
7. Tell the editor how long it will take you to deliver the article after the proposal is accepted.

The first item, opening your letter with the lead you propose for the article, is probably the most important point. If you can do that well, you demonstrate that your idea is interesting and that you write well. This is especially important if you do not have much in the way of clips or citations of earlier work; a really good lead is itself an excellent credential.

Making It Pay

Since you are probably new to writing for profit as a freelancer and, moreover, working in low-pay markets, how can you make writing for publication by others pay you at all? Here, again, we have to look to the professionals for guidance.

Most professionals agree that, at the rates you can earn in trade journals and similar markets, you cannot afford to spend time in extensive rewriting and polishing.

But that does not mean that you can get away with crude and hasty drafts. The writing must be of professional quality. Some professionals become skillful enough to do first-draft writing that is acceptable for less demanding markets, but you should do at least one rewrite if you are not yet that skilled. Fortunately, if you are using a word processor, that is not a difficult chore. Facilitating and simplifying rewriting is one of the principal benefits of using computers.

You can also not afford to spend a great deal of time in research for an article that will pay you perhaps $150 to $200. Yet, you cannot get by with an inadequately researched article either; your article must be a complete and accurate presentation of the facts.

The efficient professional approach to handling this is simple enough: Don't undertake articles (or books) in fields about which you know so little that it would be impractical to research them without the prospect of a large return. Many writes do invest years in research for a single book, which may or may not provide an adequate return on that large investment. But, more appropriate to our case, many others specialize in some given field, as consultants do, and write only in that field.

In general, then, do not undertake an article or book that would require excessive research. There is another, more practical side to that coin, an alternative: Don't settle for only a single article (or book) from a research effort.

Earlier I applied that principle to the writing of articles, and later to books. For example, in researching transducers for an article, I came up with material for three more articles, all from one modest research effort.

You can plan all of this in advance, as a series. Suppose that you are a computer expert and you plan an article on how to buy the right computer in today's market. Using the data gathered initially, you might do articles also on troubleshooting computer problems, finding software, using public databases and electronic bulletin boards, newest trends in software, ideas for using computers, and sundry other subjects. Or you might write and rewrite the article for different readers—the accountant, the writer, the hobbyist, the executive.

The idea works in writing books, too. In writing a first book on selling to the federal government, I covered it all, from procurement regulations and practices, to solicitation and contract forms, to bids and proposals, to reference data. Soon after, I realized that I had a mountain of residue, remaining files of data that I had not used, and that chapters in the original book could easily be expanded into full-blown books themselves. There followed then a book on proposal writing, a directory of government purchasing offices, a book on selling computers and computer services to government agencies, and others. I wrote two books on proposal writing, one for defense contractors and others who pursue government contracts, one for independent consultants, whose requirements are entirely different.

On the other hand, much of the residue of book-writing projects becomes material for profitable magazine articles, so it works both ways. The idea is to gain volume, by organizing the writing processes for efficiency. As I mentioned earlier, part of the solution lies in using your computer and word processor efficiently; the computer can double your output.

The Lead

That term lead is not exactly cryptic—it does mean introduction, in a general sense—and yet it is a special term, having special meaning. And perhaps that meaning is not universal even among writers, although it should be. To me, the lead is an essential key to unlock my thoughts. It is my philosophical summation, the theme of my work, the road map to my destination. On occasion, when I have traveled many pages down the road and decided—or discovered—that I was on the wrong road, I retraced my steps to the beginning and started over. I discarded the pages that represented my miles along that road, all the pages, as many as 50 of them. The lead is that important. And there are many leads: They are the first sentence of a paragraph, the first page or paragraph of a chapter or article, and the first chapter of a book.

The lead is, to me at least, thinking on paper. I doodle with words, and the computer, with its word processor, is totally conducive to doodling with language. I doodle with ideas, perhaps, even more than with words, thinking the matter out. What is my objective? Where am I trying to go? What do I wish to demonstrate? To point out? To explain? How can I best make my points? Do I really know what I am trying to do?

In my struggles for a lead, I juggle words and sentences—ideas. I move words and sentences, even paragraphs, around. I cut and paste, cut and try. I go on, and I come back again. And again, until I am satisfied. Like a sculptor, manipulating the soft clay endlessly, searching for that configuration that I cannot define but know that I will recognize when I find it. For it is the process in finding—yes, finding the lead. It's immeasurably important to many writers. To me, anyway.

The lead is just as important to an editor. It tells the editor where you intend to go, how you intend to get there, what you intend to say along the way, even why you bring the whole subject up. Why his or her readers—and he or she—ought to be interested, too.

It is important to the reader. It says, "Hey! What do you think about this? It concerns you, you know. Here is what it's all about."

The editor who sees that in your lead is going to be interested. Whatever grabs the reader will grab the editor. No question about it. That is what an editor thinks about: what readers want to read. Learn to write proper leads, no matter what else you do or do not learn. The lead is the sine qua non of all commercial writing. If the lead captures the readers' attention and addresses a need or concern that the reader is currently struggling with, the editor is going to look favorably on placing that article in the publication.

Most bad writing has failed because the writer had not done either enough research or enough thinking, usually the latter. (The purple prose of the neophyte can be corrected easily enough; that is not the real problem. Thinking, or the lack of it, is the problem.) Writing a lead, a proper lead, requires you to think. You can't write a decent lead without thinking your subject out thoroughly and plotting a course to reach an objective.

To put this yet another way, the lead is a reflection of your strategy for the presentation. Consider, for example, these three different leads for a price on selling to the government:

The essence of government procurement is *competition.* The concept is that free and open competition results in the government being offered the best quality at the best prices.

The chief difference between selling to private industry and selling to the government is that private-sector organizations can buy where, when, and how they please, but government agencies are controlled by statute.

Selling to government agencies is different from selling to private companies more in the size of the orders than in anything else.

Note the different themes and strategies of these three leads. The first focuses on competition as the underlying concept of government purchasing; the second makes the point that public laws and regulations control government spending; and the third says the difference is only of size, not of kind. All are legitimate positions, but they are different positions. Each would have to proceed to prove or justify the premise of the opening statement—and lead. Each would then result in an entirely different argument, and a given publication might accept or reject your proposal entirely on the basis of their editorial policy, which might dictate agreement or disagreement with the premise of your lead.

What You Sell

When you sell your writing for publication in a periodical or book, you usually sell the publisher certain rights, but not all rights. Most periodical publishers buy *first rights,* allowing them to be the first to publish the work, but not granting *secondary rights,* rights for you to sell your work again as reprints, as part of a book, translation into other languages, or other further use. Authors must also be aware of who possesses the "rights" to using the material for reproduction on Internet sites, international opportunities, other media aside from print, and so on.

There is another way to turn your writing talents to profit: Become your own publisher. Let us have a look at that prospect.

PUBLISHING YOUR OWN BOOK

Many writers have published their own works. Edgar Allen Poe is a classic example, but modern writers have also found it necessary or desirable to publish their own books. It may be because they can't reach agreement on terms with a commercial publisher or even that they can't find a commercial publisher willing to publish their books. Commercial publishers are not infallible, and self-published books sometimes turn out to be great successes.

To have your book typeset and manufactured so as to appear thoroughly professional requires a substantial investment in setting type, printing, binding, and distribution to wholesalers and retailers. A typical first-run printing order would be about 3,000 to 5,000 copies, and the complete investment for editing, typesetting, and manufacturing may easily be from $15,000 to $20,000. On the other hand, with today's ordinary office resources—computers, laser printers, desktop publishing programs—it is feasible to do your own typesetting and even printing by laser for small books, if you plan a limited number of books for direct sale. That is a viable plan for an initial effort to test the book and the market. (If the book sells well, you can get it printed in quantity or offer it to a commercial book publisher; if not, relatively little is lost.) Through the advent of these technologies, the cottage industry of print-on-demand books has sprung up to permit small run or even individual books to be published at a time. The downside to this is that it often requires the author to do all of the proofreading and copyediting, a task that may overwhelm many first time authors, or result in sloppier final products than desired.

There is one important caveat to be noted here: Avoid the vanity press. These are firms who call themselves publishers and who will produce your book for a rather large fee, but who will sell virtually none and who you will probably have to pay again to get all the copies, other than the few you were entitled to under the original contract. This is not a viable alternative, and it is most definitely not what is referred to here as self-publishing.

MARKETING BOOKS

The larger book publishers have established avenues and methods of distribution through libraries, bookstores, wholesalers, their own in-house mail-order programs, bulk sales to companies and associations, and various kinds of dealers. Small book publishers often arrange to have their books distributed by larger book publishers. Many of these methods are not the exclusive province of large businesses, but are available to you, too, as a self-publisher of your own books.

Distribution to Bookstores

There are three ways to get your books into bookstores: sell them directly to bookstore owners by personal calls and mail, sell them through book wholesalers, and/or make arrangements with an established publisher to distribute for you. (*The Literary Marketplace,* listed in the chapter on references, will furnish names and addresses of book wholesalers.)

Bear in mind that when you sell to bookstores and wholesale distributors, you must not only extend terms—wait 30 or more days for payment (and many bookstores are notoriously slow in paying)—but you must accept returns of unsold books for full credit, a well-established industry practice.

Libraries are a good market; they are usually given only 10 percent discount, and often not even that, that there is no question of returns. Newsletter and other periodical

OTHER PUBLISHING VENTURES   **345**

publishers who run mail-order bookstores (usually specialized to fit the slant of the periodical) generally want their orders drop shipped, and therefore get a discount smaller than the usual 40 percent. (However, not all publishers allow 40 percent. Some of my own publishers allow only 25 percent discount.) On the other hand, many self-publishers have used the PO/PI type of promotion.

PO/PI Programs

PO and PI stand for *per order* and *per inquiry,* respectively. In the PO arrangement, the periodical runs an advertisement, using camera-ready copy supplied by the author/publisher. Orders are sent to the publisher of the periodical. The periodical publisher keeps his or her share of the money—40 percent to 60 percent, usually—and sends the remainder to the book publisher, along with a shipping label, and the book publisher then ships the book. (This is known as *drop shipping.*)

PI works somewhat similarly. The periodical runs advertising soliciting inquiries, to be sent to the periodical publisher, who forwards them to the book publisher with a bill, charging a rate per inquiry, such as $2 each.

This plan—gathering inquiries at a per-inquiry charge—is also used by other entrepreneurs, people who gather inquiries through means other than advertising in periodicals and make mailings of advertising literature, so that the clients who pay for the inquiries can follow up with direct mail to the inquirers. This, like the per-order method, is a means readily available for selling books or, for that matter, for selling anything by mail. Very much related to this PI approach is the use of Internet sites such as www.amazon.com to sell books. Amazon will "post" your book and retains a relationship with the publisher and will fulfill requests on a per request basis.

OTHER MARKETING MEANS

If you are publishing a newsletter of your own, you can sell your own books through your newsletter, which is usually an excellent medium for doing so. And if you are presenting seminars and/or lecturing, you can sell many books through that back-of-the-room sale (which will be discussed in greater detail in the next chapter).

OTHER PUBLISHING VENTURES

Many independent consultants publish newsletters, reports, and other specialty items. Unlike book publishing, the publishing of such materials is much more the province of very small businesses. And I use that adjective *very small* because the government's definition of small business is totally out of proportion to our discussions. According to the U.S. Small Business Administration, which is responsible for establishing the many different standards that define small business in different industries, the smallest of small business is one which employs not more than 500 people or has sales not greater than $3 million annually. That is hardly what we refer to here when we speak of small business. There are a few major publishers of such ancillary materials, but by far the majority have annual sales of a great deal less than $3 million—or even $1 million. The very nature of specialty publishing is such that it does not require a great deal of capital, and it can be run as an adjunct to a related profession or as a part-time enterprise, so a great many newsletters are of the Mom-and-Pop variety.

Newsletter Publishing

Newsletter publishing is inherently a small-business, self-publishing enterprise, despite the fact that some newsletter publishers have developed large, multimillion dollar publishing enterprises. To some extent that is because newsletter publishing is a growth industry. The ever-developing technologies and attendant complexities of life on the planet dictate the need for specialized media of communication and information just as they dictate the ever-growing need for consultant specialists. In that regard alone, the development of a newsletter by the independent consultant is a natural; the newsletter complements the consulting service—is, in fact, itself a consulting service, one of the many a modern consultant ought to provide. The two, consulting and newsletter publishing, are based on the same concept of a need for specialized knowledge and skills. Newsletters were founded on that idea: They furnish information passed over by the popular press as not having interest for the general public. Take the subject of superconductivity, for example: It is important enough to merit many special articles in the general press explaining it to the public, but the engineers, physicists, and potential manufacturers and marketers of superconductive devices cannot depend on the popular press for information; they must subscribe to specialty publications, such as engineering trade journals, to keep up with developments in a field of great interest to them. Eventually they seek a periodical that is even more specialized by being devoted exclusively to the single subject of greatest interest, and covering it regularly as a special field of interest; that periodical will almost invariably be a newsletter. Many consultants view the Internet as a *real-time* tool for collection of information relevant to a particular target audience, and then repackage it (with their own spin on things to make it unique) and send it out as an e-newsletter to a distribution list of e-mail names culled from either personal experience or from a list broker. The costs of sending electronic newsletters is infinitely smaller than having to produce paper copy and incur costs of printing, mailing, and so on.

A newsletter can spring into being almost overnight. Again, that is its nature; it responds to needs of the moment and can be launched—birthed—with modest investment and on short notice. When the federal government created the Occupational Safety and Health Administration, newsletters on the subject sprang out of the ground, just as the birth of new government agencies—the federal Consumer Product Safety Commission and the Department of Energy—mandated the birth of newsletters on those subjects. (Should these agencies vanish on Monday morning, the newsletters would vanish on Monday afternoon.) Whatever your field, there are surely relevant newsletters published in it, and there is probably room for one more—yours. One writer on the subject of newsletters (his own newsletter was about batteries and dry cells, a special field that had not yet been covered by its own newsletter) suggested that if there were fewer than five newsletters extant on the field (whatever the field), there was probably room for one more. But that is an impracticable measure: some fields are popular enough to support far more than five newsletters—investment counseling, for example, supports many newsletters—while others will support fewer than five.

It is not easy to generalize about newsletters, especially as to their basic concepts and subjects. Newsletters are of a wide variety of configurations and concepts. Here are a few of the basic characteristics of some newsletters:

- Roundup summaries of relevant information drawn from a wide variety of other published sources.
- News items only—personnel changes, new developments, and so on.
- Advisory service—answers to questions, general counseling, and so on.
- Interpretive discussions of events and developments.

Formats and Related Matters

While many consultants use electronic means of distribution, there are still many who feel that there is more impact when the publication arrives in the mail to the intended recipient. Therefore, we examine the format most often used for newsletters. The typical format is in an $8\frac{1}{2}$ by 11 inch format, 4 or 8 pages, composed by one of the software applications commercially available, and printed on white bond or offset paper. Often, it is published monthly or at least quarterly. There are many exceptions to that standard, however. Some newsletters are of tabloid size, formally typeset, printed on newsprint or smooth calendered stock, on white or colored paper, published more or less frequently than monthly, and of more or fewer than four or eight pages. Moreover, subscription rates vary quite widely, ranging from free subscriptions, to nominal rates, to quite extravagant rates, sometimes upwards of $100 annual subscription rates.

The newsletter is a stern master. Even on a bimonthly schedule, deadline time for each issue comes with startling frequency and competes with other, often unanticipated demands on your time. Your equipment takes a holiday, and you lose days from your schedule. The help you rely on to take care of editorial and production problems fails to show up, costing you more delays. And even when you have surmounted all your internal problems and the newsletter is ready for the press, your troubles are not over. The printer has problems too, for example, and is unable to meet the schedule; that, too, becomes one of your problems.

On the other hand, the newsletter is an asset in more than one way—in at least three ways, in fact:

1. It may become a valuable property in terms of the income it produces directly.
2. It may become valuable in terms of supporting your consulting practice generally, helping you gain clients and contracts for your services.

3. It may become—usually is, if managed for it—an excellent medium for the sale of your books, reports, seminars, and/or other products and services you offer.

Even the newsletter that does not produce a direct profit is often a valuable asset in the other benefits it delivers. In fact, there are marginal or unprofitable newsletters supported by the publishers—subsidized, in fact—because they are such excellent media for other ventures that are quite profitable.

Sources of Material

Newsletter readers do not pay the relatively high price of subscription for amusement; the appeal of a newsletter is its usefulness. And unlike the daily newspaper, the newsletter cannot base its appeal on different features for different readers; the reader expects to find all or nearly all the content relevant to his or her needs. That is the very nature of a newsletter, specialized as it is, high-priced as it is (relative to size and frequency of publication), and limited in size and number of pages as it is. The reader is paying for information, not writing style, and your editorial work must maximize both the quantity and quality of the information offered.

That is not an easy goal to reach. In fact, the newsletter is possibly the most difficult form of writing. (Someone—it has been credited to many noted writers—is reported to have apologized to a correspondent for the length of his letter, pleading that he had not had time enough to compose a short note.) Newsletters cannot be chatty and cannot waste space on trivia. Material must be scrupulously evaluated and information not of direct use to readers ruthlessly discarded. Even that which is used must be condensed, boiled down to essentials, and even phrased in telegraphic style, which omits articles and conjunctions, and keeps adjectives and adverbs to an absolute minimum.

Sources of raw material inevitably include other publications—periodicals, new books, other newsletters, press releases, and whatever other sources you can find, including the Internet or web sites devoted to industry issues of interest. It calls for a great deal of reading, but that is part of the job.

You may have to go out of your way to get at all that information at first, but it is rather easy to induce a heavy flow in your mail every morning. One thing to do is to send out many complimentary copies of your newsletter, especially to the publishers of other newsletters that cover matters relevant to your own coverage. Most small newsletter publishers send out many comp (complimentary) copies, swapping comp subscriptions with others, often with mutual permission to copy each other's material (with attribution). Before long, you will be getting press releases, several newsletters, some of the many free trade journals (many are free to qualified subscribers), and much other useful material. Press releases are particularly useful when they are relevant and contain good information. (A great many do not, unfortunately, because they are thinly veiled puffery.) They are relatively easy to edit and boil down to their essentials, so that they do not have to be rewritten as much as they need to be trimmed. (It is probably true that effective editing, even when done for printing in a more capacious vehicle than a newsletter, should eliminate about one-third of the original copy.)

You must be concerned with copyright protection and plagiarism. It is a rather weary, if humorous, platitude of writing that plagiarism is stealing material from one or two sources, but stealing from 50 sources is research! There is a nugget of truth underlying the sardonic humor here: Using information published elsewhere is not plagiarism; it is research. Copyright protection covers a given combination of words and phrases. It does not cover information itself. Plagiarism is, therefore, stealing another's writing, not information. There is in the copyright law the doctrine of fair usage, however, that allows you to quote published work briefly. The problem is that there is no firm definition of what constitutes a *brief* quotation. (It varies with individual circumstances.) Caution is advised, and the safest course is either to get permission to quote or to rewrite, putting the information entirely into your own words.

It is the wise consultant who only uses photographs of others with their express permission. The allure of adding pictures to a newsletter to spice it up or make it more compelling must be tempered by the necessity to seek approvals before using someone's photograph in your newsletter. Unless the person has granted permission to use their image, it is not only poor form to do so, it may also be illegal.

Press releases are another matter. They are issued for the express purpose of being reproduced. You need not rewrite them nor worry about copyright infringement. Of course, all of this, especially abstracting and/or rewriting material from other published sources, takes up a great deal of your time, but there is another source that will not take as much of your time. That is soliciting material from writers, both professional, free-lance writers and others. To attract contributions from professional freelance writers, you need merely advise the editors of *Writer's Digest, The Writer,* and *Writers' Journal* that you are in the market for contributions, explaining just what you are looking for and what you are willing to pay. (Read sample issues of those periodicals for models of the kind of information they publish in such notices.)

There is a certain other benefit in this. It compels you to think out exactly what you do and do not wish to publish, an exercise you might not otherwise engage in. (A surprisingly large number of newsletter publishers do not have firm editorial policies or well-established definitions of what they will publish.)

That latter is an important consideration. Your subscribers subscribed with the expectation of getting certain kinds of information in each issue. If you fail them in this respect, they will be unlikely to renew their subscriptions. (The renewal rate is one of the key factors in the success or failure of a newsletter.) To maximize the appeal of your newsletter, you must work constantly at discovering what appeals most to your readers and what appeals least to them, and be governed by that. Take the time to read letters from your subscribers, and encourage them to write and let you know what they like, do not like, and would like to see in your newsletter. Let your readers tell you how to run your newsletter; their opinions count for more than yours in that respect.

It is also possible to get many free contributions from other professionals who will write material for the privilege of being published. Unfortunately, there is a hazard here: Much of what you get in this fashion is not what you want or can use. You run the risk of offending the well-intentioned contributor when you do not use the material he or she has supplied. You must be prepared to cope with this. You can, however, minimize this if you ask for specific factual information only, such as personnel changes, news of new products, or other such items. The tendency of many contributors who are not professional writers is to editorialize, trying to use your vehicle as a medium for expressing their opinions publicly.

Publishing Other Specialties

There is no firm definition of the word *book*. Some publications referred to as books are slender volumes, bound publications of less than 100 pages, while others are massive tomes. In any case, many consultants who become publishers choose not to undertake the considerable labor and cost of producing formal books, even the relatively inexpensive paperback books. They do, however, produce a variety of other publications, publications that are inexpensive and easy to produce, despite sometimes being large enough to publish as a book. These publications usually require a limited investment, and usually produce a profitable return on investment. These are often referred to as reports, white papers, special reports, or folios.

The key to these is that they rarely look like books; they look like internal reports or memoranda, typed (or computer printed) on ordinary white paper (bond or offset paper), bound with a corner staple or enclosed in a proprietary paper or plastic office binder readily available. In some cases, where they are thick reports, of interest to a small population of high-placed executives and providing valuable information not easy to come by elsewhere, they can fetch a rather high price. In most cases, however, these are small publications, marketed at reasonable prices, and highly profitable because they are inexpensive to produce. While fairly expensive to market, their selling price is high in relation to production costs.

The Economics of Specialty Publishing

The difference in manufacturing and distribution costs of a hardcover and a trade (quality) paperback edition of a book is not great, probably a dollar or two. Yet, the selling price reflects a much greater spread. That is because the customer for a book is buying the physical product and perceives a difference in quality that is not in proportion to reality. On the other hand, customers buying reports, newsletters, and similar specialty items are encouraged to ignore the aesthetic qualities of the physical product and concentrate on the information content as the value being purchased. Your advertising must have that focus.

A handsomely bound book of 300 pages may sell for $35.95, while a simple, stapled report of 10 pages may bring $5. I developed over 30 such how-to reports, ranging from 2 to 20 pages, covering a wide variety of subjects related to my services, and had no difficulty in getting from $2 to $10 for them. I also developed a series of special reports on new federally funded public works projects, reports that merely identified the projects, their dollar value, and other such data, and I found a brisk market for these.

Later, I developed a series of three books on selling to the government, composed by Selectric typewriter and paperbound, and I sold many of these as a package (via mail order and a newsletter I published) at $89.95. In retrospect, the reports were more profitable and certainly less trouble than were the books.

Conventional wisdom in direct-mail marketing dictates that you should set a selling price of not less than three times your product cost, and be prepared for selling costs of approximately one-half the selling price. That means that if the item costs you $5 to produce, you must ask at least $15 for it and be prepared to spend up to $7.50 in advertising and related costs. That leaves you with an approximate 16.66 percent gross profit—$2.50/$15.00 × 100—which is none too generous a margin. Therefore, even the 3 to 1 markup is thin, and it is wise to give yourself a wider margin if at all possible.

Fortunately, specialty publishing allows you that wide margin, which is why it is a relatively low-risk enterprise. The typical report can be produced at a cost of about 4 to 5 cents a page, and you can usually get about 50 cents per page without difficulty, giving you a gross profit of about 20 cents per page or 40 percent on investment.

You can see from such figures how it is possible to make PO deals in which you allow the other party to earn 50 percent of the selling price, while you still earn a substantial profit. If you sell your reports on such a basis, you get 25 cents per page, while the product costs you 5 cents, for a gross profit of 20 cents. You also have the labor and cost of packaging and mailing the product, which, if you mail first class, can add about 4 cents more per page for postage alone, still leaving you an adequate margin to pay overhead costs and amortize your original development costs.

Each time you fill an order, enclose advertising literature, offering your other publications and other services—seminars, for example, as well as your regular consulting services. If you give good service and your reports contain useful information, you will find soon that you get repeat orders and that many of your customers want to buy other reports—some even decide to buy all of them. You will find, in fact, that you may lose money on first orders—first orders are small and the cost of winning them proportionately large—but repeat business is profitable and more than compensates for the cost of first orders. Always bear in mind that the purpose of marketing is not to make sales; it is to make customers. When you make customers—buyers who return to buy again—you can afford to lose money on first orders.

That consideration should dictate the entire configuration of what you publish: You should think in terms of the interests of your typical customer and design your entire line of publications for that typical customer. In short, make the line of publications mutually supporting. They should have a linkage, offering a complete complement of information to encourage and stimulate follow-on (repeat) business.

It is not only your publications that should be mutually supporting—with each other, that is—your publications and seminars can and should be mutually supporting. You should use each to help sell the other. If first orders for publications can produce customers for other publications of yours, they can also produce customers for your seminars, a venture with a relatively high price tag and profit margin.

It is for this reason that the consultant's web site must also link into the marketing messages contained within the reports. (The message being "I can help you do X better.") Having the ability to process product sales from a web site also allows the consultant to make money at all hours and all days, without having to physically be available to answer a phone call or address a question about the product. At minimum, the consultant's web site must direct the person browsing to what products are available for purchase, and how to go about acquiring them. A web site that is integrated with a consultant's marketing plan would advise prospects how to contact you for speaking engagements, consulting assignments, and, if appropriate to your business, list other consultants that provide complementary services that you work with synergistically. The web site and specialty publishing opportunities should be unified to promote sales that are add-ons to what the prospect may have originally been looking for, or was unaware you provide.

Your basic consulting service and your ancillary profit centers ought also to be mutually supporting. That is a large part of the strength you gain from multiple activities. If you work at seeing to it that they do, in fact, support each other, you often gain a synergistic effect: The whole becomes greater than the simple sum of the parts. Moreover, as I have pointed out, you may discover that you are better suited to, prefer, or are more successful at one of these other activities than at the original consulting practice you set out to build. This happens often enough. But now on to still another major profit center: public speaking and the many opportunities it offers.

21 | Additional Profit Centers: Seminars and Public Speaking

*Public speaking ability is not only a marketing asset; it is
the basis for additional profit centers.*

SPEAKING FOR PROFIT

Public speaking is an industry in itself, not as large or diverse as writing and publishing, but still a major activity that supports many individual full time and provides extra income to many others. The stars of public speaking—referred to in the
speaking profession as celebrity speakers—are well known public figures; athletes,
astronauts, and actors to name only some of the A list (The B list includes beautiful
people, business executives, and burglars caught in the Watergate scandal) earn upwards of $100,000 for a lecture or speech. (Former President Bill Clinton and for-
mer Mayor Rudy Giuliani are currently reputed to be asking those fees for a speech
or lecture.)

On the other hand, there are thousands of speakers who are not well known and
who earn far less than these many-zeroed figures, but are still rewarded handsomely,
earning at least $500 minimum for a speech, with fees of $1,000 to $5,000 not at all
uncommon. Many are full-time professional speakers; others are part-time speakers
from a variety of fields. Many speakers are also consultants, and it is not always easy
to determine whether one is a professional consultant who speaks frequently for fees
or a professional speaker who consults often for fees! In fact, some are specialists in
fields in which public speaking is an integral part—educators, trainers, theologians,
and radio or TV announcers and commentators, for example.

There is a broad parallel between writing for profit and speaking for profit. Both
can be packaged and sold to the public as a fee-paid standard package or series of
packages. This is especially true for seminars and other training programs. It is interesting to note, however, that many professional speakers are also writers and self-
publishers, earning much of their income through selling their books at their

presentations. The three activities—consulting, writing, and speaking—are a commonly encountered combination.

THE PUBLIC SPEAKING INDUSTRY

Despite striking similarities between the two, public speaking is different from freelance writing in several ways. The professional writer, especially a writer of books, is likely to have a literary agent who represents the writer on an exclusive basis; every book the writer produces is marketed by the agent, and all the writer's business dealings with publishers are handled by the agent. In the speaking industry, only the most high-rated speakers, principally celebrity speakers in heavy demand, are represented by agents or managers. (It is usually one or the other, not both.) The rest of the speakers rely primarily on their own marketing, with some engagements arranged via lecture bureaus.

Lecture bureaus are nothing like literary agents, but are more like brokers. For one thing, they do not represent the speaker at all; they represent the client who wants to engage a speaker. That is, they perform a service for the client, although they usually earn a commission on the speaker's fee. The client may request that the bureau arrange for the services of a specific individual or that the bureau supply candidates of a given type or to speak on a given subject. It's an anomalous situation in that the bureau provides a service to the client, but it is the speaker who actually pays by permitting the lecture bureau to collect his or her fee and deduct a commission (usually from 25 percent to 40 percent, but often less when the speaker is in demand and commands a large fee).

There are no exclusive agreements between the lecture bureau and the client or the lecture bureau and the speaker. It is considered unethical, however, for a speaker to arrange future engagements with a client originally booked via a lecture bureau without paying the bureau a fee each time.

Most professional speakers get only a small percentage of their engagements through lecture bureaus, winning most through their own marketing efforts. There are a few exceptions, especially when both the speaker and the lecture bureau are highly specialized in their subjects or types of presentation.

On the other hand, many lecture bureaus are the creations of the speakers, with the speaker as the principal, perhaps sole, speaker offered. In short, many speakers create their own lecture bureaus as a marketing device, a perfectly legitimate approach to this special market.

This does not mean that you should not register with as many lecture bureaus as possible; you certainly should. But do not expect to get the bulk of your bookings in this manner.

Who Are the Clients?

The clients for speakers are almost as varied as the speakers, their subjects, and their presentations. They include colleges and universities, companies, government agencies, cruise ships, resorts, civic groups, unions, associations, and many others. This will become clearer as we explore the subject.

Marketing Yourself as a Speaker

Basic marketing tools for speaking engagements are a brochure and some kind of audition tape. Many speakers also have videotapes made up for auditions, and still others have included small video clips of presentations on their web sites. An audiotape is generally still adequate for most needs, and even that is not always necessary, once you have become established and have adequate bona fides (being able to cite prestigious speaking engagements you have fulfilled and have testimonials to furnish). Much of what is needed to market yourself depends on certain factors and circumstances, which can be illustrated in part by my personal experience, as well as that of many others. There is the question, however, of what kinds of presentations you make, who want such presentations, and why they want them. Here are just a few general types of speakers in descriptive terms that suggest the kinds of presentations they make:

- The famous and the infamous.
- Motivational speakers.
- Humorists.
- Entertainers.
- Experts.

These categories and classifications are arbitrary, and often overlap. But the characterizations differentiate the major appeals of certain kinds of speakers, the different reasons for engaging a given speaker; consequently, they help to explain and delineate the markets for public speaking. A closer look at each of these types helps in understanding this.

The Famous and the Infamous

Curiosity probably explains the major appeal of the famous; many celebrities are not especially good or interesting speakers, and do not have anything especially interesting to say, although there are exceptions. The same considerations apply to the infamous, such as the former officials who took the lecture circuit for handsome fees after they had served their time for Watergate crimes.

Very often the appeal to the hosting organization to have these speakers is for the photo opportunity that it permits for attendees. Being in the presence of a well-recognized person is sufficient motivation for attendees to participate. Many athletes, coaches, or others fit this category.

Motivational Speakers

Theologians and sales trainers tend to be motivational speakers, sometimes referred to as inspirational speakers. (When they write, their books are usually of the self-help variety.) They appeal to the emotions, preaching brotherhood, positive thinking, and similar topics and exhortations. They try to encourage certain helpful attitudes, to make listeners feel better about themselves and their lives, to inspire listeners to more lofty goals and thoughts. Many people find their messages both inspirational and entertaining, especially when they come from gifted presenters like Dr. Phil McGraw (Dr. Phil) or Tony Robbins. Unfortunately, these speeches rarely have the effect of changing attendees' behaviors or improving circumstances, but are nonetheless entertaining ways to engage an audience, and have a value, albeit temporary, more times than not.

Humorists

Probably the most famous and popular American humorist was the late Will Rogers, who perceived humor in many well-known situations, especially those in the news. One who probably rivals him is newspaper columnist Dave Barry, but there are many speakers who are humorists, albeit less well known than these two men. A really good humorist has little trouble being booked frequently.

Entertainers

Many professional entertainers accept public speaking engagements. (Now you know where they are when you don't see them for months on the big or small screen.) In the parlance of the entertainment industry, this is sometimes referred to as "doing industrials." Big name entertainers such as David Letterman, Jay Leno, Dennis Miller, or Mark Russell can often book themselves around their television shooting schedule for high-dollar speeches. The current rage within industrials is to have comedy troupes who specialize in extemporaneous presentations that are slightly tailored to the audience's interests perform (along the lines of Second City Television, etc.).

Experts

Many speakers are engaged on the basis of their reputations as experts in some field, especially when an expert in that field is not easy to find. That, more than talent as a speaker, accounts for most of my own engagements. Very few true experts in marketing to the government and writing proposals are willing to lecture even briefly on the subjects, let alone conduct an all-day seminar to train others.

These characterizations and categories overlap, as already noted. Many speakers who are not professional entertainers are engaged because they are entertaining speakers, even when their subject is a serious one. While one speaker may find it necessary to have a videotape and outstanding printed literature to win speaking engagements, another needs rather little. Jay Leno, Tony Robbins, and former President Bill Clinton, for example, would need no audition materials or introduction. And that is true to a lesser extent for many other experienced speakers who have testimonial letters and references that a prospective client can check. In fact, I have only once or twice been asked to audition by arranging for a prospective new client to sit in on one of my seminar sessions.

Accordingly, you will have to decide for yourself what you need in the way of marketing materials to make yourself and your offer of public speaking known. That is a typical problem in marketing, no different in principle from any other marketing problem. You must identify your prospective clients and understand their needs and desires thoroughly, and then decide what it is that you—your service or product, that is—can do for the prospective client. What you promise to do must correlate with the prospective client's needs and desires. For example, I teach marketing to the government, including—especially—proposal writing, the key to winning government contracts. But I promise to help client win contracts—that is what I promise to do for them: I promise to help them get what they want as a final result, the end, not the means. That is a most important point. Many marketing efforts fail, despite beautiful and costly brochures and other sales literature, simply because the consultant tries to sell the means and not the end. Clients always want to buy the result, not the means. They really do not care much about the means, as long as it results in the end desired.

But that promise, the right promise, is only one half the battle for the order. The other one half is proof, the evidence that you are what you say you are, can do for the prospect what you say you can do, and can deliver what you say you can deliver. That is the job of the audiotape and/or videotape, as well as of your printed literature, but it can also be accomplished by testimonials and references. My own clients do not care whether I am an entertaining speaker or whether I speak in the resonant, pear-shaped tones of the trained orator or the gravelly voice of a carnival barker; they care only whether I can produce the promised result of more success in pursuing government contracts.

THE SEMINAR BUSINESS

Attractive as the lecture circuit is, and it does attract a great many newcomers every day, for many of us in the consulting field seminars offer distinct advantages, including these:

1. You create something, packaging the seminar as a proprietary product and marketing it under your own total control, with options for profit that are not available to you as a presenter of a simple speech.
2. You create a seminar that is demonstrably a unique product or program, thus gaining an important market advantage. (It is much more difficult to establish a speech as unique.)
3. You do not wait for a client to want you as a speaker. You seize the initiative and make your program open to the general public—with open registration—something difficult to do for a simple speech.
4. You also sell it to organizations as a custom service for substantial fees.

Seminar Subjects

Seminars are learning sessions that address highly specialized and perhaps little-known aspects of some field or topic, presented by a qualified expert. Often the subject is something new, such as a new kind of computer program or a new legal requirement, and sometimes it is new only in that it has never been presented as a seminar before. When I offered seminars a decade ago in marketing to the government, I was among the pioneers—not in marketing to the government; that was already old hat; but in offering seminars in the subject, especially on the subject of writing winning proposals. I offered new and different approaches to the subject, and they produced salutary results.

I offered these seminars on an open-registration basis, open to the public; anyone could register and attend by simply paying the fee. At the time, seminar registration fees ranged from $75 to $100 per day, although many seminars were more expensive and a few cost less. Now, those same sessions, or similar ones cost between $500 and $1500 per attendee in some instances, a sure sign that the value contained within the seminars was higher than initially understood.

Who Pays to Attend?

We have identified two basic kinds of seminars: those open to the public and those presented on a custom basis for a client organization who will have certain individuals attend. However, there is another question to be answered in connection with that open-registration seminar: Who will pay for the individual's registration and attendance?

The answer bears directly on the marketing problem, for one thing, because in a very real sense the market—which means the customers—is whoever is paying the bill. Consider the following hypothetical seminar subjects:

1. Handling collection of delinquent accounts.
2. More effective selling techniques.
3. A weight-loss program.
4. A stop-smoking program.
5. Job-hunting tips and procedures.

Which of these would employers pay for? Which would attendees have to pay for themselves? Here are my answers:

1. Definitely one that employers would normally pay for. (However, and individual-owner of a small business might choose to attend and would therefore pay for him- or herself.)
2. Definitely the type of program that employers normally send employees to at company expense.
3. Most employers would not pay for this, since they would not benefit from it, but there are exceptions; some employers might be persuaded to pay for employees' attendance.

4. Same comments as for number 3.
5. Employers would probably not pay for this, although in some cases large corporations with substantial layoffs of employees might offer this kind of help.

In the case of my own government-marketing seminars, most attendees were sent by their employers at company expense, but there were also numerous individuals, in business or about to go into business, who paid their own way. They attended as managers of their own businesses, not as consumers seeking to solve personal problems. That is a significant point in marketing your seminar. It is basic in regard to understanding motivation, but it is even more critical in reaching your prospects with your advertising offer and appeal.

MARKETING THE SEMINAR

Sometimes you will find seminars advertised in newspapers, usually in the business pages. Those seminars are almost invariably addressed to individual consumers, prospects who would attend for personal reasons and pay for their own attendance. On the other hand, your name—the one you use for business—sooner or later finds its way on to many lists, and your mail often includes brochures appealing to you to attend seminars of many kinds. You are invited to learn how to become a better manger, write more clearly, learn how to use a new kind of computer program, become a direct-mail expert, and otherwise master many new and useful skills that will improve your business operations. By far the overwhelming majority of seminar promotion is by this means: an e-mail is sent to your corporate or personal e-mail address with some pithy headline or subject in an effort to get you to open the e-mail or the attachment and read how you can improve on something. Often, the e-mail is what is referred to as spam or unsolicited e-mail (so named because it is not real mail and is often just "filler"). It is recommended that you only use lists for e-mails that are comprised of people who request your e-mail—it is also the law. Sending unwanted e-mail is illegal.

Should you choose to use e-mail, be mindful that not every monitor has the same ability to handle color or sophisticated graphics. (If the recipient of your e-mail is attempting to download your graphic intensive images that you have included in your e-mail from a remote or dial-up location as opposed to from a DSL or cable modem connection, the ill will you will generate by tying up their bandwidth is such that you stand no chance of acquiring their business. In fact, all you will accomplish is their anger.)

Many printed brochures are still mailed out to business addresses, and they tend to follow a particular pattern: an $8\frac{1}{2}$-by-11-inch brochure of four or six pages, printed in colors on glossy paper, and mailed flat without an envelope in great quantity, using bulk mail. It is the marketing method of choice for most seminar producers.

Ordinarily, the seminar expected to draw individuals paying for their own attendance is the only one that is advertised in the newspaper or other general media. Seminars addressed to business executives, on subjects to improve business operations, use direct mail, usually the flat self-mailer brochure. The reason is simple: Direct mail is the more effective way to market a seminar, and it is possible to find mailing lists of business of all kinds. But there is no practical way of finding mailing lists—especially local ones, since it is unlikely that individuals will travel great distances to attend the seminar—of individuals likely to be interested enough in weight loss, quitting the tobacco habit, or writing a better resume to pay the fee of a seminar. Thus advertising in the general media, such as a newspaper, is usually the most practical way of marketing this type of seminar, inefficient though it is.

There are exceptions. More than one seminar has been offered successfully on how to become an independent consultant; start a small home-based mail-order business; or buy and sell real estate successfully, for example. In some cases, it is possible to find or build suitable mailing lists of individuals who qualify as good prospects for such seminars. But by far the overwhelming majority of seminars are on business subjects and intended for businesses. Because business and industry represent the major market for seminars, the following discussions will concentrate on this kind of seminar and its marketing. But there are at least two other important points to consider here:

1. An appeal to individuals to attend a seminar usually produces only single registrations. But it is not unusual to get several registrations from companies. I have had as many as six registrants from a single company, for example, so that even as few as a dozen organizations responding can result in a well-attended seminar.

2. The business seminar can be sold as a custom, in-house seminar for organizations—companies, associations, and others—for adequate fees. There is little possibility of doing so with seminars appealing only to personal interests.

These are powerful arguments for designing seminars to appeal to employers. Moreover, the appeal ought to maximize the number of employees who might be sent. A seminar on purchasing procedure might inspire employers to send only one employee, the purchasing agent, since that is the single individual who does all the purchasing in most organizations. But a seminar on more effective business writing is likely to inspire an employer to send a number of people because many people handle correspondence and other writing chores in most companies. This consideration alone, taken into account in conceiving and designing the seminar, may have an important influence on its success.

Marketing by Direct Mail and E-Mail

The principles of marketing by direct mail or e-mail are not different from the principles of marketing in general, but the methods of implementation are quite different, taking advantage of what the medium offers. Here are at least a few of those advantages:

1. Direct mail or e-mail lets you target your prospects more closely than do other media. You can get mailing lists of kinds of prospects—small businesses,

appliance manufacturers, retail chains, and many other such characterizations at various levels of specialization. When you use the general media—print and broadcast—the targeting is almost nonexistent, except as the readership of a given periodical. It is, by comparison, the rifle shot versus the scattergun blast.

2. In terms of cost per qualified prospect, direct mail is usually much less expensive than other media and e-mail is even less expensive.

3. Testing offers and copy via direct mail or e-mail is much more practical in terms of elapsed time and cost than it is in other medium.

4. Direct mail and e-mail afford you the opportunity to develop specialized—premium—lists.

5. Be sure that you provide an option for the recipient of the marketing effort to opt out of future mailings if they are no longer interested in receiving your mail (whether it is e-mail or a direct mail piece). It is just good manners.

6. Also be sure to provide the receiver with the way(s) to register for the offer or to seek additional information. It frustrates the recipient (and reduces the ultimate number of positive responses) when they have to search for how to respond or you have not provided them with an easy to use method for communicating back to you (either through a bounce-back card or registration form, inclusion of phone numbers, web-site address, or a combination of all of them).

The Direct-Mail Package

What has become the more or less traditional direct-mail package includes at least a sales letter, a brochure, a response device, and a return envelope. The response device is an order form, although many elaborate direct-mail packages include other response devices: seals that must be detached from one place and stuck to another place; simple quizzes or directions for the recipient to perform other chores. (The theory is that this direct involvement of the recipient improves response rates.) Direct-mail experts also maintain that including a return envelope, especially one that requires no postage (you pay the postage on each one returned to you under the special permit for this kind of postal service), also increases response.

They are undoubtedly right, as far as direct-mail campaigns directed to individuals in their homes. Many people do not have envelopes and stamps at hand in their homes, but when the direct-mail literature is directed to business executives in their offices, that problem does not exist. To test this theory, I included return envelopes in my earliest mailings promoting seminars. I found few of the registrations returned were in those envelopes. Almost all registrations were returned in the executives' own company envelopes. In subsequent mailings, therefore, I enclosed a sales letter and a brochure. One of the panels of the brochure was a registration form, perforated for easy separation. That was my response device.

By now you may have noted that I did not use the conventional flat, that four to six page 8½- × 11-inch brochure, sent out as a self-mailer—sans envelope—via bulk mail. From the beginning I thought this not the way to go when promoting seminars on a small scale; my principal reason was the difficulty of finding the right mailing lists—lists of truly qualified prospects. That meant that the brochures had to be mailed to more generalized lists, with a great waste of time and money. The discard rate for self-mailer brochures is itself high; many recipients discard what they recognize as advertising matter—junk mail—without even a glance. Couple that with mailing to generalized lists, of which a large portion of individuals have absolutely no reason to be interested in the seminar. The rate of response—registrations—is so small that to use these brochures effectively you must mail in large numbers—many thousands. The waste of this approach appalls me. I therefore decided to seek out or compile the right mailing lists and turn to the more conventional direct-mail approach of a sales letter and brochure, mailed in a conventional business envelope, using first-class postage. But first I had to acquire the right mailing lists.

Mailing Lists and List Brokers

None of the foregoing explanations are intended to deride the existing mailing list services. There are a great many such services (a short list is offered in the final chapter), and they do a good job as far as most advertisers' needs are concerned. They simply happened to be unable to respond to my own highly specialized needs. I wanted lists of people who were or wanted to be government contractors for the types for contracts that require proposal writing to win, admittedly a demanding requirement. These services may, however, serve your own needs with complete satisfaction.

How we describe or characterize mailing list services depends on viewpoint. Those who rent mailing lists to users—and the lists are not sold but are rented for one or more uses, according to agreement—rent lists that are not their property, for the most part. Most own some house lists, but the bulk of the lists they rent out are subscriber and customer lists belonging to publishers, large mail-order dealers, and other business organizations. The list service is a broker, earning a commission on the rentals. However, they prefer to be regarded by the owners of the lists as list managers, attending to the interests of owners of the lists by organizing and marketing the lists.

With today's computers, most list brokers can retrieve lists according to a variety of classifications, and most will furnish you a catalog explaining their entire offering.

Compiling Your Own Lists

Mailing lists are valued in several ways. One way is in terms of accuracy, with certain guarantees regarding the maximum percentage of nixies, those which are undeliverable for one reason or another. Lists are valued by demographic characteristics—high income, upwardly mobile, young marrieds, and/or other such indicators of qualifications as buyers. More important, probably, is the buying history of those on the list. Lists of those who are on the list because they are inquirers—they responded to offers of information—are not as valuable as lists of people who spent $20 or more on mail-order merchandise. But there are those who have spent $50 or more, and son on.

In this environment, the compiled lists, derived from such sources as directories and membership lists, are low on the totem pole. They have relatively little value because little data, except origin or source, is available about those on the list; neither demographic data nor prior purchasing history are known. (This is not to say that rented lists are never created through such compilation; many are compiled lists.) I decided that in my own case I would do better with compiled lists, as long as I did my own compiling. I had the advantage of knowing my field well enough to be able to judge with a fair degree of accuracy which companies and other organizations (e.g., unions, associations, nonprofit corporations, and agencies of state and local governments who pursue federal contracts) would be suitable for my purposes. In many cases, I recognized the organization by name and knew a little about it; in other cases their name or the circumstances in which I learned their name gave me a good clue. For example, I compiled many names and addresses from the help-wanted sections of major daily newspapers, especially from professional opportunities display advertising. The wording of the advertising itself furnished an excellent clue as to whether the advertiser was the type of organization that would pursue the negotiated type of government contract, which is the type where marketing success depends largely on proposal-writing skill. I was also able to get a list of contractors from a Navy department, a list of minority-owned firms from the Small Business Administration, and a list of the subscribers to the *Commerce Business Daily,* the government's own publication in which it announces bid opportunities and contract awards. And, naturally, I compiled many names from the contract-awards section of my own daily copies of this publication.

It was a great deal of work, but it paid off. I experienced results others considered phenomenal in being able to win 30 to 60 registrations from mailings of fewer than 5,000 pieces, often even from mailings of less than 3,000 pieces. I had, in fact, developed a premium list for my own needs.

I chose to use first-class mail and mail in a plain white business envelope that did not announce itself as advertising literature. This is expensive, compared with bulk mail, which runs roughly about one half the cost of first-class mail. (Some seminar producers make cooperative arrangements with small colleges or other organizations that add more than the [presumed] prestige of their name by enabling them to mail literature out under the special nonprofit rate.) Obviously, if you use an e-mail list, you need to collect that information from sources as diverse as a corporate home page (many sites have a "How to Contact Us" page), as well as from other sources that may require more networking and creativity to collect. Once established though, this list should never be provided or given to someone else for their use. This breaks a trust that you have established with the recipient.

Copy and Ideas

Over several years, I developed various ideas and techniques that improved response or otherwise reduced risk and added to overall success. First of all, although advertising experts often stress the need to get attention first and then arouse interest, I consider these to be the same thing. That is, getting attention should not be through some unrelated gimmick, as it unfortunately is in some promotions; it should be through something directly related to the main promise of benefits—should, in fact, be the main promise expressed as dramatically or as commandingly as possible.

Headline Copy

Consider the following headlines with respect to developing copy that gets attention but also arouses interest and addresses the main promise, all at the same time:

THE GRADUATE COURSE IN WINNING CONTRACTS!
HOW TO WRITE WINNING PROPOSALS
BE A CONSULTANT. EARN $1,000 AND MORE A DAY
HOW TO BECOME INDEPENDENT

Headlines are often made more compelling by subheads or blurbs. In some cases, they require such additions to convey meaning and complete their impact:

THE GRADUATE COURSE IN WINNING CONTRACTS
Secrets of the most successful professionals revealed!

HOW TO WRITE WINNING PROPOSALS
It's Marketing Strategy, Not Writing Skill,
That Makes the Difference

BE A CONSULTANT. EARN $1,000 AND MORE A DAY
Successful Consultants Earn at Least That Much

HOW TO BECOME INDEPENDENT   Here are dozens of ideas
and reams of how-to information
on starting your business IN YOUR OWN HOME!

Figure 21.1 illustrates that. It is the front panel of a brochure, sent out by one of the sponsors of my seminar programs.

Note the direct appeal of the headline, with its focus on secrets of success, followed by a series of subordinate headlines, summarizing the major points of the program. Note, too, the final item, which promises insider tips and secrets, repeating the main promise made in the headline. (In fact, this was an $8\frac{1}{2} \times 11$ inch brochure, the choice of the sponsor of the seminar, whereas I always preferred a 3×9 inch brochure. The copy used illustrates the points made here.)

Body Copy

Once you have established the main promise (and premise)—the major benefit which is your principal argument for registration and attendance—the rest of your literature must follow logically from that introduction, for that is what your headline purports to be and what a reader is entitled to expect. The body copy of your

---

"Proposalmanship"

The graduate course in
Winning
Government
Contracts
through
Strategy

8:30 a.m. - 4:30 p.m.

June 22, 2003

Francis Scotte Key Room
Key Bridge Marriott
Arlington, VA 22202

Figure 21.1   Front panel of brochure illustrating headlines.

brochure should now expand on the main promise, buttressing it with some proof
or evidence.

Figure 21.2, the second page of the brochure, indicates how that was done,
building the case primarily on the presenter's credentials as an expert, but also listing
the names of well-known organizations that attended previous sessions. (In some

Key Benefits of Attendance:

- Hear one of the nation's most successful consultants tell you how to turn your present knowledge and experence into marketable skills.
- How government cutbacks benefit you.
- Find out how to penetrate the $200 billion market of federal contracts and billions of dollars in industrial and professional services.
- Get the facts from Herman on how to win contracts—he has won over $260 million in federal contracts alone.
- Learn how to write proposals that win.
- Find out why it is now easier for you as a consultant to penetrate the federal contracts market and win as a result of the "Competition in Federal Contracts Act," and what your largest competitors don't want you to know about it.
- Learn how to market your services with confidence.
- How to locate government markets.
- Understand the key to mastering sales and marketing skills.
- Leave armed with the tools you need to get started immediately—the knowledge and a seminar handbook, personally developed by Mr. Holtz.

   "A large portion of those who enter into consulting services as a profession do not survive the first year, the chief reason being the failure to market their services effectively."—Herman Holtz

   The above quote is but a sample of the straight talk you will hear from Herman Holtz at this seminar. You will learn how to market your skills effectively and much more. That's why you can't afford to miss this opportunity to consult for a full day with Herman Holtz.

- How to turn your talents to profits
- How to inventory your technical assets and your talents
- How to cash in on trends
- Where the money is today

Some Previous Participants

Alcoa	Kenton
Bethlehem Steel	General Kinetics
Sikorsky Aircraft	Pitney Bowes
General Reserarch	DSI Computer Services
Western Union	Dynamic Data Processing
Computer Sciences Corporation	Digital
Memorex	Marriott
Boeing Computer Services	Owens Corning Fiberglass
Bionetics	Sperry
Burroughs	Tele Sec Temporay Personnel
Raven Data processing	AT&T
Finalco	Techplan
Tracor	Control Data Corporation
Watkins-Johnson	Color-Ad
Genasys Corporation	Systematic General
Illinois State OMBE	Scientific Applications
Flow General	The Maxima Corporation
Rolm Corporation	Battelle Memorial Institute

Figure 21.2   Body text on inside panel of brochure.

cases, the brochure would quote former participants who had favorable things to say in commending or recommending the seminar.)

The evidence must demonstrate that yours is not an empty promise. It must show that you can and will deliver what you promise by revealing some details of your plan of presentation and of your own credentials as the presenter and expert. The brochure copy illustrates this principle. Along with the accompanying sales letter, it suggested that attendees would learn some not-very-well-known truths about the subject (a valid claim) and would also learn some insider secrets (an equally valid claim). The literature included such startling and motivating blandishments as teaching attendees how to appear to be low bidders when they are not, and how to gather the priceless and necessary marketing intelligence. These are the kinds of items that not only command attention and arouse interest, but virtually demand registering for the session. A detailed seminar outline (Figure 21.3) lends great weight to this.

Persuasive Blandishments

The results of advertising—of any marketing and sales promotion—are never completely predictable because the reaction of the public (any public) is never predictable. We do learn, however, that some things work better than others and work most of the time, for example:

1. The credibility of your claims and promises is in almost direct proportion to the amount of degree of detail you furnish in explaining them. The public senses instinctively that anyone can generalize, but only those who know what they are talking about can furnish the details of what they promise and how they will do it. But don't overdo it; too much becomes tedious. The art is in judging how much detail is just right.
2. Excessive hyperbole has the same effect; it suggests vain boasting. Minimize your use of adjectives and use factual data, especially quantitative data, to impress the prospect. (Example: the $260 million in contracts won, cited in the brochure illustrated.)
3. Prospects are usually strongly attracted by the words and ideas of insider information, secrets, and other promises of getting information not commonly available and difficult to get. Such words as new, free, special, and sale also seem never to wear out in their appeal.
4. The more appealing the promise, the stronger the wish to believe it; but the more elaborate or dramatic the promise, the stronger the evidence backing it up must be. Sometimes it is better to downplay your promise, actually offering less than you believe you will deliver, simply because the truth is sometimes difficult to believe or to prove.

The Sales Letter

I am a believer in sales letters as the main element in a direct-mail program. They furnish the opportunity for chatty communication with the prospect, in direct contrast

SEMINAR OUTLINE

Proposals for Government Contracts
How to Develop Winning Proposals

6:30 a.m. - REGISTRATION: coffee and pastries
9:00 a.m. - Session Begins

I. The $160 Billion Market
   a. Understanding the market.
   b. What the government buys.
   c. How to sell to the government.

II. Locating Sales Opportunities
   a. How to uncover selling opportunities.
   b. Getting on the appropriate bidder's list.
   c. How to use the *Commerce Business Daily* as an effective marketing tool.
   d. How to use the Freedom of Information Act to market.

III. Proposal Strategy Development
   a. Why proposals?
   b. What is a proposal?
   c. What does the customer want?
   d. What must the proposal do?
   e. What makes a winner?
   f. Why strategy makes the difference.

IV. The Stages of Proposal Development
   a. Bid/no-bid analysis and decision.
   b. Requirement analysis—understanding the requirements.
   c. Identification of the critical factor(s).
   d. Formulation of the approach and technical/program/pricing strategies.
   e. Formulation of the capture strategy.
   f. Establishing the theme.
   g. Design and presentation strategy.
   h. Writing the proposal.

V. Persuasive Proposal Writing
   a. What is persuasion?
   b. The art of persuasive writing.
   c. What makes others agree?
   d. What turns them on? And off?

VI. How to Write a Winning Proposal
   a. Writing to communicate.
   b. Writing to sell.
   c. Writing to arouse and sustain interest.
   d. Your proposal should promise desirable end-results.
   e. Your proposal should, preferably, be a unique claim, one your competitors can't match.
   f. Your proposal must be able to prove it's validity.

VII. Formats and Proposal Content
   a. Recommended format.
   b. Front matter and other elements.
   c. How to use format for best results.

VIII. Cost Justification in Proposals
   a. Understanding costs.
   b. What the government expects in cost proposals.
   c. Technical vs. cost proposal.
   d. Construction of the quote.
   e. How to make bids.

WHO SHOULD ATTEND: If you are a small business executive and would like your company to increase its sales or profits in the enormous government market, or if you're a marketing executive in a major corporation, this seminar will be of tremendous benefit to you. New employees will shorten their learning curve. This seminar is designed to benefit marketing executives, contract administrators, engineers, systems analysts, computer specialists, trainers, editors, proposal writers, accountants, lawyers, contract specialists, manufacturers, service companies, consultants, and individuals seeking government contracts. Our faculty's expert advice has helped companies win contracts worth $1 million to $25 million and that expertise can be yours by attending this fact-filled seminar. Just one tip or one idea can be worth thousands of dollars to you.

MATERIALS: Each participant will receive an exclusive Handbook on Proposalmanship, authored by Herman Holtz, along with a host of other valuable materials.

Figure 21.3   Seminar outline.

to the formality of a printed brochure. In keeping with that idea, the sales letter should be typed and printed from a high-quality laser printer. In fact, with typical office computers and printers, it is easy to use proportional spacing and mix fonts so that your letter appears formally typeset. Many sales letters now include handwritten messages scrawled in margins on the page, or in different colored inks to try to draw attention to specific sections of the marketing piece (as well as give the appearance of it being personalized for the recipient). One of the more frequent pieces that crosses my desk contains an article from some publication touting a consultant's ability to improve an executive's public speaking with a Post-It Note affixed

EXCELSIOR ASSOCIATES	Mktg Mgr_____
4722 Lincoln Drive	
Pleasantville, OH 44444	

HOW TO WIN [MORE] GOVERNMENT CONTRACTS

ANYONE CAN DO BUSINESS WITH THE GOVERNMENT—YOU, TOO!

The Federal government right now spends about $200 billion a year to buy just about every service and product known. The nearly 80,000 state and local government entities (that number comes from the U.S. Census Bureau) account, altogether, for more than twice as much, so the federal, state, and local governments of the United States spend over $600 billion a year—every year —buying almost every kind of goods and service known. Are you getting your share of this enormous market? If not, you are missing out on something you could easily share in.

There are several reasons that many marketing people shrink from approaching the government markets. The first reason is mythology: There are many false stories circulating, to the effect that the paperwork involved in doing business with the government is impossibly difficult, that you must "know someone" to win government contracts, that there is little or no profit in government contracting, that the government takes forever to pay its bills, and many other myths. Yes, myths, for most of these stories are totally untrue, at least for all practical purposes.

The simple fact is that you are as much entitled to pursue government business as anyone is, and the law clearly requires the governments to give you equal consideration with everyone else; public money—your taxes and mine—are being spent, and we all have a right to compete for a share of the business. The paperwork is no worse than you will encounter with any large organization, and many private-sector corporations take longer than the government to pay their bills.

How do I know this? I know it because I have over 25 years's experience in this field. I have won and managed many dozens of government contracts for former employers, for my own account, and for my many clients, organizations who have retained me to help them win government contracts.

(MORE)

Figure 21.4   Sales letter with routing box.

to the bottom of it with what appears to be a note on it saying that someone named "J" recommended that I review this (the fact that no one I work with or know signs their name or is referred to as "J" is not lost on me . . . but I am assuming it does work to get others to investigate further).

Figure 21.4 is one example of a letter, using a routing box suggesting the first person to whom the letter and accompanying brochure should be sent.

A Few Special Promotional Ideas

One idea that paid dividends was a postscript to the letter along the following lines:

> If you must miss this important event, there will be later opportunities. We will be pleased to put your name on a special list that will absolutely ensure your being advised of future sessions. In fact, I invite you to return the following brief form, suggesting times and locations that would be most convenient for you and your staff.
>
> Name & Company: _____
>
> Address, city, state, zip: _____
>
> Preferred times & locations: _____

Another idea that paid rich dividends was the inclusion of literature advertising a newsletter and special publications, offering the option of ordering individual items or ordering all in a special package deal. Many who did not register for the seminar forwarded checks and orders for the publications. In fact, the total of such orders usually produced enough income to cover all the front-end expenses of the seminar, making it not only virtually risk-free, but most profitable as well.

Cancellations plague seminar producers. Most seminar producers exact a penalty for last-minute cancellations, but even so they believe that they are impelled to guarantee refunds. I found it possible to avoid the problem of refunds entirely through issuing rain checks. I guaranteed anyone canceling full credit for attendance at any future presentation of the seminar. That satisfied the registrant and eliminated refunds.

Most seminar producers charge a flat fee for attendance at a seminar, with a reduced fee for additional registrants from the same organization. Some, however, charge two kinds of fee, one for registration and a second one for attendance. The registration fee covers the organization; attendance fees are identical for as many participants as the organization wishes to send. And refunds are made of attendance fees only; registration fees are not refundable.

Most seminars carry a slightly higher fee for registration at the door than for prior registration and payment by check or credit card. Today, with telephone payments and Internet processing of credit cards possible, it is a good idea to invite registrants to enter their own numbers into the payment processing process to avoid your having to track down transposed numbers and other errors. That removes you from the burden of that administrative hassle.

Fees and Costs

Typical seminar fees are approximately $500 or more per day, although many independent consultants offer seminars at a lower fee. Usually the fee includes coffee and cakes in the morning and cold drinks in the afternoon. A few seminars include a lunch, often with a luncheon speaker, but that has become quite expensive. Most seminars include handout materials, including special seminar manuals. But some seminar producers also sell books, newsletter subscriptions, and tape cassette programs in back-of-the-room sales. That has become a common practice among professional speakers, especially those who publish their own books and other, related materials. Many derive as much income from these sales as they do from speaking.

Best Days for Seminars

In presenting seminars to business firms, I soon learned that Mondays and Fridays were the worst days for attracting attendees. Not the least reason is that attendees from out of town do not wish to travel on Sunday to attend a Monday session, nor do they wish to fight the Friday evening crush in most airports. Tuesday and Wednesday were best days. I also recommend that seminars do not last beyond whenever the local rush hour traffic begins to build. Your participants will appreciate a 4 P.M. ending and will likely remain engaged with the material as opposed to starting to worry about the commute home, or slinking out of the room before you have finished.

Summer is not a good time either, for the usual reasons of travel difficulties and conflicting vacation schedules.

Presenting Custom Seminars

Many organizations will book you to present your seminar on a custom basis as an in-house event. I have been fortunate enough to present my seminars for many organizations and at various events throughout the United States. In many cases, you can generate a full free plus all expenses. I would suggest either a per attendee fee of no less than $200 to $500, or if you are inclined to charge a flat fee regardless of number of attendees (or will conduct the seminar for up to a certain number of attendees), then I would recommend no less than $2,000 per day (and if your seminar is truly worthwhile, that number can often be increased upwards to $5,000). In some cases, however, it will pay you to undertake such sessions even at very much reduced fees because they represent excellent PR opportunities that lead quite often to highly profitable sessions.

The following are all potential opportunities:

- Business and industrial corporations.
- Local community colleges.
- Special education programs at four-year colleges and universities.
- Nonprofit corporations.
- Associations and annual conventions.
- Special schools and courses.
- Trade associations, industry conferences, industry exhibitions, and others.

22 | Consulting and New Technologies

There has never been a time when the independent consultant could be as independent—self-sufficient—as he or she can be today, with all the facilities and resources available for even the most modest office

THE NEW MEANING OF INDEPENDENT

There have always been independent practitioners in every field, including consulting. Never before, however, has that word *independent* meant what it means today. Today, the independent consultant is more independent than ever, and that independence is increasing steadily. The well-equipped office makes the consultant increasingly independent of suppliers and support of all kinds, even independent of information technology suppliers, accounting/finance/accounts payable or receivable service providers, and human resources vendors, in addition to printers, copy shops, and part-time helpers. Nor does the consultant of today have to travel as much as in the past. The only catch is the need to learn what is available and how to use it.

DESKTOP COMPUTERS

Few new inventions have caught on or developed as swiftly as the personal computer or PC. In fact, technology has developed so rapidly that the PC is now far more than a personal computer. PC's rival all but the larger mainframe computers, and are used as central computers in millions of small offices today, often linked to other computers in the office or in a local area network.

The computer is the greatest boon yet to office efficiency, especially in the small office and especially if you have a reasonably modern machine. That adjective, modern, has special meaning here. The desktop computer has evolved and is still evolving so rapidly that I retired my first computer, vintage 1983, in 1986. It was still functioning well, but the newer machines offered so many greater capabilities that I felt as though I were writing with a quill pen! My first machine was a CP/M, with only 64k memory (although that was a giant step from the earlier 4k, 16k, and other smaller memories).

372

Still, 64k memories soon became a memory—no pun intended—as the new machines started at 128k, and soon ranged to 640k and beyond.

All that began when Big Blue—IBM—entered the picture with its machines using a new operating system, PC DOS (personal computer disk operating system) and what computer experts refer to as *open architecture.* Revolutionary changes followed. The enormous market power of IBM was such that almost everyone except Apple Computer Company and a few others soon abandoned their CP/M designs and began to produce machines nearly 100-percent compatible with IBM's PC computers. (Those who opposed the trend or were too slow to join in perished or were absorbed into other companies.)

The compatible machines were called clones because, with their MS DOS operating system, almost a double for IBM's PC DOS, they could do almost anything and everything that the IBM machines could do—frequently even more than the IBM computers—and they sold for considerably less money. The marketing battle was joined. (Most of the clones and their components soon began to come to America from Asian countries.)

The original IBM PC soon evolved into an XT—extended technology—model and then into an AT—advanced technology—model. And soon the industry settled, for a period, on IBM XT and AT models and XT and AT clones. Now Pentium IVs or similar technology is considered de rigueur on most computer purchases.

Admittedly, I am presenting these facts and arguments with reference to the general case, and there is always the possibility that yours is a special case in which the capabilities of a Macintosh would be more suitable. Generally speaking, applications or business needs that require higher order graphics (CAD/CAM, advertising, etc.) tend to gravitate toward using Macintosh machines, but even that is not always the case. (Some nongraphic intensive users prefer the interface of the Macintosh, and there are heavy graphics users that prefer a non-Macintosh machine.) You will have to make that decision, basing it on the principal functions for which you can and should use your desktop computer.

Why all this history? Because it is germane. The consultant of today is all but required to have remote computing capabilities through a laptop or portable computer, a personal digital assistant (PDA), a cellular phone that can also double as a data transmission device in a pinch, and access to a web site for the uploading/downloading of pertinent information to or from clients. The open architecture standards of software and communication devices allow for products created by different manufacturers to work together without proprietary computer code needing to be written (in most cases, that is).

The strength of Microsoft in creating an operating system (Windows) and various business applications and platforms that are nearly universally accepted allows a consultant to share files or work products with clients with full confidence that it can be read and/or used by the client without having to go through arduous translation processes.

Most recently, the technology revolution has allowed computer users to increase the memory resident in their computers exponentially for essentially minimal cost. It is now uncommon to see a laptop computer in use that is not at least a 2-gigabyte machine (substantially more memory than provided in large mainframes of only a few short years ago). Additionally, through the advent of different storage media, the floppy disk has been replaced and improved on by CD-ROMs, DVDs, and other devices that have leapfrogged past the zip drive that used to be able to store multiple floppy disks worth of data on one small portable hard drive that could be disconnected for transport.

Other advances have included major improvements in the bandwidth performance for communication between computers so that telephone dial-up modem service has been replaced by cable modems, fiber optics, DSL lines, and the like and is readily affordable for even the entrepreneur working in a garage or basement. The use of the Internet for business (and personal) applications has also pushed manufacturers of technology to improve their capacity to handle audio transmissions, video feeds, and do so in ways that allow nearly any machine to play (regardless of manufacturer).

THE MOST POPULAR FUNCTIONS

Word processing is still the number-one use of desktop computers. Any word processing software designed by or for a Windows operating system will work on a computer using Windows. Periodically, Microsoft upgrades their operating system with new features, so depending on the time the computer was purchased (often, the Windows operating system is "bundled" or preloaded with the computer at purchase), or if the user installed an upgrade to a later version of the operating system, the version being run may not allow as full functionality as is potentially available. However, rarely is it so significant a difference that not having the latest upgrade prevents a consultant from conducting business on an on-going basis.

Currently, the word processor program most often used by consultants is MS-Word (often packaged with the office bundle of applications from Microsoft that include other frequently chosen business applications, including a presentation application, a spreadsheet function, and a database management capability). Word provides assistance in writing and formatting common business communication (be it letters, envelopes, outlines, or other common business needs). With a dictionary and grammar checker resident, users are able to be prompted as they type to review potential errors in their text (and I emphasize that it is a *prompt*. It is not foolproof and is designed to have you confirm you meant what you typed). While not a replacement for good editing and proofreading skills, it still provides the busy consultant with a first line of defense in ensuring that the written work is properly formatted, spelled, and adheres to the grammatical structures required for professional correspondence.

DESKTOP PUBLISHING

Desktop publishing is increasingly popular, probably inspired in part, at least, by the advent of laser printers, but logically an extension of word processing. Desktop publishing programs have special capabilities for newsletters and other publications in that they offer a variety of type fonts and facility in layouts, printing in multicolumn, justified type, generating and integrating graphics (including clipart), and otherwise moving several steps toward computer automation of both the typesetting and the formatting/layout functions. There is a growing number of such programs, and several periodicals on the subject of desktop publishing indicate the rapidly rising interest in this field.

When looking at Desktop Publishing applications or other presentation-specific programs, the consultant needs to be aware of how colors will be seen when printed by lesser quality printers (a black ink only printer may not provide a sharp enough distinction or "grayscale" between a maroon text or object and the black lettering labeling it, so important data gets lost when printed). Another caveat is that when an image is projected if used as part of a presentation, be aware that some colors will not appear on the screen as they are on your monitor. Be sure to test how your final product looks under multiple conditions to make sure that it can be read by all levels of technology and by all people (a large percentage of people have at least a slight degree of color blindness and may not recognize the differentiation between two colors you choose).

Adobe Systems Inc. has a product called Acrobat that creates a PDF (Portable Document File) that permits any machine to "read" a file regardless of the manufacturer. For times when documents must be shared across different users, this application permits sharing of files and information without worrying about having to re-create it so that some other machine can access it. This is a highly useful tool and allows a consultant to more easily move between and among clients without having to acquire specific components or technology that is customer specific (and may not be used by any other client).

DATABASE AND SPREADSHEET FUNCTIONS

Database use is another heavity function of computers. Where word processing functions and word processor design are fairly standardized, database functions and database designs are variable. First of all, there is the definition of the term itself; a database is any collection of information, and you, the user, decide what belongs in the collection and what is/are the common factor/s that make the information a collection. Thus, a database may be a simple list of names and addresses, a client list, a list of invoices, a file of letters, or any other information you wish to record and preserve. If your database needs are simple and the size of the collection of data not especially great, the simpler variety of database, the *flat file database,* will probably suit your needs. If your collection is so great and complex as to be unwieldy, you are more likely to have a set of databases—separate name and address lists, invoice lists, client lists, prospect lists, inventory lists, sales records, and others. If you wanted to find all the clients who both attended one of your seminars and subscribed to your newsletter, you would have difficulty, if that information was in separate flat file databases. However, if you have a *relational database,* you can search in and summon up information from other files and databases. That ability is the distinguishing feature of the more sophisticated relational database.

Database software is that it lets you design your files to suit your own preferences. Each individual data item (name, address, telephone number, etc.) is known, technically, as a *field,* and the entire set of fields for a given entry—for a client or a project—is a *record.* You decide (within the bounds of the software) how many fields you can have in a record and how large they can be, thus establishing the size of a record, how data will be entered, and so on. That determines how you can search the database and retrieve information. You thus do your own design.

Spreadsheet software is also most popular, enabling you to make projections, do modeling, and conduct what if studies—see what the total effect on business is likely to be if you raise your rates or make some other changes in your practice. For some consultants, this is an indispensable asset.

The majority of small businesses are not specifically created around technology issues (and therefore, may have unique or more complex needs), but rather use technology to facilitate their effectiveness in their chosen area of expertise. They use the bundled spreadsheet application—Excel—that came pre-loaded with their office suite of applications. This spreadsheet has become the de facto standard for most light to moderate users of spreadsheets and is commonly used to track multiple variables about particular people, events, or other critical data. Microsoft also offers a database management application (Access) that many consultants may find useful for integrating data into larger informational or research needs.

COMMUNICATION SOFTWARE

The most essential communication software used by all businesses, consultants included, is e-mail software. Regardless of which application is preferred (and there are many commercially available through various providers, be it an Internet Service Provider (ISP), commercially available, or the prepackaged options already loaded on your computer), the ability to communicate in real time with others who are geographically remote from your location, and also attach files, presentations, photos, or any other business communication, is a requirement.

Next on the list of communication software is not really software at all, but the Internet itself. Only the most backward thinking consultant would ignore the power of the Internet to communicate with or to clients, conduct research, or acquire much needed access to others. Today's computers are used for gathering information. Physicians can consult medical data—using the MEDLARS program to research fields at the National Library of Medicine, for example. Lawyers can ring up LEXIS or WestLaw in search of legal precedents and other helpful data. Investors can get up-to-the minute market information. Writers can track down books and magazine articles. (Recently, I used this method to track down a magazine article on a sales promotion, and then had a copy of the article itself sent me by fax.)

You can do all these things without leaving your desk if your computer is equipped with a modem and communications software. In some cases, the information exists only in printed form, and you must have it transmitted to you by fax or by mail. More often, the information is in a computer and can be transferred to your own computer and/or printer. (In the case when you are actually charged for connection time to a site, it is normally more efficient to use the faster transfer to your own computer files, then print out later, at your convenience.) The necessity of having at least a presence on the Internet with a web site cannot be overstated. It levels the playing field between you and your competitors (regardless of the inequity in size of the businesses), and may actually give you an advantage if done correctly. Of utmost importance though, is what you wish to communicate with your client and prospects. Think through what you want the visitor to your site to think of you as a result of the visit and weave that message throughout the site. Think of how your site will be navigated and used and be sure that you make it easy and intuitive for the user to find what he or she is seeking, and also to communicate back to you with further questions, ideas, and so on. The web site can sell for you if you allow it, but at minimum, it should always market for you! Of course, you need to drive traffic to your web site and registering with search engines, cross-linking with complementary web sites, and including your web address (URL or universal resource locator), on all correspondence are good ways of doing that.

Within communication software discussions, it is also important to make reference to various search engines. There are various search engines available on the Internet to guide users to find the information sought. Among the more popular are www.Yahoo.com, and www.Google.com. There are also specialized search engines that are specific to niche needs (usually highly technical), but they all operate on the same principles. The user identifies the topic or information desired, and depending on the specificity of the request, the search engine then scans the Internet for related documents/sites, or areas of information on that topic. The more narrow the request, the fewer documents are found (and hopefully, the more targeted and appropriate the information will be to the user). For instance, if I were to enter "Beatles" in a search engine, I may get information on Paul McCartney, or I may also receive information on the whole group. By entering multiple words, I eliminate references to the whole group.

Another communication software application that many consultants that travel frequently use is an application that converts a fax into an electronic file so that you can receive faxes on your e-mail server and not have to rely on the hardcopy being received. In this way, you can be anywhere remotely, and still receive faxed transmissions without having to have someone else receive it at the office or place of receipt and then resend it.

PDAs

One of the more useful technological advances has been the personal data assistant (PDA). These handy devices condense the essentials of most business professionals into a device the size of a deck of cards. Contained within these battery-operated devices or rechargeable units are typically the following: addresses and phone numbers or contact list, a calendar of upcoming meetings or travel scheduled, the ability to jot notes to yourself, and the ability to transfer information from one device to another or to a computer. Some of the more enhanced units also include cellular telephones, navigation systems, various games, and other business programs. These devices "synch" or communicate with a computer so that data can be constantly updated as situations or plans change.

Archives

One of the folders I keep on my hard disk I call ARC, or archives. In that folder I keep materials I can use again and again in my work (especially in writing books), either directly or with suitable modification and adaptation. Here are descriptions of a few of these files:

- Trademarks and registered trademarks. The list, to which I add as the occasion arises, is a great time saver.
- Charts and graphs. Many of the charts and graphs I have developed laboriously can be adapted to new uses far more easily than new ones can be created, so I store many of these.
- Glossaries of special terms. Like the other items, these can be adapted to new needs.
- Bibliographic listings. Again, a file that is maintained and from which I draw what is appropriate to the occasion.
- Listings of various kinds, such as association and suppliers (other than those I would maintain in a database).

GRAPHICS DEVELOPMENTS

Desktop-publishing technology has not stopped with improvements in type and formats. The technology is applied also to graphics, which can be produced by both laser and dot-matrix printers with a good degree of quality. Even photographs can now be downloaded from digital cameras specifically designed to create computer files for use on computers. These photos are then *digitized* (made readable by a computer that can then print them, incorporate them into presentations, or modify them as needed). The desktop-publishing technology has produced a special acronym, WYSIWYG, which stands for "what you see is what you get" and is pronounced "wizzywig." It refers to the fact that modern desktop-publishing programs can display on the screen the full, composed page exactly as it will be printed. Most of the advanced software that produces all of this requires a graphics card, usually a color graphics card. Everyone has a color monitor, though they are not all at the same caliber and so what may be WYSIWYG for a higher end monitor or printer, may differ for a lower end monitor or a printer with less capability. The graphics adapters have been improved to the point though, where the distinctions between lower end equipment and the higher end equipment is becoming less noticeable all the time.

PRINTERS

The rise of desktop publishing coincided with the introduction of laser printers. The laser printer provided true letter-quality printing without a daisy wheel or ball type of element. It produced its characters, in fact, by converting the digital code to laser pulses that painted the electrostatic pattern on the transfer medium for transfer to paper a la the conventional xerographic copier found in most offices today. It is a xerographic dot matrix, using a much denser population of dots and so achieving a much higher fidelity or resolution than the older 9-pin dot matrix printers; in its best implementation, the product approaches the quality of formal typesetting by traditional means.

Despite the quality of their output, laser printers do not have the market to themselves. Ink-jet printers (where the ink is actually "shot" at the paper in a dictated pattern according to the image) are less expensive and still are purchased by many users. Many printers costing under $100 used for reports or less graphic intensive applications are more than sufficient and it is only those consultants who require the more sophisticated of faster printing capabilities purchase machines that are $1,000 or more.

Because many small office or home office businesses have minimal space for equipment (referred to as the "footprint" of the equipment), vendors have integrated multiple functions into a single machine. The fax capability, telephone, printer, and scanner are often contained in one machine (and while there are tradeoffs in quality between the various components with the integrated or multifunction units, the difference is insignificant enough to not really matter to the user).

MODEMS

To communicate through the Internet, receive e-mail, and exchange files between computers without having to physically have access to both computers to copy information on a diskette or CD and then transfer it to the second computer yourself (or have someone else do it for you), you need a device that can permit electronic transmission of data. A modem (modulator/demodulator) permits data to be transferred electronically between computers at varying speeds (depending on the device and other conditions that can impact speed of transmission). Most businesses are at minimum using a 56kbps (bits per second) and more are using cable modems or DSL (Digital Subscriber Line) that permits much faster transmissions (a necessity if your business requires sharing large files or graphics/photos between users).

FACSIMILE MACHINES

The fax has become a fact of life; few business people do not know what it is and what it does. It has also become inexpensive enough for most of us in any kind of business venture to have our own. As in the case of modems, you can have a stand-alone or internal fax (on a board), and that can be the combination fax-modem card. The combination is an obvious efficiency because both need a modem to send and receive information over telephone lines. As mentioned earlier, the options available to the small or home-based businessperson include integrated units that also include a scanner so that hardcopy faxes can be "read" into the computer as a file and stored electronically, or a software application that permits faxes to be received through an e-mail server can also be used to prevent the problem of not having access to information due to the form in which it was received.

TAPE DRIVES, COPYING TO CDS, AND BACKING UP

The random access memory—RAM—is a *volatile* one: When you turn your machine off, whatever is in RAM disappears. The disks, both floppy and hard or fixed disks, retain what has been stored there, and that information is available the next time you turn your computer on. Hard drives wear out, however, as do all things, and sometimes they fail suddenly—crash. Then all your stored data is lost. (Some experts can retrieve much of the data on a crashed disk, but for most of us it is a lost cause.) Because of that possibility—and many computer experts say it is a certainty that every hard disk will fail eventually—it is necessary to make copies of whatever is on the disk that is otherwise irreplaceable.

Many people back up their data by making copies on floppy disks. That becomes less and less practical as the size of your hard disk and the volume of data stored there increases.

There are several viable options available to back up data (a task that anyone with experience with computer crashes would insist is essential). Additionally, with the frequency of hackers and viruses infiltrating computer systems, it is likely that at some point, you will be confronted with the need to replace damaged or lost files, information, or applications. It is not only prudent to back-up frequently, in many instances it may be what saves you from going out of business entirely. Options include:

- Internet services that will store your data on a remote server and will warehouse it for you for a fee.
- CR-ROM or DVD, given the capacity that these storage media have, their easy portability, and their relative inexpensive cost, many businesses choose to periodically save their data through these.
- Applications that are resident on the computer and create parallel or duplicate files. (This only works if you have access to the computer and it is only information within a file that you seek. If your computer itself is damaged, the ability to access this application is lost as well.)
- Many businesses still use tape drives to store back-up information (either internal or external tape drives that can be connected to the computer and files are replicated onto the magnetic tape).

Regardless of the method used, backing up information is something that must be done (the downside is worse than you may even imagine) and should be a part of your regular maintenance and computer use. Daily is not too frequent in many companies to conduct a back-up, and in very fast-moving environments, that may be too infrequent.

THE COMPUTER AS A GENERAL AIDE

Finding Software

The business market for software continues to evolve and become more user friendly and more comprehensive. Whether looking for software that instructs on how to complete a particular IRS form in preparation for tax payments, or software that increases your proficiency with a particular software application and everything in between—there is likely to be commercially available software at a relatively reasonable price (as low as $19.95 to a more pricey, but still affordable $300 for higher end applications). Compare that to the cost of proprietary software or having to pay a computer programmer to create code to do a task that is relatively mechanized and already created for others and the merits of paying even $300 for software becomes clear.

There are today some public-domain software (also sometimes referred to as freeware) programs written by individuals who generously donated them to the world at large; in many cases, the author retained copyright but licensed everyone to use the program for personal use—specifically not for commercial use—free of charge.

That kind of software was particularly abundant for the early CP/M machines. Today, most of those freelancing, independent programmers offer their software as shareware, a designation that requires a bit of explanation: The author copyrights the program and makes it available to all on a trial basis, with the proviso that he or she—the author—expects payment for continued use of the program beyond a trial period. The payment is voluntary, of course, although the author suggests a specific figure (usually quite modest) for registering (and paying for) the program and promises some additional benefits, including a printed user's manual and free updating (providing a copy of subsequent revisions or updated versions of the program).

Much of the shareware is of poor quality; much is highly specialized and of little interest to the average user; but much of it is quite good, perhaps even better than expensive commercial versions. Most of the leading shareware communications programs are probably at least the equal of anything sold through regular commercial channels, for example, and there are many excellent utility programs, programs for copying files, displaying directories, recovering accidentally erased files, and many other methods for manipulating files. One that I use, for example, displays the entire contents of my hard disk in one large directory of the directories, while another does an excellent job of copying all hard-disk files to floppies as backup files—insurance against loss. Such shareware is almost superabundant. The authors encourage free distribution to encourage trial by new users, and much of it is made available through the thousands of electronic bulletin boards (most of them are operated by enthusiasts as a hobby, although many are sponsored by government agencies and private business firms). Anyone equipped with modems and communications software can ring up such bulletin boards via telephone and download—have transmitted—the programs of interest.

It is also possible to buy such programs from services who advertise in computer periodicals. They do not sell the software; the author's copyright specifically enjoins against this. But they sell the service and the disks on which they copy the programs, usually on the basis of about $3 to $5 per disk.

23 | Business Ethics in Consulting

As a consultant, your image and reputation are among your greatest and most valuable assets. You must guard them carefully.

A STANDARD OF CONDUCT

We live in an increasingly cynical age, one which has had to invent the term white collar crime to identify acts that represent a gross betrayal of trust by high-placed officials in government, business, and industry. In fact, in most of these cases it is that very position of trust that makes the criminal act possible. Enron, WorldCom, and Andersen Consulting are among the latest examples of corporate malfeasance written about in the business and popular press.

By the nature of your work as a consultant, it is almost inevitable that you are often entrusted with the proprietary and confidential information of your client's business affairs and perhaps even of his or her personal affairs. Even when the information is not specifically identified as confidential, you can usually recognize it as such. But even when that is not the case—when there is doubt in your mind as to the confidentiality of certain information you have become privy to in your consulting work—wisdom dictates that you play safe by assuming that the information is confidential.

There is undoubtedly temptation to use such information for your own ends. Perhaps you have gained information that can be directly profitable for you in a variety of ways—to guide investments, perhaps, or to make your services especially valuable to another client. The temptation to profit, especially when business is in a lull, is great. Just your sense of self-preservation should enable you to resist temptation and impel you to hold the information in strictest confidence, although your professional integrity should represent an even higher priority in motivating your actions.

In actuality, even harmless gossip about a client is unwise, for clients are likely to infer from such gossip that you do not have that lofty degree of professional integrity—are not to be completely trusted. The only safe course is to refrain completely from discussing a client with anyone.

That creates something of a problem for you in citing a list of clients and types of projects you have handled—information essential for marketing. The way around that problem is simple enough: Ask each client or former client for permission to cite the work you have done for them. Some clients may wish to review the specific citations you propose and edit them or comment on them, but if that is the case you do not have a problem with it; the client is not opposed to being named.

You must not only respect confidentiality in fact, but you must not even appear to compromise it. Appearing to be loose-lipped about a client's affairs is most dangerous, and that is why you must go to extremes to avoid that appearance.

CONFLICTS OF INTEREST

There are many situations in which you can have conflicts of interest. These are simply situations where you find yourself with two interests, both of which offer tempting possibilities, but that cannot be reconciled because they are in conflict. There are many such situations possible. Here are five hypothetical cases as typical examples:

1. You are supporting Client B, who is a direct competitor of another client of yours, Client A. You can increase the effectiveness and worth of your services by utilizing what you know about Client A, even without telling Client B what you know about Client A. Is it ethical to do so?
2. In the situation just described, Client B demands to know what you know about Client A. He or she will fire you—cancel your contract—if you don't come through with the information. It is a sizable contract, and Client B is a much more profitable account than Client A. Yielding to Client B's demands makes good business sense. Should you yield?
3. You meet an executive at a convention, and you discuss the executive's needs vis-à-vis your services—the possibility of becoming your client. The executive reveals information about his or her organization, but not—not yet, anyway—to retain you. Are you obliged to treat the information as confidential?
4. You are under annual retainer to a client company, giving them a priority call on your services. One day they call to ask your help with a project. But you have already begun work with a new client who is a direct competitor of the first company. Can you—should you attempt to—handle both assignments?
5. You are working with clients who are direct competitors of your former employer. You were in a relatively senior position, and you possess confidential information about that company. Are you bound by any ethical considerations in using that information to achieve maximum success in your own enterprise?

The first two cases should require little discussion. Whether you disclose information about Client A directly to Client B or use that information in Client B's interest without disclosing the information or its use, the use of it is definitely a violation of confidentiality. The only safe course is to so compartmentalize your thinking that you can manage to forget, at least temporarily, the information concerning Client A. That is not easy to do, but it is necessary, in this connection, to have a good forgetter in consulting work, especially if you work for clients who are in direct competition with each other. (It is best to try to avoid having directly competitive clients, if that is practicable.)

Case number 3 is a much more difficult problem. Inasmuch as you have not been retained nor compensated in any way by the prospective client, you are probably not legally and certainly not morally obligated in any way to that executive. Still, there are two serious considerations here, the more important of which is that your basic integrity—ethical code—ought to extend to all conversations with prospective clients, as well as with actual clients. Prospects are unlikely to speak openly with you and discuss possible assignments unless they believe that the conversation is privileged, and that alone tends to foreclose or at least limit your marketing prospects. That, your interest in gaining new clients, is the second consideration, and it is by no means a minor one. The safest course is to treat all relationships with clients and prospective clients as privileged.

Case number 4 is even more difficult. There is only one sensible thing to do here, and that is to avoid the problem entirely by pursuing a clear policy of prevention. If you have accepted an annual retainer or any other arrangement that provides a client priority rights to your services, you should recognize what this obligation means in its entirety. Morally, it means more than a priority right to call on you; it must be translated also as an obligation to anticipate possible and potential conflicts of interest and take preventive measures. That is, before agreeing to an assignment that may mean conflict of interest, such as that hypothesized in case number 4, you should call the client who pays you a retainer and get his or her approval.

I do not mean by this that a retainer-paying client has the right to dictate your policies or actions. But such a client usually does have the right to claim your services under such retainer agreements, and you should consider this in contemplating new assignments. For example, suppose that you are a marketing consultant and another client wants help in pursuing some important new contract, but that is the kind of contract your retainer-paying client might also pursue. You should not accept the new client without checking with your retainer-paying client to find out whether that client intends to pursue the same contract and therefore want your help. (In fact, I have had prospective clients inquire into my policies with regard to whether I would handle two clients competing for the same contract. It is a concern of prospective clients, at least when they seek help in marketing, that you will not represent a competitor for the same contract.)

Case number 5 represents a typical situation, such as the case of former government executives becoming consultants to organizations seeking to do business with government agencies, and sometimes even becoming consultants to the very agencies from which they have retired. (This has been referred to as the *revolving door of federal employment,* and sometimes such people are referred to as *double dippers.*) These situations have become the subject of many mini-scandals reported in the *Washington Post* and elsewhere, despite legislative controls that have been established over the years.

Apparently many independent consultants believe that they owe nothing to former employers, especially if they were civilian and private-sector employers. This may be true enough technically, but you have an obligation to yourself to maintain an ethical code and apply it without exception. Bear in mind also the practical consider-ations that you must safeguard your reputation and that a former employer may be-come a client. This happens quite commonly, and may happen to you if you nurture good relationships with former employers.

An Exception

There is at least one exception to this, one case in which it is perfectly ethical and honorable to use any information you have acquired in the course of earlier employ-ment or in pursuing your consulting assignments. It is this, briefly: You may use all the information you acquire anywhere to benefit your own enterprise in any way gen-erally, provided that you keep the information itself in confidence and do not use it in any way that would embarrass, compromise, or injure your former employer or client. You might, subject to that latter qualification, use such information to do any of the following:

- Compile a list of prospective clients.
- Prioritize a list of prospective clients by arranging it in order of estimated probability of closing.
- Compile information about prospective clients that will help you market to them successfully—to win their agreement to retain you.
- Develop marketing plans in general.
- Design or identify specific consulting services or modify your normal modus operandi to improve your practice in some way.
- Identify and pursue special market segments or niche markets.

However, in situations where you are prospecting for additional business with an existing client, blatant huckstering for project work is unethical, unseemly, and is to be avoided. While it is expected and even appreciated that you will be vigilantly looking for opportunities to further assist the client in meeting needs, it is not per-missible to go hunting within the confines of an organization for future business as if it was an Easter Egg hunt.

FEES AND RELATED ETHICAL CONSIDERATIONS

There are different schools of thought about standardizing fees. One school has it that it is a sharp and unethical practice—or, at the least, unprofessional and unbusi-nesslike—to have different fees for different clients and different situations. The other school has it that flexibility in setting fees is a practical necessity and certainly not dis-honest, nor reprehensible, and not unethical. A case can be made for both schools.

ETHICS AND FEES

Without providing insight into *what* to charge for your services (that is too variable to address with readers having different needs, offering varying services or products, and who may be content with different reward compensation structures), it may be insightful to review some of the more commonly confronted issues faced by consultants in setting their fee policies. In establishing the fee structure for a client or project, the issues to be addressed are:

- Noncompete agreements and their value.
- Variable rates.
- Good customer rates or new customer rates.
- Barter.
- Partial ownership of client (stock or bonds).
- Project fee versus day or hourly rate.

Noncompetes

Depending on the industry, it may be a requirement of a potential client that you as the consultant *do not* work with that prospective client's major competitor. It is easy to understand that PepsiCo does not want their consultants to be in a position to share insights gleaned or have access to information that could wind up in Coca-Cola's hands. In my own practice, I have offered "category exclusivity" to a client in exchange for an increased fee. In effect, I am agreeing not to pursue business opportunities, or to refuse business from another prospect or client and only work with the one client in that industry.

This is not always possible to agree on with a prospect and the consultant must gauge the necessity of agreeing to this formally and assessing the risk or potential risk to refusing to do business with all other competitors. If a major manufacturer were to offer a small project, but demand exclusivity, it is possible that much larger business (and conceivably business that did not mandate exclusivity) opportunities would be missed.

Variable Rates

As covered earlier in this book, there are some consultants who view their fees as commodities (I sell my time and it has a value of "x" and my fee is simply the number of units of my time you purchase). Still other consultants prefer to assess the value of a project to a client and then charge based on the urgency, number of people impacted, or some other value measurement. So, assuming Project A is exactly similar to Project B with the exception of number of people who will be expected to read the report and take action based on it, it is possible that there would be two different prices charged.

The core difference in these two scenarios is that in the first commodity consultant pricing example, the product is the consultant's time and that has a relatively fixed cost associated with it. This scenario tends to push down pricing and value as it diminishes the "worthiness" of the consulting. In the second example, the purchase is a *result* and not the work product itself. The pricing is based on the value to the client and not on the number of hours it took to get it accomplished.

This is usually relatively to justify on the basis that it is rare that two projects are *exactly* alike, so it is not easy to challenge.

I don't want to lead the reader to one or the other, but just want to expose both methods to you and allow you to judge the inherent risk, reward, and ethics of each.

Good Customer—New Customer Rates

There is nothing wrong or unethical about offering preferred rates for companies you are hoping to attract, be they new clients or existing ones that you prefer to do business with. Of course, realize that if you do work with the government, they are entitled to your "best price" in the market, so any market provided to another private industry client is required to be offered to the government, should you wish to do business with them.

One issue worth considering when changing or offering preferential rates to a client is that you may inadvertently establish a precedent for future pricing with that client. You set the benchmark for future projects with that price and it becomes difficult to change it upward once you have consented to a lower fee. Where possible, don't lower price, but rather, offer more services to provide additional value to the client (and provide the fees "normally" associated with those services so that the client associates the worth of what you are offering), but maintain the integrity of your pricing.

Barter

When working with other vendors or suppliers, it may occasionally seem like a worthwhile idea to exchange services with one another instead of money. So, for example, in exchange for providing insight into how your printer's energy use could be minimized, you receive printing for a direct mail campaign you are planning to drum up support for a new offering you are creating.

As long as both parties agree on the inherent value of what is being provided to each other, this is perfectly fine from an ethics perspective and may actually lead to additional business based on the other vendor's personal experience with you and your services so that he or she recommends you to their clients. Be sure your accountant knows what was bartered and the value of those services so that it can be correctly accounted for on various financial or tax related forms.

Ownership

Every so often, on a cyclical basis, there is a movement within consulting where an aggressive consultant or consulting firm decides to offer services in exchange for a partial ownership of the client company. Some clients like it, because it seems to "force" the consultant to only provide advice that is truly meaningful and productive, and no longer look to just "pad" the bill to extract as much money from the client as the consultant can, since they are now also an owner and have an incentive to ensure there is prudent spending for services rendered. Consultants may like this arrangement, because they see a "sure" thing and can now be in on the ground floor of an opportunity that will lead to growth and prosperity. This last had a ground swell of support during the heyday of the Internet boom when money was in short supply, but ownerships were easy to come by in many companies.

As a consulting purist, I am opposed to this and vehemently feel it is an inappropriate approach for a consultant to take with a client. The dynamic is no longer objective counselor aiding the company, but it now is of self-interested owner looking to maximize the investment. I am a strong advocate of "managers manage, and consultants consult." When those roles are intertwined, it is my belief that neither role is properly served and that both suffer.

It is one of the stronger beliefs that I have that consultants are accountable for their actions and the appropriateness of their advice and that managers are responsible for the actions they take with the advice (or if they choose to ignore it). A physician is responsible for telling you the benefits of a healthy diet and the downside to ignoring your nutritional needs. That same physician is *not* responsible for doing the patient's grocery shopping or ordering off of the menu when the patient goes out to eat.

The Middle Road

I happen to be middle-road on the question of rigidly uniform rates versus more than one scale of rates. I do not believe it to be unethical or dishonest to offer different fee bases for different kinds of situations—in fact, I can find and will shortly present rational justification for it—but I think that it is a bad business practice to vary rates spontaneously on the basis of expediency. That can lead to unethical and dishonest practices, such as misleading and deceiving clients about your fees. That sort of deceit is inevitably exposed, and that destroys your credibility—your very image—with all who learn about your practice.

If you decide to have different rates for different circumstances, it ought to be based on a clear and consistent basis and applied uniformly. Bear in mind that each consultant has to evaluate his or her own circumstances, and there are a number of factors that must be considered.

My assignments tend to be short-term, from a few days to several weeks at most. I find it most practical to set my rates on a daily basis for the typical assignment. However, I do not wish to be compelled to keep time records and do complex calculating in making up invoices, so I charge a flat day rate, one that is the same for an 8-hour day as it is for a 12-hour day, and the same for Wednesday or Thursday as for Saturday, Sunday, or Labor Day. In short, I do not charge for premium time or overtime; I simply set my standard day rate large enough to permit me to work this way.

Occasionally it becomes necessary for me to charge an hourly rate. I have a fixed hourly rate that is less than my day rate divided by 8. The reason? My day rate is not based on 8 hours, so my day rate divided by 8 would not yield an accurate figure. (In fact, my hourly rate is my day rate divided by 10, which is much more representative of my working day.)

Once in a while I undertake a relatively large project, one that may occupy months of my time. In that case, I prepare an estimate for the entire job, based on rates that have nothing to do with daily or hourly rates, but consider direct labor, overhead, and profit, which I believe is a much more realistic basis on which to estimate costs for a long-term project.

Each of these bases for setting rates and billing reflects a fixed and consistent policy, based on a rationale that I can explain to a client and that is unchanging or standard operating practice. For the typical short-term assignment, my overhead rate is high, the natural consequence of briefly tenured assignments. The occasional long-term project involves a greatly reduced overhead. More to the point, the client usually requires a detailed estimate and, quite often, a fixed price for the large project.

For such reasons, I find it impractical to have a single, fixed rate for every situation. Clients judge you by appearance, however, so you must always consider the client's perception. I recommend that you set a client's mind at rest and demonstrate that you have a consistent rate structure and are not bargaining to charge what the market will bear. One way to do this is to have your rate explained in some printed form that you can display or furnish to clients.

Personally, I have no hesitancy about explaining all of this to a client or prospective client. I have never found a client or prospective one resentful of my efforts to conduct business in a businesslike way. Frankness about what I am doing and why tends to make questions and objections fade rapidly. Clients are usually comforted and reassured by an objective and businesslike manner.

The Ethical Considerations in Billing

In my own practice, clients usually require me to furnish an estimate, often including a not-to-exceed figure, before approving an assignment and issuing a contract or purchase order. It's usually difficult to make that estimate, and of course the tendency is to make the estimate and not-to-exceed figure as large as possible, yet not so large as to lose the contract. So it is not surprising that you often need more time than you estimated, while once in a while you get the job done in less time than estimated. And often the client is unaware of whether you ran over or under the estimate, especially when you do some or all the work on your own premises.

What do you do when you need another day or two? Ask the client for more time? Finish the job and then ask to be paid for the extra time? Finish the job and eat (don't mention) the expense of the extra time?

There is no absolute answer. Either the first or second alternative is correct for most cases, however, although there may be occasions when the third choice is the right one. But there is this to consider: The second choice—finishing the job and then asking for payment for the extra time is viable only if you are prepared to eat the extra time if and when the client objects to paying for it; it is rarely sensible to get into a major dispute with a client.

If you can justify the need for extra time—if you can demonstrate that it is not the result of a deliberate underestimate by you (to win the contract) nor of an incompetent performance by you—that is, if you can justify the overrun—clients will usually grant you the extra time. I have often asked for the time but indicated that, while I thought I was justified, I was prepared to accommodate the client by eating the extra time. So far, I have never had to do so. I believe that reflects typical clients' appreciation of my being totally up front with them.

The one thing you should never do when you have exceeded an estimate or a not-to-exceed figure is to simply bill an overrun without explanation and, especially, without previous discussion with the client. That almost always leads to a dispute that can polarize positions swiftly, making it most difficult to reach a resolution that satisfies either party. Even when the client is willing to pay for the extra time, your invoice often creates an administrative problem in that the invoice is for a different amount than that authorized by the purchase order. The purchase order must be voided and a new one written, the original purchase order must be amended, or an additional purchase order must be written. No client appreciates your making new problems; the problem would have been minimized had you discussed it in advance.

There is the opposite problem, the other side of the coin: What do you do when you finish the project ahead of schedule—when you were authorized ten days and finished the job in nine days? Should you bill for ten days? For nine days? Talk to the client?

There is a temptation to bill for ten days, as authorized. It is not necessarily dishonest to do so, either. It depends on the contract you have with the client. If it is a fixed-price contract, one in which you guarantee to deliver for a fixed price and in which you must suffer the loss if you run over—you are clearly entitled to bill the full ten days, and you need not feel guilty nor apologize for it. But if the contract was clearly based on a daily rate and your estimate of the time needed was ten days, you are not entitled to bill for more than nine days.

A RECOMMENDED CODE

Not to belabor these points unduly, for they are dependent on your own sense of fair play and moral behavior as well as on accepted standards, I recommend the following code of ethics for your serious consideration:

- Make no extravagant promises, not verbally, not in correspondence, and not in your literature, that you would be unwilling or unable to live up to.
- Do not withhold important facts or make weasel-word statements in which you are not, technically, telling untruths or hyping the truth, but are nevertheless deliberately misleading the client or prospect and inducing him or her to believe something you did not explicitly say.
- Be scrupulous in respecting the confidentiality of every client's proprietary information and what your business relationships with clients have been.
- Make a strictly honest accounting of hours, when the contract calls for it, and otherwise up front dealing with all clients and prospective clients.
- Do not poison the well for all consultants; refrain carefully from denouncing, condemning, or otherwise derogating competitors, either in general or specifically.
- Make it a firm policy to deliver everything you promise a client.

- Conduct yourself with professional dignity in all matters and at all times.
- Deal with your vendors and/or brokers as you would with clients.
- Provide clear communication throughout projects. Even if you are the bearer of bad news, your candor, openness, and honesty coupled with clear communication will reinforce your professionalism and trustworthiness.
- Be quick to take responsibility for correcting errors (even if not your doing or making), and to offer congratulations or credit to others for successful projects. The client will remember that you "saved" the project from the error (especially if it is the client's mistake that caused it), and will appreciate the sharing of the kudos when the project delivers beneficial results.

e Reference File

One benefit of education is learning how and where to seek out information you need, especially in this information age. This chapter is written with the hope that it will help you in that.

Within these pages, I have tried to pass on what I know and have learned about consulting and, especially, what additional knowledge I have gained since I wrote earlier editions of this book. It is not an easy task. Being an independent consultant is not easy; it is an anomaly, in fact, requiring you to be both specialist and generalist, master of some given discipline and yet highly competent in a dozen complementary disciplines. In this final chapter, I identify other sources—books, periodicals, computer programs, services of many kinds, and miscellaneous tips to help you cope with the many fields of knowledge essential to your success. These items and tips are certainly not all, nor necessarily even the best, information available. But I pass them on in good faith, and I recommend them as at least a starter list. (I include some of my own books where relevant.)

BOOKS ON RETIREMENT AND SECOND CAREERS

What Do You Want to Do When You Grow Up, Dorothy Cantor, Little, Brown and Co. (Pap), New York, 2002.

100 Best Retirement Businesses, David H. Bangs Jr. and Lisa Angowski Shaw, Upstart Pub. Co., Denver, CO, 1994.

Jobs and Activities After Retirement, Vincent A. Miller, Writers Club Press, Lincoln, NE, 2001.

Retiring Right 2003, Lawrence J. Kaplan, Square One Publishing, Garden City, NY, 2003.

Second Acts; Creating the Life You Really Want, Building the Career You Truly Desire, Stephen A. Pollan and Mark Levine, HarperResource, New York, 2002.

BOOKS ON WRITING AND PUBLISHING

Consultant's Guide to Proposal Writing, The, second edition, Herman Holtz, John Wiley & Sons, New York, 1986.

Contemporary Business Report Writing, Shirley Kuiper and Gary F. Kohut, South-Western College/West, Belmont, CA, 1998.

Elements of Style, The, William Strunk Jr. and E. B. White, Macmillan, New York, 1972.

Getting Down to Cases: Scenarios for Report Writing, Gilbert Schectman, Prentice-Hall, Englewood Cliffs, NJ, 1992.

How to Start and Run a Writing & Editing Business, Herman Holtz, John Wiley & Sons, New York, 1992.

The Freelance Success Book: Insider Secrets for Selling Every Word You Write, David Taylor and Bob Teufel, Peak Writing Press, Savannah, GA, 2003.

On Language, Edwin Newman, Warner Books, New York, 1980.

Writer's Market, The, Writer's Digest Books, Cincinnati, OH, an annual.

The Successful Writer's' Guide to Publishing Magazine Articles, Eva Shaw, PhD, Loveland Press, Loveland, CO, 1998.

BOOKS ON PUBLIC SPEAKING

Money Talks, Alan Weiss, McGraw-Hill Trade, New York, 1998.

Speak and Grow Rich Revised and Expanded, Dottie Walters and Lilly Walters, Prentice Hall Press, Upper Saddle River, NJ, 1998.

Speaking for Profit, Herman Holtz, John Wiley & Sons, New York, 1985.

OTHER BOOKS OF INTEREST

Internet Direct Mail: The Complete Guide to Successful E-Marketing Campaigns, Stevan Roberts, Michelle Feit, and Robert Bly, McGraw-Hill Trade, New York, 2000.

Successful Direct Marketing Methods, Seventh Edition, Bob Stone, Ron Jacobs, and H. Robert Wientzen, McGraw-Hill Trade, New York, 2001.

Databased Marketing, Herman Holtz, John Wiley & Sons, New York, 1992.

Direct Marketer's Work Book, The, Herman Holtz, John Wiley & Sons, New York, 1986.

The Expert Witness Marketing Book: How to Promote Your Forensic Practice in a Professional and Cost Effective Manner, Rosalie Hamilton, Expert Communications, Inc., Clearwater, FL, 2003.

National Directory of Addresses and Telephone Numbers, The, Concord Reference Books, Bothell, WA, an annual.

Business: The Ultimate Resource, Perseus Publishing, Cambridge, MA, 2002.

The Successful Business Plan: Secrets and Strategies, Running R Media, Rhonda Abrams, Palo Alto, CA, 2000.

Start Your Own Business, Rjeva Lesonsky (Ed.), Entrepreneur Media, Inc., Irvine, CA, 1998.

Executive Temping: A Guide for Professionals, Saralee Terry Woods, John Wiley & Sons, Hoboken, NJ, 1998.

Secrets of Practical Marketing for Small Business, The, Herman Holtz, Prentice-Hall, Englewood Cliffs, NJ, 1983.

Speaking for Profit, Herman Holtz, John Wiley & Sons, New York, 1987.

Incorporate!: An Easy Step-by-Step Plan for Entrepreneurs, Karen B. Nathan and Alice Magos, McGraw-Hill Trade, New York, 2003.

PERIODICALS OF DIRECT INTEREST

Many of these publications also have electronic versions of their publications, so be sure to inquire about those options or conduct a "web search" to learn more.

Meeting News, VNU Business Publications, 770 Broadway, NY 10003-9595, a trade paper of hoteliers and others with an interest in business meetings and relevant enclaves.

Meeting News, Gralla Publications, 1515 Broadway, New York, NY 10036, a trade paper of hoteliers and others with an interest in business meetings and relevant conclavces.

Corporate Meetings and Incentives, another publication focused on meeting planners and hoteliers. Primedia Publication, 2104 Harvell Circle, Bellevue, NE 68005.

Meetings and Conventions, a slick industry periodical published monthly, 500 Plaza Drive, Secaucus, NJ 07094.

Sharing Ideas!, published by Dottie Walters, P.O. Box 1120, Glendora, CA 91740. This is bimonthly, generally runs on the order of 30 pages, is the bible of the public-speaking industry for many readers.

DM News, a monthly tabloid on direct marketing, read by members of the industry, 100 Avenue of the Americas, New York, NY 10013.

Target Marketing, a North American Publishing Company publication, is focused on helping to narrow the communications or selling efforts so that inefficient spending is avoided, 401 N. Broad Street, Philadelphia, PA 19108.

Direct Response Specialist, a monthly newsletter of direct-marketing ideas and guidance by direct-mail consultant Galen Stilson, P.O. Box 1075, Tarpon Springs, FL 34286-1075.

Writer's Digest, a monthly magazine, in existence for many years, the bible for many professional writers. (I have been reading it since 1937.) You can find it on your newsstand, but you may want to write to the magazine at 4700 E. Galbraith Rd., Cincinnati, OH 45236.

Consulting Magazine and Consultant News, Kennedy Publications, 29 West 35th Street, New York, NY 10001.

WHOLESALERS AND DISTRIBUTORS

BookMasters, Inc., 30 Amberwood Parkway, Ashland, OH 44905.

Consortium Booksales and Distribution, 1045 Westgate Drive, Suite 90, St. Paul, MN 55114.

Greenleaf Book Group LLC, 8227 E. Washington Street, Suite 2, Chagrin Falls, OH 44023.

Koen Book Distributors, 10 Twosome Drive, Box 600, NJ 08057.

MidPoint Trade Books, 1263 Southwest Blvd., Kansas City, KS 66103.

Publisher's Group West, 1700 Fourth Street, Berkeley, CA 94710.
SCB Distributors, 15608 S. New Century Drive, Gardens, CA 90248.

These are organizations who distribute others' books. Also, some established publishers will occasionally distribute others' books. St. Martin's Press is one who does so, although there are others.

PEOPLE AND ORGANIZATIONS IN PUBLIC SPEAKING

Many successful consultants are also speakers, lecture agents, publishers, and trainers of speakers. Some conduct seminars for experienced speakers, where veterans of the platform get guidance to help them increase their success. The following, a small sampling, offer related products and/or services.

Dottie Walters, 18825 Hicrest Road, Glendora, CA 91740, (818) 335-8069.
Simply Speaking, 111 Berkeley Road, Avondale, GA 30002.
LJL Seminars, 106 Schoolhouse Road, Newington, CT 06111.
Elliot Essman, Albuquerque, NM, (505) 323-5890.
TJWalker Media, 488 7th Avenue, Suite 4B Broadcast Studio, New York, NY 10018.
Toastmasters (in every major city, see local telephone book).
Dale Carnegie (in every major city, see local telephone book).
Alan Weiss, PhD Summit Consulting Group, P.O. Box 1009, East Greenwich, RI 02818.
Sandra Schrift (The Podium, 3940 Hancock Street, Suite 207, San Diego, CA, 619-688-9467 or www.schrift.com).
Nido Qubein, CPAE, Creative Services, Inc., P.O. Box 6008, High Point, NC 27262.
Mike Frank, Speakers Unlimited, P.O. Box 27225, Columbus, OH 43227.
Bobbie Gee, Orange County Speakers Bureau, 31781 National Park Drive, Laguna Niguel, CA 92677.
SRI International, 333 Ravenswood Avenue, Menlo Park, CA 94025.
Masters of Ceremonies, P.O. Box 390, Monrovia, CA 91016.
Dean Howard, Success Seminars, 1539 Monrovia Avenue, Suite 14, Newport Beach, CA 92663.
Meeting Masters, Inc., 4000 MacArthur Blvd., Suite 3000, Newport Beach, CA 92660.
The Podium (women speakers only), Sandra Schrift and Jill Henderson, 3940 Hancock Street, Suite 207, San Diego, CA 92110.

CONVENTION MANAGERS AND PLANNERS

There are a great many convention planners, managers, consultants, and others who support such events. A small sampling is offered here.

Adelle Cox Convention Services & Consultants, P.O. Box 69-4770, Miami, FL 33169.

Association of Independent Meeting Planners, 5103 Wigville Road, Thumont, MD 21788.

Cummings Meeting Consultants, 155 East Market Street, Suite 700, Indianapolis, IN 46204.

Meeting Planners International, 1950 Stemmons Freeway, Dallas, TX 75207.

Professional Conventions and Meetings, 6145 Crawfordsville Road, Suite 400, Indianapolis, IN 46224.

Society of Company Meeting Planners, 2600 Garden Road, Monterey, CA 93940.

Trade Show Bureau, P.O. Box 797, South Beach Road, East Orleans, MA 06243.

SPEAKERS ASSOCIATIONS

There are a number of speakers associations. Here are several you should know about.

National Speakers Association (NSA), 1500 S. Priest Drive, Tempe, AZ 85281.

International Platform Association (IPA), P.O. Box 250, Winnetka, IL 60093.

Toastmasters, International, Inc., P.O. Box 9052, Mission Viejo, CA 92690.

MAILING LIST BROKERS

There is a great abundance of mailing list brokers, and you can find them listed in the Yellow Pages as well as in many other media. Here are just a few of them, many branch offices of mailing list firms.

American List Council, 4300 US Highway 1, Bldg. 5, Princeton, NJ 08543.

Chilcutt Direct Marketing, 802 West 16th, P.O. Box 1182, Mt. Pleasant, TX 75455.

Direct Media Inc., 77 Milford Drive, Suite 209, Hudson, OH 44236.

Edith Roman Associates, Inc., Blue Hill Plaza, 16th Floor, Pearl River, NY 10965.

Leon Henry, Inc., 455 Central Avenue, Scarsdale, NY 10583.

IDG List Services, 492 Old Connecticut Path, Framingham, MA 01701.

LIST, 320 Northern Blvd., Great Neck, NY 11021.

Kroll Direct Marketing, 101 Morgan Lane, Suite 120, Plainsboro, NJ 08536.

Mal Dunn Associates, Hardscrabble Road, New Falls, NY 10519.

RMI Direct Marketing Inc., 20 Birch Hill Lane, Kent, CT 06757.

Worldata, Inc., 300 N. Military Trail, Boca Raton, FL 33431.

Zed Marketing Group, 416 Autumnwood Court, Edmond, OK 73003.

A FEW TIPS ON WRITING DIRECT MAIL COPY

Here are a few reminders, as a checklist or, do's and don'ts list, to refer to when preparing direct-mail copy:

- Always make things as easy as possible for the customer, as for example:
    a) Make it easy to understand what you are saying. Use short words, short sentences, short paragraphs. One thought in a sentence, one subject and

one main point in a paragraph. (Be sure first that you yourself fully understand the main point.)

b) Make it easy for the customer to order, ask for more information, or otherwise reveal interest by providing a return card, telephone number, or other convenient means for responding. All of your materials (brochures, ads, mailers, etc.) should include your e-mail address as well as your phone number and mailing address.

c) Make it easy for the customer to understand what you want by *telling* the customer what to do. A great many sales are lost by advertisers who fail to tell the customers what they want the customers to do.

- A direct-mail cliche (which is nonetheless true) is "The more you tell the more you sell." Don't stint on copy. Be sure to include a letter, a brochure or flyer of some sort, and a response device (envelope and/or order form) as an absolute minimum, and there is no harm in enclosing even more. The experts claim that three-quarters of the response results from the letter, and that a good circular or brochure can increase response by as much as one-third. My own experience bears this out emphatically.

- Don't tell it all in the letter. Split the copy up among the various enclosures, or at least provide additional details in the various enclosures. Make it clear that additional information/details are to be found elsewhere in the enclosures. Give the reader good reason—inducements—to read everything, if you want maximum impact.

- Geography makes a difference. Prospects who are nearby tend to respond better than those at a distance. Know nearby zip codes and use them. But do test, for there are always exceptions. Example: when it comes to consulting and speaking services, there is some appeal, even a kind of mystique, to the expert from a distant place, especially if you are mailing from a major industrial or business center, such as New York, Chicago, or Washington. If you are, take advantage of it, somehow, by giving it prominence in your copy. If you use envelope copy—advertising and sales messages on the outside of the envelope—do two things:

a) Use both sides of the envelope. If you are going to make a bulletin board of the envelope, you might as well get full use of it; copy on both sides pulls better than copy on one side only—if the copy is powerful.

b) Now that you've served notice that the envelope contains advertising matter, why pay first-class postage? You might as well save money by using something less expensive.

ASSOCIATIONS OF CONSULTANTS

Many of those who belong to speakers' associations (listed earlier) and to many other kinds of associations and professional societies are consultants. But there are also a number of consultants' associations, over 30, in fact.

Association of Consultants to Non-Profits, P.O. Box 2449, Chicago, IL 60690.

American Association of Healthcare Consultants, 5 Revere Drive, Suite 200, North-brook, IL 60062.

Association Management Consultants, Suite 218-409, Granville Street, Vancouver, British Columbia, V6C 1T2.

Association of Professional Consultants, P.O. Box 51193, Irvine, CA 92619.

American Association of Professional Consultants, 9140 Ward Parkway, Kansas City, MO 64114.

American Association of Hospital Consultants, 1235 Jefferson Davis Highway, Arlington, VA 22202.

American Association of Political Consultants, 600 Pennsylvania Avenue, SE, Suite 330, Washington DC, 20003.

American Consultants League, The, 1290 Palm Avenue, Sarasota, FL 34236.

American Society of Agricultural Consultants, 950 South Cherry Street, Suite 508, Denver, CO 80246.

Association of Bridal Consultants, 200 Chestnutland Road, New Milford, CT 06776.

Association of Executive Search Consultants, 12 E. 41st Street, 17th Floor, New York, NY 10017.

Institute of Management Consultants, 2025 M Street NW, Suite 800, Washington, DC 20036.

Society of Professional Consultants, P.O. Box 785, Westford, MA 01886.

MISCELLANEOUS RESOURCES

Prosavvy, www.prosavvy.com (a clearinghouse of consultants and their services matched to client needs).

www.connect4training.com (a site specific for consultants in HR, training, or related fields).

American Home Business Association, 4505 South Wasatch Blvd., #140, Salt Lake City, UT 84124.

Service Corps of Retired Executives (SCORE), 409 3rd Street, SW, 6th Floor, Washington, DC 20024 (SBA-sponsored volunteer consultants).

Small Business Administration, 1441 L Street, NW, Washington, DC 20416 (now in nearly every major city and can be reached at 1-800-8-ASK SBA).

INTERNET RESOURCES

www.addeccotechnical.com

www.cadjobmart.com

www.monster.com

www.hotjobs.com

www.durham.com

www.kennedyinfo.com (publishes a directory of Temporary Executive Placement Firms)

A FEW SEMINAR TIPS

As one of the most important tools available to you to build your income base and market your services, seminar production deserves some thought, and for that reason a few tips and reminders are offered here for ready reference:

- There are two kinds of seminars you may consider conducting; the first is a "public" workshop where you invite attendees from either multiple companies to attend, or attendees' participation is not based on a corporate affiliation. In those instances, a typical day's session runs approximately six hours, three in the morning and three in the afternoon, with midmorning and midafternoon breaks of about 10 minutes. The lunch break is thus usually from 90 minutes to two hours. The other is when you do a workshop for multiple attendees from the same organization. In this instance, it is often more tailored to the specific needs of the host organization and exercises, references within the materials, and anecdotes shared with participants are usually client specific. In that instance, the workshop may extend for more than a single day, and breaks and meal times are controlled by the host organization (often catering the lunch to keep participants in the room and not permit them to go back to their desks and get busy with other work).
- Back-of-the-room sales may be conducted prior to the start of the morning session, during the lunch break, and after the close of the afternoon session.
- Whether you sell books, tapes, or other materials, you should include handout materials as part of the seminar. These are themselves often a major inducement to registration and attendance. It helps, from that viewpoint, if they are exclusively available to attendees. However, in many cases you can get excellent materials free of charge from government agencies, associations, community groups, large corporations, schools, and other sources.
- Often visual aids are also available from such sources as those just named— movies, slides, film strips, transparencies, and posters of various kinds.
- One profitable idea was the mini-seminar. I held these two- to three-hour sessions for 10 to 15 people in my offices on Saturday mornings, charging what was even then a modest $25. If your offices are at home and unsuitable for the purpose you can usually arrange to rent an inexpensive room somewhere.
- A variant on that idea is to conduct two such sessions, one in the morning, another in the afternoon, enabling yourself to register twice the number of attendees for a single day. (The total cost is only slightly greater for two sessions, and the income is thus doubled.)

PROPOSAL DO'S AND DON'TS

Nothing is more important to marketing your professional services than the proposal, used properly and with a few tips in mind in addition to those already presented in an earlier chapter on the subject:

- Analyze the client's problem closely and be sure that you understand it fully before committing yourself to a plan of action. Don't rush to the word processor too soon. There should be no surprises in the proposal. Everything you plan on doing or suggesting be done should have been discussed with the prospect beforehand. If you still have not provided the client with information that you plan on introducing in the proposal, you are not ready to write a proposal.
- Devise a specific strategy upon which to base your proposal.
- Be highly specific in what you propose to do and furnish to the client.
- Shun hyperbole. Stick with nouns and verbs, using adjectives and adverbs as sparingly as possible—especially avoiding superlatives.
- Quantify as much as possible by providing details.
- Avoid potential disputes by being sure to specify exactly what your quoted cost estimate covers.

OUTLINE FOR THE PREPARATION OF A BUSINESS PLAN

Although the subject of preparing a proper business plan was discussed in an earlier chapter, a more detailed outline is offered here for reference. It is unlikely that you would ever have occasion to write a business plan that included all the items listed here, however. The purpose of presenting such detail is to enable you to select the items most appropriate to your own situation.

I. Nondisclosure Agreement

A nondisclosure agreement should appear in the front matter of the plan. It states that the information in the plan is proprietary and is not to be shared, copies, disclosed, or otherwise compromised. It calls for the reader to agree to respect those conditions. The actual agreement can be verbal or can take the form of signed documentation. It may, in fact, have a line for the reader's signature. Investors are often hesitant to sign such agreements, however, believing that the agreement ties their hands too much; you may have to negotiate on that matter.

II. Control Numbering

Number each copy of the plan and keep a record of each copy—to whom issued and when. Much of the information in the plan is proprietary, whether the prospective investor has signed an agreement or not, and it is a good idea to keep track of all copies.

III. The Executive Summary

In a way, this is the most important part of the plan because it is what investors read first. It should be the hook that will capture the investor's interest and persuade him or her to study the entire plan.

In practice, the executive summary will be the last thing you write because you do not have anything to summarize until you have drawn up the plan! Moreover, the executive summary must include the most important and persuasive elements of your plan, and you can't be sure in advance what these will be. However, this outline is in the order in which the elements of the plan will appear, and so will be discussed here.

Keep the executive summary as short as possible: 1 to 3 pages. It should summarize the main points, but focus on the heaviest assets, for while its ostensible purpose is to give the investor a brief overview, its hidden agenda is to generate immediate interest and enthusiasm. It should include the following specific information, albeit in summary style:

I. The company
   A. When formed (or when to be formed)
      1. For what purpose:
         a. Design a new product
         b. Manufacture
            (1) market
            (2) other

II. The product(s)/service(s)
   A. What are you selling?
   B. What makes it better/unique?
   C. Is it a proprietary product?
   D. At what stage is its development?
   E. Comparison with competition
      1. pricing
      2. quality
      3. other

III. The market
   A. Current/estimated size (basis for figures)
   B. Domestic/international
      1. Recent growth (cite sources)
      2. Projected growth (cite sources)
   C. Estimated company market share

IV. Financial
   A. Financing sought
      1. for what purposes
      2. will carry company how far
   B. Five-year revenue and net income projections
   C. Projection of when profits will begin (2 to 4 years?)

V. Management
   A. How complete is the team
      1. Brief past experience
      2. Highlight strengths

IV. Other Front Matter

The principal other front matter (in addition to the non-disclosure statement and the executive summary) are the title page and the table of contents. The title page is usually a replica of the cover, with the addition of a date and a control number. The table of contents lists chapters or sections by title, and usually includes a list of tables and a list of illustrations. The latter would include graphs and charts, in most cases, but might include drawings and photographs, if they are relevant or necessary to help the investor understand the venture and develop faith in it and in the founders.

V. The Organization

In this section, a more detailed description of the company is made, but it is essentially the full details which were reviewed briefly in the executive summary, including most or all of the following:

- When the organization was (or is to be) founded and by whom? Who are the principals and main executives?
- What is the organization structure to be? (Charts?)
- What markets will be pursued?
- Is the company creating/planning to create new demand, anticipating new demand, or responding to existing demand? (Cite sources bases for conclusions.)
- What will the products do for buyers? Reduce costs; improve efficiency; other.
- Who are the buyers (not specifically, but in general, i.e., disk drive manufacturers, appliance retailers, other)?
- How many people in the company now; how many expected in the future?
- What technologies being used in production?

Generally, this section will run two to five pages in length and will serve to highlight details covered in greater depth in later sections.

VI. The Market

This is for many by far the most difficult section to write because it is difficult to foresee marketing developments—opportunities, changes, and problems in the markets. Consequently, this section may require the greatest effort, for it must be specific and detailed. Moreover, it is most important to cite sources and explain the basis for estimates.

  I. Market size
   A. Recent
   B. Current
   C. Projected (5 to 10 years)

II. Market trends
    A. Where is the market going and why?
        1. What are the relevant trends?
        2. Maturity of market—growth stage or level?
    B. Products in the market
        1. What is available?
        2. How many suppliers?
    C. Market players
        1. Who is buying? OEMS, wholesalers, end users, others?
        2. Why are they buying?
        3. What are they looking for?
        4. On what factors are buy decisions made?
    D. Market segments
        1. Natural splits—geographic, industries, volume versus unit buyers and so on.
        2. Growth prospects within each segment
III. Market distribution
    A. How products are delivered to buyers
        1. Direct sales
        2. Manufacturers' representatives
        3. Distributors
    B. Competition
        1. Who are they?
        2. Strengths?
        3. Weaknesses?
        4. Markets addressed (segments)?
        5. Reputation?

The better you know your competition, the better you'll be able to plan around them (and the more you'll impress potential investors). Good information about competitors adds a great deal of strength to the plan. Here are just a few of the many possible sources for gathering intelligence about the market and the other players (competitors) in it:

- Existing manufacturers (competitors) and their product brochures.
- Interviews with marketing people (which requires a degree of brashness, but don't be timid in asking a potential competitor to lunch to pick his or her brain). You can succeed at this surprisingly often.
- Trade publications; if you don't know what's available, ask someone who does; call editors for further suggestions on sources; visit your public library; there are many directories of trade publications.
- Analysts' reports and annual reports; available from many securities brokers (Merrill, Lynch; Hambrecht & Quist, others).

- Users of existing products
  - —Purchasing directors
  - —Manufacturing directors
- Potential customers; it is an absolute must that you have as many discussions as possible with users before, during, and after formation of the company. Their feedback should be incorporated into both your products and plans.

VII. Marketing/Sales Strategy

After describing the market, explain here how you plan to reach prospective buyers and sell them.

- Target market by segment:
  - —Geographic
  - —Industry
  - —Type of buyer

Identify the market niche you will pursue and explain your rational for the decision. What is it about the segment that makes it right for your company? Is it a niche ignored by competitors or ill-served by competitors? If you go into it and make a profit, why won't a larger competitor enter it, also. (Furnish reasons for your conclusions.) Cover the following topics also in presenting the rational for your marketing decisions and plans:

- Credibility: company and product, why should customers buy a new product or buy from a new and unproven company?
- Pricing strategy: high, medium, or low relative to market? Why?
- Warranty policies: standard or non-standard?
- Image targets: quality, reliability, service, response time—all are key components in imaging and should fit neatly with other strategies. Be especially careful to explain and justify apparent anomalies, such as the promise of highest quality at lowest prices.
- Advertising and public relations: Again, these strategies should match with other strategies and tactics. For example, are you choosing the most appropriate media for advertising and other marketing activity?
- Distribution channels (getting the product/service to the customer)
  - —Factory distribution
  - —Company-owned regional distribution
  - —Independent remote distribution
  - —Order long-lead items
- Servicing (service of products—how, where?)
  - —Factory-only service
  - —Company field service engineers
  - —Contracted service

    —Service contracts
    —Profit centers
    —Loss leaders
- Sales
    —Direct sales
    —Reps
    —Distributors
    —Hybrid

How are you going to actually sell the product? If you use manufacturer's representatives, rather than house salespeople, what kind of incentives will you use to get them to handle, learn, and promote your products? Is special skill (e.g., engineering or computer knowledge) required to sell it? At what level in the buyers' organizations will sales be made? Should senior management in your company participate directly in the sales effort to establish company and product credibility? How will you compensate sales—commissions? bonus? salary? other?

VIII. Products

Provide a detailed description of existing products and plans for future products. Are products market-ready and, if not, how long until they will be? Description (illustration, if appropriate) and following:

- Bill of materials (major components, not too detailed)
- Potential component supply problems
- Proprietary protection (trademark, copyright, patent)
- Advantages/disadvantages to competing products
- Price and cost
- Differentiation from competition. Here, a high level matrix comparing your products' capabilities, strengths, and characteristics to your competitors' is useful. (Be sure your product is more easily visible in the matrix—bold face print at top of matrix is appropriate.)

Future Products
- Innovations to existing line
- New products
- Development time lines

IX. Manufacturing/Research and Development

Depending on the nature of your company, these two areas might more appropriately be separated.

Index